THE EARLIEST NORWEGIAN LAWS

BEING THE GULATHING LAW AND THE FROSTATHING LAW

Translated from the Old Norwegian

BY

LAURENCE M. LARSON
PROFESSOR OF HISTORY, UNIVERSITY OF ILLINOIS

THE LAWBOOK EXCHANGE, LTD.
Clark, New Jersey

ISBN 9781584779254 (hardcover)
ISBN 9781616191047 (paperback)

Lawbook Exchange edition 2008, 2011

The quality of this reprint is equivalent to the quality of the original work.

The Lawbook Exchange, Ltd.
33 Terminal Avenue
Clark, New Jersey 07066-1321

Please see our website for a selection of our other publications and fine facsimile reprints of classic works of legal history:
www.lawbookexchange.com

Library of Congress Cataloging-in-Publication Data

Gulaþingslög hin eldri. English.
The earliest Norwegian laws : being the Gulathing law and the Frostathing law / Translated from the Old Norwegian by Laurence Larson.
p. cm.
Originally published: New York : Columbia University Press, 1935.
Includes bibliographical references and index.
ISBN-13: 978-1-58477-925-4 (cloth : alk. paper)
ISBN-10: 1-58477-925-X (cloth : alk. paper)
1. Law--Norway--Sources. 2. Law, Medieval--Sources. 3. Manuscripts, Old Norse. I. Larson, Laurence Marcellus, 1868-1938. II. Frostaþingslög hin eldri. English. III. Title.
KKN136.G85 2009
349.481--dc22 2008041289

Printed in the United States of America on acid-free paper

THE EARLIEST NORWEGIAN LAWS

BEING THE GULATHING LAW AND THE FROSTATHING LAW

Translated from the Old Norwegian

BY

LAURENCE M. LARSON
PROFESSOR OF HISTORY, UNIVERSITY OF ILLINOIS

NEW YORK: MORNINGSIDE HEIGHTS
COLUMBIA UNIVERSITY PRESS
M • CM • XXXV

Published 1935

PRINTED IN THE UNITED STATES OF AMERICA
GEORGE BANTA PUBLISHING CO., MENASHA, WIS.

TO CHARLES HOMER HASKINS

the master of American medievalists who first
directed my attention to the unique
treasures of medieval law

FOREWORD

When Professor Austin P. Evans asked me some years ago to contribute to the *Records of Civilization* a translation from the Old Norwegian, there was little doubt as to what materials might best be chosen for such a volume. The laws of a race provide a record of its progress which is in many respects more enlightening than most other documentary survivals. Though primarily a statement of ethical principles, the law must of necessity be concerned with all the many varieties of human relations and consequently enters into the entire scheme of organized life. Since the North is comparatively rich in documents of this sort, it seemed most expedient to select a volume from the legal sources.

The oldest Norwegian laws, those of Gula and Frosta, go back to a time when the culture of the Middle Ages was still a somewhat novel experience in Northern Europe. Though the copies that have survived seem to date from the twelfth century and later, the codes must, in considerable part, have taken form in the eleventh century, or as early as the first generation of the Christian age. Heathendom had by that time been outlawed, but one seems justified in believing that the cult of strength and valor was for some time yet a force that had to be taken into account; for the principles that governed life in the heathen age retained much of their ancient vigor, and the old civilization, rooted, as it was, in the soil itself, was able in large measure to maintain both life and validity.

These principles and this civilization were not exclusively Norwegian: they were essentially more perfect developments of those that ruled in earlier Germanic times. King Olaf Haraldsson who did more than anyone else to bring his people within the pale of Christendom is also credited with the earliest effort to bring the laws into written form. Whether tradition is correct in this matter is of little moment; the important fact is that when the lawmakers of the eleventh century began to formulate their codes they must have found most of their materials in the folk laws of the time which were essentially Germanic.

Saint Olaf was a missionary king somewhat after the manner of Clovis, but he lived five hundred years later. The earliest Norwegian written law is at least five hundred years younger than that of the Salian Franks. In those five centuries great changes came into Germanic civilization. In the North, however, where the development along heathen lines was unhampered by a hostile religious system, thought continued in the old grooves; and while the newer forms of life became progressively Norse or Scandinavian, fundamentally they remained Germanic.

While the importance of these codes lies primarily in their detailed presentation of Norwegian life in the two greater centuries of the Middle Ages, they do have this earlier interest leading back into Germanic origins which no scholar can afford to ignore. It is quite true that they belong to a Christian age, but it is also true that the secular laws are not in accord with Christian ethics on every point. Much was added to Norse jurisprudence when the bishop arrived in Norway, much was discarded when the Northmen deserted the old faith, but even more was retained. For, Christian or heathen, the dwellers on the North Way continued to live in the old environment, and they kept what they could of the familiar system, since that alone seemed to fit into the circumstances of their social and physical life.

The Great King Alfred in his famous preface to the *Pastoral Care* states that he translated "sometimes word by word, sometimes meaning by meaning." A translator can scarcely devise a better formula. In dealing with the materials in this volume it has sometimes been possible to give what is approximately a literal translation and to do so with entire confidence. But in most of the enactments the problem has been to determine exactly what the scribes intended to say and then to phrase their meaning in intelligible English without losing entirely the flavor of the original statement.

This has not been easy to achieve. The scribes wrote for their own time and in the terms of their own age. They wrote in the terse, compact style which characterizes the writings of the medieval North and which sometimes defies successful translation. They took for granted certain forms of knowledge which are not readily acquired at this distance. The translator cannot hope, therefore, to have produced a version that is absolutely correct on every point; it is believed, however, that in most places it will be found reasonably accurate.

A serious difficulty has been the fact that in Old Norway there were institutions and conditions of life that had no close parallels in medieval England and consequently have not been noted by modern lexicographers. With these matters I have dealt as seemed most expedient. I have at times made use of terms in their Old Norwegian form; at other times I have been compelled to use words or phrases which are not nearly so exact as the work demands. It is with reluctance that I use "baron" for *lendr maðr*, but there seems to be no alternative. For terms of this sort and for other unfamiliar combinations of words, the reader is referred to the glossary, which I hope will prove helpful in difficult places.

In preparing this translation I have received valuable assistance from my two colleagues, Professor George T. Flom and Judge Sveinbjörn Johnson, who have allowed me to draw on their abundant knowledge of Old Northern linguistic usage and jurisprudence. From Professor Evans, the editor of this series, and Miss Ida M. Lynn of the Columbia University Press I received fruitful advice and criticism when the manuscript was receiving its final touches preparatory to publication. I am indebted to Mr. Donald Goodchild of the American Council of Learned Societies for material assistance in securing a grant from that organization. My wife, Lillian M. Larson, has read the proof sheets and has otherwise assisted in the prosecution of the work. To her and to all the others whom I mention above I desire to express my most appreciative thanks.

L. M. L.

University of Illinois
January 21, 1935

CONTENTS

INTRODUCTION

INTRODUCTION

The backbone of the Scandinavian massif is a more or less continuous series of mountains and groups of mountains usually called *Kjölen* or the Kjölen Range. Kjölen is, however, not exactly a range of mountains; it is rather a broad belt of arctic and subarctic highlands (one hundred and fifty miles across), a wild complex of hills and moors that has never been inhabited to any extent; indeed, on the whole, it can scarcely be regarded as habitable. These highlands begin a little to the south of Hammerfest and continue south-southwestward for a distance of about eight hundred miles. Except in the southern part of the peninsula, where the elevation is not so high, they form the actual, and in part the political, boundary between the kingdoms of Norway and Sweden.

On its eastern side the Kjölen crest slopes gently down into the Swedish plain. On the Norwegian side throughout most of its extent it runs closer to the edge of the sea, and here the slope is more abrupt and decisive. Farther to the south where the peninsula broadens out toward the west, the crest is flanked by a wide plateau which spreads out till it meets the tidal waves of the North Sea.

Norway is, therefore, a highland country, the greater part of which is wholly unfit for human habitation. In two areas only are there any important depressions: in the southeast and in the region bordering the Trondheim Fjord. In the southern part of the kingdom there are a number of considerable valleys, each a long, narrow trench worn out of the ancient rock by the eroding forces of geologic time. Similar forces have been at work along the coast where they have produced the most ragged and sinuous shore line in all Europe, perhaps in all the world. Here the rocks have been worn and riven in hundreds of places, and hundreds of fjords and other inlets have found their way miles and miles into the land.[1]

[1] The largest of these, the Sogn Fjord has a length of about 130 miles.

In this way Norway has come to have a coast line of extraordinary length,[2] and at the same time the area available for the building of homes and farms has been materially increased. The great mass of the Norwegian population has always lived within an easy distance of the great sea.

Men and women began to build homes in Norway three thousand years or more before the beginning of the Christian era. Some time in the Later Stone Age, Germanic tribesmen began to move northward along the southwestern coast of Sweden and were soon finding their way into the lowland region around Oslo Fjord and into the neighboring valleys farther inland. It seems quite probable that immigrants have also come across from Jutland[3] and even from more distant regions, such as the British Isles, as some would have us believe. There are those who have held that the Germanic peoples were not the first to occupy the land and that they found a more primitive dark race in possession on the west coast;[4] but this theory seems not to be in great favor at present. Whatever the truth may be on this point, one may feel sure that Germanic thought, culture, and civilization have dominated life in the North as long as the Teutonic race has dwelt in the land.

The character of the Norwegian coast line was such that anything like a continuous settlement was impossible. The same was largely true of the inland country, where each valley, in itself a unit, lay in comparative isolation. This fact was no doubt responsible for the forms that were taken by the earliest social and political organizations.

The most ancient unit of this sort seems to have been the *bygð*, or settlement, sometimes also called the *herað* (herath). One cannot know why these early pioneers felt called upon to form political bodies; but the term herath (probably from *herr*, an armed body of men) points toward an early recognition of a need to provide for local defense. Another motive that led to a like result was, no doubt, the desire to make adequate provision for local worship. While these may have been the determining considera-

[2] About 12,000 miles.

[3] Brögger, *Det norske folk i oldtiden*, pp. 127 ff.

[4] See especially A. M. Hansen, *Oldtidens nordmænd*, Christiania, 1907.

tions, one should also remember that most men have within them a strong urge to be with and among those of their own kind.

In the course of time it was evidently found expedient to group some of these primal units into a larger organization, and the *fylki*, or shire, came into being. Like herað, the word fylki has a military significance: the fylki is the folk in warlike array. When the Norwegian monarchy was formed (toward the close of the ninth century), there were about thirty shires along the North Way[5] and in the highland valleys. Each one of these had come to look upon itself as a little state and insisted on a large measure of autonomy. In some of these the freemen recognized the authority of a chieftain who might be called *jarl*, and sometimes even king. This chieftain was no doubt a leader, rather than a lord; especially was he expected to lead the men of the fylki on the battlefield and to represent the folk in their bargainings with the divine powers. He was not, however, entrusted with sovereign power; sovereignty, if that term can be applied to the political arrangements of Teutonic times, was held and exercised by the public assembly in which practically all the farmers held membership.

It seems quite clear that some of these shires were built on a geographical basis, as for instance *Firðafylki* (the Firth fylki) and *Sygnafylki* (the Sogn fylki), of which the latter derives its name from the great fjord. A safe conjecture seems to be that some of the southeastern shires were formed by conquering jarls or chieftains. Again, there are those that evidently grew out of a distinctly tribal consciousness; the best examples being *Hǫrðaland*[6] and *Rogaland* on the southwestern coast. At some early date, possibly during the migration period, the Hords came into the Hardanger Fjord (the fjord of the Hords), settled the coast, and thence spread northward to the limits of Sogn. South of Hordaland was the land of the Rugians[7] who may have come into the country

[5] The Northmen spoke of the sea routes to the east Baltic, to the south Baltic, to the British Isles and to the Arctic lands as the East Way, the South Way, the West Way, and the North Way, respectively.

[6] Hordaland (*Hæreðaland*) is mentioned in the *Anglo-Saxon Chronicle*, *anno* 787.

[7] In its catalog of Germanic tribes the Old English poem *Widsith* mentions the Holmrygas (*Holmrygum*, l. 21), who are usually identified with the inhabitants of Rogaland.

about the time when the neighboring tribe was giving its name to Hordaland.

About two hundred and fifty miles north of Hordaland, in the lovely basin of Trondheim Fjord was the Trondelaw, or Trondheim, the home of the Tronders,[8] a tribe of great power and influence in the Norse kingdom. The Tronders had divided their country into eight shires, each of which had the usual institutions that belonged to a self-governing unit; at the same time the tribal unity was maintained in certain other institutions which were recognized throughout the Trondelaw.

The Northmen of the early Middle Ages all spoke what was virtually the same language and accepted the belief that all the various Norse tribes had sprung from a common stock. At the same time they can scarcely have had any conception of national unity. Of the ordinary geographic conditions that favor the building of states, only one was present: this unifying influence was the North Way, the long sea route northward of which nearly all the freemen of the coastal shires made common and frequent use. A step in the direction of larger unities was taken, perhaps in the earlier Viking age, by the organization of a group of shires into a "law," or "jurisdiction." But so long was the distance from north to south, and so arduous was the travel on the inland highways, that one single law court and one single lawmaking body for the whole people could not be established. Accordingly, Norway came to have not one, but four, such provincial jurisdictions. Only the will of a conquering monarch could weld the tribes and shires into one united kingdom.

The Icelandic historian, Snorre Sturlason, informs us that the oldest of these laws was the Heidsævisthinglaw (later called the Eidsivathinglaw), the origin of which he ascribes to Halfdan the Swart, who flourished in southeastern Norway in the first half of the ninth century. But Snorre, though often remarkably well informed, wrote nearly four centuries after the event, and the tradition that he reports may not be entirely reliable. It is even quite likely that this law was already an old institution in Halfdan's day. The Eidsivathing dispensed justice to the Norse farmers

[8] Probably the Throwendas (*Þrowendum*) referred to in *Widsith* (l. 64).

who lived on the banks of Mjösen[9] and in the neighboring districts. In its earlier organization the law thing of this province may not have differed much from an ordinary shire thing; but in the course of time the representative principle was introduced and the assembly was assimilated to those of the other provinces.

Next in order of time came the Gulathinglaw in the southwest and the Frostathinglaw with its center of gravity in the ancient Trondelaw. These are both credited (again by Snorre) to the statesmanship of Hakon the Good, whose dates are generally given as 935-61. But here again it seems quite probable that tradition has confused organization with a later reorganization, for there is evidence that the Gulathing, at least, was a lawmaking body some time before the accession of the good king.[10] In the next century Saint Olaf brought about a grouping of the southeastern shires into a new law, the Borgarthinglaw, with headquarters at Borg (Sarpsborg). Further the organization of provincial assemblies did not go, though there remained several shires that did not send representatives to any one of the four law things. These unattached shires did not, however, undertake to build up legal systems of their own but accepted the older laws and the later enactments of some neighboring jurisdiction.

The Gulathinglaw is believed to have had its origin in the sacrificial festivals which were held periodically on Tysnes Isle in honor of Njord, the divinity that ruled the waves and the sea.[11] How this local body developed into the Gula confederation cannot be known; but early in the tenth century three shires, Hordaland, Sognfylki, and Firdafylki, appear to have composed the union. Later on, the lands of the Egdir and Rogaland to the south, and still later, South Möre to the north were admitted to the fellowship. It may have been in part the addition of the southern shires which the historian should have credited to Hakon the Good.

The business of the Gula republic was transacted by a representative assembly which met once a year. In the eleventh and

[9] Mjösen is a large lake (sixty miles long, the largest in Norway) lying some fifty miles north of Oslo Fjord.

[10] See A. Taranger, "Alting og lagting" in *Historisk tidsskrift* (Norwegian), XXIX (1930, 3), 137–38.

[11] See *Haskins Anniversary Essays*, pp. 133–34 (Larson).

early twelfth centuries the time of meeting was Thursday after Easter; but when the reforms of Magnus Erlingsson were written into the Gulathing law (1164), the date was changed to the eve of Saint Peter's day (June 28). Where the law thing met in the earlier centuries of its history cannot now be determined; but the later sources all speak of the assembly as the "Gulathing," and the inference is, therefore, that the name of the meeting place in Christian times was "Guli" or some name derived from Guli.

Among the place names of the southwestern coast country there are several which seem to have some such derivation; but most of these can be ruled out on topographical considerations. The consensus of opinion among the investigators at present seems to be that the famous thingstead was located somewhere near Gulen Fjord in a parish which was throughout the Middle Ages the northwest corner of Hordaland, but which, in 1773, was transferred to Sogn. Gulen Fjord joins the Sogn Fjord on the south side near the point where the great inlet opens out into the North Sea. The shores of Gulen were therefore accessible to all parts of the province; for in those days the fjords and the outer fairway were the only important highways on the western coast.

There is a local tradition in the Gulen country that the great court held its sessions on Gulöy (Gul Isle), a little peninsula on the north side of the fjord about six miles from the entrance into the inlet. There seems to be no good reason to question the accuracy of this tradition, except that physical conditions on the peninsula do not seem to meet the requirements of a large assembly. Efforts have therefore been made to find a place in the neighborhood where the conditions are more satisfactory but without unqualified success.[12]

Like the other three provincial courts, the Gulathing was a representative assembly, each fylki sending a prescribed number of degelates. In the legislation of Olaf the Quiet the number was fixed at about 400; two generations later the total was reduced to 258; a century later (1274) the number was further reduced to 148. The more important shires were evidently Hordaland and

[12] The problem of the site has been discussed by Gustav Indrebö in the Norwegian periodical *Syn og Segn*, XXII (1917), 374–84.

Rogaland, the two being allowed more than one-half of the entire representation. The delegates were chosen by the king's barons[13] and stewards in each fylki; at least, such was the case in the time of the older laws. Heavy fines were levied for non-attendance; on the other hand, the laws provided that each thingman should be allowed a payment in produce and money, enough to meet his expenses and perhaps a little for wages. These payments had to be made by the general citizenship of the fylki.[14]

The first important business of the session was the appointment of a committee, called the *lǫgrétta* (law court), whose duty it was to look into the causes and the proposals that were to come before the assembly and to recommend what disposition should be made of each. It is believed that in the earlier history of the law thing, when only three shires made up the law, twelve men were chosen from each, and this number, thirty-six, continued to be the strength of the law court even after the shire membership had risen to six. The original method employed in selecting these men cannot be determined; but in the eleventh and twelfth centuries they were chosen by the king's representatives. The law court was an important and influential body; but it seems not to have had the power to render final decisions: its recommendations became final only when they had been confirmed by the law thing, as they probably were in nearly every case.

The land of the Tronders differed materially, both in character and in appearance, from that of the Hords and the Rugians. Instead of a narrow strip of rock-built coast with uncounted islands fronting the mainland toward the sea, they rejoiced in a broad lowland, which in places became a fairly level plain. Unlike their brethren to the south, who were much addicted to roaming the sea as traders and pirates, the Tronders preferred to remain at home on their fertile farms and found in their own tribal affairs and relations such an outlet for their energies as the Hords and the Rugians sought in foreign climes.

Since time immemorial the tribesmen of Trondheim had had a "thing" which met every summer on the sands (*eyrr*) near the mouth of the Nid river, where the city of Nidaros (Trondheim)

[13] Barons; see below p. 22 and Glossary, "Baron."

[14] *Gulathing law*, c. 3. Elsewhere Gulathing law will be abbreviated to *Gul.*

was later built. The Eyrathing was never a representative law thing; it was an "althing," or primary assembly, which all able-bodied farmers were expected to attend. Early in June the freemen of the eight shires would begin to assemble to hear difficult lawsuits and to transact such other business as might arise in rural communities.[15] In 997 Olaf Trygvesson founded the borough of Nidaros close to the thingstead. Trondheim was in those days regarded as the heart of the kingdom, and for a time the king maintained his chief residence at Nidaros. During this period it became customary, when the throne was vacant, for the claimant to summon the Eyrathing and ask that his rights be recognized and confirmed.[16] In 1164 Magnus Erlingsson promulgated a new law governing the succession to the throne; but the principle of election was in a measure retained and in order to be legal the choice had to be made in Nidaros.[17]

There is some reason to believe that Hakon the Good may have wished to enlarge the Eyrathing by the admission of representatives from the neighboring shires; but if such a proposal was actually made the Tronders must have refused to acquiesce in it, for the Eyrathing long continued to function in its ancient form. As a compromise, perhaps, though this is conjecture merely, a new provincial organization was formed—one composed of the eight shires of Trondheim and in addition those of Naumdale, North Möre, and Raumdale. South Möre may also have belonged for a time; later it was added to the Gulathinglaw, as noted above.

The new law held its court on the Frosta peninsula, a comparatively level area some twelve miles northeast of Nidaros. The assembly convened about midsummer on Lagatun farm, which is thought to have been a royal estate. It was a large body: four hundred thingmen came from the Trondelaw and a smaller number from the other shires.[18] There were also certain functionaries present whose membership was *ex officio*.

[15] *Frostathing law*, I, c. 4. Elsewhere Frostathing law will be abbreviated to *Frost.*

[16] Ordinarily the new king would also present his claims at such other things as were deemed important. See Keyser, *Norges stats- og retsforfatning*, pp. 52 ff.

[17] *Gul.*, c. 2.

[18] The *Landslov* (common law) of Magnus Lawmender continues the representation from Trondheim at 400 and gives 85 to the other (four) shires.

Close to the thingstead was Lagatun church, where a copy of the provincial law was kept and daily brought to the court by the priest who had it in his keeping. A bell was rung when the priest set out for the meeting place with the law book, and so long as the sessions continued this bell could be rung for no other purpose.[19]

Like the assembly at Gula, the Frostathing had its law court only it was a much larger body. The Frostathing law seems to set the number at 400 all of whom were to be chosen from Trondheim; in fact it looks as if all the representatives from the eight shires had places in the law court as well as in the law thing itself. In this way the Tronders were able to keep control of all the provincial business: "they had secured for themselves an absolute majority among the representative thingmen and had the law court as their own monopoly. In addition they had a monopoly on the elections to the kingship at the Eyrathing."[20]

The functions of a law thing were chiefly legislative and judicial. Ordinarily such litigation would come to the great assembly as had failed to be settled properly in the lower things. The Old Norsemen appear to have been quite insistent on what they regarded as their rights; consequently the legal system of the times had to provide for eventualities of many kinds. Of the laws applied and enforced by the Borgarthing and the Eidsivathing, only those that concern the church have survived; but of the Gulathing law and the Frostathing law, there are extant versions which seem to be quite complete and reliable.

In the earlier centuries of Norwegian history the population was almost exclusively rural. This does not mean that the urban elements were wholly unimportant, for traders and trading centers are mentioned in some of the earliest sources, and the profession of the merchant was regarded as highly honorable even in the days when valor was counted as next to godliness. On some of the older trading sites important towns can be found today, several of which can trace their history back to the eleventh century or even ear-

[19] *Frost.*, I, c. 3.

[20] Taranger, *Trondheimens forfatningshistorie*, pp. 21–22. Maurer rejects this interpretation: *Vorlesungen über altnordische Rechtsgeschichte*, Vol. I, Part 2, 15.

lier.[21] In these trading centers, at least in those that had received royal recognition, the life and the activities of the citizens were regulated by a special code of laws, the so-called "Birch-Isle code," which has survived only in a fragmentary form. But while the municipal laws were an important part of Old Norse legislation, they did not directly concern more than a small part of the population. In medieval Norway freeman and farmer were almost synonymous terms.

Unlike the rural classes elsewhere in the North the Norwegian farmers did not live in villages, though farmsteads grouped in what may be called hamlets were evidently quite numerous. The provincial laws appear to assume that the freemen lived in small settlements or on separate farms, often at some distance from other homesteads. The laws also recognize the fact that travel by land, as well as by sea, was often difficult and might be quite perilous; and they are therefore quite specific as to the time that must be allowed to pass before an action may be begun or legally terminated.

As elsewhere in the Germanic lands the stratification in Norwegian society was clear and definite. In a survey of the social order one begins with the *hauldr*, whose class was the most important in the kingdom. The holdar were the members of ancient families whose ancestry, so far as was known, was of free origin on both sides of the house; but to be a hauld one must also be the possessor of allodial land or able to possess such land. He must be born to odal right.

Next below the hauld stood the *bóndi*, *búandi*, or common freeman.[22] The freeman might also be the owner of land; but if he was, it was land that had not yet been long enough in the family to be regarded as an ancestral possession. More often he was a

[21] Trondheim (Nidaros) celebrated its nine hundredth anniversary in 1897. Oslo is said to have been founded by Harald the Hardruler who fell at Stamford Bridge (1066); Bergen dates from about 1075; Tunsberg seems to have developed into a town in the tenth century; and Sarpsborg belongs to the eleventh. These towns seem all to have been trading centers long before they received recognition as boroughs.

[22] The Frostathing law recognized two classes of freemen: the well-born man who could claim a free ancestry and the "reksthegn" whose family had a servile origin; IV, cc. 49, 53.

tenant farmer occupying land to which the title was held by another. Ordinarily his landlord would be some member of the hauld aristocracy; but he might also be tilling land that belonged to the church or even to the king.

Lower still stood the freedman, one whose family, though no longer servile, had not yet attained to a status of complete freedom. In the act of emancipation the liberated thrall entered the borderland between slavery and freedom; but this was a broad realm and could be completely crossed only after several generations, usually four. The last traces of dependence would, therefore, disappear only with the freedman's great-grandson; and his great-great-grandson would be the first of his decendants to enjoy the unqualified rights of a free man.

There is no need in a survey of this sort to discuss the status of the slave, since he had no place or membership in the social body. Nevertheless, thralldom was a very important factor in the social and economic arrangements of the time. The Gulathing law leaves the impression that in the twelfth century the slave population was quite numerous. Earlier, especially in the Viking period, the number must have been considerably larger. It is difficult to understand how the activities of that virile age could have been carried forward to achievement without a large element of unfree men and women bound to labor and service of every sort. But the forces of civilization were hostile to slave economy; when the Frostathing law was taking its final form (in the thirteenth century), the provision for public emancipation at the lawthing was evidently regarded as wholly obsolete.[23] Slavery was becoming a thing of the past.

A curious though a thoroughly characteristic Germanic conception was the theory of personal right. In general the term *réttr* (right) was taken to mean what it means today; but it was also used in the sense of rank, and it was further used to indicate the material compensation for injuries to which a citizen of some particular rank was entitled.

The scale of "right" in its simplest form is stated in the Gulathing law. In the Gula province a baron enjoyed a right of six

[23] *Frost.*, III, c. 19

marks.[24] That of a hauld was three marks. A common freeman could claim one and one-half marks. A freedman who had given his freedom ale[25] had a right of six oras, or half as much as a freeman. His son, who was farther along on the road to freedom, was rated at one mark (eight oras). But if the freedman had not given his ale, his right was only four oras. In the Frosta law there is some difference in details but the general plan is the same.

The medieval Norseman held firmly to the ancient principle that the life and the honor of a free man were sacred and must be regarded as inviolable by his fellowmen. Every injury, therefore, demanded satisfaction either in blood or in a monetary payment. "No one, either a man or a woman" says the Gulathing law, "has a right to claim compensation more than three times, unless he has taken revenge in the meantime."[26] This was doubtless good law even in the twelfth century; but it seems unlikely that the duty of revenge was consistently enforced. Usually the injured man would be satisfied with a certain sum of money (or the equivalent) which in the earlier days would amount to the right due to a man of his rank. Lesser injuries might be satisfied with half a right; in graver cases the compensation might be doubled. In the course of time the lawmakers had come to recognize wrong in many degrees, and the provincial laws provide elaborate tariffs of fines which frequently seem to take only slight account of the ancient personal right.

The same principle governed in cases of manslaughter: to take revenge was not only a right but a sacred duty. Men had come to feel, however, that even manslaying might be atoned for with a suitable and sufficient payment, though all would grant that in many cases the right to choose and to decide still rested with the kindred most concerned. The taking of a life deprived the slain man's family of potential wealth, power, and prestige; while the slayer's kinsmen gained in strength and riches to the same degree. Somehow this unfavorable balance would have to be redressed. The safest way to achieve this was to exact a fine, wergeld, or man money, which the slayer and his kinsmen paid to the family of the

[24] The mark was the highest monetary unit used in the North. See Glossary.
[25] That is, had published his emancipation.
[26] *Gul.*, c. 186.

slain man. The amount levied always had some relation to the rights of the parties involved and was in every case a considerable sum. In the Gulathing law there are at least two, and probably three, wergeld tariffs[27] one of which is highly detailed.[28] In the later law only one scheme is presented but this is exceedingly elaborate and shows clearly what an appalling business the practice of exacting wergelds had come to be.[29]

Originally, no doubt, each individual, with the aid of his kindred, was expected to enforce all his rights, and this theory was by no means obsolete even as late as the thirteenth century. But by this time, and long before, certain judicial organs had come into being which stood ready to assist any one who believed himself wronged in person, honor, or property. This help was rendered for the most part in and by the public assembly, or moot, which the Northmen called a "thing." Of such moots there were many kinds: regular things were held in the province, the fylki, the herath, and the borough; but moots of the more local type could also be called and held at any time when the need was evident, as in cases of theft or homicide.

In the twelfth century the Norwegian state was still almost without machinery for the apprehension and prosecution of persons accused of crime. Normally it was the business of the injured man, or of his heir, to find the one who was believed to be guilty of having done wrong to him and to bring the man before the assembled farmers of the settlement at a regular or special moot. If a man was found killed, his wife, or someone acting in her behalf, could summon the freemen to a thing.[30] When the moot was called a summons was also sent to the accused, warning him to appear at the assembly to hear the charge and to make what answer he could. In those parts of the country where the herath system prevailed, it is likely that the call went forth through all that area. Elsewhere the procedure must have been somewhat different.

It was the business of those who came to the thing to hear the facts that were alleged and to note carefully the evidence that was presented. Ordinarily the thingmen took no further action

[27] *Gul.*, cc. 218–52, 316–19.

[28] *Ibid.*, cc. 316–19.

[29] *Frost.*, VI.

[30] *Gul.*, c. 151.

at the initial moot, but left the actual hearing to a later moot when a final decision would be reached and declared. Whenever possible a case was concluded on the testimony of witnesses. If the facts were not known and the defendant persisted in his denial of guilt, the court might order him to clear himself with oaths and oath helpers, or by an appeal to the judgment of God.

Norwegian history has recorded several interesting cases of an appeal to the ordeal. In 1128 Harald Gillecrist proved his claim to royal blood by walking over nine hot plowshares. Ninety years later Inga of Varteig carried the hot iron to prove that her son, the later King Hakon IV, was the son of Hakon III. But this expedient seems, on the whole, not to have been employed very extensively in the North.[31] Compurgation was, on the other hand, a very popular method and, when better proof was lacking, this was the one that was generally used.[32]

The number of oath helpers required depended entirely on the gravity of the charge. In some instances the accused could clear himself with his own unsupported oath; in more serious cases he would need the support of two, four, five, six, or eleven compurgators. The nature of the charge would also determine how the oath helpers were to be chosen: they might be selected by the accused, in part by the accused and in part by the accuser, or they might be chosen by the court itself. It is provided in the Gulathing law that in cases of murder and arson, six men shall be chosen and placed "on either side of the accused, all to be men of equal rank with him; and let him have two of them and his nearest two kinsmen; let [the accused] himself be the fifth, and let him find seven oath helpers."[33] How the initial group was selected cannot be determined; but the probabilities are that they were chosen by the two parties to the suit. It was in all cases necessary that the compurgators should be unanimous in their declarations: if one oath failed, the entire proceding was a failure, and the defendant stood convicted of guilt.

When a man had taken the life of another he had at the same time destroyed the sanctity of his own life and had forfeited his

[31] See *Haskins Anniversary Essays*, pp. 152–53.
[32] On the subject of compurgation, see *ibid.*, pp. 144–52.
[33] *Gul.*, c. 132.

right to live in peace among his fellow men. The logical penalty was usually not exacted, however, before the men of the locality had heard the charges and had examined the circumstances alleged in formal moot. In cases of this character the findings of the thing-men might take one of three directions. They might conclude that the slaying was justifiable and dismiss the indictment. Or they might find that the crime was of such character that the charge could be satisfied with the payment of a fine, and they would therefore order the accused to make atonement as provided by law. But, if the crime proved to be of a peculiarly heinous character they had no choice but to declare the accused an outlaw.[34]

There were two forms of outlawry recognized in Old Norwegian law. Sometimes a sentence of outlawry would mean something like involuntary exile from which one might return on the payment of a series of heavy fines. This payment was called *skógarkaup*, or money paid for the right to return from the forest. The second form was final and irrevocable and was reserved for persons whose crimes were particularly odious and atrocious. The sentence extended, moreover, to the outlawed man's property, which was immediately seized in the interest of the complainant and the higher authorities, which in the twelfth century meant the king.

Though capital punishment was not unknown in the Northern lands, it seems to be less in evidence than one should expect. The practice of mutilation appears to be far more common. The old laws often prescribe the loss of an arm or a foot or some other important part of the body as worthy and suitable punishment. There can be little doubt that such operations were too often equivalent to a death sentence. Flogging is also found in the category of penalties; it was a common punishment for offending thralls and was also applied in certain cases of petty thievery.

To the Germanic mind the most odious crimes were such as were committed in secret. Theft was such an offense and seems to have given the law makers much concern. The laws of the Gula-thing and the Frostathing both contain lengthy and detailed titles devoted to this subject. If the amount stolen was of considerable value (an *ertog*[35] or more) the thief forfeited both life and property,

[34] Keyser, *Norges stats- og retsforfatning*, p. 396.
[35] See Glossary, "Ertog," "Monetary system."

though in rare instances the law would be satisfied with outlawry. For theft in smaller amounts the thief would be flogged or made to run the gauntlet. In all such cases the crime led to a complete loss of personal rights.

In legal actions involving the title to property or caused by the infraction of property rights, the principles applied were quite similar to those that governed in criminal actions. The procedure was, however, far more elaborate and required a careful attention to legal details. It was ancient law that no action could be brought against anyone except in his own house. The complainant, accordingly, had to begin his suit by looking up his opponent and summoning him to be at home by his fireside and in his highseat on a specified day to hear the claim which the plaintiff wished to present. This was called a "home summons" and had to be served in the presence of witnesses. On the appointed day the plaintiff would again take witnesses and go to his opponent's home to summon him to appear at the public court. If the claim was one that was not clear in all its details he would present it as a demand; and if this was refused, the suit would probably be heard by a "doom,"[36] a sort of private tribunal, the aim of which was to ferret out the circumstances and to bring the contending parties into a friendly agreement.

As the suit began to go forward in the normal way, witnesses to the various forms of summons had to be heard in their turn. If it appeared to the satisfaction of the thingmen that the case had been brought before them in a legal manner, they would allow the trial to go on. The plaintiff would bring forward a group of men who could testify to the facts involved in the contention and would ask for a favorable judgment, which the thingmen would render or refuse to render, according to the decision which the evidence appeared to justify.

The witnesses heard at court were usually men who had been invited to hear the terms of a transaction and to watch its consummation; they were witnesses by request or by appointment. Throughout all the Old Norse legislation one finds the same fundamental principle: that the dealings of man with man should, as

[36] *Gul.*, c. 37; see Glossary, "Doom."

far as possible, be made a matter of public knowledge. To achieve this it was necessary to have a record made of the important features of every transaction that might later become a subject of litigation. Inasmuch as it was not possible to make a written record in every case, even after the Christian clerk had brought an improved art of writing into the land, the record had to be made on the minds of men. All purchases therefore had to be made in the presence of men called in to hear the terms of the bargain and to observe the payment of the price. Land was leased and rent was paid under the same conditions. All important matters of economy involved in marriage and guardianship had to be settled in this way. A certain number of neighbors were always invited to hear the terms of a betrothal, or of a legal separation, if such there had to be. The children of a bondwoman could be disposed of only in the presence of witnesses. Illegitimate children were adopted into the family at a ceremonial feast and in the presence of neighbors who came to witness the ceremony and to taste the ale.[37]

When the decision was finally rendered, the duties of the court as such had been performed. The execution of the judgment, if the complaint was held to be well founded, was the plaintiff's own affair. If there should be fear that his opponent might offer resistance, he had the right to ask the assistance of as many thingmen as were thought necessary to enforce the decree, and such a demand could ordinarily not be refused.

It may be thought strange that these provincial jurisdictions did not develop some sort of executive or administrative institutions; but of such there seems to be no trace, except, perhaps, in the arrangements for public worship in heathen times. What might have happened in this field if their development had been allowed to go on without interference from outside forces cannot be known. But quite early in the history of these republics a new variety of institutional arrangements was planted alongside the older growth, and the constitutional development was deflected into newer lines.

[37] For a somewhat more extended discussion of the use of witnesses in medieval Norway see *Haskins Anniversary Essays*, pp. 135–43.

The history of monarchy in Norway goes back to the second half of the ninth century when Harald the Fairhaired undertook the task of consolidating the tribal units into a single kingdom.[38] There had, of course, been kings in the land long before Harald's time; but these must have been chiefly of the shire-king variety and their kingship may have been little more than military chieftainship. Harald's ambition seems to have been to build a state in which the king and his officials should be real, controlling forces. But the Norwegian holdar could not brook a strong kingship, and Harald's son, Hakon the Good, was forced to retreat from his father's position and to restore to the freemen some of the rights that Harald had taken away.

Early in the eleventh century, Olaf Haraldsson, usually known as Saint Olaf, mounted the royal highseat and ruled the land intermittently for a period of fourteen strenuous years (1016–1030). Under his firm and somewhat heavy hands the constitution of the young kingdom was forced into new molds. The national worship, dear though it must have been to strong and valorous hearts, was driven into hiding, and Christianity with all its many social and political implications was made the official religion of the land. Bishops and priests came to take places alongside the jarl and the hauld in the councils of the king and in the assemblies of the freemen. At first the priest seems not to have exercised much influence outside his own order;[39] but the bishop was a power to be reckoned with from the very beginning.

The change in religion led to important changes in the provincial laws. Many human activities that were formerly allowed, and even enjoined, were now forbidden; on the other hand, the new Christians were ordered to observe a variety of religious practices with which they were unfamiliar. The old laws bear witness that offenses against religion and morals were quite common; and, since the church in Norway never had courts of its own, at least not in the continental sense, the amount of business to be transacted

[38] Harald's work was completed by the victory of Hafrs Fjord (near the modern Stavanger), the traditional date of which is 872. Some writers reject this date and hold that the battle was fought about twenty years later.

[39] It is stated in the Gulathing law (c. 15) that the priests were no longer subject to corporal punishment; this does not indicate a high social status.

in the public assembly was measurably increased. Another fact of real significance was the appearance in the folkmoot of a new official in the person of the bishop's bailiff to whom the prosecution of offenders against the laws of the church was largely entrusted.

It was inevitable that the introduction of the new faith would seriously influence the character of the royal institution. Norwegian kingship in its earlier phase was of the older Germanic type. The king had risen to a high place in the state. His functions were important and of considerable variety. His wealth was great and his power was not to be challenged. He enjoyed the right to a fine for injury to his person and to his personal rights sixteen times as great as that allowed a common freeman. In the eyes of the law he was the first citizen of the realm; but he was a citizen none the less. His person was not sacred, for the Norsemen had never been taught that the king can do no wrong. If he did evil, he would have to suffer the same penalties as any other citizen. If the king attacks a man in his house, says the Frostathing law, "[men shall] go upon him and slay him, if they are able to seize him, and if he escapes, he shall never be allowed to return to the land."[40]

Throughout the more distinctly medieval centuries of Norwegian history the institutional arrangements that had been carried over from heathen times continued to serve as the framework of the government. Even as late as the first half of the thirteenth century the people, organized in fylki and province, continued to be the decisive power in the state. Ordinarily the freemen alone could give a legal sentence and they alone could add to the laws of the land.

With the accession of Magnus Lawmender (1263–1280), the royal office shows that it has come to have a new meaning. The king is now the Lord's anointed and holds his office by the grace of God. He is gradually coming to be regarded as the fountain of justice and the source of law. Soon after 1263 the old provincial codes ceased to be operative; for early in his reign King Magnus and his lawyers began seriously the work of building a new legal system which was to have authority throughout the entire land.

[40] *Frost.*, IV, c. 50.

In the new common law the shifting of emphasis is clearly apparent. Certain powers that once could be exercised by the deputies of the law things only are now passing definitely into the hands of the king's own local officials.

In the Middle Ages the kings were often great landowners and derived a very considerable part of their income from their many estates. The Norwegian kings were no exception in this respect. The royal fisc appears to have extended into every part of the realm; and, as the ruler of a decidedly rebellious folk, the king found many opportunities to add to his holdings by forfeiture and other forms of confiscation.

The king disposed of these lands in various ways. Many of his farms were let to tenants who were allowed to occupy and till them for a year or a term of years in return for a specified rent. Some of his more desirable estates or groups of estates he would frequently grant to prominent chieftains on certain conditions which recall the arrangements of the feudal contract. The tenants of this class were called *lendir menn* (later barons)[41] because they were endowed with land. The remaining lands formed what may be called the royal demesne and were managed wholly in the king's interest by his stewards or bailiffs.

The dignity of the baronial estate was, it seems, more a matter of rank and honor, than of official duties. A baron was allowed to keep a certain number of armed retainers or housecarles (forty was a common number) and was allowed a personal right of six marks, which was twice that of a hauld and half that of a jarl or bishop. As a king's tenant he enjoyed the right to be summoned to the royal council chamber. Most of his functions, however, were of a local character and were concerned with his own shire, where he was expected to guard the king's interests, especially in the matter of the coast defense. The number of barons was never large: Gustav Storm believes that thirty was probably the maximum.[42]

Although the baron's office was not hereditary, the honor was usually granted to prominent members of the local aristocracy; it was, therefore, quite natural that these men should come to ex-

[41] See Glossary, "Baron."

[42] *Historisk tidsskrift*, Ser. 2, IV, 129–88.

ercise a definite influence in the administration of local affairs. They had a part in the appointment of delegates to the provincial law things. They saw to it that the shire thing was properly conducted and that its decisions were respected and carried out. At the same time the freemen were determined that the influence of these worthies should not become controlling. No baron was allowed to sit in a doom or "to approach so near to a doom that his voice could be heard."[43] A baron could not act as attorney for a woman.[44] He could not appear in the law court at the Frostathing.[45] In other ways, too, the provincial laws indicate that the freemen regarded the power of this order with something like fear if not suspicion.

It is not likely that Harald the Fairhaired and his immediate successors took a very live interest in the work of the local courts. The situation is quite different in the thirteenth century when the king's rights appear on almost every page of the law books. Just how this change came about is a difficult question; but one may conjecture that financial necessities had something to do with it. The central authorities must have discovered at an early date that the folkmoots might become important sources of revenue. It was in the nature of things that the king should seize the property of any man whose crime was directed against the royal person or office. But the king did not stop at that point; in the course of time the category of pleas in which the head of the nation might have a direct interest was widely extended, until the number of crimes that yielded fines payable to the royal treasury grew to be very large.

The king's authority in local affairs was entrusted for the most part to the royal bailiffs who were to be found in every part of the country. In addition to managing affairs on the king's garth, and providing for his needs when he came into that part of the country, the bailiff had important duties in connection with the administration of justice. It was his business to make sure that the regular things were held at the proper time, and he was expected to attend the most important ones.[46] A man accused of

[43] *Gul.*, c. 37; *Frost.*, X, c. 16.
[44] *Gul.*, c. 47.
[45] *Frost.*, I, c. 2.
[46] *Ibid.*, I, cc. 1, 2.

crime might be delivered to him for custody, and he could not refuse to receive him.[47] He was the proper prosecutor in all cases in which the king had an interest, and he collected the fines that were awarded to the royal office. It was his duty, on occasion, to administer flogging and even to act as public headsman. But he did not as a royal official have any judicial functions; the freemen retained their ancient power to declare the law.

The old system was not, however, to endure much beyond the twelfth century. It may be that, as the laws grew more complex and refined, the efficiency of the old courts could no longer be maintained. Or it may be that, on account of the prevalence of crime in the thirteenth century, the leaders of the folk had become disposed and willing to allow the enlargement of the royal dominion. But whatever the cause, it is quite evident that in the thirteenth century the folkmoot was losing much of its old authority. The change appears first in the provincial assemblies: certain powers that once could be exercised only by the delegates from the various shires are now passing definitely into the hands of royal functionaries, among whom the most important in the judicial field was the lawman.

There is no mention of the lawman in the Gulathing law, and he is referred to only incidentally in the main body of the Frostathing law;[48] still, there can be little doubt that the history of his office goes back into a much earlier time, though it may have had a different name and title. Originally he seems to have been one who was learned in the law and who was, therefore, able to give authoritative opinions whenever he was asked by the court to do so. His first notable advance toward independent authority came in the reign of King Sverri when certain lawmen received the status of royal officials.[49] In the course of the thirteenth century the functions of this official take on a more definite character: in the Common Law he is recognized as the presiding officer of the

[47] *Gul.*, c. 152.

[48] Professor Taranger regards these references to the lawman as later interpolations. *Trondheimens forfatningshistorie*, p. 28.

[49] For a discussion of the various theories presented with respect to the early history of the lawman's office, see Hertzberg, *Grundtrækkene i den ældste norske proces*, pp. 156–77.

provincial assembly and before long he is competent to act in a judicial capacity (to a limited extent, at least) without regard to the older rights of the lawthing.

In the early history of the office the lawmen seem to have been appointed in varying numbers. It was therefore likely that each jurisdiction would have more than one lawman. This fact no doubt led to an informal arrangement which allowed each lawman to act as legal adviser and authority in his part of the province. In time what had been informal became formal; for in the fourteenth century it was found expedient to divide the old jurisdictional areas and to create new law things. Soon there were nine or ten instead of the historic four.[50] By that time the people had almost ceased to be a real power in the state.

The changes that came in the dawning hours of the new age were many and far-reaching. The ancient institutions of the organized folk were transformed or taken away. The local aristocracy to which the folk had entrusted power and leadership lost the virility that it had once displayed. More and more the emphasis came to be placed on the royal office. It would be a mistake, however, to conclude from this that all parts of the earlier system disappeared; on the contrary, the new régime was in large part built on the old foundations. The new legislation was essentially a revision and codification of the earlier provincial laws. Though the changes in details were many and important, the old framework remained and judicial business continued for a long time to find its chief guidance in the ancient principles of Norwegian jurisprudence.

Of the four codes that had authority before the reign of Magnus Lawmender, only two have survived in anything like a complete version. As stated above, only those parts of the laws of the Eidsivathing and the Borgarthing that deal with the church have escaped destruction. Of the other two, the laws of the Gulathing and of the Frostathing, fairly complete versions have come down to us. There are also extant copies of two municipal laws and various gild regulations which are also important for the history of the judicial system of Old Norway. But these do not come into

[50] During the years 1632-1719.

this discussion; this volume is concerned almost exclusively with the two ancient folk laws, the Gulathing law and the Frostathing law.

Of these two books that of the Gulathing is the older: the most satisfactory manuscript that has come down to us dates from about 1150. It is quite evident, however, that both laws have gone through a long process of change and development. In both there are legal formulas and ceremonies which have the appearance of great age. Such are the rites that are employed in the legitimation of baseborn children;[51] in the manumission of thralls and bondwomen;[52] in the transfer of odal land and odal right,[53] in the use of the law billet;[54] and in the persistent employment of the five-day week in secular affairs.[55] The chapters dealing with social classification, land tenure, theft, and man money are often based on principles that are much older than the twelfth century. The laws relating to marriage contain provisions which are Germanic rather than Christian. And certain parts of the church law, such as the permission to expose a child that is born with a serious deformity[56] and the rather lenient attitude toward carnal sins,[57] reveal a background that is distinctly Germanic and heathen.

The Gulathing law begins with a title devoted to the statutes of the church, which, inasmuch as it is based on a code that seems to have been enacted in the reign of Olaf the Quiet,[58] must in large part go back to the closing decades of the eleventh century. The law furthermore contains allusions to an older church law, which it ascribes to Saint Olaf (who fell in battle in 1030), and it seems more than likely that the missionary king gave law, as well as organization, to the young Norwegian church. Olaf the Quiet's legislation was amended in several important respects by Magnus Erlingsson in 1164, when he bought the crown from Archbishop Eystein.[59] The amendments were submitted with royal and epis-

[51] *Gul.*, c. 58; *Frost.*, IX, c. 1.
[52] *Gul.*, c. 61; *Frost.*, IX, c. 12.
[53] *Gul.*, c. 292.
[54] *Frost.*, IX, c. 30.
[55] *Gul.*, cc. 22, 159, *et passim*. See Glossary, "Five-day week."
[56] *Gul.*, c. 21.
[57] *Ibid.*, c. 25.
[58] Olaf the Quiet shared in the expedition that came to grief at Stamford Bridge. He died in 1093.
[59] The Concordat of 1164 was the price paid by Erling Skakke (the Wry One) for the coronation of his young son Magnus, who, though his mother was of

copal recommendation to a meeting of magnates and provincial deputies who came together in Bergen later in the same year. The will of the church and the kingship prevailed.

The provisions in the Gulathing law that are most recent in origin are no doubt the new schedule of man fines attributed to Bjarni Mardsson, which makes up the closing pages of the code.[60] Bjarni Mardsson, if he is correctly identified, was an able and highly influential magnate who flourished in the far north of Norway in the earlier decades of the thirteenth century. That he was learned in the law is well established; but there is no evidence that he was at any time associated with the court that assembled at Gula. One may therefore be permitted to doubt whether this division of the code should be actually regarded as law; it has more the appearance of an appendix added by the scribe who edited the materials in the extant copy of the code.[61]

The Frostathing law, both in language and in legal details, gives the impression of belonging to a somewhat later age than the Gulathing code. The version that has come down to us is prefaced by a series of amendments drawn up by the lawyers of the elder Hakon and accepted (as seems to be generally believed) at a law thing held at Frosta in 1260.[62] This "introduction" takes the form of a charter and is addressed not only to the freemen of the Frostathinglaw but to all the king's subjects, "clerks and barons, freemen and farmers, those now living and those to come." Its provisions are therefore intended to have authority throughout the land and were doubtless in due time incorporated into the laws of the other provincial jurisdictions.

The titles that deal with the laws of the church have long been regarded as an amended version of the so-called *Gullfjǫðr* (Goldfeather), a revision of the older legislation by Archbishop Eystein, who apparently was not wholly satisfied with the concordat of 1164. There is no doubt a close relation between the two

royal blood, was not the son of a king and is therefore rated as a usurper. Magnus was eight years old in 1164. [60] Cc. 316–19.

[61] On the general question of the composition of the Gulathing law see Taranger, *De norske folkelovböker*, pp. 1–29, especially pp. 20–26. (Originally published in *Tidsskrift for retsvidenskab*, XXXIX, XLI.)

[62] Taranger, *Udsigt over den norske retshistorie*, I, 44.

documents and there can also be little doubt that many of the newer provisions in the church law had their origin in the reforming labors of the strenuous archbishop.[63] It was Eystein's purpose to bring the laws of the Norwegian church into a closer agreement with canon law which had quite recently been codified in Gratian's *Decretum*.[64] This purpose was in great measure achieved. Since the archbishop went into exile in 1180, the Christian law of the Frostathing book must have taken form before that date.

In his introduction King Hakon alludes to the "old plan according to which the Frostathing book had been arranged";[65] it is therefore evident that the new book was based on an older statement of what was law in the northern province. This earlier book, with the exception of Title vi, is believed to have been prepared in the decade following 1170.[66] Title vi is a new and quite elaborate schedule of wergeld payments, which was probably drawn up by one of the lawmen early in the thirteenth century. But though there are these large sections of the Frostathing law which can be shown to have had a comparatively late origin, one may still be allowed to believe that many of its most characteristic enactments go back into a hoary past, when the legal principles of the Germanic system of law were not hampered in their development by the insistent demands of Christian ethics.

The old laws of the Gulathing have come down to us in five manuscripts, four of which are fragments only.[67] Fortunately the fifth manuscript seems to be entirely complete except for three missing sheets. In the days of the famous Icelandic collector, Arna Magnusson, this book was in the possession of Count Otto

[63] See Taranger, *De norske fokelovböker*, pp. 33 ff.

[64] The *Decretum* dates from *ca.* 1140. See Taranger, *De norske folkelovböker*, pp. 39–40.

[65] C. 25.

[66] Taranger, *Trondheimens forfåtningshistorie*, p. 21.

[67] Manuscript C includes several sheets from various parts of the code and is of interest to the historian chiefly because it is no doubt the oldest fragment that has survived; the copy itself may not be much earlier than 1200, but the material that it contains is scarcely later than 1150. E is a trifle later; it comprises three sheets only. The two sheets of manuscript D are credited to the first half of the thirteenth century. B is a copy of the church law to chapter 29; it belongs to the middle of the fourteenth century. For further details see Keyser's account in the Norwegian edition of the old laws, *Norges gamle love*, IV, 641–44; Taranger, *De norske folkelovböker*, pp. 4–6.

Rantzau and was accordingly christened the Codex Ranzowianus by the great antiquarian. The manuscript has since become the property of the library of the University of Copenhagen. It is a parchment of 146 pages in small quarto and seems to be a product of the second half of the thirteenth century, though it probably should not be dated much later than 1250.[68]

The published text of the Frostathing law is based almost entirely on a copy of a thirteenth-century manuscript, the Codex Resenianus, so called because in the seventeenth century it was the property of Count Peder Hansen Resen,[69] a man of great eminence as royal official and professor of jurisprudence at the University. Count Resen was an untiring collector of books and manuscripts; especially was he interested in Old Northern literature and law. In the course of his search for old parchments he came into possession of many rare treasures, which he finally presented to the University library and which were all destroyed in the great fire that devastated Copenhagen in 1728. Fortunately, several copies, more or less complete, had been made of the Codex Resenianus, and these with the aid of other sources have made it possible to reconstruct the text of the Frostathing book almost in its entirety.[70]

The existence of these legal monuments was a fact well known to Norwegian scholars one hundred years ago, though little had been done to make them accessible to students. In 1830 the attention of the national parliament was called to the need of a scholarly edition of these laws and the Storthing (the national legislature) appointed a commission to bring the documents into printed form; at the same time it made a small (and wholly inadequate) appropriation to finance the undertaking. Nothing of importance was achieved, however, before 1835, when Rudolf

[68] Taranger, *De norske fokelovböker*, p. 6.

[69] Count Resen's dates are 1625–88.

[70] In addition to the Codex Resenianus five manuscripts of the Frostathing law have come to light; but these are all slight fragments except one, a codex from about the same decade as the Resen book (1260–70), which it corrects and supplements on various points. It is published in *Norges gamle love*, IV, 501–14. The various manuscripts and copies are described in *ibid.*, pp. 393–94, 449, 489–90, 503–4, 673. See also I, 120, and Taranger, *De norske folkelovböker*, pp. 30–33.

Keyser and Peter Andreas Munch[71] betook themselves to Copenhagen and other literary centers in the North to begin a search for manuscripts and to make the necessary copies.

The plan was to prepare a text with all possible care and accuracy of all the Norwegian laws that had been accepted or enacted before 1387. After ten years of intermittent labor the work had reached such a state of preparation that the commission might proceed with plans for publication. Volume I, containing the Gulathing law and the Frostathing law with some other materials from the same age (before 1277), was published in 1846. Three other volumes followed in the course of the next forty years; Volume IV appeared in 1885. The work closed ten years later with an extensive glossary which was issued in 1895.

The translation that is presented in this volume is, so far as the writer can learn, the first attempt to give a complete version of these two old laws in any modern language. It is based on the text prepared by Munch and Keyser and published in 1846, as stated above. This text has been followed consistently except in places where the scribe seems to have omitted or repeated a word or a phrase, or has otherwise manifestly fallen into error. Careful note has therefore been taken of the many emendations suggested by the learned Norwegian editors, and most of these have been incorporated into the translation. Changes of this sort are particularly numerous in the sixth title of the Frostathing law, where scribal errors, especially in the statement of numbers, are quite numerous.

The versions included in this translation are those of the Codex Ranzowianus and the Codex Resenianus. As noted above there are extant fragments of other codices, some of which have the authority of greater age than those of the more complete copies; these have been left untranslated for the reason, chiefly, that they contribute very little to the knowledge of legal details and principles afforded by the principal codices. In the Frostathing law each title is prefaced with a list of chapter headings; these

[71] Rudolf Keyser (1803–64) and Peter Andreas Munch (1810–63) were the founders of the Norwegian historical school. Munch is perhaps the most eminent historian that his country has produced. See Gjerset, *History of the Norwegian People*, II, 493–96.

lists have been omitted as serving no necessary purpose. On the other hand, the larger divisions, or titles, of the Gulathing law have been provided with headings which are not in the original text.[72] These and all other materials introduced by the translator into the body of either law have been placed in brackets. In other respects the purpose has been to include all the materials included in the Old Norwegian edition prepared by Rudolf Keyser and Peter Andreas Munch.

[72] In the Codex Ranzowianus the chapters or sections are not numbered. Since some form of numbering is a convenience if not a necessity, the Norwegian editors thought it expedient to supply this defect.

THE OLDER LAW OF THE GULATHING

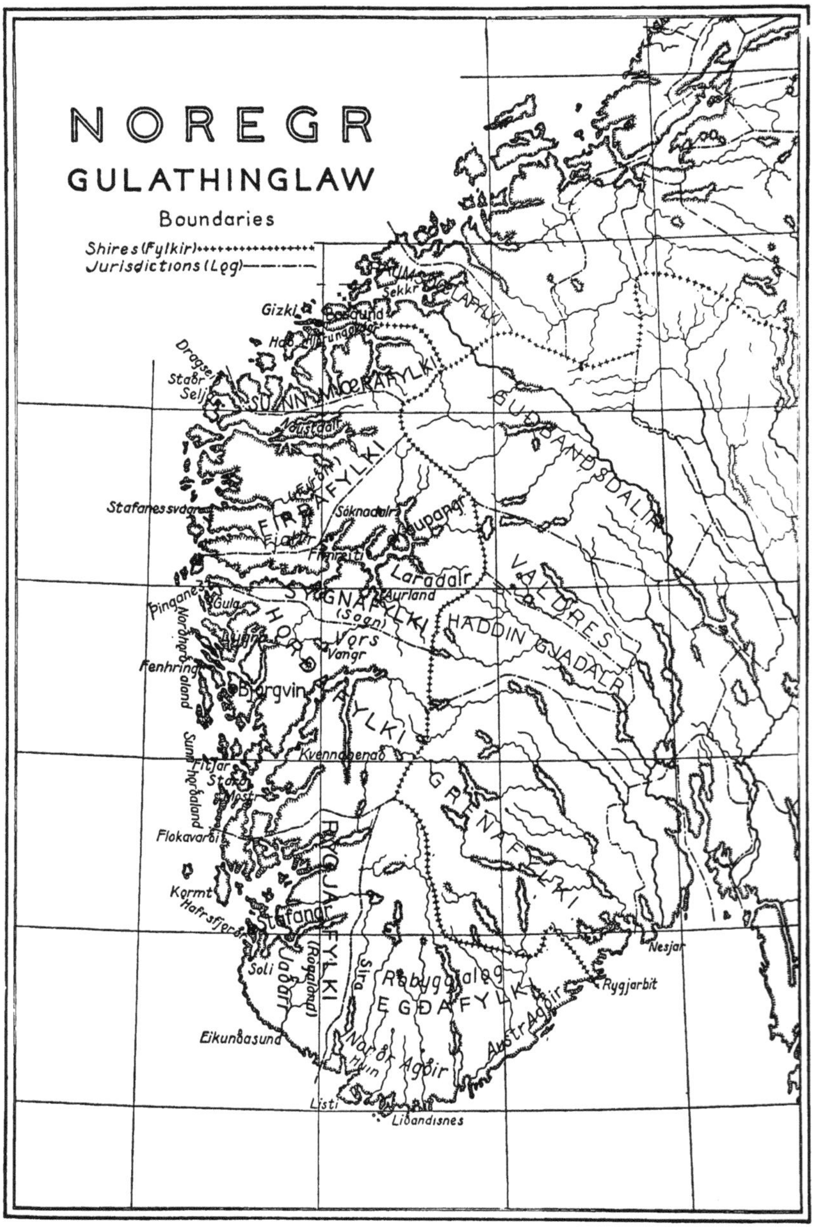
NOREGR
GULATHINGLAW
Boundaries
Shires (Fylkir)
Jurisdictions (Lǫg)
Gizki
Staðr
Selja
SUNNMŒRAFYLKI
FIRÐAFYLKI
Stafanessvágr
Sóknadalr
Laradalr
Aurland
SYGNAFYLKI
(Sogn)
Vǫrs
Vangr
Gula
Fenhring
Bjǫrgvin
HǫRÐAFYLKI
Norðhǫrðaland
Sunnhǫrðaland
Fitjar
Kvennaherað
HADDINGJADALR
VALDRES
GUÐBRANDSDALIR
GRENAFYLKI
Flokavarði
Kormt
Hafrsfjǫrðr
Stafangr
RYGJAFYLKI
(Rogaland)
Jaðarr
Soli
Eikundasund
Sira
Róbyggjalag
EGÐAFYLKI
Norðr Agðir
Austr Agðir
Hvin
Listi
Líðandisnes
Nesjar
Rygjarbit

HERE BEGINS THE BOOK OF THE GULATHING

[THE CHURCH LAW]

1. THE FIRST TITLE IN THIS BOOK DEALS WITH THE KEEPING OF OUR CHRISTIAN RELIGION

The first commandment in our legislation is that we shall bow toward the east and pray to the Holy Christ for peace and a fruitful harvest and that we may keep our country settled and tilled and that our sovereign lord may have strength and health; may he be our friend and we his friends, and may God be a friend to us all.

2. THESE ARE NEW ORDINANCES WHICH WERE PUBLISHED BY K[ING] M[AGNUS][1] ON THE ADVICE OF ARCHBISHOP EYSTEIN,[2] ERLING JARL,[3] AND ALL THE MOST PRUDENT MEN IN NORWAY

The next is this, that the king of Norway shall be one who is born a legitimate son of a king of Norway, unless he be dominated by evil-mindedness or lacking in discretion. And if such faults shall deprive the oldest of the kingship, it shall pass to that one of his brothers, a son of the same father, who shall seem the best qualified to the archbishop, the bishops, and twelve of the most prudent men of each bishopric,[4] whom the bishops shall appoint [to act] with them. And the laymen shall proceed to the business after having taken oaths that they will select the one whom they believe before God to be the best qualified. And though

[1] Magnus Erlingsson, 1162–84. The amendment dates from 1164.

[2] Eystein Erlendsson was elected archbishop of Nidaros in 1157 but was not consecrated till some later year. He ruled the province from 1161 to 1188, except for a period of years when he was in exile.

[3] Erling Jarl, a powerful magnate who had married a daughter of Sigurd the Crusader; he was King Magnus's father. He fell in battle in 1179.

[4] The province of Nidaros, established in 1152, included five bishoprics in Norway and six in the Norwegian dependencies. The latter were probably not expected to send representatives.

the bishops take no oath, they shall be answerable to God for this oath, just as those are who swear the oath, that they shall base their decision on what is right and proper, just as the laymen do, who swear that they will act as God gives them light to discern most rightly. And if the king of Norway leaves no legitimate male issue, the one who stands next in the line of inheritance shall be chosen king, subject to the judgment of those who are duly authorized [to determine] whether he is a suitable man. But if this one does not seem qualified, let him be king whom the men, who are appointed [to decide], believe most likely to regard the rights of God and the laws of the land. If they disagree, the decisions of the majority shall prevail, provided that the archbishop and the other bishops are in accord [with them]; and let them confirm their choice with their oaths. On the death of a king all the bishops and abbots and the chieftains of the royal household with the entire "hird" shall without further summons make the journey north to [the shrine of] the holy King Olaf[5] to take counsel with the archbishop; and each bishop shall appoint twelve of the most discreet men [to go] with him; and let them all have entered upon the journey within the first month after they have learned of the king's decease. And the crown of the departed king shall be offered up there for the health of his soul; and let it hang there forever to the glory of God and the sainted King Olaf according to the promise of King Magnus, the first king to be crowned in Norway.[6] And if any one has [allowed] himself to be chosen [king] in some other way, he and all those who support him in this shall have forfeited peace and property and shall be in the ban of God and of all the saints, of the pope, the archbishop, and all the bishops. And if the men appointed by the bishops to be with them shall neglect the journey, they shall be in the lesser ban, and shall owe the king a fine of forty marks, and if they die in the meantime they shall not be buried in hallowed earth. And let every man make this journey at his own expense; but the king will reimburse those who have at no time

[5] Saint Olaf, who held the Norwegian kingship from 1016 to 1030, fell in battle, July 29, 1030. His shrine was in the cathedral at Nidaros (Trondheim).

[6] Magnus Erlingsson.

held land from the crown. If the archbishop is abroad or is deceased, these men shall [nevertheless] all go to this conference as has now been ordered.

3. BOTH OLAF[7] AND MAGNUS[8] ORDAINED THIS

Now the next is this, that we have ordered a meeting to be held here at Gula[9] every year with as many thingmen [in attendance] as we have now agreed to, that is, *M[agnus]*: sixty (*O[laf]*: one hundred and two) from Hordafylki, and the same number from Rogafylki; *M[agnus]*: fifty (*O[laf]*: eighty) from Firdafylki; *M[agnus]*: forty (*O[laf]*: sixty-four men) from Sognfylki; *M[agnus]*: twenty (*O[laf]*: twenty-seven) from Egdafylki, all appointed as the law provides; and from South Möre sixteen freemen (*O[laf]*: as many as wish [to come]). *M[agnus]*: Two barons shall remain at home in Egdafylki, two in Rogafylki, one in South Hordaland, one in Firdafylki, and one in South Möre to protect the homes of men from thieves and pillagers. But all the barons (*M[agnus]*: the other [barons]) *both:* who live within our jurisdiction shall attend the law thing from these six shires unless prevented by the king's necessities or by their own. And the mass priests whom the bishop selects (*O[laf]*: all from whom men buy the divine services), two from each shire,[10] and all the [king's] bailiffs shall attend without fail. But they shall have valid excuse, if the king comes into the fylki and orders his bailiff to collect the entertainment dues in

[7] Olaf the Quiet (1066–93). [8] Magnus Erlingsson.

[9] See Introd., p. 8.

[10] In tabular form the two schemes of representation will appear as follows:

	Olaf, 1066–93	Magnus, 1164
Hordafylki	102	60
Rogafylki	102	60
Firdafylki	80	50
Sognfylki	64	40
Egdafylki	27	20
South Möre	?	16
	375	246
Priests	?	12
		258

In addition, an indefinite though not very large number of barons would be expected to attend. This would bring the total in Olaf's day to something like 400 or perhaps a few more. Magnus reduced the number by about one hundred and fifty. See above, pp. 8–9.

the neighboring fylki. Now the next is this that *both:* before sunset, *M[agnus]*: on the eve of Saint Peter's Day[11] (*O[laf]*: Thursday in Easter week) they shall come together here, as many thingmen as we have now enumerated. But if they do not come, every man appointed to attend the Gulathing is liable to a fine; or if he comes later and after the oaths have been sworn. If a man comes earlier than this but later than our appointed day, he shall pay a fine of one ora. If all the shiremen neglect [to come on time], they shall bring forty marks with them the next spring, and we who are of this law shall have one-half of this fine and the king one-half. And if a fourth of the men from a fylki, or an eighth, neglect this, let them count out of that fine as [large a part as] their numbers indicate. If individual men neglect this, they shall pay a fine of three oras. *Olaf:* And we shall provide food and money for this journey from the six shires: half a month's provisions for each man, unless the journey takes longer time, a *sáld*[12] of malt and an ora in silver. If some man fails to contribute, and the journey is hindered on that man's account, he shall pay a fine of three oras for that [neglect]. *M[agnus]*: And from Egdafylki one man shall go from each ship district; and let the districts be equalized so that twenty men will go; and they shall be provided with victuals for two months: butter and meal and a sáld of malt and an ora in weighed silver, or as much in current money as is coined from an ora. And they shall make the journey whom the barons or the bailiffs or the king's officials shall appoint. Every one shall pay in proportion to [his] wealth, but three pounds of butter shall go into the contribution. And in Rogafylki fifteen men [shall go] from each quarter; and let victuals be provided for each man for a month and a half: meal and butter[13] and a sáld of malt and an ora weighed. The same number [shall] go from Hordafylki; and let each man be provided with victuals of both sorts for a month; also a sáld of malt and an ora weighed. In Sogn ten men shall go from each quarter; and let each man be provided with victuals of both kinds for a month; also with an ora weighed and a sáld of malt. Thirteen men shall go from each

[11] June 29. The court met on the 28th.
[12] See Glossary, "Sáld."
[13] See *ibid.*, "Meal and butter."

quarter in Firdafylki; and let victuals of both kinds for a month be provided for each man; [also] an ora weighed and a sáld of malt. And from South Möre let each of the sixteen men go provided with victuals of both kinds for two months and with a sáld of malt and an ora weighed. And if some man fails to contribute and the journey is hindered on that man's account, he shall pay a fine of three oras for that [neglect]. *Olaf:* In case a thingman is ordered to pay a fine at Gula, the money shall be paid there; and the money shall belong to the whole body of Gulathing men. Then it is well, if the man pays it himself or if his friends pay it. If he refuses to pay, the king's bailiff or the baron shall pay it, each in his bailiwick, and shall collect double the amount at [the man's] home.

4. OLAF ORDERED THIS BUT MAGNUS REVOKED THE ORDER

The next is this, that every year we shall give a man his freedom here at Gula. And we have distributed this duty among the shires so that each one shall in its year present a man for manumission. And the man shall be given his freedom on the first Sunday in the Gulathing session. And we Gulathing men shall all [together] contribute six oras to this. And if a man is not given his freedom on that Lord's Day, the men who were to provide such a man shall pay a fine of twelve oras to the bishop; and let them buy a man and give him his freedom, even if it [has to] be at a later time.

5. AND THIS LIKEWISE

Now the next is this, that we shall give freedom to a man in every fylki in the Gulathinglaw; and we have distributed this duty among the four divisions [of each fylki]. And the men whose duty it is to provide such a man shall have given [him his] freedom before Holy Night. But if they have not given it, they shall pay a fine of twelve oras to the bishop and shall buy a man and give him his freedom, even if it [has to] be at a later time.

6. BOTH OLAF AND MAGNUS

Now the next is this, that we have promised an ale feast, such as men call a "neighborhood ale"; [there shall be] ale from one measure of malt for each freeman and another for his wife. And let three householders at the fewest give the ale in common, unless they live so far out among the isles or so high up on the mountain side that they are not able to bring their brewing to the homes of other men; in such cases they shall brew as much ale singly, *Magnus:* as would be their share (*O[laf]*: as all three should). But if a man occupies a farm supporting fewer than six cows or [needing] less than six sálds of seed grain he shall give the ale feast only if he wishes to do so. *Both:* This ale shall be given before the mass of All Saints at the latest. The ale shall be blessed with thanks to Christ and Saint Mary for peace and a fruitful harvest; and if one fails to do this at the appointed time, he shall pay a fine of three oras to the bishop and shall give his ale even if it [has to] be at a later time. If he fails to do it and if he is accused and convicted of having allowed a twelvemonth to pass without sharing in a neighborhood ale, he shall pay a fine of three marks to the bishop.

7. BOTH OLAF AND MAGNUS

We have also promised that every husbandman and his wife shall join in an ale feast, all sharing equally, and bless it on Holy Night with thanks to Christ and Saint Mary for peace and a fruitful harvest. And if this is not done, they shall pay a fine of three marks to the bishop. And if a man allows three winters to pass without giving this ale feast, and he is accused and convicted of this, or [if he fails to heed] the penalties that we have added to our church law, he shall have forfeited his goods to the last penny; and the king shall have one-half of it and the bishop one-half. But he has the choice of going to confession and doing penance; [then he may] remain in Norway; but if he refuses to do this, he shall depart from the king's dominions.

8. MAGNUS ALONE DECREED THIS

We have entered into this agreement with our bishop that he shall provide us with the divine services, and that we [in turn] shall reward him by granting him the right to a full and complete tithe, both of all the harvest and of other increase, and of all our rightful catch of fish and game. And the tithe shall be divided in this wise: the bishop shall have one-fourth, the poor one-fourth, the church one-fourth, and the priest one-fourth. The bishop shall come into the fylki every twelvemonth without fail to render such services to the folk as are fit and needful. But the bishop has a valid excuse if he is ill, or the king requires him to make a journey, or the archbishop sends for him to assist in consecrating another bishop, or if some other important contingency shall arise. And if a man allows a twelvemonth to pass without paying his tithe, he shall owe a fine of three marks to the bishop. And if he allows twice a twelvemonth to pass without paying his tithe, he shall owe a fine of six marks to the bishop. And if he allows three winters to pass without paying his tithe, he shall forfeit his property to the last penny, his land as well as his movables; and one-half shall go to the king and one-half to the bishop.

9. OLAF ALONE DECREED THIS

We have entered into this agreement with our bishop that he shall provide us with divine services. And we shall buy these [services] from him [with an] ertog for every forty persons within our law. And the bishop shall earn this money in this way, that he shall come into every fylki once in a twelvemonth to render such services to the folk as are fit and needful. When the bishop comes into a fylki or into a quarter, he or his deputy shall summon a thing, and shall appoint a day when he wants to have his dues paid; then it is well if the men pay him. But if they refuse to pay him and if all the men of a muster group shall neglect this [duty], they shall [each] owe a fine of three oras; and the bishop or his deputy shall demand [the payment of] these fines at the thing. But if a smaller number [only] are neglectful, the bishop's bailiff shall go to their homes, taking with him the two neighbors who live nearest [in each case]; then it is well if they are willing to go with him. But if they refuse, he shall make a formal demand upon them and they shall owe the king's messenger a fine of three oras. And he shall himself take witnesses and go to the house of the man [concerned] and demand the bishop's fee along with the fine [for nonpayment], an ora for every penny. Then it is well if the man pays; but if he will not [pay], he shall be summoned before the thing on the charge of robbery, and he shall then owe the king's messenger a fine of twelve oras. And the bishop and his bailiff and all the priests shall carry forward their actions at law in the manner that I have just described.

10. BOTH HAVE DECREED THIS ABOUT CHURCHES

The next is this, that we shall keep our Christian religion and maintain all the churches which were established by Saint Olaf and Bishop Grimkell[14] at the Moster thing[15] and all those which have been built since then. And in each fylki there is one church which we call the head church and which it is the duty of all the men of that fylki to maintain. But if the church falls into disrepair and the corner posts come down, it is our duty to haul timbers to the site within a twelvemonth. And if these are not brought, we shiremen shall jointly pay a fine of fifteen marks; one-half of this shall go to the king and one-half to the bishop. But if a smaller number only are neglectful, the men of a quarter or of an eighth, let them pay such a part of the fine as their numbers indicate. If individual men neglect this duty, they shall pay a fine of three oras for every piece of timber that is needed and [they shall] provide the timbers even if it [has to] be at a later time. An ora shall be paid for every meal[16] [that is not provided] and an ora for every nail that is wanting. Now the church is built.

11. BOTH ORDERED THIS

It shall be the duty of all the men of the fylki to build a fence about [the church]. The bishop or his deputy shall summon the men to the building of the fence and shall appoint a day for its completion; then it is well if it is completed. But if it is not completed and the church remains for a twelvemonth without a fence, the men of the fylki shall all pay a fine of three marks to the bishop. But if individual men [only] neglect this duty, they shall pay the bishop a fine of three oras for every piece of timber that is lacking and shall provide the timbers and build the fence, even if it [has to] be at a later time. When the church is built and the fence is raised, the men of the fylki shall join in buying consecra-

[14] An Englishman, bishop at the court of Saint Olaf.

[15] Held on the island of Moster (about fifty miles south of Bergen) in 1024 (?).

[16] Evidently the workingmen were provided with meals.

tion from the bishop, [paying for] three nights' entertainment for thirty men.

12. LIKEWISE THIS ABOUT THE BUILDING OF CHURCHES

Now these are the other churches that are all to be maintained: the churches of the quarter and of the eighth [of the fylki], those of the herath, and the private chapels. These churches must all be maintained, and the site must not be left vacant. But if a church falls into disrepair and the corner posts come down, the men who own the church shall have timbers hauled to the site before the passing of a twelvemonth. And if they are not brought, those who own the church shall pay the bishop a fine of three marks for this [neglect]; and let them bring the timbers and build the church, even if it [has to] be at a later time. If individual men neglect this, they shall pay the bishop a fine of three oras for every piece of timber that is needed; and let them bring the timbers and rebuild the church, even if it [has to] be at a later time; and let no site be left vacant. If individual men build the church, if a baron builds it, or a freeman, or whoever it [happens to] be, they shall maintain it and never let the site become vacant. But if the church falls into disrepair and the corner posts come down, he [the owner] shall have timbers hauled to the site before a twelvemonth has passed; and if they are not brought he shall pay the bishop a fine of three marks for this [neglect] and bring the timbers and build the church. But if he fails to do so and leaves the site vacant another twelvemonth, he shall pay the bishop a second fine of three marks for this [neglect]. And if he lets the site lie vacant for three winters, he forfeits the land on which the church was built; then the king has the land and shall attain complete ownership by having the church built within the following twelvemonth. But if he fails to do so, the freeman shall take back the land and shall rebuild the church. But if the freeman has not done [so] within a twelvemonth, the king owns the land and it shall never again come into the freeman's control.

13. CONCERNING THE CHURCH FENCE

The men whose duty it is to maintain a church shall build a fence about it and shall have it built within a twelvemonth; and if it is not built within a twelvemonth, they shall pay a fine of twelve oras to the bishop. But if individual men [only] neglect this duty, they shall pay three oras for every piece of timber that is wanting and shall provide the timber even if it [has to] be at a later time. Now all the churches are built with fences about them.

14. CONCERNING THE CONSECRATION OF CHURCHES

Consecration shall be bought from the bishop. If in any case the site is hallowed but the church is not, [consecration] shall be bought from the bishop for twelve oras. But if neither the church nor the site is hallowed, consecration shall be bought from the bishop for three marks and three nights' entertainment for [the bishop and] fifteen men. Now the churches are all built and the consecration is paid for.

15. CONCERNING THE SUPERVISION OF CHURCHES

The next is this, that the bishop shall govern the churches as Saint Olaf allowed Bishop Grimkell at the thing on Moster Isle,[17] and as we [king and thingmen] have later come to agreement. The bishop shall appoint to all churches such priests as he knows will be able to provide the parishioners with the right divine services. And we shall give the priests such maintenance as Saint Olaf and Bishop Grimkell ordained at the Moster thing. In the herath churches [this shall be] as the freemen shall come into agreement with the priests whom the bishop appoints; and the priests whom the bishop appoints shall remain in charge twelve months and shall provide the folk with the right divine services. If the priest builds a house and forms friendships and is pleasantly situated,[18] the bishop shall not remove him from his parish; for we do not want to make our churches the subject of [profitable] bargaining. But if at any time during the twelvemonth he gives his people wrong directions with respect to fast days and holy days, he shall atone with a fine of three marks to the bishop. And if this happens a second time he shall again pay the bishop a fine of three marks. The bishop then has the right to remove him from his parish and to appoint one who is competent to provide the people with the

[17] See above, p. 42.

[18] See Hertzberg, *Glossarium* (*Norges gamle love*, V), p. 859, *hagi.*

right services. And as often as the priests give us wrong directions or disobey the orders which the bishop puts forth in the interest of our Christian religion, they shall atone to the bishop with a money fine; for we have abolished [the custom of] punishing them with blows,[19] since we have entered into marriage relations with them and allow [them] to give our sons instruction. Our priests shall enjoy the same security in their persons as we all enjoy [in our dealings] with all other men in the land.

16. CONCERNING THE KEEPING OF SUNDAY

The next is this, that every seventh day is holy and that day we call Sunday. And the Saturday just before shall be [counted] holy from noon on, when a third of the day remains; also the [following] night till dawn on Monday. [So holy is the day] that one shall neither hunt birds nor catch fish, nor labor in field or meadow; but there is this exception that men may row their usual course with nets cast over the side of the boat or they may row with wares that were loaded on a work day. And if they come home at holytide but find no haven, they shall cast the freight up on the dry shore and secure their ships. Or men may travel their course on the highway, driving horses laden with packs, if these were bound on a work day. If a man is accused and convicted of having done labor on a Sunday, he shall atone for it with six oras and he shall go to confession and do penance. If a bondman of alien race does [such] labor without his master's consent, [his master] shall have him flogged or pay the bishop three oras.

17. CONCERNING MASS-DAYS

These are the days which Saint Olaf and Bishop Grimkell appointed at the Moster thing to be preceded by a fast and to be [counted] holy from the preceding noon. They shall be honored as Sunday [is honored]. The first is Saint John's Day.[20] The second [is] Saint Peter's Day.[21] The third [is] the Mass-day of the holy men of Selja.[22] The fourth [is] Saint James's Day.[23] The fifth [is]

[19] This punishment was apparently administered by the bishop or at his command. [20] June 24. [21] June 29.

[22] July 8. Celebrated in honor of Saint Sunniva and her companions, who were believed to have suffered martyrdom on the isle of Selja (near Cape Stadt) some time in the tenth century. [23] July 25.

the earlier Saint Olaf's Day.[24] The sixth [is] Saint Lawrence's Day.[25] The seventh [is] the earlier Saint Mary's Day.[26] The eighth [is] Saint Bartholomew's Day.[27] The ninth [is] Saint Matthew's Day.[28] The tenth [is] Michaelmas.[29] The eleventh [is] the Mass-day of the Two Apostles.[30] The twelfth [is] All Saint's Day.[31] The thirteenth [is] Saint Andrew's Day.[32] The fourteenth [is] Saint Thomas' Day.[33] Now all those days which are to be preceded by a fast and [are to be] counted holy from the preceding noon have been enumerated. And let him who does labor on those days atone with a fine as for labor on Sunday.

18. MORE ABOUT MASS-DAYS

Now there are other holy days which are not preceded by a fast and are not counted holy from the preceding noon; nevertheless, as regards labor they shall be kept as holy as Sundays. If men do labor on those days, they shall pay a fine of three oras to the bishop. If a bondman does [such] labor, without his master's consent, the fine shall be one and one-half oras. Now these days shall be enumerated. They begin with the first four days of the Yuletide. The fifth [is] the eighth day of the Yuletide. The sixth [is] the thirteenth day [in the Yuletide].[34] These shall all be regarded as equally sacred; but, on the intervening days one may look after the live stock, if there should be such need. Next following Christmas is the "Brittifumass."[35] Then there is Saint Paul's Day.[36] Then there is Candlemas.[37] Then there is Saint Matthias' Day.[38] Then there is Saint Mary's Day.[39] Now come four days on which one is not allowed to open the earth to bury the dead: the first is Holy Thursday after noon; the second [is] Good Friday, the entire day; the third [is] Easter eve till noon; the fourth [is] Easter Day, the entire day. And if one does bury a body [on any

[24] July 29.
[25] August 10.
[26] August 15; the Assumption.
[27] August 24.
[28] September 21.
[29] September 29.
[30] October 28; Simon and Jude.
[31] November 1.
[32] November 30.
[33] December 21.
[34] January 6.
[35] January 11. Saint Brittifa has not been identified.
[36] January 25.
[37] February 2.
[38] February 24.
[39] March 25; the Annunciation.

of these days], he shall pay a fine of three oras to the bishop. In Easter week there are two days, Monday and Tuesday, on which one shall do no labor except caring for one's live stock, if there should be such need. And all day Wednesday shall be kept holy. Next comes the Mass-day of the Two Apostles.[40] Then there is the Mass-day of the Holy Cross.[41] The gang days shall be kept in such a way that one may do labor till midday on the first three days; but the Thursday[42] is sacred all day, like Easter. Now comes Saint Halvard's Day.[43] Then there is Saint Botholf's Day.[44] Then there is Saint Swithun's Day.[45] Then there is Saint Knut's Day.[46] Then there is the later Saint Olaf's Day.[47] Then there is the later Saint Mary's Day.[48] Then there is the later Mass-day of the Holy Cross.[49] Then there is Martinmas.[50] Then there is Saint Clement's Day.[51] Then there is Saint Nicholas' Day.[52] [All] these shall be kept holy within our law.[53]

19. OLAF ALONE ORDERED THIS

Now the priests shall send forth the crosses[54] before the holy days, each in his own parish where he reads the divine services whether this be a shire church, a quarter church, or the church of an eighth. And the crosses shall be sent forth after such a plan that they will come to all the places where the priest has duties. A cross shall come to every house where smoke rises. And every man shall carry it forward to another except where several men live on the same homestead; in such cases each one in his turn shall carry it from the farm. The crosses shall be carried about among the winter dwellings but not up on the mountain. Every householder shall be responsible for one house, lest the cross fail to go forward, though he may own several [houses]. If he fails to

[40] May 1; Philip and James.

[41] May 3; the Invention of the Holy Cross.

[42] Ascension Day.

[43] May 15. Halvard was a native saint belonging to the region about Oslo in southern Norway.

[44] June 17.

[45] July 2.

[46] July 10.

[47] August 3.

[48] September 8.

[49] September 14.

[50] November 11.

[51] November 23.

[52] December 6.

[53] See Glossary, "Law."

[54] See Glossary, "Cross."

send the cross forward, he shall atone for this [neglect] with a fine of three oras to the priest who sent the cross forth. But if the man denies the charge and states that the cross did not come to his house, while his neighbor affirms that he carried it to him, the accused may swear that it did not come. And the one against whom the oath is sworn shall pay a fine; then it is well if he pays the cross fine. But if he refuses, the priest shall take two of the man's neighbors and proceed to his house and demand the cross fine; and he shall summon him to the thing for robbery, and for that he shall owe a fine of twelve oras.

20. BOTH OLAF AND MAGNUS

The next is this, that every seventh day we shall abstain from eating flesh; that [day] we call Friday. And whoever is accused and convicted of having eaten flesh on Friday shall pay a fine of three oras to the bishop, unless he ate it in ignorance. And if a man comes in and asks him why he eats flesh on Friday, then, if he has a bite in his mouth, he shall spew it out and state that he ate it unwittingly, not knowing what day it was. Then he shall be free from punishment, but he shall go to confession and do penance. But if he swallows [the bite], he shall pay a fine of three oras to the bishop. If it happens again that he eats flesh on Friday, he shall pay a fine of three marks to the bishop. If after having paid a fine twice he still refuses to honor the Friday and our Christian religion, he shall forfeit all his chattels to the last penny, but he shall be allowed to go to confession and do penance. If he will not do so, he shall depart from the king's dominions. If a man eats horse flesh[55] he shall pay a fine of three marks to the bishop, and let him go to confession and do penance. [This applies to] all men of our speech. If a bondman eats flesh on Friday or on forbidden days, [his master] shall have him flogged for it or pay a fine of three oras to the bishop. If the bishop or his deputy charges a man with having eaten flesh on Friday or on forbidden days, and he denies the charge, the bishop's bailiff shall go to his house and summon him before the thing and bring action against him at the

[55] Horseflesh was quite generally eaten at the great sacrificial festivals of heathen times. It was doubtless for this reason that Christians were forbidden to use it as food.

thing. But if he denies it, he shall offer to support his denial with a threefold oath. If a man eats flesh during Lent, he shall pay a fine of three marks to the bishop, unless he ate because of great need. And if he has no other food to eat, let him go to three of his neighbors and offer to trade provisions with them; then it is well if he gets [food]. But if he gets nothing, he may eat flesh to preserve his life; for it is better for him to eat [even] a dog than that a dog should eat him. If a man eats horse flesh in Lent, he shall forfeit all his property to the last penny and shall depart from the king's dominions. And if the bishop's bailiff accuses him of this, he shall offer to defend himself with a threefold oath; if the oath fails, the failure leads to outlawry. If a bondman eats [horse flesh] without his master's consent, his master shall sell him beyond the king's dominions and use the price for his own benefit. But he must not break bread with him; and if he does break bread [with him], he shall pay a fine of forty marks. If the bishop's bailiff charges him with this, he shall defend himself with a threefold oath.

21. MAGNUS REVOKED THIS IN PART

The next is this, that every child that is born in our land shall be reared [and cared for], *O[laf]*: unless it be born with some serious deformity, the face turned around to where the neck should be, or the toes to where the heel should be; in such a case the child shall be brought to church to be baptized, and then [it may be] laid down in the church and be left to perish. *Both:* Every child that is born after Holy Night shall be baptized before Septuagesima; if it is born in Lent, it shall be baptized by Easter; if it is born after Easter, it shall be baptized before Saint John's Day; and every child that is born after Michaelmas shall be baptized before Holy Night. It shall normally be baptized by the priest from whom men buy the divine services. But if the child is stricken with sudden illness and this priest is out of reach, the priest who can first be secured shall perform the baptism; and no priest may refuse to do this; if he does refuse, he shall owe a fine of three marks to the bishop. If the child is so weak that no priest can be reached in time, the men who are bringing the child shall give it a name and plunge it into water, speaking these words over it: I baptize thee N. in the name of the Father, and of the Son, and of the Holy Ghost; after that it may be buried in the churchyard. *M[agnus]*: If water cannot be obtained, the child may be baptized in any fluid that can be found. If there is no fluid at hand, one may spit in the palm [of his hand] and make the sign of the cross on the [child's] breast and between the shoulders. And such a baptism a woman may perform as well as a man, if no man is available. *Both:* If a child is not baptized within the appointed term, the father shall pay a fine of three oras to the bishop and have it baptized, even if it [has to] be at a later time. But if he refuses to let it be baptized and keeps an unbaptized child in his house over two terms, he shall pay a fine of three marks to the bishop and shall have the child baptized. But if he still refuses and keeps the child in his house unbaptized for a twelvemonth, he has forfeited all his property to the last penny. His [only] choice is to go to confession and do penance. And if he refuses to do this, both [he and the child][56] shall depart from the king's dominions.

22. HERE MAGNUS PROVIDES PERMANENT OUTLAWRY FOR A CRIME FOR WHICH OLAF HAD DECREED A PENALTY OF THREE MARKS

If a man exposes a child, whether [it be] baptized or not, and allows it to perish, and if he is accused and convicted of this, he has forfeited peace and property, for we call that [crime] murder in the highest degree. And if a bondman allows his child to perish, whether it be baptized or not, his master shall have him flogged within five days or sent to the kingsmen. And he shall be allowed to sell him abroad, if he likes, but he must not break bread with him; if he does break bread [with him], he shall pay three marks to the bishop. If the bishop or his deputy charges a man with having allowed his child to perish, whether it be baptized or not, and he denies it, he shall have to clear himself of this as of any other murder. And if the oath [fails], the failure leads to outlawry. And if the bishop or his deputy charges a man with having buried an unbaptized child in hallowed earth, and the charge proves false on investigation, the man who brought the accusation shall pay

[56] Fr. Brandt, in his lectures on the Old Norwegian Constitution, reads the law to mean the parents, not the father and the child. *Forelæsninger over den norske retshistorie*, II, 15.

the bishop a fine of three marks, [thus paying] the penalty [maliciously] intended for the other. If a heathen man comes to our kingdom, stating that he has a desire to be baptized and has in mind to seek a place where there are priests, he shall be given food, but let him partake of it alone. But if he travels past churches and priests and does not seek baptism, the bishop's bailiff shall arrest that man and take him before the thing; then it is well if he submits to baptism. If he refuses, the thing shall allow him a grith[57] of five days [in which] to leave the king's dominions; and let him have no food on any night where he tarried the night before. But if men entertain him longer and break bread with him, they shall pay a fine of forty marks. And in case the fine for violating the laws of the church is more than three marks, one-half goes to the king and one-half to the bishop. And if a man fails for three successive winters to pay his dues to the priest or to the bishop and gives no heed to the other payments that we have added for the support of our Christian religion, he has forfeited his chattels to the last penny.

23. CONCERNING BURIAL IN THE CHURCHYARD

The next is this, that every man who dies shall be brought to church and buried in hallowed earth, excepting only evildoers, traitors, murderers, truce breakers, thieves, and men who take their own lives. And those whom I have now enumerated shall be buried on the shore where the tide meets the green sod. Bodies shall ordinarily not remain unburied longer than five days; but if a corpse does remain longer [unburied], the one responsible shall pay the bishop a fine of three oras and shall bring the body to the church. But if he refuses to do so and leaves the corpse at home to decay, he has forfeited his chattels to the last penny; and his only choice is to go to confession and do penance; and if he is unwilling to do this, he shall depart from the king's dominions. But if he lives high up on the mountain side or very far out among the isles, and the stress of the conditions, be it stormy seas or [bad] mountain [roads], prevent him from transporting the body, he shall carry it into an outhouse and fasten it up; for a corpse must not be allowed to lie on the ground. If a man has buried a body in a

[57] See Glossary, "Grith."

mound or a heap of stones,[58] he shall disinter it and pay three oras to the bishop and bring the body to the church to be buried in hallowed earth. If a man falls ill and wishes to have a priest summoned, let him send for the one from whom he buys the divine services. If he desires unction, the priest shall go to him and anoint him, *O[laf]*: and he shall have two oras as a fee for the unction. *Both:* But if the illness comes on so suddenly that it is necessary to send for a nearer priest, this priest shall go to him and anoint him *M[agnus]*: without charge. But if he fails to come, he shall owe a fine of three marks, unless he is prevented by a serious hindrance or [the needs of] his own parishioners, and the fact is known to witnesses. And every man who has paid his tithe shall have unction if he confirms his desire for it while still able to speak. *Both:* When the man is dead and his heir goes to the priest and asks him to come to chant the death mass at the bier, he shall go and sing [the chant] at the bier; *O[laf]*: for that he shall have half an ora, which men call the fee for the death mass. *Both:* When the body comes to the church, the priest shall go to meet it and shall chant before it such prayers as the ritual prescribes; he shall place the body in the grave; *O[laf]*: and for that he shall receive the burial fee. *Both:* But if the priest refuses to perform the rites, the heir of the deceased shall take *M[agnus]*: the tithe (*O[laf]*: the burial fee) and [use it to] buy masses for the soul of the deceased. If the priest is away from home the body shall be interred nevertheless; and, when he returns, a stake [shall be driven] down to the coffin, and holy water poured down upon it, and the priest shall chant the death mass over it. In no case ought a priest to enter the parish of another priest for the sake of gain. But if he is accused and convicted of [having done] this, he shall restore the fees to the one to whom the parish belongs, and he shall atone for it with a fine of twelve oras to the bishop. And whenever, on the death of a man, his heir wishes to give an ale feast, whether on the seventh or the thirtieth morning, or even later, that is called an inheritance ale. But if men give an ale and call it a soul's ale, they shall invite the priest from whom they buy the services; they shall invite him as one of three at the fewest; and the priest

[58] This was heathen practice and forbidden for that reason.

ought to attend an inheritance ale or a soul's ale as a matter of course. If he refuses to attend, he shall forfeit the tithe (*O*[*laf*]: the payments) that he should receive in a twelvemonth from the levy district[59] where the feast was given. And the man who is the heir after him for whom the feast was given shall take *M*[*agnus*]: the tithe (*O*[*laf*]: the payments) and use it for the spiritual welfare [of the deceased]. *Both:* If there are several funeral feasts, the priest shall go first to the one to which he was first invited and shall remain there the first night; in the morning he shall go to the second. *Both:* Even if there be three gatherings and he will have to travel the same road twice in one day, he shall, nevertheless, bless all the ales. But if he cannot [do this], let him go to the second feast and drink there while the ale lasts.

24. BOTH DECREED THIS

The next is this that none shall have a kinswoman as his wife. And if a man is accused and convicted of having a wife of nearer kinship than the law allows, he shall atone for it with a fine of three marks to the bishop and forsake the woman and go to confession and do penance. But we are allowed to take a wife among our kinswomen in the seventh degree of kinship and in the seventh "knee";[60] and among other women, the widows of our kinsmen,[61] in the fifth degree and the fifth knee. The same [rule] applies to wives that are of kin, the wife that a man had before and the one that he takes. And if [a man] takes a wife of nearer [kin] than I have now indicated, *M*[*agnus*]: or takes another man's wife, or a woman in addition to his wife, *both:* he shall pay a fine of three marks to the bishop and cease from the woman and go to confession and do penance. But if he refuses to do this, they shall both depart from the king's dominions. And if the bishop or his deputy charges a man with having a wife of nearer kin than the law allows and he denies the charge, he may refute it with a threefold oath. There are other women who have an even greater right to respect and honor from us, and we do an evil deed with them, if we have

[59] See Glossary, "Levy." [60] See *ibid.*, "Knee," "Kinship."

[61] The original has *frændkonor* (kinswomen). Maurer suggests that this should be emended to *frændleifur* (widows of kinsmen), otherwise the statement seems inconsistent, *Vorlesungen über altnordische Rechtsgeschichte*, III, 22.

carnal dealings with them. The first is a man's mother; the second [is his] sister; the third, [his] daughter; the fourth, [his] stepmother; the fifth, [his] daughter-in-law; the sixth, [his] brother's wife; the seventh, [his] son's daughter. There are other women who are of the same [near] kinship; with all these, too, men may commit evil deeds. *Magnus:* These are stepdaughters, a brother's daughters, a sister's daughters, a daughter's daughters, the mother's mother, the father's sister, the mother's sister, the father's mother, and the sister of a man's wife. *Both:* And if a man is accused and convicted of having lain with a woman of such near kinship, the man and the woman are both outside the law and they shall depart from the king's dominions *M*[*agnus*]: and [remain away] till they have completed a penance laid upon them by the bishop. *Both:* And [they shall] forfeit all their possessions, both land and movables, to the last penny; and one-half of these shall go to the king and one-half to the bishop, *M*[*agnus*]: unless the king or the bishop wish to deal more mercifully [with them] on their return. *Both:* If a bishop or his deputy shall accuse a man of having done this evil and the man denies it, he shall refute [the charge] with a sixfold oath. Let twelve men of his own rank be selected and let him choose one of the twelve; he himself shall be the second; his nearest kinsman shall be the third; and [there shall be] three [others], men who can be held to account for pledge and promise[62] in our speech. This oath shall be taken before the church door, and if it fails the accused is guilty of the evil deed. *M*[*agnus*]: But [even if] the oath fails, the man shall have permission to go to the ordeal before he is finally [adjudged] guilty of the charge. *Both:* And every man who is put to the proof, whether by taking the oath or going to the ordeal and is convicted, shall have grith for five days from the door of the church.

25. THAT A MAN SHALL POSSESS ONE WIFE

The next is this, that each one of us shall possess one wife, the one that a man has bought with the "mund"[63] and according to agreement. If he pays the mund for two women, he shall cease from the woman whom he took last; and he shall pay a fine of three

[62] See Glossary, "Pledge and promise."
[63] See *ibid.*, "Mund."

marks to the bishop and go to confession and do penance. And no child that he begets with the woman whom he took last shall take inheritance from any man except his freedman only. If he refuses to give up the woman whom he took last, they shall both depart from the king's dominions, and they shall have forfeited their possessions to the last penny. If a man keeps a bondwoman as a concubine and [keeps her] by his own fireplace, or whatever kind of woman he keeps in addition to his wife, and if he is accused and convicted of this, he shall pay a fine of twelve oras to the bishop and he shall go to confession and do penance; and he shall forsake the woman.

26. CONCERNING SPIRITUAL KINSHIP

There are six persons of spiritual kinship from whom we shall abstain as we do from our kinswomen. Now the first [is the one who] holds the child when it receives the sign of the cross [in baptism]; the second [the one who] receives [the child when the priest lifts it] out of the water; the third [the one who] removes the white robe;[64] the fourth [the one who] leads the child to the bishop [at confirmation]; the fifth [the one who] loosens the chrism band;[65] the sixth [the one who] leads the mother into the church. In the last case the kinship concerns [the priest and] the woman [only] but in the other five cases the spiritual kinship must be respected both as regards the father, the mother, and the child. And if a man is accused and convicted of having possessed a spiritual kinswoman, he shall pay a fine of three marks to the bishop, and go to confession and do penance; and he shall cease from the woman.

27. CONCERNING WEDDINGS

Wives shall be taken at proper and not at improper times.[66] If a man buys a wife with the mund and according to agreement but at an improper time or at a time when the bishop has forbidden us to take wives (Sunday eve, Friday eve, or Wednesday

[64] On the eighth day after baptism.

[65] After confirmation.

[66] The provisions of this chapter apply not only to weddings but also to carnal relations on the part of those already married.

eve, or on the nights before fast days or holy days, or during the minor fasts that cover the three weeks before Saint John's Day and the three [weeks] before Michaelmas and the three [weeks] before Christmas *M*[*agnus*] (*O*[*laf*]): and in the thirteen days of the yuletide), if a man takes a wife on any of the days that I have now enumerated, he shall pay a fine of three oras to the bishop. And if a man takes a wife in Lent, that is, the nine weeks during which the bishop fasts, or in the tenth [week] which is Easter week, he shall pay a fine of three marks to the bishop.

28. CONCERNING SORCERY AND SOOTHSAYING

The next is this, that we must pay no heed to soothsaying, incantation, or wicked sorcery. And if a man is accused and convicted of having practiced soothsaying or of having told fortunes, he shall be an outlaw and shorn of all personal rights; and all his chattels to the last penny shall go, one-half to the king and one-half to the bishop. And if any man gives heed to soothsaying and the charge is proven, he shall owe a fine of forty marks, one-half to go to the king and one-half to the bishop. And if a man practices sorcery and witchcraft, and he is accused and convicted of it, he shall depart from the king's dominions, for men must give no heed to such doings. But whoever does pay heed [to such things] has forfeited his chattels to the last penny; and his [only] choice shall be to go to confession and do penance. If the bishop or his deputy accuses a man of practicing soothsaying or sorcery or witchcraft and he denies the charge, a method of defense has been provided. If a man is accused of practicing soothsaying, let him refute [the charge] with a sixfold oath: let twelve men of his own rank be selected, and let him choose one of those twelve; he himself shall be the second; his nearest kinsman shall be the third and [there shall be] three others, men who can be held to account for pledge and promise; and if the oath fails, the failure leads to outlawry. *Magnus:* And if a man is accused and convicted of having sworn a false oath, or of having led other men with him [into perjury], he shall owe a fine of fifteen marks and three marks additional for each one who swore with him, if they were not aware that the oath was false; but if they knew that it was false before they swore it, they shall pay as he pays, fifteen marks each. *Both:*

If a woman is accused of practicing sorcery and witchcraft, let six women be appointed, housewives whom men know to be good [women], three to stand on either side of her; and they shall bear witness that she knows neither sorcery nor witchcraft. But if this testimony fails, she becomes liable to outlawry, and the king shall have one-half of her property and the bishop one-half. And her heir shall convey her out of the king's dominions.

29. CONCERNING HEATHEN SACRIFICES

Heathen sacrifices are also banned for we are not permitted to worship any heathen god, or [on any] hill, or [in any] heathen fane. And if a man is accused and convicted of this, he has forfeited all his chattels to the last penny, and he shall go to confession and do penance. But if he refuses to do this, he shall depart from the king's dominions.

30. CONCERNING EVILDOERS

We are also forbidden to commit any sort of evil deed, and we may therefore have no carnal dealings with cattle. And if a man is accused and convicted of having had carnal dealings with cattle, he shall be castrated, *both:* and he shall depart from the king's dominions as a malefactor and shall never return. *M[agnus]*: And the officials who have bailiwicks there [and can act] both on the king's behalf and the bishop's shall have him castrated. *Both:* And the owner of the beast shall drive her into the sea and shall make no further use [of her]. But if he does make use [of her], he shall pay a fine of three marks to the bishop. And if the bishop or his deputy accuses a man of having had carnal dealings with cattle, and he denies it, the bishop's bailiff shall go to the man's house and summon him before the thing [to answer] for that evil deed. If he offers to clear himself with a sixfold oath, *both:* he shall have sworn this within ten weeks of oath days,[67] for the term allowed for the taking of oaths is [nearly] always the same, if they are legally offered. He shall deal in this way with these oaths, he shall go to the man's home who is to witness the oath taking and notify him to appear after five nights at the church where he [the defendant] is to take the oath; then it is well if he comes and hears

[67] See Glossary, "Oath day."

the oath taken. But if he does not come, he [the accused] shall take the oath before witnesses. He shall take the oath before the church door; a Gospel book shall be laid on the threshold and [let him] take it up from the threshold; then it is well if he takes the oath correctly. But if the oath fails, he is an outlawed man, shorn of all personal rights; but he shall have grith for five days after he leaves the church door. In this way shall all oaths be sworn which men offer to refute charges of having violated the laws of the church.

31. CONCERNING FORBIDDEN MEATS AND ANIMALS THAT HAVE DIED OF THEMSELVES

M . . . it[68] we are also forbidden to eat. If a man is accused and convicted of having eaten the flesh of animals that have died of themselves, he shall pay a fine of three oras to the bishop and shall go to confession and do penance. We speak of those animals as having died of themselves whose bane is not known to men. But men may eat what wolves rend and deprive of life; and men may eat the flesh of beasts attacked by bears or bitten by dogs. Men may also eat the flesh of a beast that is drowned in running water or falls out over a cliff or is choked by the halter. But there is this to add about the flesh of animals that are killed in this way, that salt and water shall be consecrated and sprinkled upon the carcass, and it shall be hung up till the blood dries up. It is proper to sell the hide and divide the money in such a way that the owner keeps one-half; but with the other half let him buy wax and send it to the church where he buys the divine services.

32. MAGNUS MADE THIS NEW ORDINANCE

All those who violate the pledges of peace and security which men give to each other in settling cases of manslaughter are to be regarded as outlaws who have permanently forfeited all rights to peace and to property, to land and chattels, odal land as well as other land. And those who are killed as thieves and bandits, whether they plunder men on shipboard or on land; and [those who are killed] for [deeds of] murder or for [the practice of] witch-

[68] The word is illegible but is probably *mortit*, a beast that has died of itself. See Hertzberg, *Glossarium*, "mortit."

craft or for going abroad at night to call forth evil spirits and to promote heathendom thereby; and assassins who assist in the slaying of men with whom they have no quarrel and take money for it (unless the king [makes use of them to] rid the land of criminal vagabonds and to promote peace); and the men who take women by violence or [carry off] other men's wives or their betrothed, or their daughters without the consent of those who have authority over them or without their own [consent], no matter how those who control the marriage may later change their minds;[69] and also those who take revenge for outlaws of this sort or demand blood money for them, and the facts are known to witnesses; all such men are in permanent outlawry and have forfeited all rights to peace and to property, to land and chattels. But those who defend their goods and their kinswomen against such men shall be in the protection of the law; and no fines shall be owing for the others, either to king or to kinsmen, whether they be wounded or slain. All the dooms that are appointed to deal with manslaying or with adultery of the sort that gives men a legal right to kill shall be set according to law and with grith assured till the first payment is due. And whoever disregards the legal decision of a doom without cause before [the first] payment or at the first payment violates his own grith and is a truce breaker and has forfeited his right to peace and property. A man may be excused [only] if he is ill or wounded or has some other serious reason, which, as good men testify, prevents him from being present. And the first payment shall be forthcoming within the same month and it shall be brought to his [the plaintiff's] home and shall be proffered before two witnesses. And let him or his agent receive it there, unless he who is to have it wishes to ease the matter for the other. But in all other cases in which men join in appointing legal dooms[70] the one who disregards [the decision] shall owe a fine of eighteen oras to the prosecutor and fifteen marks to the king; and the decision shall stand as before. And let the king or his officials bring suit in behalf of both, but let him [the complainant] be paid his dues first according as the doomsmen

[69] Cf. *Frost.*, V, c. 45.

[70] *Lagadómr:* a doom of six or twelve men chosen by the thing, not by the parties involved in the action.

have decided. In either case the fine shall be assessed according to the [defendant's] ability to pay. If the man refuses to comply with the award, the king's officials shall summon him before the thing and declare him an outlaw, unless he pays according to the award. If a man comes to a settlement with one who has lain with his wife, he [the husband] shall bind himself to keep the peace; but if the man lies a second time with the woman, he is a truce breaker like one who commits murder after he has given a peace pledge. If a man slays his son, or a son his father, be he Christian or heathen, or [if he slays] his mother or a brother or a daughter or a sister, he shall suffer permanent outlawry, as provided above, unless he is a madman, and men know him to be demented. If two men practice sodomy and are accused and convicted of it, they shall both suffer permanent outlawry; but if they deny the charge while common rumor affirms it, let them deny it with the hot iron; and if they are convicted of the charge, the king shall have one-half of their possessions and the bishop one-half. If men come to blows in a church or in a consecrated churchyard, they shall suffer permanent outlawry; and the bishop shall have three marks [from their property] and what is needed for the churchyard, and the king shall have what remains. But if there should be no remainder, the king and the bishop shall divide the property, each [taking] one-half, unless they wish to show greater mercy. If a man has become liable to permanent outlawry but the prosecutor has neither force nor knowledge to send forth the arrows,[71] the other shall be regarded as an outlaw just as otherwise.

33. CONCERNING RIDING HORSES FOR THE BISHOP

Now the next is this, that when the bishop lands from his ship and goes up into the country to consecrate churches or to render other services to the folk, whether the distance be long or short, the freemen shall provide him with eighteen riding horses and [with] thirty if he is coming to consecrate a shire church. And if they refuse to provide horses, every one who joins in this refusal shall owe a fine of three oras. If the bishop or his deputy charges a man with having broken some part of the church law, the fines for which are due to the bishop, and if he denies it, the bishop's

[71] See Glossary, "Arrow."

bailiff shall go to his house taking with him the two neighbors who live nearest his house; then it is well if they are willing to go with him. But if they refuse, he shall make a formal demand on them; then each one of them shall owe a fine of three oras to the king's official. And he shall himself take witnesses and proceed to the man's house and summon him to answer the charge at the thing, and he shall bring action against him at the thing. And the accused shall offer to defend himself with a threefold oath; but if he fails to offer compliance with the law or to appear at the thing, he shall owe a fine of twelve oras to the king's official. And the bishop and his bailiff and all the priests shall bring their legal actions in the manner that I have now described.

[THE MERCHANT LAW]

34. HERE THE MERCHANT LAW BEGINS

Now this is the next, that none of us shall take goods away from another nor shall we be guilty of taking the law into our own hands; every man is entitled to legal judgment in [what concerns] his possessions. But he who deprives another [of goods] shall restore them and atone to the king with a *baug* for unlawful seizure; after that let him [who has been despoiled] sue for his own according to law. If a man has a cause of action against another, and this one refuses to pay what he owes, he shall summon him to be at home to hear his demand and the testimony of witnesses; and let him offer to accept the prescribed compensation. Such a debt may be demanded three times like any other debt. If the debtor still refuses to pay, let him be summoned before the thing for robbery and contempt of law; and the men shall condemn him to outlawry with respect to him who brought the action and to all the men of that thing district,[1] until he shall offer atonement at the thing or in the presence of assembled men and have the money there to pay over.

35. CONCERNING HOME SUMMONS[2] AND SUING FOR DEBTS

Now the next is this, that if a man owes money to another and the debt is known to witnesses, he [the creditor] shall summon him to be at home in his highseat, if [he is] a householder, to hear the demand for payment and the statement of witnesses. If [the debtor is] a single man [he shall summon him] to [the home of] his heir, if this one lives in the fylki, or to the place where he was on Holy Night. [He may give him] as brief a respite as he likes, but fifteen nights at the longest. Now he shall say that he will be at home when he comes there. The entire day is available for the appointment, whether the summoner comes early or later in the

[1] In this case the outlawry was limited; the right of revenge did not extend to those who lived outside the outlaw's own district.

[2] See Glossary, "Home summons."

day but [comes] openly and [while] there is yet daylight. Then the witnesses to the home summons shall be heard at once and after that the complainant shall offer testimony as to the amount of money owing to him. If he [the debtor] refuses to make payment, he shall make a formal demand[3] upon him and [threaten to] charge him with robbery, unless he shall pay at once. Now if the debtor pleads that "I do not know the law but I will comply with whatever the thingmen think lawful," he [the creditor] must summon him before the thing after five nights, at the shortest, and five times five at the longest, if he knows when the thing is to meet; if he does not know, the business will have to wait till he does know. Any man who needs a thing may summon one if he will. And when the dispute comes before the thing, the complainant shall present his witnesses to the thing summons; it is then the duty of the thingmen to decide the matter and to award him his money. But if they refuse to give judgment, they shall owe a fine of fifteen marks, if the plaintiff insists on a judgment. Now if no agreement is reached at the quarter thing, the case may be sent with [the aid of] two witnesses to the shire thing; and if one [of the litigants] feels that he does not get justice even there, he may appeal from the shire thing to the Gulathing, [though only] in case one-fourth of the men withdraw from the thing, declaring justice to be what the appellant claims; then the appeal is valid, but otherwise not. But in case the thingmen agree that the plaintiff has [properly] demanded his money and that his evidence is sufficient, it is their duty to award him his money. But if the debtor did not meet the demand with an offer to accept the decision of thingmen, he shall owe the king a baug[4] and the complainant shall increase his claim to the double. If the debtor appeals to the judgment of thingmen, he escapes the [payment of the] baug by that move. Then he [the plaintiff] shall bring before the thing the witnesses who heard him demand his money in legal manner; then it is well if he [the debtor] is willing to pay the money at the thing or to appoint a day and to pay it then. But if he refuses to pay, [the plaintiff], if he has sued for his money according to law, shall ask the men who are at the thing and the

[3] See Glossary, "Demand."

[4] See *ibid.*, "Baug."

king's bailiff and as many freemen as he thinks necessary to go upon the debtor and to seize the double of what he sued for and a baug to be paid to the king. And he shall have six oras for having to proceed with distraint. But if men resist and support the debtor with point and edge [and are slain], they fall as outlawed men deprived of all personal rights; while those who sue at law and wish to uphold the law shall all remain in the peace. Even if they be not [outlawed], the leader shall owe a fine of forty marks and all the others three marks each; and the one whom the complainant points out shall be [considered] the leader. But if men refuse to go with the plaintiff from the thing to seize the goods [that he] sued for, each one of them shall owe a fine of three oras to the king; and if the bailiff refuses to go, he loses the fines that were due him.

36. CONCERNING LEASED OR BORROWED CHATTELS

Now there are borrowed chattels and leased chattels and hand-sold[5] chattels and chattels awarded by the court and debts owing on an appointed day, and all those demands that witnesses have knowledge of—all these shall be sued for by the formal demand. In the case of a debt that is due on a specified day, you may produce your witnesses on that day as if you had given the debtor a home summons. If the one who is to receive the money does not appear, but the man who is to make the payment is present, he shall offer the payment on that day; and if there is some one present who has been authorized before witnesses to receive the money, he shall pay it into his hand. But if none such is present, the debtor shall renounce the hire, the keeping, and the responsibility, if [what is owing is] a borrowed chattel. But let him who had the chattel continue to keep it and be responsible for all neglect, till the creditor comes to get it; he shall then give it into his hands.

37. CONCERNING AN APPEAL TO A DOOM[6]

The next is this, that if a man owes another a debt of which witnesses have no knowledge, [the creditor] shall summon him

[5] See Glossary, "Hand sold."

[6] See *ibid.*, "Doom," "Doomsman."

to be at home to hear his claim, and he shall formally demand what is due him. The debtor shall [then] either acknowledge the debt, *Olaf:* or meet the demand with a request for a doom, lest he risk a fine for ignoring the demand. Now, every man shall accept the offer of a doom when it is made by a free man of mature age, if the one who should offer it is not at home. In every case when a doom is offered within the limits of the garth, a doom shall be appointed to meet after five days before the door of the defendant's house. And the doom shall be set for a time that will not fall on a Sunday or a mass-day, otherwise the action that the complainant has brought has no force. Now the doom shall be set before the defendant's door and not behind his house. He [the plaintiff] shall place his doomsmen no nearer the house than that the defendant can place his doomsmen between the door and the other man's doom and [leave room for] a load of wood to pass between the doom and the door. Now it is well if the one who has the defense goes out to set the doom with his opponent; otherwise he [the plaintiff] shall go in with two witnesses and summon him to come out and set a counter doom. When the doom is set, the defendant shall purge the doom of the plaintiff. And if this one has taken into his doom any near kinsmen on either side or any one closely related by marriage or some one who has a suit against the defendant, these shall arise and leave the doom; and the suitor shall find disinterested men in their stead, if such there are; if there are no such men, his doom is worthless. If he has taken a baron into his doom or the son of a baron, one who is younger than forty years, or a king's bailiff, he loses by default and shall never be allowed to bring the case up again. And these men shall not be allowed to approach so near the doom that their voices can be heard. Now the plaintiff shall purge the defendant's doom as the defendant has purged the plaintiff's doom. When both dooms are purged and neither side is able to invalidate the opposing doom, the plaintiff shall present witness that he summoned the defendant with a proper home summons to be at home to hear his claim; [he shall] also [present] witness that he demanded his money. It then becomes the duty of those who sit in the doom to pass judgment and to order him who denies the debt to present as great an oath of refutation as the law demands for the amount requested from him. One [oath] will deny [a debt of] one ora; two, [one of] two oras; three, [one of] three oras. The debtor shall clear himself with a threefold oath till the amount rises to half-a-hundred [oras], that is, to seven marks and a half,[7] [if it is] more than that, the threefold oath shall be repeated. A book shall be laid on the threshold and the defendant shall take it up and swear the oath, and the [other] men [the oath helpers] [shall take] the same oath. A doom shall be conducted in such a way that no one shall [be allowed to] rise up to leave the doom or to depart, except on necessary errands; if one goes away [for such a reason] he shall leave his gloves, or a weapon, or something else of value behind; he shall tell his needs and shall return immediately to the doom. But if a man rises and leaves the doom before all have come into agreement in the case, the one who had him in his doom loses his case by default. If a man demands his money and the debtor is unwilling to submit to a doom, he shall go outside the garth or shall walk along the shore's edge and return to the house to present his claim a second time. If the debtor is still unwilling to submit to a doom, [he shall] ask him to be at home the following day in the morning and [let him] then present his claim a third time. Four witnesses are needed at the third demand. If the debtor still refuses to submit to a doom, he shall owe a fine of eighteen oras to the king, six oras for each request. The claimant shall thereupon summon the debtor to the thing and present his witnesses at the thing, all the witnesses that he would have presented to a doom. If he still refuses to pay, the thingmen shall award the plaintiff his money. He shall then ask them to go upon him and take from him eighteen oras due the king and for himself double the amount that he sued for, *M[agnus]*: or [let them demand] the oaths that the law requires. If he refuses both [payment and oath], he admits the validity of the claim. The plaintiff shall then call this to the attention of witnesses and summon him before the thing for robbery; and let him bring two men to the thing to testify that the debtor has refused both to pay the money and to defend his case with oaths. It is then the duty of the thingmen to award him his money and [to add] a baug of twelve oras for

[7] The ancient hundred was sometimes one hundred and twenty.

the king. But if he will neither pay at the thing nor promise to pay, he [the plaintiff] shall call upon the king's bailiff or official and upon as many freemen as he thinks necessary to go with him to seize double the amount that the debtor owed him; and whoever refuses to go with him shall owe a fine of three oras to the king. One oath will deny [a debt of] one ora; two, [one of] two [oras]; three, [one of] three [oras]; *usque*.[8] And the other men [the oath helpers] shall take the same oath.

38. CONCERNING DEBTS TO WHICH THERE ARE NO WITNESSES

If a man who has a debt to pay shall die and the one to whom it is owing survives, the latter cannot obtain his dues unless he comes with witnesses; for no one shall swear a [negative] oath on a dead man's behalf. But he [the heir] shall take an oath that "to my knowledge the debt did not exist"; then he swears only to what he himself knows and not to the knowledge of the deceased.

39. CONCERNING STALE OR OUTLAWED DEMANDS

If a debt remains unpaid for twenty winters or longer than twenty winters, it has become too old for testimony. But the creditor may compel the debtor to [a negative] oath all the same, for a suit retains its vigor if the prosecutor is capable.

40. CONCERNING PURCHASES MADE BEFORE WITNESSES AND HAND SOLD

Now all purchases that are hand sold or known to witnesses shall hold, if those who make the bargain have the right to do so; but if a man sells what is not his to sell, or if there is fraud in the sale, the purchase goes back to the seller and the buyer shall have his money returned. None of us shall sell counterfeit or worthless goods to another and whoever deceives [in this way] shall owe a fine of three marks. Whatever men deem to be a fraudulent sale shall be counted fraudulent, as [in case] a man buys sand and rubbish when he believes that he is buying meal or butter, or [if he buys] something that cannot be inspected from the outside. All agreements that are concluded with the handclasp shall stand,

[8] And so forth; see above, pp. 65–66.

if they are such as ought to stand. An agreement shall not stand if you are selling to one what you have already sold to another; but if he who made the purchase last has it [the thing sold] in his possession, he may ask a legal judgment in defense of his title. The purchase shall belong to him who bought it first, if his witnesses appear satisfactory at the doom; the bargain is then worthless to him who made it last, but let him bring the facts to the attention of impartial men. It is also fraud when a man buys that in which the seller has no right of ownership, unless the sale is made with the owner's permission. Now he [the second buyer] shall look up the man who made the sale to him and recover his own from him; but if he will not return it to him, he shall summon him to his home and shall have witnesses that you gave up possession in obedience to law, and you shall demand your money and charge him with robbery.

41. CONCERNING A COW THAT IS HIRED

If a man lets a cow for hire, the one who receives her shall be held accountable for her in all matters and shall return her in the condition in which he received her, except that she will be older. Now he shall have the cow, if the contract is right, till the gang days in the following spring; for after that time the cow shall be on the [return] journey, unless the men specified another day when the cow was hired. If the cow shall die and the owner holds another cow as a pledge, he shall have this one in place of the other; for a cow shall take the place of a cow; but if she is alive he shall have his own. If the cow shall suffer injuries, though it be only a broken horn or a torn tail, he [the borrower] shall make the damage good. If he wishes to keep the cow no longer, let him find the owner, if he is in the fylki, and offer [to return] the cow. If he [the owner] is not in the fylki, he shall bring the cow home and call in men to inspect her [and to determine] whether she is intact and fit to be received by the owner. Let him then renounce all responsibility [as a renter], but he shall give her such care as he gives his [own] cattle and he shall have the use of her for the care and the grass, being accountable for negligence only. If the owner of the cow has left the land but has committed his property to a keeper, he shall offer the cow to this keeper, if he is in the fylki; if there is no such keeper, [he shall offer her] to the [man's] heir, if he does not care to keep her for hire any longer.

42. CONCERNING THE PAYMENT OF INTEREST

If a man borrows gold or silver from another, or whatever the goods [may be] that he borrows, he shall pay the interest that was agreed upon, till he terminates the loan in a legal way. Interest shall not be collected on interest money unless that is specified in the contract and the parties are agreed upon it.

43. CONCERNING THE KEEPING OF FARM ANIMALS

If a man undertakes to keep farm animals for another with a proper understanding as to foddering,[9] he shall be held to account for all forms of negligence. It shall be [counted] negligence if the animals are starved or maltreated by him or by those for whom he is responsible with pledge and promise. It is also his negligence if the herdsman fails to find a beast before it has perished; likewise, if a bear attacks [it] or wolves rend [it], or if it falls out over a cliff, no herdsman being near—that too, is his negligence. But if the beast falls out over a cliff and the keeper shows the fact to men before he has flayed the skin off, that shall not be counted as negligence. Furthermore, he shall be regarded as negligent if the beast drowns in a well, the herdsman being absent. It is also counted his negligence if the beast dies of starvation or is choked by a wooden collar; but if there is a swivel in the halter or a pole for the halter [to slide upon], it is not a case of negligence. Now, you shall feed [the animals] till they are able to find food out in the open; then you shall seek the owner and tell him to take charge of his beasts, and call men to see that they are able to find their food, and renounce all responsibility for them. If a man takes a horse to keep [over winter] or to pasture and wolves attack it out in the open, it is [counted] his neglect unless other men allow their horses to be out. If a man takes cattle to fodder, his responsibility shall be the same as for those taken to keep through the winter. But he shall not be held accountable if a cow fails to become gravid, if he keeps a bull among his cattle. If a man has been

[9] Brandt believes that this refers to winter foddering (*Retshistorie*, I, 311), which is likely to be true, though the terms used are quite general.

promised a cow in payment of a debt, one that is lacking neither in value nor in [the possibility of] money rent, she must not be older than eight winters nor younger than her second calfing; [she must be] in good condition with healthy teats, and should have had a calf the winter [before].

44. CONCERNING LATENT DEFECTS

If a man buys a horse or other farm beast from another, all responsibility [for the beast] rests with the purchaser as soon as he has led it away. In the sale of live stock let no one deal dishonestly with another by concealing defects. It is a latent defect if a cow sucks herself. If the purchaser discovers this flaw during the first month, the seller shall take the cow back or swear that he was not aware of such a latent defect.

45. CONCERNING RESPONSIBILITY FOR GOODS

If a man buys something unseen from another, the responsibility for it rests with the seller until it has come into the hands of the buyer or [into the hands] of one whom he has authorized before witnesses to receive it, unless the parties have arranged otherwise before witnesses.

46. CONCERNING THE HOME SUMMONS

If there comes into the fylki a man whom you wish to bring into court on account of some claim, but who was not in the fylki on Holy Night and who has no heir in the fylki, he shall be asked as to his abiding place, and if he names it, you shall summon him to that place; but he shall not name a baron's farm unless that is [his abiding place]. If he refuses to name it, the fact shall be called to the attention of witnesses, and you may summon him to any homestead that you like, except to your own, and after that you may bring action against him there. A man is also correctly summoned if he is summoned to the place of purchase, where the parties entered into the bargain. A single man shall be summoned as one summons a householder, [namely, to the place] where he has had his abode for two half years. If there is no such [place], let him be summoned to the place where his heir lives, [if it is] in the fylki, or he shall be asked to name an abiding place; and it shall be as he names it, if within the quarter, unless he names a baron's [farm].

47. CONCERNING LAWSUITS AND HOME SUMMONS

All legal actions shall be at rest while the levy is out [at sea] and till the ships have been five nights upon the beams. Legal actions shall be at rest during Lent, [except that] violations of the church law and fresh crimes may always be prosecuted. No one may follow up a suit on holy days, except only to serve a home summons. A man may serve a home summons in behalf of another as for himself, if he is authorized to do so before witnesses. Within the realm every man who is free and of legal age shall prosecute his own lawsuits; but, if a man leaves the land, his possessions shall remain for three winters in the keeping of whomever he has authorized before witnesses to hold them, and this man shall have the right of suit and defense in his behalf. But if the man goes to the Greek Empire, his nearest heir shall hold his property. A woman may bring an action at law just as a man may, if she is unmarried; but she has the right to assign both suit and defense [to another]. She shall not appoint a baron or a man more prominent than her opponent to prosecute her cases. A man may carry forward her suits as he would his own, if he has been authorized to do so before witnesses. If a man wishes to bring action to enforce some claim, but another has brought an earlier suit against the [same] man, let him yield who began last, for one cannot defend twice at the same time, unless [it be that] the earlier suit is a mere pretense.

48. IF A MAN MAKES AN UNWARRANTED SALE

If two men or more hold a certain chattel in joint ownership and one sells [his share] without consulting those who own it with him, and if his fellow owners wish to nullify the sale, they shall determine by lot on which side the decision shall lie. If the one who made the sale wins the lot, the sale shall stand; but if those win the lot who wish to nullify [the sale], they shall declare it null and void within the first month after they have become aware of it.

49. IF A MAN LENDS CHATTELS TO ANOTHER

Whoever receives anything as a loan shall be held accountable for it and shall return it intact. If he refuses to do so, the owner may sue for it as for notorious property. Any form of property to which the title is known to witnesses is notorious property. If a man lends [to another] what has been lent [to him] and thus abuses [the loan], he [the owner] may claim [the value of] it, as he prefers, from either [borrower]. And thus it shall be whenever a man disposes of the property of another; the owner may claim it from whomever he prefers, from the one who sold it or from the one who bought it.

50. CONCERNING PLEDGES

If a man hands over a pledge in return for something of value, the one who receives the pledge shall be accountable for it. If they have appointed a day when it shall be redeemed, the holder shall offer it on that day, having witnesses present. If no one redeems it, the pledge is forfeited. If a man has a debt owing him by another and takes a piece of property as a pledge for what is due, whether it be land or something else of value, and if he hands the pledge over to another, the one who owned the pledge shall have witnesses as to his [right to the] pledge within the following twelvemonth, if he is in the fylki. But if he is not in the fylki, he shall redeem it within the twelvemonth following his return to the fylki; otherwise he shall have no right to renew the claim later. If a man gives the same pledge to two men, the one who received it first shall have it, if the facts are known to witnesses; but the one who received it last has nothing.

51. THE MARRIAGE OF WOMEN

Now, the next is this, that we must learn how we shall buy our wives with the mund in order that a child may be capable of inheriting property. A man shall pledge himself to pay the lowest mund [at least], which is twelve oras, and there shall be witnesses present, and let him have bridesmen and let her have brideswomen [at the wedding]. And in the morning after they have been together during the night, he shall give her such a [morning] gift as he has pledged to her; then the child that is born after that shall be capable of inheriting. The next is this, that a man may wish to arrange a marriage that calls for greater outlay; in that case the father shall himself betroth his daughter, if she is a maid; but the brother [shall betroth her] if the father is dead. If the father refuses to wed his daughter to the man who has betrothed her, he [the fiancé] shall give him a home summons and appoint a day on which he wishes to have his betrothed. But if the father refuses to let him have her, he shall make a formal demand for his betrothed and summon him [the father] before the thing for robbery; and it shall be the duty of the thingmen to declare him an outlaw. A maiden has by no means the right to decide whether she will fulfill the obligation. The man [who controls the marriage] shall keep an affianced woman twelve months for her betrothed. If leprosy appears on either side, the betrothal is annulled. If a man lies with his betrothed, he shall pay atonement to her rightful heir; after that he may have her as wife. A widow shall betroth herself but with the advice of kinsmen; then she may not break the contract. But if she has not had the advice of kinsmen, she may break it, but she shall pay three marks for breach of promise to the one who had affianced her. Every man shall have his betrothed if she is affianced to him by the one who has the right to give her in marriage; but if a man pledges a woman whose marriage is not in his control, he shall pay three marks to the man to whom he pledged her. If there are brothers, two or more, who have the right to give a sister in marriage, and if one of them betroths her to a man and the other wishes to annul [the contract], they shall determine by lot who shall have the decision. If the one who made the agreement wins the lot, it shall remain valid, otherwise not; and he shall pay three marks for breach of contract. If either one [of the betrothed] falls ill or is wounded, let them wait twelve months and then do one of two [things], either proceed according to contract in spite of the defect that has come into it, or annul the betrothal. The woman shall not be given in marriage [to another] before a twelvemonth has passed unless [the earlier fiancé] is willing; nor shall he take another woman to wife sooner than that unless [the guardian] is willing. If a man refuses to wed his betrothed, he shall be served with a home summons and a day shall be appointed when he must take her; he shall then be summoned to make answer at the thing for having avoided his betrothed; and the thingmen shall declare him an outlaw and he shall be known as *fuðflogi*.[10] In the same way a day shall be appointed for a woman who has affianced herself to a man, in case she has failed to come on the day agreed upon to marry the man to whom she had pledged herself. If she refuses to come on the appointed day, she shall be summoned before the thing to answer for having fled from her betrothed; and she shall be outlawed at the thing, and she shall leave the land and shall be known as *flannfluga*.[11] If a hostile force invades the land, every man shall make provision for his betrothed, if she is offered to him before witnesses; but if he refuses and will not provide for her, he breaks the betrothal with that refusal. If a man's betrothed is carried off in a foray, it is his duty to go after her and to give three marks toward her ransom, her heir to supply what more is needed. If a man takes another man's betrothed and has her [as his own], both having consented to this, let him who had affianced her summon the one who has taken her to appear before a thing; and it shall be the duty of the thingmen to outlaw them both. But if the woman did not give her consent, she has nothing to answer for.

52. HOW A MAN SHALL MANAGE HIS WIFE'S PROPERTY

No man shall carry his wife's property out of the land unless she is willing. He shall manage all the property belonging to both and to their advantage. Neither of the two shall damage the possessions of the other by word or deed. Every man has the same right to atonement in his wife's case as in his own.

53. CONCERNING COMMUNITY PROPERTY[12]

A woman must not deny her husband the right of community ownership. If a man marries a maid, they shall not establish community property unless the men who are to inherit from them give their consent. But if they beget children to inherit from them,

[10] One who flees from the female sex organ.

[11] One who flees from the male sex organ.

[12] Norwegian scholars are in disagreement as to the meaning of this chapter; some believe that actual ownership was formed while others hold that the income only was concerned in the agreement. See Brandt, *Retshistorie*, I, 116; Keyser, *Norges stats- og retsforfatning*, p. 311.

they may establish community ownership on whatever terms they like. If a man marries a widow who has children to inherit from her and these are minors, but the husband wishes none the less to enter into community ownership with her, the paternal kinsmen of the children shall be summoned and the arrangement shall be made with due regard to the family wealth. Land shall be set over against land and money against money and let the husband's income be estimated [to make sure] that it is greater than his wife's income, and whatever is established in this way shall not be disturbed. But if community ownership is formed in any other way, the arrangement shall be voidable at the election of whomever wishes, his heirs or hers, by the expedient of going before the thing ere the two have lived twenty winters together and declaring the arrangement void; but if it is not annulled before they have lived twenty winters together, the man can never bring the matter into court again. Whenever two married people wish to form a community, they shall publish [their intent] in the presence of assembled men. If two married people have lived together twenty winters or longer than twenty winters, a legal community is formed by implication, if that has not been done earlier; and the wife shall have a third in this and the husband two-thirds. And if a community was formed but not published before the passing of twenty winters, it shall be as if it were not formed.

54. CONCERNING THE MYNDING

The gift that is given to a woman shall remain her lawful property, no matter how the marriage is terminated. *Olaf:* The husband shall [by the payment of mund] acquire [control of] all the goods that come with a maiden, but for every ora an ora shall be given [by him] in return. But of a widow's property [he acquires] one-half.[13] This balancing of mund and marriage portion shall remain in force in all cases except two: if the wife dies without children or if she leaves [her husband] without cause. *Both:* No man shall strike his wife at the table or at an ale feast; if he strikes her in the sight of assembled men, he shall pay her such an atonement as he could demand in his own case; and the same the second

[13] See Hertzberg, *Glossarium*, *mynda.* The significance of mynda has long been in dispute.

time and the third time, [if he repeats the offense]. *Olaf:* After that she has the right to leave him, taking with her the husband's gift[14] and the property set aside to balance the marriage portion. And if a man wishes to separate from his wife, let him announce the termination of the marriage so [distinctly] that each one can hear the other's voice, and let him have witnesses present.

55. OLAF AND MAGNUS

If a man demands the payment of a debt from one who is in the fylki and the debtor gives him a valid order on some other man, he has discharged the debt so far as it concerns him, provided that the arrangement was made before witnesses.

56. HOW LARGE A PURCHASE MAY BE MADE BY A WOMAN

No minor can make a purchase or a valid bargain. A thrall may bargain for nothing but his knife only; nor may a freedman who has not yet given his freedom ale make a bargain involving more than an ertog. Now it shall also be told how large a purchase may be made by a woman. A freedman's wife may make a bargain [to the amount] of an ertog, if he has given his freedom ale,[15] and his son's wife [to the amount] of half an ora. The wife of a freeman may bargain to [the amount of] one ora; the wife of a hauld to [the amount of] two oras; a baron's wife to [the amount of] half a mark. If a larger purchase is made, it may be annulled within the first month following; and if he [the husband] is not at home, he may annul it within the first month after his return.

57. FREEDMAN'S LAW

The next is this, that if a man buys a thrall from another, let them make a valid bargain according to law.[16] He who sold him shall give warrant for the time of the waxing and the waning of the next moon that he does not suck cows and that he is not epileptic or does not have a stitch in the side or any other serious ailment; also that he can retain his own water and does not befoul his clothes; and he shall give warrant covering all latent defects

[14] See Glossary, "Husband's gift."

[15] See below, c. 62, and Glossary, "Freedom ale."

[16] *Lagakaup ok lýrittar:* according to common or folk law.

for the following month. Now if any such defect is found, the buyer shall return the purchase within the following month in the presence of witnesses. If the thrall has a bastard child, the one who sells him shall provide for the child. If the thrall has been paid wages, let him have that as foster money. If the thrall goes without concealment to his wife's bed, the one who buys him shall provide for the child that she is pregnant with, but the seller shall care for the earlier [children]. If a bondwoman is with child and the purchaser was not informed of it, that, too, is a concealed defect. He who has the child with her shall then be held to account, if she suffers injury or death when she goes to child-bed, and until she can carry two buckets of water from the well. He [the new owner] shall then take the child and the mother with it [and go] to the one who sold her; and he shall offer him the bondwoman and shall hand the child over to the father. He [the owner] shall lend him the bondwoman,[17] if he finds it necessary to charge another man with the paternity; he has then disposed of the child in a legal manner, but there must be witnesses. Every man, if his thrall lies with a woman, shall make such reparation as he would in his own case. The heir shall in every case receive the atonement for a woman, unless she has a husband. The one whom the mother points out as the father shall be [held to be] the father of the child. If she charges a thrall with the paternity, she shall summon his master to be at home and she shall present her witnesses to the summoning; and the master shall then offer to take a threefold oath in his man's behalf or take the child; but if he will do neither, let the child be laid down in that place and all responsibility passed on to him. The child of a free woman shall be disposed of in the same way as that of a bondwoman. If a bondwoman charges a free man with paternity, he [her master] shall summon him to be at his home to [hear her] claim and to receive the infant. The one [who served the summons] shall go to him on the day to which he had summoned him, bringing his witnesses to the home summons. And when a woman charges a man with the paternity, she shall demand compensation from the

[17] This seems to be Gjessing's interpretation. See his discussion of the probable origin and the history of slavery among the Norsemen in *Annaler for Nordisk Oldkyndighed* (1862), pp. 28–322.

one whom she has thus charged and [also demand] that he receive the infant; for no one shall carry a child out into a highway to offer it to a man there. Now it is well if he admits the charge, for then it is his thrallborn child; but if he denies the charge saying that he has no claim to it, and will neither promise compensation nor receive the child, then the child shall be laid down in that place, for his denial is naught unless he offers to clear himself with a threefold oath; but if he agrees at once [to purgation], the suitor shall take the child away and the oath may be taken [any time] within ten weeks of oath days. A threefold oath shall be required in every case of illegal carnal dealings except when the man is somehow related to the woman with whom he worked the misdeed; in that case it shall be a sixfold oath. Now if the man takes the oath, he swears the child off his hands so that no responsibility for it remains either with him or with his kinsmen. If the child comes to resemble him and he sees that he has taken a wrong oath, let him go into a gathering of men and acknowledge the child as his own, and let him do penance for his perjury; then the child is his thrallborn child. If he has agreed to take an oath but refuses to swear, he shall pay the suitor six ells to the ora[18] for every month that this one fosters his infant child. Now this failure to take the oath must be prosecuted like any other [such failure] within the next twelvemonth; otherwise it is as if the oath were taken according to our laws. If the man who fails to take the oath also fails to claim the child [as his own] within the twelvemonth, the suitor shall foster it as his thrall or his bondwoman; for none of us shall rear a thrall as he would a calf to another's profit. If, when the child has been reared, the man desires to confess [paternity] and to acknowledge the child [as his own], he shall redeem it with such a sum as judicious men deem to be its worth as a thrall who has no free time. If a man acknowledges a child to be his and carries it to church before it has seen three Holy Nights and gives it freedom and brings it up in his family, it shall have the same right to atonement as the father has. In the same way the child's kinsmen may give it freedom on the father's behalf, and bring

[18] The amount is not stated. Hertzberg suggests one-half ora. *Glossarium*, *ǫln.*

it up in the kindred; it shall then have the same right to atonement as the father has.

58. CONCERNING LEGITIMATION[19]

Now a man may improve the status of his [illegitimate] son by bringing him into the kindred, if he wishes [to do so] and the nearest heir gives consent. If he has sons by a mother whom he has bought with the mund, though but one of these is of major age, and this one gives consent, he gives consent for all those who are still minors and also for those who are unborn. The one who shares in the odal shall give consent for the odal land. He [the father] shall then give a feast with as much ale as can be brewed from three såld of malt by the standard of Hordaland. And he shall butcher a three-year-old ox and flay off the skin in the cleft of the front hoof on the right side and make a shoe of it which he shall set beside the large ale bowl. The one who brings the man into the kindred shall first put on the shoe; next the one who is being brought into the kindred; then the one who consented for the inheritance; then he who consented for the odal; and finally the kinsmen. No one shall give away the inheritance of another; a fraudulent contract has no value. No one shall cheat another out of his inheritance. Now the father shall put on the shoe if he is bringing a son into the kindred; his son who is of major age [shall next put it on]; then the legitimation is complete. If there is no [such] son, the one who consents for the inheritance shall put on the shoe; next the one who consents for the odal shall put on the shoe. He [the father] shall now make a statement in this wise: "I conduct this man to the goods that I give him, to geld and to gift, to seat and to settle, to bót[20] and to baug, and to all personal rights, as if his mother had been bought with the mund." A brother or a sister may bring a brother into the kindred and a father's brother [may legitimate] a brother's son. A "corner lad" or a "bush lad"[21] shall be brought into the kindred in the same way as a thrallborn son. Other kinsmen may bring [a man] into the kindred in the way that I have described and make him competent to inherit, if the nearest heir gives his

[19] Cf. *Frost.*, IX, c. 1.

[20] Fine, reparation, wergeld.

[21] See Glossary, "Corner lad," "Bush lad"; see also below, pp. 108, 326.

consent. If a father gives his son his freedom before he has seen fifteen Holy Nights, he, too, may be led into the kindred; but consent must be secured from all those who are in the inheritance with him. Now he shall have everything that has become his by legitimation as long as they are living who stepped into the shoe with him; after their death he shall take both inheritance and odal. A man shall make public announcement of his legitimation every twenty winters [or] until he has received an inheritance; after that the inheritance shall testify for him and for all time.

59. CONCERNING TESTIMONY

Every lawsuit shall be decided by the testimony of witnesses and the gains[22] [that come to a litigant in the course of the action]. If only one man bears witness for a man, it is as if no one has testified; but two [are as good] as ten if there is no danger of opposing testimony. Now there are witnesses that are not to be met by counter witnesses: witnesses to a home summons and to thing summons, to a formal demand [by a claimant], to legal excuses, to a demand for the surrender of odal land, and witnesses as to quarrels among men at an ale feast. If a man demands money from another, the latter may assert in his defense that the debt has been paid and name the witnesses who were present [when the payment was made]. If [these] witnesses are in the fylki, they shall be given sufficient time to make the journey; but if they are outside the fylki, they shall have a legal summons to come and testify as to what they had observed. If they bear witness that they were present when the debtor cleared the debt off his hands, the defendant has successfully met the demand. That is evidence of legal payment and there shall be no counter witnesses [in such a case]. But if they [the witnesses] fail to appear, the debtor shall owe the claim. Near kinsmen on either side of the house or near relatives by marriage may not bear witness with a man unless they are equally related to both parties.

Two men may receive the evidence from one [witness] if this one was [actually] present [at the transaction]; then their evidence becomes as competent as if they had all been present.

[22] *Gagn:* that which is helpful and advantageous; as a legal term its use is about as given above. See Hertzberg, *Glossarium,* "gagn" (3).

60. CONCERNING COUNTER WITNESSES

If men bring counter witnesses forward, they shall increase [the number] by one witness; then those who testified earlier shall be [regarded as] false witnesses. If both sides produce the same number of witnesses, those who testify last are to be [regarded as] false witnesses. They shall never again be allowed to testify in such a case and each one of them shall pay a fine of three marks to the king.

61. IF A MAN LIBERATES A THRALL

If a man takes a thrall to church or seats him on his chest[23] and gives him his freedom, and if he gives it free from all debts or dues, he [the freedman] need not give his freedom ale any more than a man who is born to freedom. After that he shall himself arrange his marriage and his business affairs; he shall, nevertheless, remain in dependence upon his master as another must who buys his freedom. If a man gives freedom to a thrall or a bondwoman who buys and pays for it, then whoever receives this freedom is free, if it is given by one who has the right to give it. If a thrall walks in the ways of a free man for twenty winters or longer than twenty and no man complains of his dealings or his marriage or his purchases, whether he moves about within the fylki or without, he is a free man if he wishes to be called free. A man who receives his freedom from the king need not give his freedom ale; nor [shall this be required of] one who received his freedom before he had [seen] three Holy Nights and has grown up without encumbrance [of any sort]. If a thrall or a bondwoman are to pay their value in money, they shall be taken to church, a [Gospel] book shall be laid on the head of each, and they shall be given [their] freedom. Now a man shall continue to labor a twelvemonth for his master; but if he received his freedom on such terms that one-half of his value or even more might remain unpaid, the king shall have no claim, even if the master shall proceed by corporal punishment to force the payment of what still remains unpaid.

[23] Agnes Wergeland understands this to be the chest of arms "which was below the seat of the head of the family." *Slavery in Germanic Society*, p. 132.

62. CONCERNING MANUMISSION

If a freedman wishes [full freedom] to control his marriage and his business affairs, he shall give a freedom ale[24] brewed from at least three såld of malt and let him invite his master in the hearing of witnesses but let him not invite any of his [master's] opponents in a lawsuit, and he shall place him in the highseat. And let him put six oras into the scales the first evening, and let him offer his master these as a ransom fee. If he takes the money, then it is well; if he gives it back, it is as if all is paid. But if the master refuses to come, the freedman shall call upon his witnesses to testify that he did invite him, and let him leave the master's highseat vacant. And let him place six oras in the scales the first evening and let him offer the money to the vacant chair; that is called the ransom fee. If the master has authorized some one to receive the money, then it is well; but if no man takes it, he [the freedman] shall keep it till the morning and offer it once more at the meal. But if no man takes it then, he shall have it and keep it till the one who is to have it comes for it. Then the freedom ale is given complete.

63. CONCERNING THE MARRIAGE OF A FREEDMAN

If a freedman who has given his freedom ale takes a well-born woman to wife, and they separate, all the children shall go with the mother. If she dies first, all the children shall return to the father and subsist on his goods as long as there are any; and when all is consumed, they shall all go to the better kindred, and the father shall return to his master. If a freedman who has not given his freedom ale takes a well-born woman to wife, all the children shall go with the wife no matter how the marriage may terminate. If a freedman who has not given his freedom ale marries a freedwoman who has given hers, the children shall inherit from neither one. But if his freedom ale has been given and hers has not, but her master holds out a hope of emancipation, the children shall inherit from both. If a freedman marries a freedwoman and the master of the one has given his consent but [the master of] the other has not, then, if there are goods to divide, the one who has not con-

[24] Cf. *Frost.*, IX, c. 12.

sented must reckon up his share; but if there is great need he may renounce every claim. If a freedman marries a freedwoman, both having celebrated their freedom ales, the children shall inherit from both; but if they come to extreme want, they [the children] shall be [regarded as] ready for the grave: a grave shall be dug in the churchyard and they shall be placed within it and be allowed to perish. Let the master take out [of the grave] the one that lives longest and provide it with food from that time on. If a freedman marries a freedwoman, neither having given the freedom ale, and they beget children, these shall have the same personal rights as their father [has] and they shall perform the labor for their father and mother. And if any one of them shall desire to go away, let him leave three marks in his stead.

64. CONCERNING A THRALL AND A BONDWOMAN

If a thrall and a bondwoman who live together [in marriage] shall both receive their freedom, two parts of the goods that they acquire shall belong to the husband and one part to the wife. The mund that he gave her when they were in bondage shall be kept intact for her[25] whether it is more or less.

65. CONCERNING THE INHERITANCE OF TWO UNFREE BROTHERS

If two brothers are brought up in bondage in the same man's home, they are both brothers and foster brothers; and if they are released by their master, but continue the common life, sharing the same work and wages, then each becomes the other's heir; but their children do not [inherit] from them unless they have given their freedom ale.

66. CONCERNING THE RESPECT AND DEFERENCE THAT A FREEDMAN OWES HIS LORD

Now a freedman shall owe respect and deference to his lord. He shall not join in any designs on his life or his goods, nor [shall he be found] opposed to him in a doom unless he has a

[25] Gjessing understands this to mean that the mund "shall serve for her maintenance" which seems unlikely, when one considers how inadequate this maintenance would be. See *Annaler for Nordisk Oldkyndighed* (1862), p. 240. Cf. Hertzberg, *Glossarium, halda* (14).

law-suit of his own to promote, in which case he shall act in defense against his master as against any other man. He must never [undertake to] measure words with him and never turn point or edge against him. He shall never join a band of his lord's enemies or bear witness against him, and he shall not enter the service of a man more powerful than his lord unless he has permission; and he shall not set a hostile doom for another man. But if he does any of these things, he shall return to the seat where he sat before and shall redeem himself thence with a full payment; he shall also forfeit his property. Two generations of the freedman's family shall remain in dependence on two [generations] of the master's [family]. If a freedman's son does any of these things, he shall owe his master the same sum that his father paid. For twenty winters the freedman shall have the duty to produce witnesses that he has given his freedom ale; and if no one complains of his doings for twenty winters, that which is not done shall be [regarded as] done, if he wishes to have it so. A freedman may purchase the right for his children to inherit, and if an agreement is reached, it is equivalent to making his own status clear. But if great distress comes upon him and his wife, and [freedom] has been bought, the children shall work for them [their parents] while they are still on earth; [after that] they may depart without [further] obligations. But if they will not do this, let those who wish to leave pay the cost of their [parents'] board and keep.

67. IF A FREEDMAN LEAVES THE FYLKI WITHOUT HIS MASTER'S CONSENT

If a freedman leaves the fylki without his master's consent, and acquires property and transacts business [in his new location], his lawful master shall go after him with witnesses, and if he is willing to return, it is well. But if he refuses to return, let the master prove with witnesses that he is his freedman; and let him bring him back as he likes, bound or unbound, and set him again in the seat that he occupied earlier.

68. IF A THRALL RUNS AWAY

If a thrall runs away and a man captures him within the fylki, but outside the quarter, he shall have an ora. If he captures him outside the fylki, but within our law, he shall have two oras. If he takes him within the realm, but outside our law, half a mark is owing to him. If he brings him home in bonds, he shall have the captor's reward; otherwise nothing.

69. CONCERNING RESPONSIBILITY FOR ANOTHER MAN'S THRALL

If a man hires a thrall from another he shall be held accountable if he sends him out upon an impassable stream, or upon dangerous ice, or into a bruin's lair, or upon impassable mountains, or upon stormy seas, or into other perilous places. If he perishes in such a place and none of his [employer's] thralls or other workmen are with him, the man shall compensate the owner for his thrall. He shall send him home at the close of the half year; but if, in sending him home, he lets him travel alone and he runs away and fails to come into his master's keeping, he shall compensate him [the owner] for his thrall. No man shall help a thrall to escape from his master; if he does, he will have to risk the consequences; but every one shall send such a one home to his master without fear of punishment. Every man shall take a warrant from the master of his hired thrall respecting his labor; otherwise he shall [himself] be accountable in every respect. If the thrall falls ill or is wounded, let him lie seven nights; later he shall be returned to his owner. If the owner has gone out of the land, he shall be brought to the one who has the keeping of his property. If he [the employer] is willing to let him lie longer, the hire shall be reduced as much as the reckoning shows; but he shall not be allowed the food that he consumes while he is lying ill. If the thrall runs away from the one who has him, information shall be sent to the owner; otherwise the employer shall pay the hire, even though he does not have [the thrall].

70. CONCERNING FREE LABORERS

If a man hires the labor of a free man, he shall carry out all [the terms] that they have agreed upon. And if a farmer refuses to keep his agreement with his hired man but dismisses him from house and service, he shall demand his keep before two witnesses and offer to labor as they had agreed. If the farmer refuses the offer, he shall owe a fine of twelve oras and the man shall have his pay and the value of the board that has not been consumed. Now if the laborer refuses to keep his agreement with the farmer, he [the employer] shall demand of him such labor as he had hand sold to him and shall offer him his keep before witnesses; and if he then refuses [to work], he shall owe a fine of twelve oras. And the farmer has the right to collect from him as much as he was to pay him [in wages]; and the workman shall have no board for he has waived his claim to that. If he undertakes a man's work but is not able to perform it, men shall determine how much the hire shall be reduced on that account. If a hired man falls ill or is wounded, but lies [only] five nights, there shall be no reduction [in wages] on that [account]; but if he lies longer, men shall determine the value of the labor [that has been] lost and the food that the man has consumed; or let him be sent into the keeping of his heir. If a man takes a minor into his service, that [agreement], too, shall stand; and if he dismisses him and the man goes [begging] from house to house, he shall pay three marks and care for the man according to agreement. In the same way as I have now set forth, all shall pay who let their dependents go begging from house to house.

71. CONCERNING DEBTORS

A debtor shall be taken to the thing and shall be offered first to his kinsmen if they should want him, [for] he is nearest [in duty] who is nearest of kin; otherwise to the one to whom he [the creditor] wishes to give him. A woman must never be forced to serve for a debt unless her kinsmen have agreed to it. A freedman's children may be offered in any [public] gathering that one prefers. All such [contracts] shall stand as men have agreed upon and are known to witnesses. No one shall force a debtor with blows to work unless he is unable to collect his dues from him; and after that the debtor has no right to claim atonement either from him or from his wife or from any one of his household; and the same is true of each with respect to the other. But if other men do injury to him, he [the creditor] has the same right to compensation as in the case of [injury to] his chief bondman. The man himself has a right to such part of the compensation due his rank as exceeds the payment, and his claim to atonement shall be as great as if he were not a debtor. If a woman held to labor for debt lies with a thrall, the bailiff has no claim to a fine from her until she has paid the debt. If a man sells a debtor at a man sale, except he be a fugitive from debt, he shall owe a fine of forty marks; and the same [shall be due] from any one who sells a free man. If a baron sells [a man], he shall pay one-half the fine to the king and one-half to the shiremen. If the king's bailiff sells [a man], he shall pay forty marks to the shiremen. A well-born man may give his child for a debt if he gives it at a thing or an ale feast or a gathering at church; and he may give it for a debt of three marks but no more. For that sum the contract shall be valid and neither the child nor any other person shall annul it. A man shall have the same use of a debtor servant as of a thrall; he shall assign tasks to him in the same way and shall give him such time for free labor as [he gives] his thralls. He shall continue in the service and work off the debt for which he is bound; if he does not like to serve, he shall have half a month to go about the fylki to raise the amount of the debt which he has to pay. If he travels with covered face or goes out of the fylki, he becomes a thrall, if the one to whom he is in debt can seize him. The king has no claim to atonement for a debtor servant when he [the debtor] can claim no [atonement] in his own right. If a free man of good birth and of major age gives himself into debt service, he may be bound for as large a debt as he wishes. If a man wants his money from a debtor, it is well if he looks after the matter himself; but if he prefers not to attend to it himself, he shall offer [the debtor] to his kinsmen, and it is well if they are willing to buy him; otherwise he may sell him [the debtor] wherever he likes within the realm, but not for a greater sum than he is held for. No one shall sell a free man at a man sale; if he is accused and convicted of such a deed, he shall pay forty marks; and the buyer [shall pay] the same [amount], if he knew that the man was free. If a debtor servant begets children, it is well if he has enough property to get them fostered and cared for; but if he does not himself have the money, the one to whom he is in debt shall arrange for the fostering, and the debt shall then be increased by so much as the fostering calls for. Let them both strive to find a place for the child. Now his debt shall be increased till his [the debtor's] full value seems to have been reached. If he begets several children [while in this state], his kinsmen shall care for them however many they be. If he proves unable to work off the debt and grows old on the hands of him to whom he is in debt and becomes dependent, he shall be his [the creditor's] charge. [The creditor] has also the choice of remitting the debt while the man is still able to work; he then returns to his kindred, if he becomes a dependent. If a man sells a free man into a heathen land, he shall pay a fine of forty marks and have the man returned or pay the atonement to his kinsmen. If the debtor servant is stubborn and refuses to work, let [the creditor] take him to the thing and ask his kinsmen to release him from his debt. If the kinsmen refuse to redeem him, the man to whom the debt is owing has the right to maim him above or below, as he may prefer. If a free man comes into debt service but has not been rightfully bound, let him go to the thing and get a release from the debt; he needs to summon no man to this [thing]. If a man takes another man's thrall and forces [him] to work for himself, he becomes responsible for him and shall pay the owner a fine for conversion, if this one demands it, unless the thrall was taken as a runaway.

[THE LAW OF TENANCY]

72. THE LAW OF TENANCY

If a man leases land from one who owns it and makes a proper contract, he shall have a legal right to occupy the land for a twelvemonth; and let him pay the owner such rent as they have agreed upon. If the payment [of the rent] is set for a certain day, but the tenant does not make payment on that day, he loses his right to that land. If he pays a part of the rent but not the remaining part, he [the owner] shall take witnesses and sue for the remainder. If he refuses to pay, the crops shall be marked with the cross to secure the payment of [delinquent] rent and the tenant shall be forbidden after five days to utilize [the crops that are] under the cross. If he does make use of them, he shall pay a baug to the king and shall pay the owner his rent all the same. He may occupy the land till moving day in the following spring. He may not convey any part of this land in return for rent, unless he made clear when he leased it, that he intended to transfer a part to another in lawful possession [in return] for rent. If he does transfer [it], the right to use the land is lost both to him and to the other who receives it; let both pay the fine for trespass, and the one who got the land from the lessee shall retire from it. But the one who transferred the land to him shall compensate him for all his losses and [shall pay] six oras for breach of contract. For every one who makes a conveyance without warrant shall make compensation in this way, unless he has other land equally good to give him.

73. CONCERNING THE UPKEEP OF BUILDINGS

Now the tenant shall keep in repair all the buildings that were on the land when he came to it, except that he shall not be responsible for the wear and tear of time. If the duty of erecting buildings is a part of his contract, he shall have it all done before he leaves the land. If he builds houses that were not included in the agreement, he builds them for his own [use]. If he has found the materials on the land let him take witnesses and offer to sell these houses to the one who owns the land, if he is in the fylki; otherwise he shall have them moved away before the moving day. If [the owner] is not in the fylki, let the tenant offer them to the one who comes upon the land. Now if a house is still standing after the moving days, the owner of the land shall have it, unless, before the moving days, it has been moved upon stony ground or upon a heap of rocks where it can cause no damage either to cornland or grassland; he may then take the house away after the moving days, as soon as he has leisure to do so. In the beginning of the moving period in the summer the tenant may occupy all the buildings for nine nights; and if he is unable to move all his belongings [in that time], he may occupy one-half of the buildings for nine nights longer. Let him travel preferably the lower highway and he shall not be required to forward summonses. He shall then move his goods away, unless there are hindrances and his new abiding place is so [located] that he has to travel over fjord or mountain; in such a case he shall store his goods in a boat house or in a shieling hut[1] and remain there a third period of nine nights. In this way he will have moved his goods without incurring penalty and [he shall] have the use of both wood and water and of the fodder [to be gathered] on the farm.

74. WHAT A MAN MAY TAKE AWAY FROM THE LAND WITHOUT INCURRING PENALTY

A man may take away from the land whatever he has the right to take away: that is, three loads of fodder for each workman[2] [required] on the farm, one load of hay and two loads of straw for the spring feeding and that we call horse fodder. He shall also be allowed to take with him all the timbers that belong to him.

75. IF A MAN CARRIES AWAY MORE FROM THE LAND THAN BELONGS TO HIM

Now the doors shall be left standing, three outer doors, three even though there were no doors when the tenant came there:

[1] See below, pp. 96, 97.
[2] Or for the area that can be worked by one man.

the living-room door, the storehouse door, and the kitchen door,[3] and all those that were there before. Now if the tenant takes any one of these doors and carries it away, he shall return it and pay the fine for trespass, if he has removed it from [the house]. If he breaks off any part of the threshold, or of the lintel, or of the jambs [in removing the door], be it only a sliver, it shall be called house damage, and he shall pay a fine of three marks. If he takes away the bench supports[4] from the house or the bench boards that are mortised together, he shall return them and pay [a fine of] three marks. [He may take away] the loose floor boards in the stable or the barn, the woodpiles, and the bridges that he has built. He shall place his buildings and his stacks where no damage will be done to cornland or grassland; and if the one who succeeds the tenant [on the farm] finds them annoying, he may have them removed whenever he likes. Floor planks running lengthwise and wainscoting and whatever has not been mortised into place or nailed to the beams or the cross-timbers may be carried away. For whatever he has torn away from any building he shall pay the owner a compensation of three marks, and he shall restore the building to its earlier condition. He must not dig up the stack supports[5] after the moving day; he may cut them off above the ground and take them away; but if he digs them up, he shall pay the fine for trespass to the owner of the land. If a man plants angelicas, he may remove [the roots] before the moving day if he likes. If a man sows the arable land with winter rye and [then] leaves the farm, he shall have nothing from it; if he has spaded up new ground for the sowing within the garth, [he shall] have the value of the seed; if he has spaded up ground for it outside the garth, let each have one-half of the crop, the one who comes to the farm and the one who sowed [the grain], if he has fenced [the field]. The man shall not allow [another to take] anything off the land itself except two loads of wood and one of scraped bark; the tenant may allow that, and the landlord, too, though the one who has taken the new lease may not like to do it. If there are

[3] Ordinarily in separate buildings.

[4] Or possibly the bedposts.

[5] These were set firmly in the ground. See Hertzberg, *Glossarium*, *hjálmróður*.

hawks nesting in the forest, the one who has leased the land shall have them, unless the owner has excepted [them]. No man shall take another man's hawks, lest he risk a fine for trespass; and he shall return the hawks. If he takes a hawk that is bound to the nest, he is a thief, if the owner has stated before witnesses that he has bound it. The fruits of unauthorized labor on land shall belong to the one who has the lease, if it is worth no more than half a mark and if he calls the landlord's attention to it, but not if he keeps the matter quiet; and let him who did the work pay the fine for trespass. One may use the land to provide a ship for his needs, [only] not one [so large] that the oar benches must be counted;[6] if he builds one so large that the benches need be counted, he builds it for him who owns the land. He shall not strip birch bark to sell unless he shall need to buy black salt.[7] He shall prepare no more salt than he needs to give his cattle, except when he has to buy birch bark [for his roofs]. He shall boil no more tar than he needs to cover his boats. No man shall give a feast on another man's land, except when a tenant shall need to give an ale;[8] but if he does give a feast, let him pay three marks.

76. IF A MAN DOES NOT WANT THE LAND THAT HE HAS RENTED

If a man takes a lease but does not take possession of the land that he has rented, the owner shall proceed, five days before the summer solstice, to sow the land and [he shall] use it as if the other had not rented it. But he shall [none the less] collect the rent from the one who leased it.

77. IF A MAN GOES UPON LAND WITHOUT A WARRANT

If a man takes possession of another man's land without taking warrant from the one who owns it, [the owner] shall give him a five-day warning to leave [the land]; and [let the man] release his belongings with the fine for trespass. If he refuses to leave the land, he shall be summoned before the thing for robbery; it is then the duty of the thingmen to award to the owner of the land everything that is on the land except the free men

[6] If it has as many as thirteen benches; smaller ships are otherwise described.

[7] See Glossary, "Salt."

[8] See above, pp. 39–40.

and [to order] the robber fine paid to the king. Now if he will not leave the land, the owner shall demand a force of thingmen so large that he will be able to remove the man from the land; whoever refuses to join in this [action] shall owe a fine of three oras. The king's bailiff is also required to join, and in this way he comes into possession of the fine.

78. IF A MAN CONVEYS THE SAME LAND TO TWO MEN

If a man conveys the same land to two men, the one who leased it first shall have it. And in every case when a man conveys the same thing to two men, the one who bought or rented it first shall have it. Let him call for a doom and let him prove by witnesses that he received it first; and he [the owner] shall provide the other man with other [land], if he has such [land], or pay six oras for breach of contract. If he owns no [land] except what he occupies, the other man shall have [this land] and not he himself.

79. IF A MAN TRIES TO BREAK AN AGREEMENT

If a man gives a lease to a parcel of land but refuses to surrender it to the lessee, the latter shall summon him as he may prefer either to the thing or to the place where the contract was made. And let him show by witnesses how he leased the land. If their testimony is satisfactory, he shall call for a doom to secure the land that he has leased. Land given in mortgage [shall be dealt with] in the same way. But if one of the parties dies, their contract is terminated, and all money for which no value has been received shall be returned.

80. CONCERNING UNTILLED LAND AND THE BUILDING OF FENCES

If a tenant on another man's land is outlawed, he [the owner] shall have the rent, if it is unpaid, and also the standing grain. If there is untilled land close by, the owner shall build a fence around this land and shall keep it in repair, for no man shall serve as a fence post for another. But if he will not build it, no one shall owe compensation if [the grass] is eaten.

81. THE LEGAL RELATIONS OF NEIGHBORS ON THE SAME FARM ARE DEFINED HERE

If two neighbors till the same farm, having rented the land from the same man, their farm is undivided land, and whatever division they arrange between themselves shall hold as long as they remain on that farm. If one of the two continues on the land while the other moves away, the one [who remains] must not refuse to make a new division with the one who comes [next] to the farm. If two men occupy [parts of] the same farm, neither one shall keep more live stock in the summer than he can feed through the winter, and let him not labor on the other man's land to this [end]. If he has more beasts in the pasture, though it be but a lamb only, he shall, unless he has the other man's permission, pay a fine for stealing grass, a fine for trespass to the landlord, and the value of the grass to the owner. All the highways and fence gates shall be kept as of old. If men live near together on the same farm, they shall drive [their cattle] out of the farm pasture [to the shieling] when two months of the summer are spent,[9] unless some other plan seems better to all. If one keeps his live stock longer [on the farm] below, the other shall forbid him to remain there [with them]; if he continues to keep them there none the less, his neighbor shall summon a thing to try him for robbery and unlawful pasturing. And it shall be the duty of the thingmen to award a baug to the king, a double fine for trespass to the landlord, and six oras to his neighbors for stealing grass. And he [the complainant] shall call upon the freemen and the men of the herath, as many as he needs, to drive the offender's cattle out of the home pasture; every one who refuses to join in this shall owe a fine of three oras. The penalty is the same if one leaves the upper pasture before the end of the fifth summer month.[10] The aftermath [that grows] in the autumn shall belong to all; but no one shall begin to graze before the rest, and whoever does shall pay the penalty for stealing grass.

82. MORE ABOUT THE LEGAL RELATIONS OF NEIGHBOR FARMERS

Now as to fences that are maintained by neighbors, [the rule is that] if two men, or more than two, occupy [parts of] the same farm, they shall maintain the fences according to the extent of

[9] Summer in the North was reckoned from April 14; the removal to the mountain pasture would begin about June 14.

[10] August 14–September 14.

their [respective] holdings and [in such repair] as they were in days of old; and the work shall be finished by the last of the moving days. And each one shall be responsible till the winter nights[11] for his part of the fence that encloses the grain fields; and the one who fails to keep his own fence in repair shall be answerable for all the damage done to the other [farmers], whether by his cattle or by those of other men. If a cow is a fence breaker or crawls through fences, the neighbor farmers shall go forth to inspect the fence. If it seems to them that the fence is satisfactory, the one who owns the fence breaker shall make good whatever the damage is. If cattle break out of a cattle yard and do damage to the other [farmers], the one who owns the cattle shall compensate for the damage according as men assess it. If men live in a neighborhood, [close together], but each one on his own homestead, and one wants a line fence built between them, but the other does not, the one who wants the fence shall summon the other to a moot to allot the length of fence to be built. And on the appointed day he shall make a statement before witnesses and shall demand the building of a fence. Now if the other refuses to come to the fence building [moot], the summoner shall produce witnesses that he did summon him, and he shall allot the length of fence to be built by casting lots in the sight of witnesses; let him build that part later that the lot assigns. Now if the other refuses to build and cattle come inside the garth and graze in the cornland and the meadow, no matter whose the cattle are, the men who neglect to keep the fence in repair shall pay all the damage that is done there. The home pasture shall be parceled out in the same way. A fence on a pasture line is properly set up if the branches reach up to the [workman's] mouth,[12] and the [straying] cattle will then have to be sent home with a warning. [One is allowed to] drive them home to the owner with a warning in the presence of witnesses, if one wishes [to do so], no matter where they are found. If he finds these cattle in his pasture [after that] and the facts are known to witnesses, he may kill them. For no compensation is due after that for cattle that have gone through a pasture fence

[11] About October 14. Winter was reckoned as beginning at that time. See Glossary, "Winter."

[12] Such fences were built of felled trees.

or a line fence, if the one [whose land they have entered] has built his part of the fence but the other man has not [built] his.

83. ONE WHO OPENS A GATE SHALL CLOSE IT AGAIN

If men pass through a fence gate, the one who opened the gate shall have the duty to close it again. And if horses or other live stock come within the enclosure and damage the cornland or the grassland, all the damage that is done shall be paid for, according as men assess it, by the one who left the gate open.

84. CONCERNING THE SHIELING AND ITS BOUNDARIES

Now the boundary markers of the shieling pasture up on the mountain shall be where they were of old. Let no one move them from their places unless it is done so that no one suffers damage thereby. [The use of] the pastures shall be [determined] in the same way.[13] No one is there allowed to send cattle home [to the owner] with a warning, for there horn shall meet horn, and hoof [shall meet] hoof.[14]

85. CONCERNING FISHING WATERS

All streams shall run where they ran of old. Let no one lead water off or upon another man's land, if it does not break out of its channel; but if one does change the channel he shall restore it and shall owe a fine for trespass. If a stream runs between farms and there are fish in it, each farmer shall control the half out to the mid-channel, if they have the land on the two sides. If a stream wears a new channel through the land of either one, the one who had the land before this channel was formed shall have [the stream] while the other shall have the shoal or the bank where the [mid-channel] was when it ran right. No one shall damage another man's fishing place or forbid him the use of it, if it has belonged to him formerly. When men have a salmon stream in common, each one shall set his fishing gear in his [part of the] stream, but in such a way that the fish are able to travel up into every part of the stream. The gifts of God shall be allowed

[13] They shall be used as they have been used in years past. See Glossary, "Shieling."

[14] Rights were equal on the mountain pasture.

to travel to the mountain as well as to the shore, if they desire to go. But if a man bars the stream, those who own land higher up shall give him a five-day warning from the thing to remove the bars if they are set up contrary to law. If he refuses to take them out, let them request a force to go to tear them out, and every freeman who refuses to join in this shall owe a fine of three oras, and the fishing gear [shall belong] to those who live higher up the stream. No one shall go to fish in another man's [stream]; if he does, he fishes for [the benefit of] him who owns the stream; and he shall pay the fine for trespass to the owner of the stream.

86. CONCERNING THE SHIELING AND PARCELS OF FOREST LAND

Whenever men are in dispute about a shieling pasture and one of them calls for a doom, the pasture shall be awarded to him, if the witnesses give it to him, unless the other man has a greater number of witnesses. If men are in dispute about a lot in the forest and one of them calls for a doom, the lot shall be awarded to him, if the witnesses give it to him, unless the other man has a greater number of witnesses. Whenever men are in dispute about a shieling pasture, or a parcel of forest land, or a boundary furrow outside the garth, he shall have the decision to whom the witnesses award it. If both have [the same number of] witnesses, let the decision go to him who is willing to swear [to his claim]. If both are willing to swear or if neither is, the matter in dispute shall be divided into halves. In cases of dispute about a boundary furrow, any man, free and of major age, shall [be allowed to] testify, if he is willing [to do so]; he shall make a formal statement that here runs [the boundary], and that is final. If men have a dispute over a shieling pasture or a lot in the forest, let him have it who has been in possession of it with a right unquestioned and unimpaired for twenty winters or more than twenty, if the facts are known to witnesses. The one who is in possession shall offer to submit to [the judgment of] a doom and the one who is not satisfied [with the situation] shall summon the possessor to appear at the forest lot and at a doom after a period of five nights at least. When the day comes he shall go to that place with his doomsmen and all the witnesses that he will need and he shall place his doomsmen where he claims the boundary to be. The defendant in the case shall set his half of the doom over against that of his opponent. The complainant shall produce witnesses that he summoned his opponent to that place and others to testify that the boundary runs as he has stated, and that shall be [held for] truth, unless a greater number [of witnesses] give stronger evidence for the other side; in that case the boundary shall be as they testify. If both sides have the same number, those who testified first shall have the decision. If there are no witnesses, let him have the decision who is willing to swear to his [claim]; but if neither is willing to swear, or if both are, the matter in dispute shall be divided into halves. And whenever men disagree about boundaries, they shall [proceed] as I have just set forth; and they shall also set their doom in the forest lot. When they have set the doom, the complainant shall produce his witnesses. Now any man may bear witness even though he may have labored on that lot as a thrall, if he has [since] been liberated. The one who has the better witnesses and the greater number shall have the lot, though the plaintiff led forth his witnesses first. If both are in possession of the land, the one who has caused the dispute shall appoint the doom.[15]

87. CONCERNING THE DIVISION OF ODAL[16] LAND

If men desire to make a division of odal land and to divide it so as to produce legal and separate ownership, and they are all of the same mind, let them divide it as they like and let them cast lots at the thing; after that such a division must not be disturbed. If men wish to have their odal land divided, let him whose right is the oldest summon them to a moot and let them divide the land [into separate holdings] in the presence of the men of the herath. The summons shall allow sufficient time so that the necessary number of men may be secured while the land [still] remains unfenced and unsown. The one who wishes to divide the land into the larger holdings shall direct the parceling. In dividing odal land, measurements may be made with the eye unless it shall seem better to measure with a rope. Boundary stones shall be set and placed in the earth where men agree [to have them].

[15] The import of this sentence does not seem to be clear.

[16] See Glossary, "Odal." The chapter seems to have in view land that is held jointly by two or more occupiers.

If one who was summoned refuses to come, the division shall proceed none the less in the manner that I have now described. The summoner shall produce witness that he has summoned the man to that place on that day to join him in dividing the land. There shall next be carried in coat laps as many lots as there are men who share in [the odal]; the men shall inspect the mark on each [lot] and shall know what each represents in house or in land. Other men shall carry the lot for those who will not themselves [do it]. They shall next proceed to the thing to publish their division of the odal; they have then divided their odal as the law demands. If one who shares in an odal with another is not in the country, the latter shall summon him from the thing to appear within a twelvemonth to join in dividing the land. Now if he has not returned by the day appointed, the man shall summon his heir to join him in dividing the land, and he shall make the division with him as [if it were] with the man himself. No one shall refuse the request of another to have the land measured with a rope, [if it is made] within [a period of] three winters, and if the land has not been measured with a rope before. The one who then has more land [than the rope allows] shall surrender a part; still, he shall have the same parcel that the lot gave him. As soon as the lot is cast, men will have to determine the boundaries. Now if one desires to have a division while the other does not, the former shall summon the one who is unwilling to the more important homestead before witnesses, and let him produce witness there that he summoned him to a division of land. The one who wishes to divide the land into the larger holdings shall direct the parceling; let them divide the farm into halves, unless some other method seems better. Later on the division shall be formally made and the lots cast at the thing by disinterested men. [Let each man] mark his own lot and let disinterested men cast the lot for any one who is too stubborn to mark his own. And from that time on the division shall be valid forever.

88. IF A MAN WISHES TO OCCUPY HIS ODAL LAND

A man shall be allowed to occupy [lease] his odal land[17] rather

[17] In medieval Norway the land was to a large extent owned by wealthy landlords and occupied by tenants. This chapter seems to provide that in

than a stranger, [that is], whatever lies close to his homestead. If the men who share in the odal refuse to sell it to him [the stranger], he shall offer them rent before the moving day, as much [rent] as the other men would pay, and let it not be a pretense, for he shall not acquire another man's [odal land] through a pretended offer. If any [other] man proceeds to occupy the land, the odal man shall forbid him to go upon it. But if a man does go upon it, he shall surrender the land and pay the robber fine. Even though the lands do not lie close to the same homestead, he [the odal man] shall have them none the less, if he has [already tilled] all the land that he had before and they lie in the same herath and are not separated by fjord or mountain or by impassable streams.

89. CONCERNING BOUNDARY STONES

If men disagree as to the boundary lines within the garth, whether it be those of the cornland or the grassland, and the one says that he has tilled only such land as he had a right to till, but [the other claims that he] has stolen the land, having dug up the boundary stones, they shall summon those men who have the best knowledge as to the boundary between them; and if it looks to them as if the boundary stones are in the right places just as [they were] set in olden times, and if they offer their testimony that the stones are in the right places, then it is well. But if the boundary stones have been dug up and not replaced and [the man has] tilled beyond them, he shall pay the [value of the] crop and a fine for trespass to the owner of the land. If he has dug up the boundary stones and set them down in other places, having moved them over on the land belonging to him whose land meets his own, he is a land filcher and an outlaw.

90. CONCERNING THE HIGHWAY

The highway, the shieling path, and all the cattle paths shall remain where they were in olden time. If a road runs across a man's farm he may move it off his farm, but [only] on the condition

---

giving a lease to land a farmer who has odal right to the land shall be preferred to one who has no such right, if the odal man's farm is contiguous to the one that he wishes to lease.

that he build another outside the garth equally good to travel in wet or dry [weather]; this shall then be followed even though it be longer. Now the width of a highway [shall be determined in this wise]: a man sitting on a saddled horse shall set his spear-shaft on the ground and move his thumb up to the joint and the span of a hand behind the spearpoint; that measure shall be laid across the road, and it shall not be wider.[18] And if the man damages a wider strip of cornland or grassland, he shall make good the loss. If a man prevents another from using the shieling path he shall pay three marks to the king and a like amount for robbery. If a man damages a bridge on a highway, he shall rebuild it and make it as good as it was before, and let him pay three marks to the owner of the bridge. If a man prevents another from using a shieling path or a cattle path which was in use of old, he shall pay a baug to the king; and let the other man use the road as before.

91. CONCERNING THE FINE FOR TRESPASS

A freedman has the right to a fine for trespass, if he owns land: a current ora for trespass within the garth. His son [has the right to] one ora; a freeman, to one and one-half oras; a hauld, to three oras; a baron, to six oras; the jarl, to twelve oras; the king, to three marks. Within the garth every one has a right [to such compensation] as I have now stated, outside the garth men have a right to one-half less. If the trespass is forbidden the fine is increased to the double, and the robber fine [is due] to the king. Where the farm is undivided the holders shall take one fine; let it be taken according to the rank of the one who is of the highest rank. If the king is an owner, let it be taken at his rank. If the land is divided into separate holdings, each owner takes a full fine for his holding. If a man goes into another man's forest and does work there without permission from the owner, he shall pay the fine for trespass. If the owner has witnesses to prove that the man was in his forest, he shall summon him to be at home (the entire day [can be used] for the summons) and bring action for trespass as for any other debt that is known, as soon as he has evidence that the man was in his forest. But if the latter denies

[18] This would give the road a width of about nine feet. The normal mode of travel in the North in the Middle Ages was on horseback.

the charge and the one who brings the action has no witnesses, he shall summon him to be at home and then he [shall summon him] before the thing. At the thing the accused shall offer either [to take] a threefold oath or [to pay] a fine for trespass. Whenever a man comes upon the fruits of unauthorized labor[19] in his forest he may carry them away with impunity. If a man finds a net on his sealing grounds and [there is] a seal in it, the net shall be his and the seal too, till he [the owner] has redeemed his net with the fine for trespass. A man may shoot a seal from his boat, if he rows the common route, whether the seal is in the water or on the land, unless it is lying on a sealing ground where a trap has been set; in that case he kills [the seal] for him who owns the ground. If a man shoots a seal from the shore where there is no trap set, the owner of the ground shall have the seal. If there was a trap set, the owner shall have the fine for trespass as well as the seal. If a man wounds a seal, the one who finds the seal shall have it; but the one who wounded it [shall have] his harpoon, if the harpoon is found with it.

92. CONCERNING UNAUTHORIZED USE OF PROPERTY

No man shall take another man's boat or his horse without his permission; if he does take it, he shall pay one and one-half oras. If the owner comes upon him in his boat or on his horse and demands the fine for conversion, then it is well if he is willing to pay him; but if he refuses to pay, [the fine] shall be increased to the double and the robber fine [shall be] due the king. If a man takes another man's ship, one that is [so large that] the benches have to be counted,[20] the one who is appointed master of that ship shall owe a fine of three marks; and [he shall pay] one and one-half oras for each thwart, whatever the [size of the] ship that he has taken; so every free man shall pay his fine for conversion. A man may claim the fine for conversion in the case of his horse, whether it has been driven or ridden or used as a pack animal; a fine for conversion is also due if the horse is used longer than it was lent for. All men have the right to equal fines in cases of conversion,

[19] Or possibly the tools used in this labor; the word used (*áverca*) may refer either to tools used in or to the fruits of unauthorized labor.

[20] See note, p. 92.

thralls as well as thegns. If a man takes another man's boat, he shall pay one fine for conversion, [to be counted as] for himself, his thrall, and those who are of minor age. The king shall neither claim nor pay fines for conversion. If a man leaps upon a saddled horse that belongs to another, he shall release himself from the saddle with a fine for conversion. If he leaps upon another man's horse [which is] not saddled and rides him forward, he shall release himself from the back with a fine for conversion. But if he does not ride him forward he shall pay no fine.

93. CONCERNING POOLS AND FISHING GROUNDS

Everyone shall have the pools and the fishing grounds that he had in former times. No man shall set traps on [another] man's land and, if he does, he shall pay the fine for trespass and deliver the catch to the owner of the land.

94. CONCERNING THE HUNTING OF BEARS

Bears and wolves are outlawed everywhere, for no man wants to be answerable for their doings, except only where a bear is imprisoned in his lair, [in which case the man shall] give notice where men come together that the barred lair belongs to him. If other men hunt [this bear], they hunt it for him who owns the lair. If men go to hunt a bear and approaching the lair above the barricade drive the bear out, they shall pay [for damages] if the bear attacks the [farm beasts of other] men; but if he runs out toward the woods, they shall pay nothing.

95. CONCERNING THE DEER HUNT

Whoever owns a forest may hunt deer there with weapons and wherever he can. When men go on a deer hunt, every man shall go to where he has forest land and run the hounds after the deer [there]. A deer belongs to him who starts it so long as he cares to pursue it, though another may bring it down. If the deer comes to a place [where it has] to swim, the one who brings it down has the right to one ham;[21] let him cut it off with the skin, or [let the

[21] *Skotbógr.* Any one who brought down a beast the flesh of which was edible could claim this part of the carcass. See Hertzberg, *Glossarium,* "skotbógr."

owner] redeem the skin uncut. If the deer leaves the course and is killed by other men, each shall have one-half, the one who started it and the one who killed it. If a man enters another man's forest to hunt with hounds, he hunts for the one who owns the forest. When men kill a deer the skin belongs to [the owner of] the hound. If a man comes upon seal or fish above the shore's edge, it belongs to [the owner of the] land; if he carries it off, he shall return it and pay the fine for trespass, if it is demanded. But if a man finds a dead beast on dry land, he shall have the find himself, whatever [kind of] beast it may be.

96. CONCERNING DAMAGE WORK

No one shall do damage to another man's property. If he does damage to the amount of half a mark, that is damage work, as is any injury [to property] which men rate as [amounting to] half a mark. If a man cuts the tail off another man's horse and cuts off a part of the rump [at the same time], that is damage work. If a man hews into the beak of another man's ship, either in the prow or at the stern, [causing damage] to the extent of half a mark, that is damage work. If he offers an oath in defense he shall offer a sixfold oath or go into outlawry. If he owns the deed, let him make such compensation as men think right. If a man does damage to a less amount and owns the deed, he shall pay such compensation as men think right and let him add six oras as a fine for unfriendly conduct. If he denies the charge he shall support his denial with a threefold oath; and if the oath fails, let him make such payment as has been provided above.

97. CONCERNING DAMAGES THAT ARE TO BE PAID FOR IN HALF [THE VALUE]

If a minor or a beast does injury to property, the value shall be paid in half; let the man to whom the beast or the minor belongs clear himself with a threefold oath. If a horse approaches another horse which is in tether, and they fly at each other and the [tethered] horse breaks loose and crowds the other over a cliff or [otherwise] kills him, there is no compensation due; if both leap out over [the cliff], the one that was tethered shall be paid for, since he would have stood quietly if the other had not come.

98. CONCERNING ARSON

No man shall burn another man's house or barn with evil intent; but if he does burn [them] and he is accused and convicted of the deed, he shall be outlawed and shorn of all personal rights; and he shall be called a "firewolf" and shall have forfeited all his property to the last penny, both land and movables. But if he denies the charge, the accuser shall go to his house and summon him before the thing for arson and to outlawry. The accused may offer to present a sixfold oath at that thing, and he shall have taken this oath within ten weeks of oath days; if the oath fails, [the failure] leads to outlawry. If a man instigates arson and he is accused and convicted of doing this, he shall restore half the value of what is burned. If he denies the charge let him support his denial with a threefold oath; if the oath fails, he shall pay half the damages.

99. CONCERNING RESPONSIBILITY FOR FIRE

Every free man of major age shall be responsible for his own fire. Fire belongs to the one who has it in his hand and gives it fuel afterwards. If a man sets fire [to something] but does not do it with hostile intent, he shall restore it to its full value; or, if he denies the charge, let him deny it with a threefold oath. If a minor sets fire to a man's property, let it be paid in half; if he denies the charge, let him to whom the minor belongs support the denial with a threefold oath. If a thrall sets fire with hostile intent, he shall be outlawed; but if he denies the charge, let his lord support the denial with a threefold oath; if the oath fails, the thrall becomes liable to outlawry.

100. CONCERNING RESPONSIBILITY IN [WAYSIDE] SHELTERS AND SOJOURNING THERE

All men have equal rights in a [wayside] shelter.[22] Now, it is well if all can be housed inside with their baggage; but if all cannot be housed inside with their baggage for lack of room, let all carry their baggage out, and then it is well if they all have room. They shall all be inside if there are seats for all. If some of

[22] These shelters were huts built at intervals along the mountain roads. They were often built by kings who would also provide for their upkeep.

them have tarried three nights without need, they shall pass out; otherwise men shall be put out by lot; then it is well if those whom the lot points out are willing to leave. But if those whom the lot points out refuse to leave, they shall owe the robber fine. And the men who refuse to leave shall pay the full wergeld if those whom the lot allowed to remain inside shall die outside. If a [wayside] shelter burns while men are sojourning there, all who were within shall share the responsibility.

101. IF A MAN MAKES USE OF LAND THAT ANOTHER HOLDS FROM THE KING

If a man makes use of land that another holds from the king, he [the tenant] shall bring action [to collect the fine] for trespass and he shall have one-half [of it]; if he does not do so, the king's bailiff shall bring action for the whole fine.

102. CONCERNING PUBLIC SUMMONS AND THE DEMAND FOR BAIL

In every case when men have to give a public summons to a man at the thing, the term of the summons shall be half a month if [he is] in the fylki but outside the quarter; a month if [he is] outside the fylki but within our law; two months if [he is] within the realm but outside our law; twelve months if the man is outside the realm. It is the duty of his heir to send him the summons; but if the heir is not at the thing, the thingmen [have the duty]. Every man has a right to a defense. Now if a man demands bail from another, he shall not refuse [to give it]; let him give the bail on the same day. If he refuses to give it, he shall owe a fine of three marks. Let his live stock be held as bail, if he has stock to the value of three marks. He shall be held to this bail for a month, if the complainant has demanded security that he will comply with the award. If he does not have live stock to the value of three marks, some one who has stock to the value of three marks shall give the bail for him. If he refuses to give bail, he shall owe a fine of three marks. If the plaintiff comes upon the defendant while he is away from home and demands a surety pledge, he [the defendant] shall give surety that he will proceed to his abiding place and later he shall give bail that he will comply with the award;

and [let him] be released from the pledge when the month has expired. If one demands bail from a man on a day when legal actions are not allowed, he shall be held to his pledge till the next litigation days; and this suit shall be heard first on the next litigation days, [even] though other men have causes to prosecute against the same man. The plaintiff shall bring up his suit within the first month in which there are litigation days, for the other shall not be held longer to his pledge. Any man who has a merchant ship resting on beams, if it is large enough to have the benches counted, may serve as surety for him. If a man demands bail to ensure the presence of another at a certain place, he [the defendant] shall name a man who will give bail for him. They shall then fare forth to where this man is, and it is well if this man is willing to act as surety. But if he refuses to do so, he [the accuser] shall point out three places in the fylki, he shall point forward and not backward. If he points out a second place, and they fail there, and again a third place, but without success, then the man who demands the bail shall secure a boat and provisions and sail the sea with the other man in fetters, one of his feet bound to his own [boot], and sail home with him. Then he shall release his own foot and bring the suit against him as against an unbound man. If a man brings action against a sailor [or other person] on board his ship, he shall have bail for half a month. If he [the defendant] has a merchant ship that is large enough to have the benches counted, it may serve as security for him.

[THE INHERITANCE LAW]

103. HERE BEGINS THE INHERITANCE LAW

The first inheritance is that which a son takes from his father or a father from a son, if death removes the one or the other. The second is that which is taken by a daughter and a son's son, each [taking] one-half. The paternal grandfather shall inherit in the same way, if there are no children [sons] of the dead who stand in the way; she [the daughter] shall inherit the movables and he [the son] the odal land. The third is that which a brother takes from a brother and which brothers and sisters take from each other, if they are by the same father and their mother was bought with the mund. The fourth is that which the mother takes from her kinsfolk by marriage.[1] The fifth is that which is taken by a paternal uncle and a brother's son, each [inheriting] from the other;[2] they both take the inheritance of one man, if it happens to be that way. The sixth is that which is taken by sons of brothers, each [inheriting] from the other, and by a uterine brother, if there is such a one. He shall inherit the money and they the odal land.

104. THE INHERITANCE OF A CORNER LAD OR A BUSH LAD

The seventh [inheritance] is that [which is] taken from a father by a corner lad or a bush lad or a thrallborn son [who has] not [been] brought into the kindred; [it includes] both movables and odal land. A corner lad is one who is the son of a free woman [whom his father has] not bought with the mund but to whose bed he has gone without concealment. A bush lad is the son of a free woman but begotten in secret. A thrallborn son is the son of a bondwoman who has been given his freedom before he has seen three Holy Nights. These enter into all rights [of heirship]. The eighth is that which is taken by the men who come next after the sons of

[1] Maurer understands this to mean that the mother inherits from her children. *Altnordische Rechtsgeschichte*, III, 221.

[2] The meaning seems to be that they share in one inheritance and that the one receives the whole if the other is missing.

brothers, each [inheriting] from the other. The ninth is that which is taken by the maternal grandfather and a daughter's son. The tenth is that which is taken by a maternal uncle and a sister's son, each [inheriting] from the other. The eleventh is that which the sons of "sistkins"[3] inherit, the one from the other. The twelfth is that which the sons of sisters inherit, the one from the other. The thirteenth is that which is called the inheritance of the unborn: if a woman is with child and the child is quick in her womb before she dies and two housewives have shared her knowledge of this, it shall inherit the husband's gift to the marriage portion, but the marriage portion [itself] must be given to her heir.

Now the inheritance groups within the kindred have all been enumerated. Those who have been enumerated shall inherit first and all the others in their order before the property can escheat to the king.[4]

105. [THE ORDER OF] INHERITANCE AMONG KINSMEN

If the men belonging to any inheritance group are wanting but there are kinsmen on the masculine and the feminine sides who are equally near, those on the masculine side shall have [the inheritance]; but if the others are nearer, they shall have [it]. If there are those who are related on both sides but in varying degrees, the one who stands nearest shall have the inheritance. If a man is counted in one line but not in the other, it shall be as if he were counted in both. Now if the men belonging to any inheritance group are wanting but there are others of a like degree of kinship, they shall have the inheritance who rank in kinship with those who are listed above. Among the women who are not enumerated a son's daughter shall inherit first.

Now there are those who may inherit but are not listed [in any group]. If there is no heir [of the class] that is listed, a son's daughter and the paternal grandmother, if there are such [persons], shall have [the inheritance]. But if there are no such [women] and none of the class enumerated, a paternal aunt and a brother's daughter shall have [the inheritance]. But if there are

[3] See below, p. 202, note.

[4] An exact translation of this sentence seems impossible to give; the text is probably incorrect.

no such [women] and none of the class enumerated, the daughters of brothers shall have [the inheritance]. But if there are no such [women] and none of the class enumerated, the daughters of a free-born concubine shall have [the inheritance]. But if there are no such [women] and none of the class enumerated, [the inheritance] shall pass to the women whose fathers were the sons of brothers. But if there are no such [women] and none of the class enumerated, the maternal grandmother and a daughter's daughter shall have [the inheritance]. If there are no such [women] and none of the class enumerated, a maternal aunt and a sister's daughter shall have [the inheritance]. If there are no such [women] and none of the class enumerated, the daughters of sistkins shall have [the inheritance]. If there are no such [women] and none of the class enumerated, the daughters of sisters shall have [the inheritance]. Now this is called the order of inheritance, but the kinship of men can take so many forms that no one can draw up a complete order of inheritance, and those who have to apply [the rules] will have to do what seems most reasonable. Now all those have been enumerated who are of parallel kinship in the order of inheritance on the masculine side; all those who have been listed shall at all times inherit in this order, except when a daughter inherits in preference to the father.

106. THIS DEALS WITH A FREEDMAN'S INHERITANCE

The fourteenth is the freedman's inheritance. His inheritance shall be taken to the ninth knee[5] before it escheats to the king. When the son of a freedman inherits from his father, each one shall inherit from the other. Now if there is an inheritance in the freedman's kindred to which there is no legal heir and there is no man living of the freedman's kin who has inheritance right after the deceased, then one of the master's line shall inherit to the ninth knee before [the inheritance] escheats to the king, even though the deceased be the eighth [in kinship] from the freedman.

107. THIS DEALS WITH INHERITANCE BY GIFT

The fifteenth is that which is called inheritance by gift. If a man has at any time disposed of his inheritance by gift, he may

[5] In his master's kinship.

cancel [this gift] and declare his will a second time at the thing; then it shall hold. And if a woman disposes of her inheritance by gift, she may cancel the gift once and also a second time and declare her will a third time; then the gift shall hold.

108. FOSTER INHERITANCE

The sixteenth is that which is called foster inheritance; that is, when a man takes another into his keeping for good or for ill and maintains him to fire and pyre,[6] as the old saying goes.

109. THE HOUSECARLE'S INHERITANCE

The seventeenth is that which is called the housecarle's inheritance. [A man is a housecarle] if he unfastens his bag in the autumn [in the house] where he fastened it in the spring. If he dies he [the host] shall keep his belongings for three winters. If no heir has appeared [by that time], he shall have them all, if the value is three marks or less; if it is more, he shall have one-half and the king one-half.

110. THE LAND[OWNER'S] INHERITANCE

The eighteenth is that which is called the land[owner's] inheritance. If a man cultivates land for another and dies on that land, the [land]owner shall keep his belongings for three winters. If no heir has appeared [by that time], he shall have it all, if the value is three marks or less; otherwise he shall have one-half and the king one-half.

111. THE SHIP[MASTER'S] INHERITANCE

The nineteenth is that which is called the shipmaster's inheritance. If a man dies on board a merchant ship on this side the middle of the [North] Sea, no matter in what direction he travels from Norway, the king shall have one-half of his goods, if [the value is] more than three marks. But if he dies beyond the middle of the Sea, the shipmaster shall have all of it, if no heir appears within three winters. But if the man's partner [in business] is on board, he shall keep [the property] and not the shipmaster. If the

[6] Unto death: an allusion to the heathen practice of burning the bodies of the dead.

ship is moored, and the man dies [on land] in a tent, the landowner shall have all that part of his belongings that is not bound [and placed] in the hold.

112. A PARTNER'S INHERITANCE

The twentieth is that which is called a partner's inheritance. If two men share the same purse, and one of them dies, the one who survives shall take charge [of his property] and shall have it, if [the value is] not more than three marks; if it is more he shall have one-half and the king one-half, if no heir appears within three winters.

113. THE GUEST INHERITANCE

The twenty-first is that which is called guest inheritance. If a man is host to another, and this one dies in his house, he shall keep his belongings for three winters. If no heir appears within that time, he shall have [the property], if [the value is] not more than three marks; if [it is] more, he shall have one-half and the king one-half.

114. THE LESSER INHERITANCE

The twenty-second is that which is called the lesser inheritance. If two brothers grow up as thralls in the same household, both sharing equally the labor due and the fruits of their own labor, and if they make no division [of what is theirs] before they are liberated, then each shall inherit from the other, unless they have children standing in the way. This inheritance does not stand in the way of another's right when there is no longer any group [to claim it].

115. CONCERNING THE SEVENTH-DAY ALE AND THE SETTLEMENT OF DEBTS

When a man is dead, his heir shall take his place in the highseat; and he shall notify the creditors [asking them] all to be present at the seventh-day [ale],[7] when they shall all receive what is owing them according to the testimony of witnesses. But if the property is not sufficient, they shall all suffer a reduction in the proper ratio; the one who has the largest claim shall suffer the largest

[7] See Glossary, "Seventh-day ale."

reduction. If a man fails to come to the ale, let him bring action for what is due him with witnesses, if there is property still remaining, and let him summon the heir to hear what the witnesses have to say. If there is no [property], he loses the debt. If there is property in the estate that belongs to a minor or is claimed by the wife,[8] it is well if there is enough for both; if there is not enough, she shall surrender her husband's gift to her marriage portion and other [gifts]. And if the property does not suffice at all points, he shall lose the most who has the largest sum due him, the wife of the deceased as other creditors. There shall be a reckoning for this purpose, except that any article of value that is held in pawn shall first be given to the holder of the pledge. The wife shall rather surrender her husband's gift [to the marriage portion] than that those [shall suffer loss] who were the man's creditors before he married her; for no one shall buy himself a wife with another man's money. Now she shall have her marriage portion, and the minor shall have his money; but if the property is insufficient, each one shall lose in proportion to his claim. If there are sons or daughters, they shall pay the debts if they have the money; but no other man [shall need to pay], unless he is heir to the property, for they [the heirs] shall have to meet both good and ill. If two married people have a community possession, and one of them dies, the other shall meet his debts according to the terms of their community. Indigent men and women and bondfolk shall be apportioned like other obligations, but their children and property shall be in the keeping of him who is their nearest heir; and the guardian, whether he be a man or a woman, shall take over the property [only] after it has been appraised and valued. He shall not carry the property of a minor out of the fylki, unless some one who has land there [in the fylki] will give surety that the goods will be restored to where they were received when the minor attains his majority. If the appraisal of the property shows that there is sufficient capital for maintenance, [namely], four marks for each minor child (it is well if there is more), she [the wife] shall take this amount and it shall not [be expected to] grow or shrink; and let her restore exactly what she received. But if the

[8] As a part of the marriage stipulations.

capital [for maintenance] is not sufficient, the minor shall be allowed half a mark every twelvemonth till he is twelve winters old; after that he shall be regarded as one who works for his board. Interest shall be reckoned on what money there may be over and above what he pays out for himself in a twelvemonth. The minor shall receive half a mark from the ground rent. Now the figures for the ground rent shall remain as it was assessed the first year, whether it grows or diminishes [after that]. A guardian shall not hand the property over to the keeping of another; but if he does dispose of it to another, the ward may bring suit against either one, as he prefers, to secure his own. If the ward has land to the value of half a mark,[9] that shall be counted as maintenance capital. If a man gives over the movables of a minor, except they be taken out of his hands by act of court, he shall secure them with his own property.

116. CONCERNING DEBTS

A debt is satisfied only when witnesses have knowledge [of the payment]. If the creditor denies [that it is paid], the debtor shall pay a second time and seek redress later by legal action.

117. CONCERNING THE PROPERTY OF A MINOR

If a freeman dies and his wife survives him and there is no more property than for her needs only, she shall none the less have the care of her children, penniless [though they be]. If the man had other children, they shall be handed over to his kinsfolk. But if the wife's children have any funds, they shall consume these first, the kinsmen advising; afterward they shall be handed over to the father's kinsfolk.

118. CONCERNING NEEDY MEN

If a freeman in the country comes to dire need, his minor children shall be gathered into three groups; let him keep two groups and let the mother [hand] the third [over] to those of her kinsmen who are nearest in the line of inheritance, if they have the necessary funds to maintain them. For each one of the minor children [there shall be] four marks; that is maintenance money;

[9] Land that yields income to that amount.

if the income shows more than four marks, he [a kinsman] shall take one minor child; let him take as many as he has maintenance money for. And let those who still remain go forward into the keeping of the one who is next [to him] in the line of inheritance, if he has the maintenance money. If he does not have the money, the minors shall pass farther out in the kindred till they find [one who has the] maintenance money. There shall be the same arrangement with respect to those who follow the father.

119. IF A MAN HAS AN UNAPPRAISED INHERITANCE IN HIS KEEPING

If a man has an unappraised inheritance in his keeping, one that was not assessed at the seventh-day ale, the minor [heir] shall go before the thing as soon as he comes of age; and let him present a sworn claim to as much property as he intends to demand under oath. And if his kinsmen have advised him so that he does not swear falsely, he shall have the property that he has thus demanded under oath, unless his opponent shall present evidence to a different estimate. Now he shall have sworn [to this claim] some time during the five winters before he fills his twentieth [year]; but if he has not taken the oath by that time, he shall have no claim to a judgment.

120. CONCERNING SUITS FOR INHERITANCES

An heir shall sue for an inheritance in the fylki where the inheritance became available. But if he brings his witnesses into another fylki than the one where the inheritance became available, or [sues] according to borough law, he has made his case void. Now in all those disputes that rise among us, townsmen or countrymen, whatever is done in a borough shall be dealt with according to borough law and whatever is done contrary to the laws of the herath and concerns the men of the herath[10] only shall be dealt with according to the laws of the herath.

121. IF A MAN DEMANDS A DOOM, WISHING TO DEFEND UNLAWFUL POSSESSION

If a man has the possession of an inheritance which is claimed by another and demands [a hearing before] a doom, he [the

[10] Or possibly: and concerns us [both], herathsmen [and boroughmen].

claimant] shall summon him with a proper summons to be at home and shall demand that he withdraw from the inheritance. If he refuses to withdraw from it, he [the claimant] shall summon him before the thing for robbery and unlawful possession. If his witnesses are satisfactory and the course of the suit is favorable and no opposing witnesses are presented, it shall be the duty of the thingmen to award him the inheritance. And he [the defendant] shall pay three marks to the king for having asked a doom to award him an inheritance to which he had no right. If he [still] refuses to withdraw from it, he [the claimant] shall call for a force of thingmen so that he may have sufficient strength to oust him from the inheritance; and everyone who refuses to join in this shall owe a fine of three oras. If, when they arrive, the possessor defends himself with point and edge, he shall owe a fine of forty marks; and everyone who joins in the resistance with him shall owe three marks. If there is a fight, everyone who resists the award and falls is an outlaw; but those who attack shall remain in the protection of the law.

122. IF A MAN FAILS TO CLAIM AN INHERITANCE

If a man who is of major age remains at home on the seventh or the thirtieth morning[11] and does not [come to] claim his inheritance, he can raise no claim to that inheritance at any later time. If one who is not of major age remains away, he shall give notice that the inheritance has come to him; another man may give the notice for him. He shall present his claim to the inheritance within the first five years after he has attained his majority; but if he fails to do this, he can raise no claim to that inheritance at any later time, unless some serious hindrance has prevented him. If he is not in the fylki or in the kingdom, he shall have his claim presented within the first twelvemonth after his return to the fylki where the inheritance became available, unless he is prevented by some serious hindrance; as to such hindrance men shall be called upon to decide.

123. CONCERNING THE DIVISION OF AN INHERITANCE

If men have an inheritance to divide, then it is well if all appear who have a share in it and join in the division. Now if some refuse

[11] See Glossary, "Thirtieth morning."

to come, they shall be summoned to join in the division; then if some fail to appear, the inheritance shall be divided before witnesses, and lot shall be cast for it, [each] one to have the share indicated by the lot. But if anyone asserts that the division is unfair and charges him [the keeper] with having concealed [a part of] the goods, he shall refute the charge with a threefold oath.

124. HOW A MAN SHALL OBTAIN HIS INHERITANCE

If it is doubtful whether a man has the right of heirship, let him summon to the thing the one who stands between him and the inheritance; and he shall be allowed to present evidence that he summoned him to the thing. Now other witnesses shall testify in this wise: "We were present when his mother was bought with the mund" (and let them state where that was) "and both groomsmen and bridesmaids were present and the gift that had been pledged was given to her, not less than twelve oras" (which is the lowest mund possible in case of indigence). If the witnesses of the defendant speak in this wise: "We were there, as well as you, and the mund was not paid to her according to contract," and if there is one more witness [to this than to the other], the plaintiff has lost his case. But if no opposing witnesses appear, it is the duty of the thingmen to award the inheritance to him. At all times when a man wishes to secure an inheritance and brings in his witnesses but fails to summon the one who is next in line for the inheritance, those witnesses are of no value. A suit for an inheritance shall be concluded where the inheritance became available, or [where] the odal land is, or where the deceased kept his household.

125. IF A MAN GOES WITHOUT CONCEALMENT TO A WOMAN'S BED

If a man lives with a free-born concubine for twenty winters or longer than twenty and goes to her bed without concealment and there has been no separation within that time, and no public announcement has been made to the contrary these twenty winters, their children shall be able to inherit and the law forms their property into a common possession.

126. CONCERNING THE DIVISION OF AN INHERITANCE

No man shall proceed to divide [another man's] property or his inheritance unless he has the owner's permission or men perceive that he is wasting it. So long as a man has his wits, knows how to manage his household and his business, and is able to ride a horse and to join in an ale feast, he shall have the control of his property and no man shall proceed to divide it; and if he does divide it, [the division] shall not hold.

127. CONCERNING THE DISTRIBUTION OF MINORS

Whenever men distribute [the care of] indigent minors and dependents, no matter how they group them, and thereafter cast lots [for them], they shall all accept the allotment [as final]. If there is a minor who has property, they shall keep his allotted inheritance. And that inheritance shall be regarded as already assumed, if notice is given at the thing that the minors are provided for.

128. IF A MAN GIVES MORE TO SOME OF HIS DAUGHTERS THAN TO THE OTHERS

If a man gives his daughter in marriage while others remain unmarried and all have a claim to his inheritance, and if he dies before they are all married, those who are not married shall take as much out of the undivided inheritance as the married one took with her from home; and let them then share equally in what remains. As soon as a woman reaches her majority, she shall have the keeping of her property and shall assume the care of it.

129. CONCERNING GIFTS

If a man gives more to one son than to another, he [the latter], when they come to divide the inheritance, shall take as much out of the undivided property as the other received who got the larger sum; let them then divide equally what remains. Everyone has a right [to recall] a gift unless it has been requited with a better payment; a gift is not requited unless an equal amount is set over against that which was given. The gifts that shall remain valid shall now be enumerated. Manumission shall hold unless he [the master] is in danger of death or a beggar's lot; in that case he shall take foster payment from him [the freedman],[12]

[12] That is, the freedman must help to support his former master.

unless he has paid his price. Payments for fostering children shall hold. Gifts that the king gives us or that we give to him shall remain valid; also tithe money[13] and a freedman's purchase money, six oras. A hauld may give his thrallborn son three marks; a baron [may give his son] six marks; a freeman twelve oras; the son of a freedman six oras. These gifts must not be disturbed, unless the one who is the rightful heir gets a smaller amount. A corner lad or a bush lad may be given as much as a thrallborn son.

130. CONCERNING THE PROVISION FOR WARDS

If a minor has been provided for in the distribution of wards, he is released from wardship when he establishes a household or gives notice at the thing that he intends to take his place in the kindred with full enjoyment of personal rights, or when he takes a wife. If a man is given [charge of] a minor whom he is not obliged to provide for, let him serve a home summons on the man to whom the obligation belongs. His witnesses shall speak in this wise: "Here is this minor whom you ought to provide for but not he who has brought him here." Then they shall pass the obligation into his hands. If a minor comes into a man's care, he may do as he prefers, let him go the same way back or take him to the thing; and the thingmen shall determine where he shall be taken. But if he takes him back the same way, he shall take him to the abiding place whence he came; and [the housefather] shall owe a fine of three oras if he refuses to receive [the minor]. Whoever refuses to receive him shall be held to account for three marks if he dies for want of care. If men have minor wards to provide for and one wishes to arrange a distribution but the other refuses, the former shall summon the latter to a [formal] division of [the duty of] wardship. If he comes, it is well; but if he does not come, let him [the summoner] produce witnesses [to testify] that he has summoned him to that place. The minors shall then be distributed by disinterested men [into two groups] and thereafter there shall be casting of lots. And the summoner shall take his lot with him, and the liability for the other lot shall rest with the one who did not come.

[13] The capital tithe only; see Maurer, *Vorlesungen über altnordische Rechtsgeschichte*, II, 287.

[MISCELLANEOUS PROVISIONS]

131. THIS DEALS WITH SUMMONS TO A THING

Any man who seems to have need for it shall have the right to summon a thing; everyone shall then carry the token[1] and none may fail [to forward it]. The token shall be carried to the winter dwellings but not to the shielings. It must not rest while the weather allows travel except at lodgings for the night, unless there be preventing circumstances. If the bearer fails to carry the token [forward], he shall owe a fine of three oras. If [he carries it] past two homesteads, he shall himself [be accountable for it].[2] Now the one who carries the token shall cut three notches into the door post or into the casing and set the token in the lintel above the door. All the freemen to whose homes the token comes shall proceed to the thing, except those who work alone;[3] they shall be held to attendance at three things: the king's [own] thing, the muster thing, and a thing called to deal with manslaying; from all other things those who work alone may be absent. A man is [still] counted as working alone if he is helped in his [farm] work by one who is younger than fifteen winters, whether he be his son or another's son, but attends him in his labors. Widows and freemen who are not able-bodied shall attend the thing only if they wish to do so; but all other freemen shall proceed to the thing when the summoning token comes to the house, or pay the thing fine. If a man allows a thing token to remain so long in his hands that it cannot go forward as far as it ought to go, because it remained so long in the hands of the one whose duty it was to forward it, then he who should have forwarded it shall owe a fine. Even though the token is late in coming to those who have the farthest to travel, they shall set out for the thing [and go forward] till they meet the [returning] thingmen.[4] If there are

[1] See Glossary, "Thing token." [2] See Hertzberg, *Glossarium, sia.*

[3] Who have none to help with the farm work.

[4] Such things usually met on the fifth day after the summons had gone forth. See Glossary, "Five-day moot."

five men, or more than five, all charged with the same offense, the token shall summon them [by name] to the thing, if they have been charged with the offense in the presence of witnesses.

132. CONCERNING TWELVEFOLD OATHS AND SIXFOLD OATHS

If the king accuses a man of treason, he may deny the charge with a twelvefold oath. Charges of murder and pledge breaking may be refuted in this wise: six men shall be named [and placed] on either side of the accused,[5] all of his own rank, and let him have two of them, and his nearest two, kinsmen. [The accused] himself [shall be] the fifth, and [let him have] seven oath helpers of his own selection.

133. CONCERNING THE SIXFOLD OATH

The sixfold oath shall be regarded as effective refutation in cases of theft, arson, damage to movables, wood slander,[6] tongue slander, and evil deeds against women; also in cases of nithing raids and of taking revenge for [convicted] thieves. Now, six men shall be named [and placed] on either side of the accused, all of his own rank; in cases of theft or arson let him have two of these, but [only] one in other cases that call for the sixfold oath.

134. CONCERNING THE GRIM OATH

If the "grim oath" [is to be taken], three men shall be named [and placed] on either side of the accused, all of his own rank, and let him have them all, he himself being the seventh.

135. CONCERNING THE THREEFOLD OATH

The threefold oath shall be taken [in this way]: the accused himself shall swear and with him another of equal rank, [one who is] not of near kinship on either side of the house nor closely related by marriage. Then there shall be a third, one who can be held to account for pledge and promise, a free man of major age. All such oaths may be taken at any time in a period of ten weeks of oath days; and a week is valid for oath taking though oaths

[5] Three on either side. The accuser and the defendant seem each to have selected three. Cf. *Gul.*, c. 24; *Frost.*, IV, c. 8, XV, c. 11.

[6] See Glossary, "Wood slander."

may be sworn on one day [only]. A failure to take a twelvefold oath [successfully] leads in every case to permanent outlawry, as do the grim oath and [the oaths taken in cases of] theft or arson. A failure to take any other sixfold oath leads to [ordinary] outlawry. A failure to take a threefold oath leads to such an outcome as [the parties involved] have agreed upon. The single oath shall be taken as soon as the one who demands it wishes to hear it and has a book[7] to offer to him [who is to swear].

136. HOW OATHS ARE TO BE TAKEN

Now, it is well if they [the litigants] come to agreement as to when the oaths shall be taken; otherwise let [the accuser] summon him [the defendant] [to appear] within five days at the longest at any one of the churches in the fylki that he may select. If the one who is to hear the oath fails to come, he [the defendant] shall call his witnesses to testify before the church door that he [the plaintiff] had summoned him to that place, and let him take the oath before witnesses. If they both appear, the one who is to take the oath and the one who is to hear it, they shall appoint men, each [selecting] two, to observe [and to judge] the oath taking. If these men disagree, some holding the oath to have been properly sworn and others, improperly, those who are willing to swear to their opinion shall be upheld in it. If both sides offer to swear, those who wish to support [the defense] have the best right to the oath; if any one raises a doubt, the defendant shall have his witnesses heard at the next thing. But if the oath fails him, his case shall have a hearing within the first twelvemonth like any other action. If the case is not presented by that time, the oath shall be [regarded as] taken in a legal manner, even though it has not been sworn.

137. CONCERNING DEFAMATION

No one of us shall defame a man to the king or to any man more powerful than oneself. And if a man defames another [in such a way] that he suffers loss of life or goods, he has slandered away his own goods and his life, too, if a life is involved in the defamation. If he denies the guilt, let him deny it with a sixfold oath,

[7] A copy of the Gospels.

and, if the oath fails, let him suffer the fate that he intended for the other.

138. IF A MAN INSULTS ANOTHER

No man shall utter tongue slander or carve wood slander about another. And if he is accused and convicted of doing this, the penalty shall be outlawry. Let him deny the charge with a sixfold oath, and if the oath fails, [the failure] leads to outlawry. No one shall circulate loose talk or impossible tales about another. That is called an impossible tale which a man tells about another, but which is not, or cannot be, or never has been true; as if he says that the other man is a woman every ninth night and that he has borne a child, or if he calls him a werewolf. If he is convicted of this, he shall be outlawed. Let him deny the charge with a sixfold oath; if the oath fails, [the failure] leads to outlawry.

139. CONCERNING DAMAGE TO WEAPONS

If a man damages the weapons of another, he shall pay him [a compensation] of six oras for evil intent; and he shall pay him for the weapons or restore them to as good a condition as they were in before.

140. IF A MAN TRAFFICS WITH AN OUTLAW

If a man traffics with an outlaw, the king shall have the goods that he bought from him, and he shall owe a fine of three marks. If he denies knowing that the man was an outlaw, let him support his denial with a threefold oath.

141. IF A BAILIFF SEIZES A FREEMAN'S PROPERTY BEFORE IT HAS BEEN CONDEMNED

If a baron or a bailiff seizes a freeman's property before it has been inventoried or awarded [by legal action], he shall restore it and pay [a fine of] forty marks; for every man is worthy of his possessions before the law.

142. IF A BAILIFF ROWS TO A FREEMAN'S HOMESTEAD

If men row a fully manned ship to a freeman's homestead, or if a gang of men go to his garth and do violence to him, destroy his house, and take away his movables, that deed leads to outlawry. If any one of these men wishes to remain in the land, let him restore to the husbandman all the goods that he took and pay a fine of forty marks; otherwise he goes into outlawry.

143. CONCERNING ASSAULT AND ROBBERY

If a man attacks another and robs him, and the deed is called to the attention of witnesses, the robber shall owe a fine of three marks. If he runs away with what he took, let the owner pursue him; and if he slays him, he falls as an outlaw.

144. CONCERNING FINDS

Every man who makes a find shall have it till the owner comes to claim it with witnesses. [But] every one shall publish his find, if he wishes to deal rightly [in the matter]. If men travel together on the highway and the one who walks ahead makes a find, they shall have it in common, he and the ones who come after; but those who walk past it shall have no share in it. If men who travel by boat make a find of some value, they shall divide it according to their number. Every man shall be held responsible for what he borrows and shall bring it back in good order. Every man has a right to his wager, if the wager was made before witnesses; let him sue for it as for any other chattel of notorious ownership. If men row or sail upon others, they shall make good all the damage that they do, unless the others rowed out in front of the prow.

145. CONCERNING DRIFT GOODS AND RIGHTS TO THE COMMON

Every man shall have the use of water and wood in the common. Every man shall have such rights in the common as he had of old. But if farms are cleared in the common they shall belong to the king. If a man has built a fence around his cornland and his grassland, he shall possess the ground as far from the fence as he can throw his sickle,[8] but what lies beyond is common. All the goods that drift in upon the [shore of the] common belong to the king. If men sailing forward along the shore or [coming] in from the ocean suffer shipwreck, every man retains ownership in whatever property he can prove by witnesses to be his, no matter who

[8] *Sniðill:* a kind of sickle used for cutting leaves.

owns the shore to which it has drifted; but all other wreck goods belong to the king.

146. CONCERNING THE LOADING OF SHIPS AND THE RIGHT TO PASSAGE

If a man loads a merchant ship at his home in the country and men take passage with him, he shall load the ship in such a way that all who have taken passage will have room. Now if the ship is loaded too heavily, the owner shall return his own wares [to the shore] and those who have taken passage shall have the necessary room. If they [still] think it unseaworthy, those who took passage last shall remove their effects, and each one shall have six oras for breach of contract.

147. IF A MAN IS INJURED BY A DOG OR A FARM ANIMAL

If a man is injured by a dog or a horse, or gored by an ox, or bitten by any other farm animal, or stricken down, the one who is hurt shall demand the beast before witnesses; and the owner shall bind it and hand it over to the one who was bitten. But if he refuses to hand it over, the injured man shall ask witnesses to note the fact and the one who owns the beast shall make such payments to the injured man and to the king as if he had himself injured him.

148. THESE ARE AMENDMENTS WHICH MAGNUS THE GOOD[9] AUTHORIZED AT LONG-ISLE SOUND;[10] BUT HAKON THORS-FOSTER[11] GAVE SOME OF THEM

The Christmas gift[12] shall never be made a precedent.

A man shall have [the treasure] that is found on his land, though another may have unearthed it.

Concerning a Man's Ship

Every man shall use and enjoy his ship in perfect peace; let him sail whither he pleases.

[9] Son of Saint Olaf; he ruled from 1035 to 1047.

[10] On the west coast near the modern Christiansund.

[11] Pretender, 1093–94.

[12] See Glossary, "Christmas gifts."

This Concerns the Harbor Dues

No man who contributes to the coast defense shall pay harbor dues.[13]

If a man leaves our kingdom he has the right to return whenever he likes, even though he has established a residence elsewhere, unless he has been associated with a band of the king's enemies. If a man goes hence into outlawry and some one dies here from whom he would have received an inheritance, had he been here in the land and not in outlawry, the one who is next in line shall receive it.

149. HERE BEGIN THE RULES AS TO WHALE FISHING

A hauld or a man of higher rank, [if he comes upon a whale that is no more than] eighteen ells in length, has the right to the entire whale; any other man [has the right] to one half as long. If a man comes upon a whale, he shall cut it up before witnesses, or let him leave behind the backbone, the head, and the tail fin; then these parts, if he has no witnesses, shall testify for him. He shall cut it up in the water and shall not carry [the parts] up on the green sod; if he does bring them up, the owner of the land shall have one-half of the whale, unless he [the finder] shall redeem it with the fine for trespass, thinking the whale of greater worth. If a man proceeds to cut up a whale where the grass is sufficient to feed a ewe and a lamb in summer, he shall redeem the parts with the fine for trespass if he brings them up [on the land]. If a whale drifts up on a man's land within the garth, it belongs to him who owns the ground. If a whale drifts up on a man's land outside the garth and it is larger than a finder is allowed to keep, the king shall have one-half and the owner of the ground one-half. If a whale drifts into a fjord where arrows may be shot past it from either shore, the whale belongs to both shores, unless there be a shoal there and the whale is therefore stopped farther out; in that case it belongs to the [nearest] shore.[14] A man may hunt whales wherever he can. If a man is chasing a whale and kills it out on the deep, the whale is his whether it be large or small. If

[13] *Landaurar:* a tax on ships and sea-borne trade.

[14] The meaning seems to be that in such a case the whale belongs to the owner of the shoal or to the owner of the shore nearest the shoal.

a man shoots at a whale and hits [it] and drives [it] up on the shore, one-half of the whale belongs to him who chased it, and one-half to him who owns the land. If a man shoots at a whale in a herring shoal and thus drives away the gift of God, he shall owe a fine of forty marks.

150. CONCERNING THE FINDER'S SHARE IN THE BLUBBER

If a man comes upon a whale close to land and it is larger than one is allowed to keep, he shall have the finder's share in the blubber. Let him cut a mark into it and go to report [the find] to the bailiff; he has then the finder's right to the blubber from that whale. Let him take an arrow shaft and let him measure out a square as long as a man's hand, and cut this down to the bone. [Let him take] the same length on the oar used amidships and let him place a rope around the oar where the blade begins, and let him cut down to the bone a rectangle as wide as the rope measure is long; [also one] as long as the steering oar [or one] as long as the bailing dish and the bottom board astern. If a man comes upon a whale and binds it with a rope, and men come by night and cut up the whale while it is still bound, each one is a thief to [the amount of] forty marks, but to [the amount of] fifteen marks, if he cuts it up by day. If a man drives a whale into another man's whale cove and bars [the entrance] with stakes, the whale belongs to the one who owns the cove, and the other man shall pay the fine for trespass. If a man drives a whale into a cove which is not a whale cove, one-half shall belong to him who drove it in and one-half to the owner of the cove. If a man comes upon a whale out on a fishing ground, let him cut off what he can, only not through the walls [of the visceral cavity], and let the carcass drift. If a whale drifts up on the shore of the common, it belongs to the king; but if men cut it up, the one who steered the boat out to it shall owe a fine of forty marks, and the others who rowed the boat with him three marks each.

[THE LAW OF PERSONAL RIGHTS]

151. [CONCERNING SUMMONS FOR MANSLAYING]

. . .[1] who first arrive to inspect the wounds. Though three men were parties to the attack, only the name that was first sent out with the arrow shall continue with it;[2] names that are added later shall be withdrawn. If only one man was in the attack, the names that were added later shall be withdrawn. The wife [of the slain man] shall send forth the arrows, or, if there is no wife, his heir shall send them forth in the presence of witnesses on the same day that the man was slain. And [the wife] may summon the thing to the place where the slaying was committed, if she [so] desires; and if as many as twenty-seven are in attendance, the men may render a decision there. But if the case is to be heard properly at the [regular] thingstead, one-fourth of all the thingmen must be present; they may agree to a verdict, though a greater number fails to come. It is the duty of all to forward the arrows, and none must neglect [to do so]; and whoever is guilty of such neglect shall owe a fine of twelve oras. And whoever is guilty both of neglecting to forward the arrow and of remaining at home on the thing day shall owe the double [of this fine]. She [the wife] shall send forth the arrows in the presence of witnesses and on the day of the slaying, unless her advising kinsmen are so far distant that she cannot reach them. If he [the accused] receives the arrow but does not appear at the thing, the guilt is on his shoulders. If he refuses to accept the arrow, he shall be summoned to a second thing and shall present his defense there. If he has kinsmen or heirs, they shall give the summons. But if he avoids the summons and fails to appear and sends no excuses, the guilt is on his shoulders.

[1] At this point there is a lacuna in the manuscript.
[2] A verbal summons to the accused to appear at the thing.

152. CONCERNING MURDER IN A CROWD AND IMPROPER RESISTANCE

There is this to say further, that if a man is slain in a crowd, it is well if he be revenged. But if he [the slayer] escapes into the woods, all shall join in the hue and cry, and no one shall hinder [the pursuit]. And if men who offer such hindrance shall be stricken down, they fall as outlaws, but their property is not outlawed. Though they do not fall, they shall, nevertheless, pay a fine of forty marks to the king for breaking the peace. If he [the slayer] is taken in this pursuit, the hand that took him shall bring him safe to the thing and thence [he shall go] to his bane. The kinsmen of the slain man may have him to keep and to bring to the thing, if they like; or they may take him to the king's bailiff, and he shall owe a fine of forty marks if he refuses to receive him. The baron shall take charge of him if there is no bailiff; he, too, shall pay a fine of forty marks if he refuses to receive him. Now the king's bailiff or the baron shall find a headsman or pay forty marks. The freemen shall have the money that the bailiff has to pay; but the fines that the baron has to pay shall go one-half to the king and one-half to the freemen.

153. IF A MAN PROVIDES CONVEYANCE FOR AN OUTLAW

If a banesman flees to a boat, anyone may with impunity throw an oar out to him or a bailing dish or the steering oar or the rear bottom board, any one of these things but nothing more. But, if he does more than this, he provides conveyance for an outlaw and shall owe a penalty of forty marks.

154. CONCERNING MANSLAYING IN A GANG FIGHT

It is called a gang when men are together [to the number of] five at the fewest. If four men are traveling the highway together and one of them attacks a comrade and becomes his banesman, the one who is alone in the lawsuit[3] shall be [counted] the banesman. If a thrall is on the journey with them, he shall be [counted] the banesman, if they choose to accuse him.

[3] Is accused by the others.

155. IF TWO MEN ARE ACCUSED OF MANSLAYING

Again, if it is this way, that three men are traveling the highway together and one slays another and two survive and each one accuses the other, they are both to be [counted] banesmen. But if one appears at the thing and the other does not, he is the banesman who avoids the thing.

156. CONCERNING THE SLAYER'S REPORT

Again, if it is this way, that two men meet at a crossroads and the one becomes the other man's bane, and if this one is still able to speak when men come to him, then the one whom he accuses shall be [counted] the banesman, unless he finds help in the ordeal. Now if [another] man reports the slaying as his own deed, they shall both be [counted] banesmen, even if the corpse shows but one wound. If a man [wishes to] report a slaying in the proper way, he shall go from the place where the deed was done in whatever direction he likes and report [the slaying] at the nearest house, unless there be found inside near kinsmen of the slain man, either on his father's or on his mother's side, or near relations by marriage. If such there be in that house he shall go on past and [report the deed] at the next house, unless the same [difficulty] is met with there; he shall then go on to the third house and report the slaying there, no matter whom he finds within. Let him not give his name as Ulf or Björn,[4] unless that be his name; let his tokens [of identification] speak for him and let him tell where he lodged the night before. Witness to such a report shall be presented at the arrow thing; one man's testimony shall be sufficient, and he may also bring a statement from his household. No one shall be accused of being a confederate [or instigator] unless his name was sent forth with the arrow and he is [formally] charged at the thing. Two shall testify that he moved about through the countryside in such a way that he could have been present at the slaying. They shall testify as to his lodgings the night before, though it is necessary to bear witness to lodgings only if the name of the one man has gone forth with the arrow and another has assumed responsibility for the crime. If the slain man's heir prefers to indict another,

[4] Common personal names. One shall not give an assumed name.

and not this one, the accused may deny the charge with a threefold oath. He shall proceed to the thing and, laying down his weapons, and agreeing to abide by the law, he shall request access to the thing and shall offer to take the threefold oath; and [if the oath fails] the failure leads to outlawry. But if they [the thingmen] refuse him access to the thing, they hallow his person and all his possessions. But if he makes report otherwise [than is here provided], he reports his own guilt as a murderer. The servants [thralls][5] and any free man may bring the indictment.

157. IF A MAN IS SLAIN IN AN ALEHOUSE[6]

If a man is slain in an alehouse in the light of a burning fire or in the light of day, the men present at the alehouse shall produce the banesman or pay a full atonement both to the kinsmen and to the king. If a man is slain at night after the fire has gone out, and if, in the morning when the men awaken, a man reports the slaying as his deed, he shall be the banesman; but if no notice is given, whoever is absent shall be regarded as the banesman. [When a man leaves] he must state his errand or return in the morning. But if all are there and no one seems more likely [to have done the deed] than any other, the men at the alehouse shall investigate the murder, and let the heir [of the deceased] accuse whomever he will; and the accused may defend himself with the murder oath. If the oath fails, the failure leads to outlawry, but if he takes the oath properly, the heir shall be allowed to accuse another and a third but only in case he can prove his guilt.[7] If he cannot prove his guilt, he shall himself suffer what he intended for the other man.

158. IF A MAN IS SLAIN ON A JOURNEY

If two men who are partners and messmates travel together in search of gain and the one is killed, the other shall seek to confer with his heir, and he shall report [the deed] to the first man whom he meets. If the heir charges him with having slain his messmate, let him refute the charge with the hot iron.

[5] The text has *hinna*, which, it seems, should be corrected to *hjuna*. See Hertzberg, *Den ældste norske proces*, p. 196.

[6] Or in a house where there is an ale feast.

[7] Otherwise he becomes liable for false accusation.

159. IF A WOMAN SLAYS A MAN

If a man slays a woman he shall be outlawed just as if he has slain a man. If a woman slays a man, she shall be outlawed and her kinsmen shall remove her from the land. Likewise, if a minor becomes a banesman, he shall be removed from the land, and his kinsmen shall have him sent on his travels by the fifth day, though he may remain with them five nights in case of necessity. If he remains longer, [they shall] pay a fine of forty marks or refute the charge with a threefold oath.

160. CONCERNING ACTION BROUGHT AGAINST A DEAD MAN[8]

There are three cases in which one may bring action against a dead man. The first case is when a man comes upon another having carnal dealings with a woman on whose account he is obliged to fight and to kill. There are seven such women: the first is a man's wife; the second [is his] sister; the third [his] daughter; the fourth [his] mother; the fifth [his] stepmother, the sixth [his] brother's wife; the seventh [his] daughter-in-law. Now if a man comes upon another having carnal dealings with any one of these, he may slay the man, if he will; but he must report the slaying to the first man whom he meets and he must state the cause. Now he shall wait until the slain man's heir has sent forth the arrow, if he is in the fylki; if not, the man may send the arrow himself. He shall then proceed to the thing and, laying down his weapons outside the thing, he shall ask for grith and shall offer to submit to what the law demands; and let him bring forward the testimony of the men whom he first met. Now if the thingmen refuse him access to the thing, they hallow his person and his chattels, all that he has. And the man who was slain is then an outlaw, but his property is not outlawed. And let the slayer depart in full security. The second case is when a man comes upon another in his storehouse and finds him laden with stolen goods and packages; he may then slay that man, if he will. He shall go to fetch his neighbors and show them the deed, and he shall have

[8] This was a legal fiction which allowed the slayer to show that the slain man had brought the misfortune upon himself by his own deed. In this way the slayer would avoid prosecution.

the benefit of their testimony at the arrow thing. There is again a third case, when a man comes upon another in his cow barn or in his cattle pen putting ropes on the cattle intending to lead them away; he may then slay that man, if he will. Let him go once more to fetch his neighbors and show them the deed, and let him again proceed to the thing with his witnesses. And in every case that I have now dealt with he shall be able in this way to outlaw [the slain man].

161. IF A MAN COMES UPON A CORPSE

Again there is this, that if a man comes upon a slain man out in the forest,[9] he shall first cover up the corpse and [then] report [the fact] to the first man whom he meets; and he shall look up the man's heir, if the heir is in the fylki; otherwise he shall send forth the thing token and shall inform the thing. Now whoever remains away from this thing shall owe a penalty of six oras; this is called the greater thing fine. But if the finder fails to proceed in this way, he places the murder guilt in his own hands, if the heir cares to indict him.

162. IF A MAN CALLS FOR A FORCE TO GO UPON ANOTHER

If a man calls for a force of men to join in going upon another man for some reason and he slays that man when they come to his house, they [his companions] shall separate from the banesman, and each one shall pay a fine of one baug to the king for his share in the crime; but if they go away with the banesman, [the fine shall be] forty marks. If a man is outlawed at a thing, he and all his live stock and all his property, the bailiff shall issue a five-day summons to all the creditors, and each one shall have what is owing him so far as the debt is known to witnesses before the bailiff takes [anything]. Whatever is rooted in the soil belongs to the land; but let the creditors have their dues there too.

163. IF A MAN'S THRALL IS ACCUSED OF KILLING

If a man's thrall is accused of manslaying, his master shall refute the charge on his behalf with such an oath as [he would have to take] in his own defense. And if the oath fails, the master

[9] See Glossary, "Forest."

himself becomes liable to outlawry. And whoever is unable to offer such an oath shall rid himself of the thrall or pay a fine of forty marks, inasmuch as the judgment has come upon his hands.

164. CONCERNING A MADMAN'S WAY OF KILLING

If a man kills another in a madman's way, [that is], if a son kills his father, or a father his son, or a brother a brother, or if a brother [or a sister] kills a brother [or a sister], or if a child kills its mother or a mother her child, the slayer has destroyed his right to the inheritance that he would have taken; and it shall pass to the one who is next in line; and the king shall have it rather than he [the slayer]. But let him remain in the land; [let him] go to confession and keep what he has.

165. IF A DOG OR ANY OTHER BEAST DOES INJURY TO A MAN

If a horn or a hoof or a dog becomes a man's bane, the owner [of the beast] shall dispose of it; but if he gives it food after judgment has been rendered, he shall pay forty marks. If he denies the charge, let him refute it with a threefold oath. [If the oath fails], the failure leads to a fine of forty marks; and let him pay the wergeld to the kinsmen [of the slain man].

166. IF MEN ARE WITNESSES TO A FIGHT

If men are engaged in a combat and other men have been watching the fight from across a stream or other impassable [space] but cannot identify the men, and if one is stricken down with his head hewn off or his brains dashed out, or if his back is broken or both his hands are cut off, then this one [shall be regarded as having] provoked the quarrel, since he shall never be able to strike another man; and let his opponent remain in peace and security.

167. CONCERNING GANG FIGHTING

It is called gang fighting when men go at each other in two bands and proceed to fight. Those who provoke the fight shall pay a fine of forty marks, while those who defend themselves [shall pay] nothing, if the facts are known to witnesses. But if both sides are stubborn and neither band will admit having begun the fight, they shall pay the wergeld to the kinsmen [of those who are slain] and each band shall pay forty marks to the king.

168. MORE ABOUT GANG FIGHTING

It is a gang when five men are banded together, or more than five. If men set upon each other and a man is wounded and gets his bane, let the others prove some one guilty of the slaying or pay the wergeld to the kinsmen and forty marks to the king.

169. CONCERNING INJURIES DUE TO CARELESSNESS

If two men are shaping timber and the ax flies out of the hands of the one and the other is killed thereby, then the injured man, if he is still able to speak when men come to him, shall have the [decisive] word; and it shall be counted accidental slaying only if he wills it. But if he is not able to speak, his heir shall have the [decisive] word.

170. CONCERNING THE SLAYING OF A BAILIFF

If a man slays the king's bailiff, he shall pay an atonement of fifteen marks, unless he slays him at the king's table while he is serving the king; in that case he shall be outlawed. And [the penalty shall be] the same if he slays him at the thing while he is prosecuting the king's lawsuits. He shall make atonement according to the rate prescribed at Gula: six ells [of wadmal] to the ora.

171. IF A MAN IS KILLED ON SHIPBOARD

If a man kills another on shipboard, it is well if the man is avenged and the banesman pushed overboard. The crew shall be allowed to bring the slayer to the shore on the mainland; but if they convey him further, each one of them shall owe a fine of forty marks. Those who wish to put him ashore shall turn the ship toward the land; but those who row outward [with him] shall be outlawed. Those who put up their oars may do so with impunity if they report to the men whom they first meet [and show clearly] that they were unwilling to row the slayer [any further].

172. IF A MAN THROWS [SOMETHING] AT ANOTHER

If a man throws [something] from a house or a ship or [from some place] where one is unable to see clearly and a man is killed thereby, he shall pay the wergeld to the kinsmen; but there is nothing due to the king.

173. IF A MAN IS KILLED ON THE BEAMS UNDER A SHIP

If men are pulling a ship up [on land] or shoving it out [into the water] and a man is killed on the beams [beneath], the men shall pay his wergeld, but there is nothing due to the king. If men are carrying planks or hauling beams for shipbuilding and one is killed, they shall atone for him with a full wergeld, though reduced by as much as he shared in the work; but there is nothing due to the king.

174. IF A BOAT RAMS ANOTHER

If men are out on the fishing grounds and have dragnets over the sides of the boat and if [other] men sail upon them, they shall pay the wergeld if any one is killed; but there is nothing due to the king. But if the men have no nets over the side of the boat and if they row out in front of the other boat, they are half-way their own banesmen, and the others shall pay half the wergeld but there is nothing due to the king.

175. CONCERNING THE HALF WERGELD

If two men are felling a tree and it falls on one of them, he is halfway his own banesman; let the other pay half his wergeld, but there is nothing due to the king. If two men go into the woods and one of them is felled by a tree so large that one alone can neither move it off nor on, the man's heir shall have the [decisive] word. And the same [rule] holds [when men are working] with large rocks.

176. IF A MAN LOWERS HIMSELF WITH A ROPE

If a man is killed while lowering himself with a rope, he is his own banesman; but if he is lowered by other men, they are his banesmen. Let them pay the wergeld to his kinsmen, but there is nothing due to the king.

177. CONCERNING ACCIDENTAL DEATH

If two men go into the woods and one of them falls out over a cliff, let the other go to the [dead man's] house and report his misfortune. If the heir [of the deceased] brings charges against him, he may refute them with a threefold oath. But if he fails to report his misfortune, he shall defend himself with the murder oath.

178. CONCERNING HOUSEBREAKING

If a man breaks into another man's house to attack him and kill him, that shall be called a nithing crime.[10] It is a nithing crime if a man slays one to whom he has given pledges of safety. It is also a nithing crime if a man slays one to whom he has given grith. It is also a nithing crime if a man kills another with a club, a rock, or a stump of wood. It is also a nithing crime if a man burns another to death [in his house]. It is also a nithing crime if a man robs a [fallen] man on the battlefield by stripping off his clothes and taking his weapons. It is also a nithing crime if a man murders a man. It is also a nithing crime if a man takes revenge for thieves; let him deny the charge with a sixfold oath. And in every case when a man is [found] guilty of a nithing crime he shall depart as an outlaw who has forfeited his personal rights and his property to the last penny, land as well as movables. And let him never return to the land either with king or with jarl, unless he comes bearing truthful tidings of hostile incursions.

179. CONCERNING MAYHEM

If a man hews off another man's hand or his foot, he shall pay with the half wergeld. If the limb remains joined [to the body], the half wergeld is also joined to it. If an eye is put out of a man's head, the payment is one-half wergeld. But if both hands and feet are hewn away, the man is worse off living than dead, and the payment shall be as if he were dead.

180. CONCERNING ATONEMENTS

Now atonements are reckoned [this way] in Gula. A hauld shall be paid for with eighteen marks in lawful money, and from that point in the ranks of men the atonement money shall increase or decrease as other fines do, and the compensation for a hand or a foot or an eye shall be assessed according to the scale that is accepted at Gula; and private compensations for criminal attacks [shall be reckoned] in the same way. Now a thumb is as dear as all the other [fingers]: a thumb shall be paid for with three marks;

[10] Literally, nithing murder. See Glossary, "Nithing crime."

the next finger with one mark and the long finger at the same [rate]; the one that is next to it with six oras and the little finger with two oras.

181. CONCERNING THE SENDING FORTH OF ARROWS

If a man is slain at the thing, his heirs shall send forth arrows summoning the men to his booth; it is then for the thingmen to pass judgment in that place. If men become involved in any other sort of quarrel, [the aggressor] shall be summoned before the thing and witnesses shall be heard as to wounds and evil intent. And the [man's] heir shall receive the compensation.

182. CONCERNING THE INSPECTION OF WOUNDS

If a man is accused of having killed his thrall, he shall be counted a murderer unless he has reported the slaying. If men charge him with it and he denies the charge, and the indictment comes early enough so that the body can be inspected, the body shall be viewed. If a mortal wound is found on it, the man is guilty as charged; but if no such wound is found on the body, the charge is false. If the indictment comes so late that the body cannot be inspected, the accused shall refute it with a threefold oath; if the oath fails, he becomes liable to outlawry. If a man slays another man's thrall, he shall pay such compensation as men deem sufficient for his naked body.

183. CONCERNING WOUNDS

Again there is this, that if a man wounds another in a crowd, and if he lays his weapons aside and offers to submit to the law, he shall be placed in fetters. If [the wounded man] dies of his wounds, the slayer shall be stricken dead at the feet of the slain man and shall be released from his fetters in that way. If the injured man is still living after a scab has formed on the wound, the offender shall pay him the wound fine and a baug to the king. If three men come together and one wounds another, men shall testify to a full wound fine for the injured man.

184. MORE ABOUT WOUNDS

If two men meet, and one gives the other a wound, [the injured man] shall go on the same day, if he can, with his wound unbound and show it to the first man whom he meets. And let him send men to the house where the offender has his abode to summon him to a thing, to a five-day thing at the very shortest, for that is proper in any case, even though the man is not at home. Bruises shall be dealt with in the same way. Now those who first met the injured man shall testify as to whether the hurt looked like a bruise or a wound and they shall name the [guilty] man on the same day, if they testify to a wound fine. But if they refuse to testify either for or against [the accused], each one of them shall pay a fine of three oras. And the one who is accused shall defend himself with a threefold oath; if the oath fails, he becomes liable to a money fine.

185. CONCERNING THE VALUATION OF WOUNDS

If a freedman wounds a man, he shall pay one baug, [that is], twelve oras; his son [shall pay] two baugs; a freeman, three baugs; a man born to odal right, six baugs; a baron or a staller, twelve baugs; a jarl, twenty-four baugs; and the king, forty-eight baugs. If a man wounds another, he shall pay the wound fine to the one whom he injured: an ora if [the weapon] touched [him]; an ora if it cut the flesh; an ora if the edge strikes the leg; an ora for every [bit of] bone that has to be removed if the silver rings in the scales;[11] an ora for every place that is burned in dressing [a wound], unless there is proud flesh [to remove]; an ora for every time the lips twitch [in pain]; an ora for every tear in the clothing an ora if the man was sitting alone [in private when he was attacked]; an ora if he was just rising from bed; an ora for every cut that has to be made [in dressing the wound], if the cut bleeds; half a mark for a wound in the chest or the abdomen; half a mark if the wound goes in to the marrow; an ora if the weapon comes out [on the other side]. And [let men] appraise the scar and [other] external blemishes, defects, or disabilities. Now, the one who caused the wound shall pay for the leech and the remedies and provide the injured man with victuals, a month's food of both kinds.[12] If a man cuts [a bit of] flesh off another and it drops to the ground, he shall pay a compensation of six oras, and six oras

[11] If the money is ready for payment.

[12] Butter and meal. See Glossary.

if rough scars form on the head. The wounded man shall have witnesses, if the other man denies that joints of the size claimed were [actually] broken. Wounds on the breast shall all be inspected [and valued], and wounds on the back [shall be] twice as dear as those on the breast. If a man is present at a fight and does not try to separate the men or give aid to either side, he shall pay twelve oras to the king as a baug for torpid indifference.

186. CONCERNING A MAN'S RIGHT TO ATONEMENT

No one, either man or woman, has a right to claim atonement more than three times, unless he has taken revenge in the meantime.

187. CONCERNING QUARRELS IN AN ALEHOUSE

If there is quarreling in an alehouse when men are drunk, those who have quarreled shall go out and return in the morning when men awaken; then the men may pass judgment in their dispute in that place as well as at a thing, if they know the law. A man's benchmates or his messmates or those who sat near him or the ale feasters, if those others were not present, shall bear witness with him; and their testimony shall stand, and let no opposing witness be brought forward. And at that place every man has [a right to] atonement twice as large as at his home. Now the men may determine the matter there, if they know the law, or they may refer it to a thing. If a bailiff or a baron charges them with having provoked a quarrel and they all deny it, they shall, each one of them, take a [Gospel] book in his hand and swear that they have all drunk decently. Those who take the oath [successfully] are guiltless, but whoever fails in his oath shall owe a baug to the king. And let every one [who is] accused of provoking a quarrel defend himself with a threefold oath; but if the oath fails, they each become liable to a fine of fifteen marks. If one-fourth of the men refuse to swear and leave the place, all the men at the alehouse shall pay the penalty. If fewer [than one-fourth] depart those who depart are the guilty ones; let them pay the baug to the king and let the others take the oath.

188. CONCERNING QUARRELS AMONG MEN

When a man is present where men have quarreled and his testimony is demanded, he shall in every case bear witness for one side or the other; otherwise he shall owe three oras to the king, if he is called upon [to testify].

189. CONCERNING HOSTILE DEEDS

If a man receives a hostile blow in a crowd and the man who struck the blow is killed, he falls as an outlaw, having forfeited all personal right. If he [escapes and] runs away toward the woods, all shall pursue him and none shall impede [the hue and cry]. If a man tries to hinder the pursuit and is stricken down, he falls as an outlaw, but his property is not outlawed. A man may, if he likes, put out a ski or a [spear] shaft or his foot once in front of one who is running in the hue and cry in order to delay the pursuit; but if he does more than that, he shall owe the king a fine of forty marks for having offered resistance in behalf of an outlawed man. If the outlaw is overtaken in the pursuit, the hand that caught him shall protect him as far as the thing; and thence [he shall go] to his bane. If he escapes into the woods, he may send back an offer to submit to the law; he shall then have such parts of his property as have not been listed and seized. If the bailiff arrives before the man has offered to submit to the law, he shall have all that he has listed and seized. If a man wishes to redeem himself from outlawry, let him pay the injured man a single atonement according to his rank. If he [the injured man] now receives a similar amount out of the hundred [oras due for release from outlawry],[13] he [the outlaw] shall be restored to his rights under the law, but only so that the man who suffered the injury shall have his entire atonement before the bailiff takes [anything].

190. IF A MAN STRIKES A WOMAN

If a man strikes a woman or a woman [strikes] a man, the offender shall pay such compensation as the injured person has a right to claim, and a baug to the king. If women come to blows no man can claim any atonement, only the women themselves [can claim it]. A minor shall neither receive nor pay atonement [for injury] till he is twelve winters old; then he is a man in the half-atonement class in either respect till he is fifteen winters old.

[13] The normal payment in such cases was fifteen marks, or one hundred and twenty oras (a great hundred).

191. CONCERNING THREATENING BEHAVIOR

If a man leaps toward another but someone restrains him, he shall pay a baug to the king. If he brandishes his weapons or swings a hammer toward the man and the latter asks witnesses to note the hostile behavior of his enemy, he [the aggressor] shall pay a half atonement to the one whom he menaced in this way.

192. CONCERNING MISSILES

If a man throws [a missile] at another and hurts him, the injury shall be called a wound if he has an edged weapon[14] in his hand; otherwise [it is] a bruise.

193. CONCERNING [BOW]SHOTS

If a man shoots a bolt at another and he is injured, the hurt shall be called a wound.

194. CONCERNING WOUNDS

If a man aims at another with an ax and strikes him with the handle, the injury shall be called a wound; [it shall be] the same if a spear strikes with the flat side [of the spearhead].

195. THIS DEALS WITH THE FULL ATONEMENT

If a man makes a thrust at another with a rail or a pole or an ax handle or a spear shaft, he shall pay him a half atonement, and if [the stroke] fells the man, he shall pay a full atonement. If he thrusts so [hard] at another that he staggers, he shall pay him a full atonement, even though he falls to his knees [only]. If a man pushes another into a fire, he shall pay him the full atonement and a baug to the king, [which is due] with all full atonements. If a man shoves another overboard, or off a bridge, or over a cliff into the sea, he shall pay him a full atonement, unless he shoves him over the outer side of a moored ship; for that the man may demand satisfaction in blood. If a man seizes another by the beard and with hostile hands, he shall pay him a full atonement. If a man seizes another by the hair and jerks him forward, he shall pay him a half atonement. But if he does this

[14] Brandt's translation in *Retshistorie*, II, 76. The literal translation would read: if he has no weapon in his hand.

and also shakes him up, that is called hair pulling, and he shall pay him a full atonement for that. Now if both men cast aside their weapons and seize each other by the hair, it is called scuffling and neither one has a claim to compensation in such a case.

196. CONCERNING INSULTING REMARKS THAT CALL FOR ATONEMENT

These are the [kinds of] insulting remarks that call for full atonement. The first is when a man says of another that he has given birth to a child. The second is when he says that the man has been used as a woman. The third is when he likens him to a mare or calls him a slut or a whore or likens him to any kind of a female beast. For these [remarks] he shall pay the man a full atonement; but the man may also seek satisfaction in blood and outlawry for the sayings that I have now enumerated, if he has asked witnesses to take note of them. Men may repent of their utterances and withdraw them if they wish, and acknowledge that they know nothing worse about the man than about [any] good man. It is an insult that calls for a full atonement for a man to call a free man a thrall or a monster or a malefactor. It is also an insult that calls for a full atonement to accuse a woman of being a whore and to call her a whore, if she is without guilt.

197. CONCERNING THE RIGHT TO ATONEMENTS

In the case of a daughter or a sister, a man can claim the same atonement as [would be due] in his own case: a single atonement if a man lies with her. And [he has] the same [right] in the case of any woman from whom he is to inherit or of any woman whom he has in his household, if she has no heirs in the country here.

198. CONCERNING THE RIGHT TO ATONEMENTS IN CASES OF CARNAL INTERCOURSE

If a well-born woman lies with a thrall, she shall go to the king's garth [as a bondwoman] and let her redeem herself thence with three marks. And every man has the right to take six oras for his freedwoman [in such a case]. A man has the right to take for a woman doing forced labor as large a compensation as for his best bondwoman; and her heir can take such part of the compensation due his rank as exceeds the payment. If a freedwoman lies with a thrall, she shall go [to do labor] in her master's garth. A freeman shall receive one and one-half oras in compensation for his most desirable bondwoman and half as much for each of the other; if he has but one she shall be [counted] his best. A freedman shall have an ora in current coin for his best bondwoman. His son shall have an ora for the best one among his; the hauld shall have three oras, and the baron six oras for his best bondwoman. Two bondwomen are counted as the best, the housemaid and the housekeeper.[15] Two thralls are counted the best, the foreman and the master's personal servant.[16] Every man has the same right to compensation for carnal intercourse on the part of his thralls as [on the part] of his bondwomen. If a man abuses a king's thrall who is employed in his household, he shall render satisfaction according to the bailiff's right. If a thrall accompanies his master to a thing or to a church service or to an alehouse and goes on command, he shall enjoy the protection of a baug [to the king]; for in those three places the compensation due for any man increases to the double. It is a thrall's right to take for himself one-twelfth part of a single atonement paid to his master, if he enjoys the protection of a baug in those three places. His master shall be responsible for his words and his deeds, if he goes with him at his command to places where many men come together.

199. CONCERNING CHARGES THAT LEAD TO A FINE OF FORTY MARKS

If a man violates a woman and is accused of the crime and convicted, he shall be outlawed, or he shall pay a fine of forty marks and a double atonement to the woman. But, if she brings the charge against him, she shall do it on the same day; and he may refute it with a threefold oath. If the oath fails, he becomes liable to such a penalty as has just been indicated.

200. CONCERNING THE RIGHTS OF MEN TO ATONEMENT

A freedman shall enjoy the right to six oras in a single atonement [for personal injury], and his son, to one mark in a single

[15] See Glossary, "Housekeeper," "Housemaid."
[16] See *ibid.*, "Bryti," "Personal servant."

atonement. A freeman [has the right] to twelve oras in a single atonement; the hauld, to three marks in a single atonement; a baron or a staller, to six marks in a single atonement; a jarl or a bishop, to twelve marks in a single atonement. The son of a baron shall have the same right to atonement as a hauld if he is not endowed with land. In every case when a man is mishandled or injured, the king has a right to fifteen marks. Every man who suffers a blow shall take a second atonement out of the hundred [oras][17] before the bailiff takes [anything]. Now all men shall inherit such [atonement] rights as their fathers had, except those for whom there is a different arrangement. The seneschal shall have the same rights as a hauld to a single atonement. The bishop's son, the jarl's son, the staller's son, the seneschal's[18] son, the priest's son, and the bailiff's son shall all have such rights to atonements as belong to their kinship, unless they have been given the rank that their fathers enjoyed. Icelanders shall have the same rights as the holdar while they are [in Norway] on their trading journeys, till they have lived here three winters and have established homes here; after that they shall have such [personal] rights as men testify to be theirs. All other aliens who come to this country shall have the freeman's right, unless men testify to something different.

201. CONCERNING THE RIGHTS OF A MAN WITH RESPECT TO HIS BETROTHED

If a man lies with another man's betrothed, the latter may claim as atonement as much money as he would have to pay to ransom her from an enemy, [or] as great an atonement as her heir can claim [in her case].

202. THIS DEALS WITH INDICTMENTS

If a bailiff accuses a man of having harbored an outlaw, one who was outlawed in the thing district where the accused has his home, he shall defend himself with a threefold oath; and if the oath fails, the failure leads to a fine of forty marks. If the bailiff accuses the man of having harbored one who was outlawed at

[17] See above, p. 141 and note.
[18] See Glossary, "Seneschal," "Staller."

the Gulathing or at sea with the fleet and he pleads that he did it unwittingly, he may clear himself with a threefold oath. The same [rule holds] if the man was outlawed in another thing district; and if the oath fails, the failure leads to a fine of forty marks. If the bailiff accuses the man of having given food to an outlaw in the woods, and he denies the charge, he may support his denial with a threefold oath; and if the oath fails, the failure leads to a fine of three marks. If the bailiff accuses the man of having had dealings with an outlaw at a thing, at church, or in an alehouse and he denies it, let him support his denial with a threefold oath; and if the oath fails, he shall pay a baug to the king. If a man is slain in a crowd or in a gathering of men, or is striken or wounded, his [the offender's] live stock may be seized, and no man shall entertain him until he has offered to meet the demands of the law; and if any one does entertain him, he shall owe a fine of forty marks. And if he has had dealings with him and the proof is clear, he shall owe a baug to the king. All those who see [these doings] are knowingly guilty; those who do not see them do wrong unwittingly; with them there is no responsibility until the judgment is declared.

203. HOW LONG A WIFE MAY PROVIDE HER HUSBAND WITH FOOD

A wife may with impunity provide her husband with food for five nights after the judgment has befallen him. If he remains longer on his own invitation,[19] let her go to her neighbors and report that he [her husband] is staying on his own invitation; then she is blameless.

204. IF A THRALL WOUNDS A FREE MAN

If a thrall wounds a free man, his owner shall make a settlement with the one who is wounded or send the thrall into outlawry. And there is nothing due to the king [in this case].

205. CONCERNING THE THROWING OF MISSILES

If a man throws [a missile] at a man and [it] strikes another, it shall be called a fool's misdoing, but he shall pay six oras to the striken man.

[19] The term used, *slímusetr*, is general for any one who abuses hospitality.

206. CONCERNING BENEFICES

If a man holds land from the king as a benefice and it is taken from him, he shall, nevertheless, [continue to] have the same right to atonement as a baron, and his son, likewise, till he is forty [years old].

207. CONCERNING CHARGES

If a man charges another with having offered resistance to help an outlaw, and he replies, "I am pursuing him just as you [are]," the woods shall testify [as to whether he escapes]: but if he escapes into the woods, he may buy his release [from outlawry] with forty marks, though the first man may buy his release for fifteen marks.[20]

208. CONCERNING THE SINGLE COMBAT

If two men come to blows when there are no witnesses at hand and the one accuses the other, let each one of them pay the king the amount of his own atonement.

209. IF A MAN HOLDS ANOTHER[21]

If a man is held under an ax and he gets his bane from it, the one who held him shall pay a half wergeld to the kinsmen of the slain man; but there is nothing due to the king in this case. If a man charges another with having held him under an ax, let him refute the charge with a threefold oath. If a man holds another under an ax and he gets a wound from it, he shall pay him half a wound fine. If a man holds another under an ax and he gets a [serious] injury from it, he shall pay him a half atonement.

210. IF A MAN TORTURES ANOTHER

If a man charges another with having tortured him, let him refute the charge with a threefold oath. If the oath fails, the failure leads to a fine of forty marks to the king and a full atonement to the complainant.

211. CONCERNING BLACK BLOWS

If a man claims to be injured but has neither blue nor bloody spots and can produce no witnesses [to the deed], he has brought

[20] The outlaw seems to pay fifteen marks, the one who gave him aid forty marks.

[21] Assists a murderer.

the trouble on himself with his lie. Such a blow is called a black blow and it gives no right to compensation. If a man charges another [with having stricken him] in this way, let him refute the charge with a threefold oath; and if the oath fails he shall pay the injured man such atonement as would be due in his own case and forty marks to the king.

212. CONCERNING BREACH OF THE PEACE[22]

If a man wounds another with three blows, or more than three, it shall be called breach of the peace; and the injured man shall have compensation for each blow to the number of three; and the king [shall have] forty marks.

213. CONCERNING DISTRAINT

If a bailiff prepares an inventory of a man's live stock or attaches property in other cases than the three that have been enumerated, he shall owe a fine of forty marks; and the baron [shall owe] fines in the same ratio, if he enters a freeman's homestead to seize property. And every man who gives them aid in this shall owe a fine of three marks.

214. IF A MAN IS ACCUSED OF HAVING CHEATED THE KING OUT OF HIS RIGHT [TO FINES][23]

If a bailiff accuses a man of having cheated the king out of his right [to fines] and [charges] the man's opponent with having suffered the injury, and they both deny the charges, the bailiff shall summon them both before the thing. At that thing they shall, each one of them, offer to deny with a threefold oath that they have come to any [private] settlement in that case. If the oath fails, they become liable to a fine of fifteen marks each. If the one takes [the oath] and the other does not, the one who takes it is without guilt, while the one who does not take it is guilty as charged. And if the bailiff summons the one but not the other, it is as if he has done nothing.

[22] Literally, a real combat; but the punishment seems to be for breach of the peace.
[23] By coming to a private agreement with his opponent.

215. CONCERNING WOUND FINES

All have equal right to compensation for wounds, a thrall, as well as a thegn. If a man wounds another man's thrall, he shall provide victuals for him as long as he lies wounded; he shall also [pay] leech money and compensation to the master for loss of labor.

216. IF A MAN EGGS ANOTHER TO ATTACK HIM

In case a man does not himself make any complaint of an injury received, there is nothing due to the king. If a man eggs another to attack him as one baits a bear, or challenges him to [a combat on] an islet,[24] and he suffers injury from that man, he loses his right to atonement, if the circumstances have been brought to the attention of witnesses; [he] also [loses this right] if he reproaches the other man with having formerly taken atonement [for a personal insult]. If a man takes anything of value from another and asserts that he will resist restitution with law and with doom though the property belongs to him from whom he took it, then he has it by robbery; and he shall pay the baug to the king. And the man shall have his property, if the ownership can be proved by witnesses.

217. IF A MAN'S CATTLE ARE BITTEN BY DOGS

If a man's cattle are bitten by dogs, the owner of the dogs shall pay one-half [the value of the beasts] the first time they are bitten and the entire [value] in later cases. If he [the owner] gives notice as soon as his dog has bitten that he has disposed of the animal, he shall pay nothing whatever. But if it shall happen that he or some one in his household throws food to the dog, he shall pay one-half the next time [the dog bites] and the entire value in later cases.

[24] A single combat was often fought on a small island from which there were no means provided for retreat or escape.

[THE WERGELD SYSTEM]

218. HERE THE HEAD BAUG IS DEFINED

The first baug[1] [in the wergeld] is called the head baug; it amounts to ten marks, that is, [to the value of] thirty-two cows if the man who is slain was born to odal right. And the man fines increase or decrease in amount from this point just as the other atonements do. If there is no son, the father takes [the head baug]; if both are living, the father takes three marks. If he is no longer able to fight, the slayer owes him twelve oras. But if the slayer is outlawed, there are no atonements; and when the slayer dies his heir assumes the responsibility for the ax.[2]

219. THE BROTHER BAUG

The second baug is called the brother baug; it amounts to five marks, that is, [to the value of] sixteen cows.

The third baug is called the cousin baug; it amounts to four marks, that is, [to the value of] thirteen cows less half an ora.

220. MORE ABOUT THE BROTHER BAUG

The baug that is rated at ten marks shall go to the son of the slain man. The brother baug shall go to his brother, if there is one; otherwise, to the son of the slain man. If the slain man leaves neither father nor son, the brother shall have the entire atonement. If there is no brother, [it shall go] to a cousin on the father's side. But if there are none such as I have now enumerated, all these atonements shall go to the heir of the slain man.

221. GIFTS TO THE WOMEN

Now there is a mark [additional] as a gift to the women; it shall be shared by four women, if there are [such] women: the mother

[1] See Glossary, "Baug" and its various compounds, Baug is pronounced very much like boug in English.

[2] The duty to pay the wergeld. The ax was a common weapon in Old Norwegian times.

of the slain man, his daughter, his sister, and his wife [shall take] two oras each, if they are all living. If [some of] the women are wanting, the son of the slain man shall have [their share]. If all the women are wanting, the slayer shall take the mark and give it to the son of the slain man. If one of the women is wanting, the son of the slain man shall take the two oras; half a mark, if two are wanting; and the [entire] mark, if all are wanting. Now the baugar have all been enumerated.

222. CONCERNING ATONEMENTS TO THE KINSMEN

The slayer shall pay the head baug to the son of the slain man. And the brother of the slayer, if he has one, shall pay the brother baug to the brother of the slain man; if [he has no brother], the slayer himself shall pay it. Now the slayer's cousin on his father's side, if there is one, shall pay the cousin baug to the slain man's cousin on his father's side; if [there is] none, the slayer [himself] shall pay it. The one who receives the atonement shall be [counted] the son of the slain man, whether he be father or brother, or however he is related [to the slain man]. Now the baugar are all defined.

223. CONCERNING CHATTELS [THAT MAY BE TENDERED IN PAYMENT]

Now the chattels [that may be tendered in payment] shall be listed. A cow shall be [valued] at two and one-half oras. If cows are to be given in payment, no beast shall be given that is older than eight winters, unless the man is willing to take [her]. Now a cow to be given in payment must be sound and whole as to horn and tail and eyes and teats and in all her feet. Bulls[3] and oxen and cows of calf-bearing age [may be given] to pay baugar and man fines. The wergeld shall be paid in gold or burned silver, if these are available. Horses may be given, but not mares; stallions, but not geldings; and no horse that has a protruding rectum or a whitish sheath or weak urinary organs or is wall-eyed or suffers from some other defect. Sheep may be given in payment, but not goats; odal land may be given in payment, but not land acquired by

[3] The original has *korn;* but since this does not seem to fit into the context, Hertzberg suggests that may be a scribal error for *þiora*. *Glossarium*, *korn*.

purchase. A ship may be given in payment, but not one that is rebuilt or is so old that the original rowlocks have rotted away; nor shall one give a ship with a broken prow or one that is patched with boards, unless they were laid when the ship was raised on supports. Nothing that is worth less than an ora shall be given in payment, unless the man has a fine of smaller amount coming to him; then he shall take the payment; but the one who pays may increase the fine to an ora and take a peace pledge in return. Weapons may be given in payment, if they have been tested by use, [and are] whole and hard and without defect; those that the man was slain with shall not be offered. Let no one pay wergeld with a sword, except it be fretted with gold or silver. Wadmal or linen cloth may be offered in payment, [if it is] entirely new, or any other cloth that is new and uncut, or even cut cloth, if it is new and the payee is willing to accept it. One may pay with cloth; for men, but not for women; new cloth, and not old. Large sheep pelts may be given in payment, [if they are] new and not worn also black sheep pelts and the finer cloth, [if it is] new and uncut. Thralls may be given in payment, if they have all been brought up at home and are not younger than fifteen winters, unless the payee is willing to take them younger. Bondwomen shall not be given to pay the wergeld. Now the [classes of] property that may be used to pay the wergeld have been enumerated.

224. [CONCERNING THE LESSER MAN FINES][4]

The [payments in the] lesser man fines shall now be enumerated. In the first *upnám*[5] are the paternal uncle of the slain man, his brother's son, his maternal grandfather, and his daughter's son; each one of these shall have a mark from the slayer, if the slain man was a hauld. In the second upnám are the son of the slain man's paternal uncle, the son of his brother's daughter, his maternal uncle, his sister's son, and the son of a paternal aunt (or of a maternal uncle); each one of these shall have six oras from the slayer, if the slain man was a hauld. In the third upnám are the son of a slain man's maternal aunt, the son of his paternal uncle's

[4] *Sakir.* The *sǫk* was a fine paid to a circle of kinsmen just beyond that of the baugmen.

[5] See Glossary, "Upnám."

son, a son of his father's paternal uncle, his mother's maternal uncle, and the son of his sister's daughter; [each one of these] shall have one-half mark from the slayer, if the slain man was a hauld. And inasmuch as every man [in this group] shall pay one-half less to atone for a homicide than he will receive [in man money] for one in the same degree of kinship, he shall pay two oras to the son of the slain man, and all who are in this group shall pay at the same rate. But in the middle upnâm each one shall pay three oras to the son of the slain man, and in the first upnâm each one shall pay one-half mark to the son of the slain man. Now all the men belonging to each upnâm have been enumerated and it shall now be set forth how the cross payments shall be determined.

225. CONCERNING WERGELD

Now the slayer's paternal uncle shall pay one-half mark to the son of the slain man and eight ertogs to his brother. [He shall pay] five ertogs and three pence to the paternal uncle of the slain man and a like amount to his brother's son, to his maternal grandfather, and to his daughter's son. All those who are counted in the same upnâm have a right to equal fines. Now the slayer's paternal uncle shall pay an ora and four and two-thirds pence to the maternal uncle of the slain man; he shall pay a like amount to the slain man's sister's son, to his paternal uncle's son, to the son of his brother's daughter, and to a son of his paternal aunt (or his maternal uncle); and all those who are in the upnâm with the paternal uncle shall make payments in the same way. The slayer's paternal uncle shall pay two ertogs and four pence to the son of the slain man's maternal aunt; and every one in that upnâm shall make payments in the same way. They shall pay in this way to a sister's daughter's son, to the son of a paternal uncle's son, and to his mother's maternal uncle.[6]

226. MORE ABOUT WERGELD

Now the slayer's paternal uncle's son shall pay three oras to the son of the slain man, five ertogs and three pence, weighed, to his brother, and an ora and four and two-thirds pence to his

[6] The editors of the Norwegian edition add: "and to his father's paternal uncle's son."

paternal uncle; [he shall pay] a like amount to the son of the slain man's brother, to his maternal grandfather, and to his daughter's son. All those who are in the same upnâm have a right to equal fines. Now the slayer's paternal uncle's son shall pay two ertogs and three pence to the son of the slain man's paternal uncle; [he shall pay] a like amount to the son of the slain man's brother's daughter, to his maternal uncle, to his sister's son, and to a son of his paternal aunt (or of his maternal uncle). All those who are in the upnâm with the son of the paternal uncle shall make payments in this way. Now the son of the slayer's paternal uncle shall pay an ertog and eight and two-thirds pence to the son of the slain man's paternal aunt; and all who are in that upnâm [shall pay] in this way. They shall make payments at that rate to the son of the slain man's paternal uncle's son, to the son of his father's paternal uncle, to his mother's maternal uncle, and to the son of his sister's daughter. Payments shall be made in this way by all who are in the upnâm with the son of a paternal uncle.

227. MORE ABOUT WERGELD

Now the slayer's maternal aunt's son shall pay two oras to the son of the slain man; and the son of the daughter of the slayer's sister, and the son of his paternal uncle's son, and his mother's maternal uncle [shall pay] in the same way. And each one of these four [shall pay] four ertogs to the slain man's brother and an ora less three pence to his paternal uncle. [There shall be payments] in the same way to the son of the slain man's brother, to his maternal grandfather, and to his daughter's son. And the son of the slayer's maternal aunt, the son of his sister's daughter, the son of his paternal uncle's son, and his mother's maternal uncle shall pay at this rate: each one of them shall pay eighteen pence to the maternal uncle of the slain man. They shall pay fines at the same rate to the son of the slain man's sister, and each one of them [shall pay] a like amount to the son of the slain man's paternal uncle. Each one of them shall owe a similar fine to the son of the slain man's brother's daughter. The son of the slayer's maternal aunt shall pay twelve pence to the son of the slain man's maternal aunt; he shall pay fines in the same way to the son of the slain man's sister's daughter, to the son of his paternal uncle's son, and to his mother's maternal uncle.[7] The son of the [slayer's] sister's daughter shall pay the same amount as the son of his maternal aunt. The son of the slayer's paternal uncle's son and his mother's maternal uncle[8] shall pay in the same way; each one of those in the lowest upnám shall pay a fine of twelve pence. I have now enumerated all the men in each upnâm. And every man shall make payments to every other man in the way that I have now set forth. And as the degree of kinship decreases outward beyond the last upnâm, the fine is decreased by one-third according as the reckoning happens to come out.

228. CONCERNING THE UPNÁMAMENN

All those who receive a mark from the slayer as [members of] the first upnâm shall receive one-third less from the slayer's brother, that is, five oras and an ertog. And all those who receive six oras from the slayer as [members of] the second upnâm shall receive one-third less from the slayer's brother, that is, one-half mark. And all those who receive one-half mark from the slayer as [members of] the third upnâm shall receive one-third less from the slayer's brother, that is, two oras and two ertogs.

229. THE LESSER MAN FINES ARE DESCRIBED HERE

In [paying] the lesser man fines the slayer shall be joined by his father's brother and his brother's son. And let him pay for them [if they are wanting], even though they have never existed; but if there are such [men], let each one pay for himself.

230. MORE ABOUT THE LESSER MAN FINES[9]

A brother's son shall be associated with the father's brother with respect to the lesser man fines. The two shall receive one fine and shall pay in that way as long as the father's brother is living; after his decease the payment shall be one-third less.

231. MORE ABOUT THE LESSER MAN FINES

All the wives who have sons and [all] the sisters [who are] capable of childbearing shall have a share in the lesser man fines;

[7] The Norwegian editors would add: "and to his father's paternal uncle's son."

[8] The Norwegian editors would make the same addition here.

[9] On cc. 230–35 see Phillpotts, *Kindred and Clan*, pp. 58–59.

and they shall all have an equal share till they are forty [years old]. In case one or more of these are wanting, the fine reverts to the sister's son.

232. MORE ABOUT THE LESSER MAN FINES

Now the slain man's paternal uncle shall have five ertogs and three pence from the slayer's paternal uncle. The son of the slain man's brother shall have five ertogs and three pence from the son of the slayer's brother. The son of the slain man's daughter shall have five ertogs and three pence from the son of the slayer's daughter. Likewise the maternal grandfather of the slain man [shall have] five ertogs and three pence from the slayer's maternal grandfather.

233. CONCERNING THE UPNÁMAMENN

Now [the men of the] middle upnâm [on the slayer's side] shall pay one ora and five pence to the first upnâm [on the side of the slain man]. And those who pay the fines for the lowest upnâm to the middle upnâm shall each pay eighteen pence.

234. MORE ABOUT THE SAME SUBJECT

Now the son of the daughter of the slayer's brother shall pay two ertogs and three pence[10] to the son of the daughter of the slain man's brother; and every one in that upnâm shall pay a similar amount. And the son of the slayer's maternal aunt shall pay twelve pence to the son of the slain man's maternal aunt; and every one in that upnâm [shall pay] a like amount. From [that point on beyond] the lowest upnâm a third is taken off as soon as the kinship becomes more remote. The degree of kinship to the slain man being the same, a man on the masculine side shall receive a third more than one on the feminine side.

235. CONCERNING THE UPNÁMAMENN

The man beyond the lowest upnâm who is nearest of kin on the masculine side shall have eight ertogs from the lesser man fine; that is, [the value of] twenty-six and two-thirds ells of wadmal; and the [nearest] kinsman on the feminine side shall have five

[10] As corrected by the editors of the Norwegian edition; the original has one ertog and seven pence.

ertogs and three and one-third pence from this fine; that is exactly [the value of] seventeen and two-thirds ells. The man who is in the second degree of kinship on the masculine side beyond the lowest upnám shall receive a like amount; but on the feminine side the payment in this fine shall be one ora and four and two-thirds pence; that is approximately [the value of] eleven and one-half ells. The man who is in the third degree of kinship on the masculine side beyond the lowest upnám shall receive a like amount; but on the feminine side the payment in this fine shall be two ertogs and three pence; that is, [the value of] seven and two-thirds ells. The man who is in the fourth degree of kinship on the masculine side beyond the lowest upnám shall receive a like amount; but on the feminine side the payment in this fine shall be one ertog and eight and two-thirds pence; that is exactly [the value of] five ells. The man who is in the fifth degree of kinship on the masculine side beyond the lowest upnám shall receive a like amount; but on the feminine side the payment in this fine shall be one ertog less one-half penny; that is [the value of] three and one-fourth ells. The man who is in the sixth degree of kinship on the masculine side beyond the lowest upnám shall receive a like amount, but on the feminine side the payment in this fine shall be thirteen pence; that is exactly [the value of] two ells. The man who is in the seventh degree of kinship on the masculine side beyond the lowest upnám shall receive a like amount; but on the feminine side the payment in this fine shall be [the value of] one and one-third ells; that is eight and two-thirds pence. The man who is in the eighth degree of kinship on the masculine side beyond the lowest upnám shall receive a like amount; but on the feminine side the payment in this fine shall be five and two-thirds pence; that is, one-fifth less than [the value of] a full ell. The man who is in the ninth degree of kinship on the masculine side beyond the lowest upnám shall receive a like amount; but on the feminine side the payment in this fine shall be three and one-fifth pence. The man who is in the tenth degree of kinship on the masculine side beyond the lowest upnám shall receive a like amount; but on the feminine side the payment in this fine shall be two and two-fifteenths pence. The man who is in the eleventh degree of kinship on the masculine side beyond the lowest upnám shall receive a like amount; but on the feminine side the payment in this fine shall be one and one-third pence. The man who is in the twelfth degree of kinship on the masculine side beyond the lowest upnám shall receive a like amount; but on the feminine side the payment in this fine shall be one penny. The man who is in the thirteenth degree of kinship on the masculine side beyond the lowest upnám shall receive a like amount; but on the feminine side the payment in this fine shall be two-thirds of a penny; they are then in the fifteenth degree of kinship to the slain man.

236. CONCERNING THE GELD EKERS[11]

Now there are three men who are [called] *geld ekers:* a thrallborn son, a thrallborn brother, and a uterine brother. A thrallborn son shall have twelve oras from the slayer and a mark from the slayer's brother; and all these three who eke the geld shall have these amounts. And all those who are of more remote kinship than these men shall receive one-half less of the man fine than those in the same degree of kinship.

237. CONCERNING WERGELD

A man has the right to three oras for his thrallborn maternal uncle, and each [has the right] to the same amount for the other. A man has the right to a like amount for his mother's [half] brother, though only [if they were] of the same mother, and each [has the right] to the same amount for the other. [He has the right to] six oras for his thrallborn paternal uncle and to a like amount for his father's uterine brother, and each [has the right] to the same amount for the other from the slayer, but to a third less from the slayer's brother than from [the slayer] himself and to a third less from his paternal uncle than from his brother. In this way each one of them will share in the lesser man fine; and all those whom I have now enumerated are called geld ekers. The sons of sisters have all a right to one fine, however many they may be and they pay [the man fine] in the same [way]. The sons of sistkins, whether on the masculine or on the feminine side, shall receive one common atonement. All the maternal uncles have a right to one atonement, and they pay [the man fine] in the same [way].

[11] See Glossary, "Geld eker."

All the paternal uncles have a right to one atonement, and they pay [the man fine] in the same [way], if they are the legitimate sons of the same father. Whenever the right of a geld eker passes to an heir, one-half of the payment drops away. Whenever atonement is paid to the father, it is [also] paid to the son.

238. CONCERNING DISHONORABLE FORMS OF MANSLAYING

The dishonorable forms of manslaying shall now be enumerated. If a man cuts into the cheek or into the bearded upper lip [of a slain man], there is a fine of an ora for every molar. If he throws the corpse into a fire or into a stream, he shall pay twelve oras for each one of the slain man's wounds. Likewise, if a man lies in wait for another where the passage is dangerous on either side or at either end of a bridge, so that the traveler must either attack his opponent with point and edge or venture upon a perilous passage, there shall be a fine of twelve oras. If a man severs the head from the body and carries it away, he is guilty of insulting arrogance and for that he shall pay three marks. If a man throws the corpse into water so deep that one's head will be wet before one can bring the head of the corpse out [of the water], he shall pay a fine of three marks. If a man deals another a blow with evil intent, he shall pay the man's heir a full atonement, and thus [it shall also be] whenever dishonor is done to the dead.

239. CONCERNING WERGELD

If a man has the daughter of a man, they are near kinsmen by marriage, and [if either is slain] they shall receive, each for the other, twelve oras from the slayer. If a man has the sister of another, they shall receive, each for the other, six oras from the slayer. If each one is married to the other man's sister, they shall receive, each for the other, twelve oras from the slayer. Now a stepfather and a stepson shall receive, each for the other, twelve oras from the slayer. If men are brothers by oath, they shall receive, each for the other, twelve oras from the slayer. If two foster brothers have grown up together, both having drawn from the same nipple, they shall take, each for the other, twelve oras from the slayer. If the mother of the [slain] man and her mother's father [are living], they shall receive, each for the other, twelve oras from the slayer, or [the value of] ten ells of wadmal, if the slain man was a hauld.

240. CONCERNING DISHONORABLE FORMS OF MANSLAYING

The first [form of] dishonorable manslaying is killing a man with the blunt side or end of a weapon; and if he is wounded [in this way] with two strokes, it is dishonorable manslaying [also] in a second [form]. The third [form of] dishonorable manslaying is wounding a man with a barbed arrow or a barbed spear, so that [the arrowhead] has to be cut out. The fourth, is wounding a man in more than seven [places]. The fifth, is striking a man dead without the shedding of blood. The sixth, is plundering the corpse. The seventh, is slaying a man while he is attending to his private needs. The eighth, is felling a man into a fire. The ninth, is shoving a man over a cliff. The tenth, is pushing a man into water. The eleventh, is leaving the body unburied so that it becomes the prey of ravens and carrion beasts. The twelfth, is failing to report the slaying properly; still, [in such a case] the deed is not counted as murder. The thirteenth, is [reckoned] the offering of atonement at the next thing in a voice so loud that he [the slayer] can be heard across the bounds of the thingstead, for in that case he has boasted of the deed. The fourteenth, is the failure to offer an atonement within twelve months; that means a tardy offer. And [a fine of] three marks is provided in all such cases as have now been enumerated.

241. WHEN THE WERGELD SHALL BE INCREASED

If the head is severed from the body and set up on a fence post or at a crossroads with the mouth wedged open, or if the corpse is bent over with the face down and the head between the feet, the wergeld shall be increased to the double.

242. MORE ABOUT WERGELD

Moreover, there shall be a fine of twelve oras if one severs the hand or the foot of a dead man, or tears his scalp away, or [breaks his skull] so that the brains drop out, or if he mutilates the sex organs or mangles the corpse about the buttocks, or if he breaks the bones of the head or cuts off any limb except fingers and toes.

[There is a fine of] an ora for every finger and for every toe till all have been severed; then it is one-half mark for each [limb]. The fine for housebreaking is forty marks, of which the king shall have one-half, if the husbandman is slain; [it shall be] six oras if the attack is within the garth and six [oras] more if the head is carried away from the place.

243. CONCERNING THE BAUGAR[12]

The wergeld of a hauld shall now be defined. There shall be six marks in the head baug, each ora [to be rated at] twelve ells of wadmal; [there shall be] four [marks] in the brother baug and two and one-half marks in the cousin baug. To every baug there shall be added two payments for the peace pledge, each payment to be one and one-fifth oras. And the payments for the peace pledge shall be distributed among the men who share the baug payments.

244. CONCERNING WERGELDS AND PEACE PLEDGES

Now the slayer shall pay [one] baug to the son of the slain man; [he shall make] a payment for the peace pledge to the slain man's brother and another to his paternal uncle's son. The slayer's brother shall pay one baug to the slain man's brother; [he shall make] a payment for the peace pledge to the slain man's son and another to his paternal uncle's son. The son of the slayer's paternal uncle shall pay one baug to the son of the slain man's paternal uncle; [he shall make] a payment for the peace pledge to the slain man's son and another to his brother as the price of the covenant, if all the kinsmen join in the peace at the same time and the baugamenn come to agreement. And [the payment] for the redemption from outlawry [shall be] three marks.

245. CONCERNING GIFTS

In addition the slayer, his mother, his daughter, and his wife shall render [gifts]; [they shall] each [make] a gift of one and one-fifth oras to the wife, the mother, and the daughter of the slain man; that will be twelve gifts. The sister of the slayer shall give half a

[12] A second schedule of wergeld payments (perhaps of later origin) begins with this chapter.

gift to the sister of the slain man, half a gift to his wife, [half a gift] to his daughter, and a half a gift to his mother; that will be two gifts. The slayer, his mother, his wife, and his daughter shall each give half a gift to the sister of the slain man; that will be two full gifts. Now there are sixteen gifts in all. And the baugar, the payments for the peace pledge, the payment for the redemption from outlawry, and the gifts to the women all told make twenty marks and two and two-fifths oras.

246. CONCERNING THE LESSER MAN FINES

There are six men of whom each one shall receive twelve oras from the lesser man fine: the first one is the father's brother; the second [is] a brother's son; the third [is] a uterine brother; the fourth [is] a thrallborn son; the fifth is a daughter's son; the sixth [is] the maternal grandfather.

247. MORE ABOUT THE LESSER MAN FINES

There are three men of whom each one shall receive nine oras from the lesser man fine: the first one is the mother's brother; the second [is] a sister's son; the third [is] a thrallborn brother. The sons of sistkins shall receive six oras.

248. MORE ABOUT THE LESSER MAN FINES

The father's thrallborn brother shall receive a mark from the lesser man fine. If a thrallborn daughter of the slain man has a son by a well-born man, he shall have one mark.

249. CONCERNING THE BAUGAR

Every baugman shall pay one-half less than he would receive and one-fifth [of this half][13] in addition. And the upnámamenn shall all receive two-thirds from the slayer and one-third from his brother.

250. CONCERNING THE UPNÁMAMENN AND THE CROSS PAYMENTS[14]

The first six among the upnám men shall receive four ertogs from the first cross payment made by those [who are] in the same

[13] Maurer, *Altnordische Rechtsgeschichte,* III, 53.
[14] See Glossary, "Cross payments."

degree of kinship to the slayer as they are to the slain man. And from the second cross payment each one shall receive an ora from those [who are] in the same degree of kinship to the slayer as those who share in the lesser man fine of nine oras are to the slain man. And from the third cross payment each one shall receive two ertogs from those [who are] in the same degree of kinship to the slayer as those who share in the lesser man fine of six oras are to the slain man.

251. MORE ABOUT THE SAME [SUBJECT]

And the men who share in the lesser man fine of nine oras shall each receive an ora from the first cross payment from those [who are] in the same degree of kinship to the slayer as those who share in the lesser man fine of twelve oras are to the slain man. And from the second cross payment each one of them shall receive one ora in current coin from those who are in the same degree of kinship to the slayer as they are to the slain man. And from the third cross payment each one of them shall receive one-half ora from those who are in the same degree of kinship to the slayer as those who share in the lesser man fine of six oras are to the slain man.

252. MORE ABOUT THE LESSER MAN FINES

The men who share in the lesser man fine of six oras shall each one receive from the first cross payment two ertogs from those who are in the same degree of kinship to the slayer as those are to the slain man who share in the lesser man fine of twelve oras. And from the second cross payment each one shall receive one-half ora from those who are in the same degree of kinship to the slayer as those are to the slain man who share in the lesser man fine of nine oras. And from the third cross payment each one shall receive an ertog from those who are in the same degree of kinship to the slayer as they are to the slain man.

[THE LAW AS TO THEFT]

253. HERE BEGINS THE LAW AS TO THEFT

The next is this, that none of us who desires to remain in the king's realm shall steal from any man. But if one steals an ertog or more than an ertog, he shall be outlawed or slain. If he denies the charge, let him deny it with a sixfold oath. If he steals a smaller amount, he shall be made to run the gauntlet and let men pelt him with rocks and turf; he has then paid [the penalty]. But if he denies the charge, let him deny it with a threefold oath; and if the oath fails, he shall run the gauntlet. And he shall run the gauntlet from the place where it is proved that the stealing was done. The course shall be as long as nine bows carried by a full-grown man. And he shall be pelted with rocks and with turf, and if he falls [on the course] he falls as an outlaw; but if he comes through safe, he has paid [the penalty].[1] If a man steals the carcass of a four-footed beast, [one that is] still fresh and bloody, he shall be outlawed, though he steals but a night-old lamb. If a man finds stolen goods in another's possession, he shall bind the stolen goods upon the shoulder of the thief, if there are witnesses present, and he shall bring him [the thief] into the thing district where the theft was committed and [he may] hand him over to the king's bailiff, if he wishes [to do so]. But if the bailiff refuses to receive him, he shall owe a fine of fifteen marks; and the fine that the bailiff shall pay, shall all go to the freemen. He [the thief] shall then be taken to the baron, and if he refuses to receive him, he shall owe a fine of fifteen marks; and of that money the king shall have one-half and the freemen one-half. Now the freemen shall pay no fines to the bailiff or to the baron before these have brought their claims into court. Now the man [who took the thief] shall summon a thing and shall bring him, with the stolen goods bound upon him, to this thing; and let him call men to testify that the goods belonged to the one who bound them and that

[1] See Keyser, *Norges stats- og retsforfatning*, p. 382.

he had reported the theft there. [He shall produce] other witnesses to testify that he bound the goods on the man; then the thingmen shall give a decision. If they deem the man to be wrongfully bound, the one who bound him shall owe a fine of fifteen marks to the king; but if they deem him rightfully bound, the bailiff shall find a banesman for him. If he refuses to do this he shall owe a fine of forty marks, and the freemen shall procure a banesman with his [the bailiff's] own money. If he [manages to] escape with his life, the freemen shall pay forty marks. If they allow him to leave the thing without a judgment, they shall owe a fine of fifteen marks to the king.

254. IF A MAN CLAIMS A WARRANTOR

If a man has lost goods by theft and he finds them in the possession of another, but if this one claims to have a warrantor and asserts that the goods are his own purchase, the accuser shall demand bail from him and surety for the goods that he claims as his own, and he shall set a day [for a hearing]. On that day he shall produce witness that the goods belong to him and that he had neither given them as a gift nor paid them [as a fine] nor conveyed them by sale. The goods are then his to take away and he may do as he prefers, either depart with his goods or look into his [opponent's] claim to have a warrantor. If he [the warrantor] fails him, the accused is a thief. If a man accuses another of thieving, he may do as he prefers, either summon him to be at home and [summon him] thence before the thing, or proceed to the thing and report the theft there. [In the latter case] the thingmen shall give him [the accused] a home summons [to appear] at the next thing, if he is in the fylki, or a public summons at the thing to appear before the thing, if he is outside the fylki; and [they shall proceed] in this way in any case, and the thing shall set a day for the hearing. If he fails to appear, the guilt is on his shoulder, unless witnesses can testify to preventing circumstances. If he appears in person at the thing, he shall offer to refute the charge with an oath; and if this oath fails, [the failure leads] to outlawry.

255. CONCERNING THE SEARCHING OF HOUSES

If a man is robbed of his goods and he can see the tracks of men leading away [from the house], let him call in the men of the neighborhood and report his loss; and let him then ask for a force of men to [go in pursuit and to] follow the track to the [other] man's garth. They shall then remain seated outside the garth but send one man to the house to state their errand and demand permission to search [the house]. If the man agrees to this and goes to fetch his neighbors, they [the searchers] may enter the house wearing their kirtles only, and without girdles; but if he refuses to allow the search, he admits that he is a thief. If the goods are found hidden away between two partitions[2] but were not purposely placed there [to create suspicion], the tenant of the house is [to be regarded as] the thief, if he is at home; if he is not at home, his son of major age [is the thief]. If neither of these is at home, the grithman[3] [is the thief], if he is at home; failing this one, then the housewife; and her daughter of major age, if there is no housewife. If these are both wanting, the ranking thrall[4] shall be [regarded as] the thief. The thief is a man, if the stolen goods are [found concealed] in a man's clothes; but a woman, if they are [found] in a woman's clothes. If the goods are found concealed in a man's bed, the thief is the one who made the bed. If they are found hidden under lock and key, the one who carries the key is the thief. If the goods are found hidden away outside in a man's barn where they cannot be reached from the outside except by breaking in, the thief is the one who stacked the barn. The same is true if they are found in a heap of wood. If the thralls in the household of a man of rank have stolen steak meat, the housewife, if she is at home and partakes of it with them, shall be counted the thief, though others have stolen the meat; but if she abstains from it, the ranking thrall shall be counted the thief. When stolen goods have been secreted [in a house by others], the occupier of the house has a right to deny the guilt and to make his oath effective.

256. CONCERNING THEFT

If a man finds his goods in another man's possession and takes the goods away, stating at the same time that he is not trying to cheat the king out of his rights, and he has witnesses present, then the other man is guilty of the charge, while the one who retrieves

[2] In a room. [3] See Glossary, "Grith." [4] *Bryti;* see Glossary.

his property is guiltless. But if in recovering his chattels he fails to report the theft, he owes a fine of fifteen marks to the king. If the king's bailiff or a baron reports that the two have made a settlement, the thief and the one who suffered the theft, thus nullifying the king's right,[5] each of them shall offer to clear himself with a threefold oath. If their oaths fail, each one shall owe a fine of fifteen marks; but one, alone, [shall owe this] if the oath fails in his case [only]. If a man finds property that was stolen from him but does not find the thief, he shall have witnesses present when he claims the property; and they shall bear witness that the thief was not nigh when the man retrieved his property.

257. CONCERNING FORMAL CHARGES

If a man charges another with theft and still another with having received what was stolen from him, the accused, if he denies the charge, shall refute it with a threefold oath; and if the oath fails, the failure leads to outlawry.

258. MORE ABOUT THEFT

If a man charges another with theft but the theft has not been reported, the accused may deny the guilt with a threefold oath; and if the oath fails, the failure leads to outlawry.

259. MORE ABOUT THEFT

If a well-born woman steals, she shall be driven out of the land into another kingdom. If a minor steals, the penalty shall be according to the deed. If a thrall of native birth steals, let his head be stricken off, or let his master clear him with a sixfold oath. If an alien thrall or the son of an alien [thrall] steals, he shall be flogged, and let his master have him flogged within five days; if that is not done, the thrall may be seized by the king's bailiff. And the bailiff shall have him flogged within five days; if he fails to do so, the owner of the thrall shall have him again, but he shall have him flogged thoroughly. Alien bondwomen shall be [dealt with] in the same way. But if their master wishes to enter a denial for them, he shall support it with a threefold oath; and if the oath fails, they shall be flogged and the stolen goods shall be restored,

[5] Cf. *Frost.*, Introd., c. 21.

all that is still intact and one-half of what has been damaged. Minors [shall be dealt with] in the same way. If a man's freedwoman steals, or a native bondwoman, one of her ears shall be cut off. If she steals a second time, the other ear shall be cut off; and if she steals a third time, her nose shall be cut off. After that she shall be called "stumpy and stubby";[6] and let her go on thieving, if she likes.

260. CONCERNING AN OUTLAWED THIEF

If a man is outlawed because of thieving, the man from whom the goods were stolen shall receive three times the value of his goods out of the belongings of the outlaw and [out of] his hidden loot.

261. IF A FREE MAN AND A THRALL JOIN IN STEALING

If a free man and a thrall join in stealing, the free man is the thief and the thrall shall suffer nothing; for a man steals alone, if he joins another man's thrall in a theft.

262. IF A THRALL IS ACCUSED OF STEALING

If a man charges another man's thrall, a native, with stealing, the owner shall offer him for examination, unless he is willing to take an oath in his behalf. And the accuser shall keep him half a month for examination; after that he shall return him intact in leg and limb; he shall not torture him, either with fire or with iron or with water. If the man is tortured to such a degree that he admits the theft, he speaks in fear; and he is guilty only if his confession bears the clear marks of truth. If the thrall brings a charge against a free man, he shall be held in durance till the man is cleared or is found guilty. And if the charge fails, the thrall shall be slain.

263. IF A MAN STEALS HAWKS

If a man takes a hawk that is bound to the nest and conceals it, he becomes a thief, if the owner reports the theft. And if a man takes mown grass from another man's land, he becomes a thief thereby. Let him refute the charge with a threefold oath, and [if

[6] *Stufa* and *nufa*. Stufa is anything that has been cut off or blunted; nufa is a nose that has been treated in this way.

the oath] fails, [the failure] leads to outlawry. The same [shall be done] in the case of hawks.

264. CONCERNING BOUNDARY STONES

If a man buys land from a bailiff, he is [counted] a thief, unless he buys [the land] at the thing. If a man sells land that he holds from the king, he becomes a thief thereby, but not the one who buys it. If a man removes boundary stones from where they stand and sets them down elsewhere by moving them over upon the lot that belongs to the man whose land lies next to his own, he becomes a thief thereby.

[THE REDEMPTION OF ODAL LAND]

265. HERE BEGINS THE LAW AS TO THE REDEMPTION OF ODAL[1] LAND

The reply [made by the defense] will determine the process to be used in redeeming odal land. Every man is entitled to have his land defended by a doom. If a man desires to redeem his odal he shall go to the house of the one [in possession] in the autumn about Winter Night, when the fences are still closed,[2] and he shall call upon him before two witnesses to surrender the land that he intends to redeem. Let him have this done before Holy Night in the presence of two witnesses; [he may do it] wherever he finds the possessor, and he need not give him a home summons. He shall allow him the choice of such an answer as he prefers. He may reply in this wise: "You order me to yield land in which you have no right of ownership; the land is mine in odal and ownership, and I shall defend [my title] with law and with doom." I may give as another reply: "I have sold the land." And I may give the third reply: "you will never get this land till you wrest it from a dead man."

266. THE FIRST DEFENSE

But if he shall reply in this wise that "I shall defend [my title] with law and with doom," the claimant shall summon him to be at home at any time that he wishes [to set] between Yuletide and Lent. Any man who maintains a household shall be summoned to be at home and in his highseat the entire day of the summons while the sun is in the sky. But if [the claimant] does not find him at home, he shall appoint a day for him, suiting the time to the distance that the man has to cover on his way home. He shall next go to procure witnesses, men who are born to odal right. No man shall refuse to serve as a witness to a formal demand; if he does he shall owe a fine of three oras to the king's official. He shall then proceed with his witnesses to the house of the man whom

[1] See Glossary, "Odal," "Odal land," "Odal right," "Odal witness."
[2] Cf. *Gul.*, c. 82.

he has summoned to his home; he shall come there on the appointed day and shall make a formal demand for his land and his odal. But the man shall reply as he replied to the earlier demand: "You are asking for land to which you have no right; the land is mine and I shall defend [my title] with law and with doom; and I meet you with an appeal to a doom." Any free man has the right to make this request for a doom, if the householder is not at home; and if there are no free men at home, the housewife shall make the request for a doom. [If the man is] inside, he must make the appeal; but if he runs out intending to use trickery, he shall be pursued and shall be offered [a chance] to make his appeal outside on the grounds. But if he gets beyond the garth before he has been pledged to a doom, he shall owe a fine of six oras to the one who served him with the demand. Now he [the claimant] shall time his home summons carefully, lest the first doom shall fall on a holy day; but if it falls on such a day, the suit is worthless to him who brings it. If a doom is pledged after a five-day respite, it shall be set for a lawsuit day and the formal demand shall be put forth at that time. In this doom there shall be [only] men with open minds. Every free man is eligible to a seat in a doom; but they [the litigants] may not have near kinsmen in the doom with them; agnates and cognates and near kinsmen by marriage shall all withdraw. If these have been invited into the doom, they shall be removed in the presence of witnesses and he [the litigant] shall summon men with open minds [to take their places]. The doom shall be set outside the door of the defendant's house; the claimant shall place his men facing the principal door, and the defendant [his men] with their backs to the door; and they shall be placed far enough away from the door so that both wood and water may be carried in and a cart may be run between the doom and the door. Now when the doom is set, [the claimant] shall enumerate his ancestors, the five who have owned the land and the sixth who had it both in ownership and in odal.[3] The plaintiff shall then bring forth his witnesses, first those whom he had when he gave the initial notice,[4] and if they prove satisfactory, he shall next bring

[3] In the Gulathinglaw land acquired by purchase did not become odal land, until it had remained in the family for five generations.

[4] *Forsǫgn:* a demand on the occupier to surrender the land that is sued for.

forth those whom he had at the home summons. If these give him complete support, he shall bring forth his witnesses to the formal demand, two men born to odal right. When the witnesses to his formal demand have spoken, and if the action is correctly brought, he shall produce witnesses to [his right to] the odal, three witnesses who had reached their twentieth year when their fathers died. [He shall] also [have] witnesses to confirm this evidence: these must have been fifteen winters old when their fathers died. Witness to odal right must be born only by men who are born to this right, men who have odal land in the fylki where the land to be redeemed is located. When the witnesses to the odal have testified for the claimant and if the doomsmen deem that the land should be awarded to him, the defendant may counter [with the plea] that "you have no right to [the land], for your witnesses have spoken falsely; but I have other and more numerous witnesses who can bear better witness and will all agree in their testimony." The defendant shall then name his counter witnesses, four odal witnesses and a greater number to confirm their testimony; thus, by producing counter witnesses he is able to break up this doom. [The defendant] shall then appoint another day for a hearing; there shall be [a space of] five nights between the dooms, unless the fifth shall fall on a holy day, in which case the doom shall be put forward to a working day, and it shall be set, as before, in front of the defendant's doorway. When the doom is set, the defendant shall bring forward all the witnesses whom he named at the former doom, four odal witnesses and a larger number to confirm [their testimony]. Now the defendant's witness is born to satisfaction, if he has produced one more odal witness and several more confirming witnesses than the plaintiff had; then those who bore witness first are worthless, unless both sides have the same number; in that case those are worthless who testified last. Then the plaintiff and the defendant shall appoint a place for the moot half way between their dwellings. [They shall] count the miles and the quarter miles and shall suit the time for holding the next doom to the distance; and this doom, men call a *skiladôm*.[5] At that moot, either side shall offer to make a wager or shall cease from its con-

[5] See Glossary, "Doom."

tention. If they want to have a doom of twelve thegns, six for each side, each one of them shall hand over two oras,[6] twelve oras in all, to be placed in the hand of a disinterested man. And they shall call their wager to the attention of reliable men who are standing outside the group of doomsmen. And those who set the doom, the plaintiff and the defendant, shall refer the wager doom to the quarter thing; and when they come to the thing they shall bring their witnesses forward, the men, [namely], to whom they appealed when they made the wager. Then the thingmen shall determine which side is nearest the truth, and it is well if they are agreed about it. Then those who wagered on the other side are of no worth as witnesses and are out of the suit. But if the thingmen are not agreed they shall refer the wager doom to the shire thing, and it is well if they are all agreed to this. But if they do not agree, and one of the litigants wants to appeal the case while the other does not, the former, though he may be unable to force an appeal, shall, nevertheless, bring to the attention of witnesses, men from another herath, who have not been sent to that thing district, the deprivation of right that the thingmen have caused him;[7] and he shall then take his case to the shire thing. When he arrives there, he shall report the deprivation of right that he has suffered at the quarter thing. "Here I have the witnesses whom I asked to note the facts"; he shall bring these forward and the thingmen shall give a decision in the case; then it is well if they are all agreed in that decision. But if they come to no agreement and one of the litigants wants the case referred to the law court,[8] while the other is satisfied with the outcome at the shire thing, the one who wants to appeal shall leave the thing and call for men to support him. If he secures the support of one-fourth of the men at the shire thing, he shall be able to force an appeal; but if he secures a smaller number [only], he will have to endure the decision of the shire men. If the case is appealed to the law court, and one side has lost its wager, and is out of the suit, then those of the other side shall take the money that was given into disinterested hands, two oras from

[6] In the payment of wergeld (see above, p. 150) a mark (8 oras) was counted the value of three and two-tenths cows. Two oras would therefore be equal to four-fifths of the value of one cow.

[7] By failing to reach a decision.

[8] That is, to the Gulathing.

each of the others, as the wager was. And each one [of the losing side] shall pay a fine of three oras to the king's official and in this way atone for their faulty judgment. The witnesses for that side are now worthless [as witnesses]; each one of them who bore that witness shall pay a fine of three marks to the king's official; and they shall never bear witness in odal cases after that. If the man who sued to redeem the land has brought his suit according to law, he shall bring goods and money to [tender for] the land in mid-Lent on the Saturday when, on the following morning, three weeks remain of Lent; and he shall place the goods on the stone where the cornland and the meadow meet. And he shall speak in this wise: "[I ask you to] be here on this land on Thursday of Easter week to receive what the land is worth according as men shall appraise that which I give in payment. I shall come here with reliable men and you shall have an equal number; these men shall appraise the land according to the rules [employed] when men are to redeem their odal land." The payment shall be one-half in gold and silver and one-half in thralls, native born and not older than forty winters nor younger than fifteen. In this way a man shall redeem his odal. Now the [process of] redemption has been described.

267. THE SECOND DEFENSE

But he has the choice to meet the initial demand with another defense as follows: "I have sold that land and am not the proper person to offer defense in behalf of that land, though the odal right remains with me." Then he shall ask to whom I have sold the land, and I shall name the purchaser, the man to whom I have sold the land, one within our jurisdiction, if I care to do so. But no one has the right to convey land into the possession of a baron. And if I reply that I have sold the land to a baron, I must take up the defense myself, for no freeman shall convey land to a baron.[9] If I have now told him to whom I have sold the land but he refuses to believe me and gives me a home summons and comes to my house with witnesses to demand the [surrender of the] land; and though I reply as I replied to the initial demand that I have no title to that land, I [shall], nevertheless, offer to submit to a doom

[9] Such a conveyance would embarrass the claimant and make redemption more difficult.

since every man must meet a formal demand with a request for a doom. If he has appointed a day for the hearing and the doom is properly set, I shall bring forward witnesses [to show] how I had replied to the initial demand and other witnesses [to show] how he made his demand and that I denied having the land [seeing] that I had sold the land, then I shall be able to break up his doom, and shall order my doomsmen to rise and pay no heed to his witnesses. But if I let the doom sit and let his witnesses be heard, and if they testify for him to satisfaction, I shall ask for three dooms. If he is awarded the land that he sued for at these dooms, I shall have to convey to him as much of mine in place of it as I have failed to defend successfully [since] I have called for a doom to defend another man's land. If he goes with his witnesses to seek the man whom I have named as the purchaser and asks him if he has bought any land of which the odal is his and which he is in the act of redeeming, he may reply as he likes. But if he gives this reply: "He has lied to you for I have no title to that land," he [the claimant] shall call this to the attention of witnesses and shall return to the quarter where the land is located that he is [trying] to redeem. He shall then summon a thing and shall go to that thing with his witnesses; [he shall] first [call] those whom he had when he made his initial demand and when he [the defendant] denied that he was responsible for the land, saying that he had sold it; next those who heard the man deny that he had bought the land. He shall then bring forward his three witnesses to his odal right and all those who are to confirm this testimony, the same that he would have called at the doom. And those who denied having responsibility for the land shall present no opposing witnesses at that time. Next, he shall ask the thingmen to appoint a doom to examine his evidence, and if it is found satisfactory the thingmen shall award the land to him and shall confirm the decision with a show of weapons [to the end] that he may be able to defend his land with law and with doom and he shall have it without payment, since his opponent has presented such a lame defense.

268. THE THIRD DEMAND

If he replies to the initial demand in this wise that "you will never get the land from me except you wrest it from me a dead man," the claimant shall summon him to be at home and shall go to his house with men to witness his demand and shall request the [surrender of the] land. If he [the defendant] then fails to propose a doom, he [the claimant] shall summon him to be at home on the morrow of the next day, when he will come with witness to his demand, other [witnesses] than those whom he had before; and it is well if he can secure both. But if he can get no other men, he shall have one of his original witnesses and another of those whom he had before and shall demand the land once more. If he [the defendant] still fails to call for a doom, he [the claimant] shall ask him to remain at home while he rows along the shore's edge or walks outside the garth. After that he shall return to the man's house and put forth his demand a third time, but he must find one new witness and have another of those whom he had before, for one must have four witnesses to three demands, if one is to make them properly. If he [still] refuses to agree to a doom, he shall owe a fine of eighteen oras to the king's official. And he [the claimant] shall summon him before the thing for robbery and for lawless dealings. And he shall go before the thing and produce his witnesses and [shall claim] such gains as have come to him in the course of the suit; how he had ordered him [his opponent] to yield possession, how he had served him with a home summons to hear his three demands, and how the defendant had not held him worthy of a doom. If the witness to this is born to satisfaction and his suit is properly conducted, he shall produce his witnesses to his odal right and [shall claim] such gains as have come to him in the suit, just as he should have done at the doom. He [his opponent] may not offer any counter witnesses at that time, but the thingmen shall award the land to the claimant. If he [the defendant] replies as before, saying that he will never get [the land], the land shall be sued for at the thing, unless the man is willing to submit to the award of a doom.

269. CONCERNING THE APPEAL TO A DOOM

If [the defendant] has called for a doom, but is unwilling to have the doom held, [the plaintiff] shall set a doom and shall place his doomsmen before the defendant's doorway; he has then set half the doom. He shall then summon him [the defendant] to the doom, if this one still is unwilling to set his counter doomsmen. If he sets some but not all, he does not have a full doom; he has then fled from his own doom and is out of his suit. But the plaintiff shall produce his witnesses none the less, and shall claim his gains [in the suit]; but [the defendant] shall not be allowed to present counter witnesses, or to transfer his case, or to offer a wager; but the doomsmen shall award the land to him [the claimant]. But if he [the defendant] will set no doom on his side and refuses to have a doom, he [the plaintiff] shall produce his witnesses and shall claim his gains from the doomsmen, just as he would if there were a full doom. When the testimony is born and the doomsmen have awarded the land to him, he shall ask those present but outside the doom to note the award. He shall then summon a thing and shall go to the thing with these auditors and have them tell how he sued for his land. If they convince the thingmen that the suit was correctly brought, they shall award the land to him. He shall then go to the land on the Saturday after which three weeks still remain of Lent and bring goods and money to [tender for] the land and notify the man from whom he is redeeming the land to be on the land on Thursday in Easter week and to bring reliable men. "And I shall be there with other men to assess the value of the land with a lawful assessment. And when the value is determined, I shall pay you such an amount as the men have agreed upon." He shall then proceed to the land on Thursday in Easter week with reliable men; then it is well if he [the other man] appears. But if he does not appear, the value of the land shall be determined by reliable men, and after that [is done] the suitor shall display the worth of the land [in money] and place it in his purse, and he shall keep it as a loan till the one who shall have it comes to get it. But if [the defendant] resists and defends his possession with point and edge, the suitor shall ask for a force of thingmen to help him remove his stubborn opponent from the land; and whoever refuses to join him shall owe a fine of three oras. And everyone who joins in the resistance shall owe a fine of three marks and their leader forty marks. And if those who resist be slain, they are slain as outlaws, while those who go upon them are without guilt. When the stubborn one has been removed from the land, the owner of the land shall have possession.

270. CONCERNING ODAL LAND

The various kinds of land that are to be regarded as odal land shall now be enumerated. The first is land that has passed from man to man for [five] successive generations. The second is [land that has been] acquired in payment of wergeld. The third is [land received as] foster inheritance.[10] The fourth is [land received as] a gift [or mark] of honor. The fifth is [land] received from the king as a gift for hospitality. The sixth is land received from some one, whoever it be, as foster payment. The seventh is land received in exchange for odal land. All these kinds of land and all odal land that has been parceled out among brothers and kinsmen shall be regarded as odal land. All other [land] is money [land].

271. IF LAND COMES INTO THE KING'S CONTROL

If land comes into the king's control,[11] we shall redeem it from that one of the king's bailiffs who has authority to bring legal actions in the fylki where the land is located. And if the king has no bailiff in that fylki, we shall redeem it from the bailiff who is nearest; and it must be redeemed before three kings have passed away. If the land is not redeemed by that time, it shall remain as it is. If there are three kings in the land at one time,[12] their lives shall be counted the lifetime of one. If the king wishes to redeem land from us, his bailiff shall redeem it just as any one of us redeems [land] from another. He, too, shall have redeemed it before three kings have passed away; otherwise the land shall remain as it is. He shall not sue to redeem it while the king is in the fylki where the land is located.

272. IF LAND LIES UNREDEEMED FOR TWENTY WINTERS

If land lies unredeemed for twenty winters, and there has been no publication [of the terms of sale], it can be redeemed for its full value [only]. But no publication is of any value unless the two [the buyer and the seller] are agreed as to [the terms of] sale and

[10] See above, p. 111.

[11] This chapter deals with crown property, not with the king's private possessions.

[12] Joint kingship was not uncommon in Norway in the eleventh and twelfth centuries. On the death of Magnus Bareleg (1103), his three sons succeeded to the kingship. See *Frost.*, VIII, c. 15.

purchase. If the one [the purchaser] disagrees, the other [the seller] shall be allowed to present witnesses [to the bargain] at the thing. If a man wants to redeem his land with the help of odal witnesses, the men who were present at the sale, whatever their rank may be, are competent witnesses, if they are still available; but if there are no such [witnesses], let him redeem his land with [other] odal witnesses of the right sort.[13]

273. HOW LAND SHALL BE REDEEMED

If a man is a minor, he shall redeem his land within the twelvemonth after he has reached his majority. If he does not care to redeem it at that time, he shall have no right to renew his claim at any later time.

274. HOW LAND SHALL BE REDEEMED FROM A WOMAN

If a woman comes into the possession of land, which men have a right to redeem from her, they shall redeem it from her if their kinship is so close that they are rated as either agnates or cognates.[14] They shall give her notice before two witnesses in the autumn before Holy Night that she must yield possession; and they shall summon her to come on Thursday in Easter week to receive such payment as will satisfy the law. And they shall have served the summons at the latest on the Saturday after which three [weeks] remain of Lent, and they shall summon her to the land that they wish to redeem from her. They shall then proceed to the land, the men who are to redeem it and the woman who is to receive the payment. Then he [the claimant] shall produce witness as to how he served notice on her to surrender the land and how he had summoned her and her guardian. If that witness is born to satisfaction, the men shall estimate [the worth of] his testimony and shall decide whether or not he has a right to redeem the land. If that is decided to satisfaction, they shall proceed to appraise the land at its full value; they shall appraise it after having inspected it both within and without the garth. When they have made the appraisal, the claimant shall offer in payment one-fifth less than the land is worth or is appraised [to be worth];

[13] Witnesses born to odal right.
[14] See Glossary, "Agnate," "Cognate."

and he shall pay one-half in gold and silver and one-half in thralls and live stock. And let him keep his odal with care and let her [keep her] money.

275. CONCERNING THE BAUGRYGR

A woman is a *baugrygr*, if she is the [lawful] heiress to both odal and movables; no man can deprive her [of land] by redemption. Now these are the women who are odal women and [as such] have a right to the odal: a daughter, a sister, a father's sister, a brother's daughter, and a son's daughter. There are two baugrygjar, a daughter and a sister, who shall contribute to the wergeld and shall share in the wergeld, just as men do, and they have the right to redeem land, just as men have. Now if they [daughters] are to inherit from their father, and if one has a daughter and another has a son, the son may redeem [land] from his kinswoman [cousin] as the law provides; but if the situation is reversed, he having daughters, and she [his cousin] a son, the latter may redeem land [from his cousin's daughter] by giving the same payment as was given when it was redeemed from his mother.[15] And the [title to the] land shall remain in quiet where it now is, seeing that it has come three times under the spool and the spindle.

276. HOW A MAN MAY SELL HIS ODAL LAND

If a man wishes to sell odal land, let him go before the thing in the autumn and offer it for sale to those who share the odal with him. They shall then come on Thursday in Easter week and pay him as much money for the land as other men outside the kindred offer to pay. [In such a case] the man's son has the first [right to] buy. If a man outside the kindred wants to buy [the land] and the one who has the first right to buy doubts that the man is willing to pay as much [as is stated], they shall both, [the seller and the purchaser], swear to terms of sale and purchase, stating that "at such a price I wish to buy" and "at such a price I wish to sell." Now if he [the other odal man] does not want to buy at that price, the owner may sell, giving full warranty, to whomever he likes. If a man wishes to convey land for a term of fifteen years, the agreement shall be valid, though it may be set aside in this one

[15] See Brandt, *Retshistorie*, I, 164.

case: if the land had been offered [to the kindred], the bargain may be annulled on that account, if the land is not already conveyed; and the seller shall owe a fine. He shall then bid the purchaser to increase his offer, that he may have the land for the term agreed upon. If he refuses to increase his offer, the owner shall ask the [other] odal men to buy the land, and if they refuse to do so, let him sell to the highest bidder. If the land remains [in the buyer's possession] till the end of the term, the seller shall demand a surrender in the autumn, and he may do two things at the same time, [order the tenant to surrender the land] and summon him to be on the land on Thursday in Easter week, if he is willing to accept such an amount of money as witnesses know that he paid him [the seller]; then, it is well if they are agreed that the seller has summoned him to come to the land to receive payment. But if he [the occupier] denies this, he [the seller] shall present witness as to how he demanded surrender of the land and how he summoned him [to come] to receive payment. If this witness is born to satisfaction he shall produce witness to show how much money the tenant has in the land; and he shall then offer him as much money as the witnesses have awarded him. After that he shall have the land in his keeping, and the other [man shall have] his money; he has now redeemed his land properly and legally. If the land remains [in the buyer's possession] beyond the term and remains thus for twenty winters and [the terms of sale] have not been published, it has become [the holder's] odal land;[16] he may then deny [the seller's] odal right and claim it for himself. He may now defend his land with a doom and the other must sue [for it] with odal witnesses. Now his odal witnesses are the men who were present at the purchase. If there has been no publication [of the terms of sale] during the twenty winters, the land can be redeemed at its full value [only]. A satisfactory publication is one in which both the buyer and the seller are agreed as to [the terms of] sale and purchase.

277. IF A MAN BUYS LAND THAT HAS NOT BEEN PUBLICLY OFFERED [FOR SALE]

If a man buys land that has not been publicly offered [for sale], the men who share in the odal may annul the bargain. If they call

[16] To be redeemed at full value, Hertzberg, *Den ældste norske proces*, p. 39.

for the surrender of the land in the autumn, they may do two things at one time, if they so desire: they may order him [the occupier] to surrender the land and summon him to be on the land on Thursday in Easter week. They may also summon him [later], at the latest in mid-Lent, on the Saturday after which three weeks remain of Lent. If the man defends his purchase with a doom, the doom shall be held on the land to which he has been summoned. The claimant shall then bring forward witnesses to show how he summoned the defendant to [come and] receive such a sum of money as witnesses have knowledge of; then if the testimony is satisfactory, it is the duty of the doomsmen to award the land to him [the claimant] and such a sum of money to the defendant as the witnesses know that he had paid to him. But if he [the defendant] claims that the land was publicly offered and has witnesses to testify that it was offered in legal manner, he shall have the land that he has bought. If he fails to come to the doom, he [the claimant] shall offer the money, and if the defendant has given power to any one in the presence of witnesses, the money shall be paid into his hands. Otherwise the claimant shall keep the money and shall not pay it over until he [the defendant] sues for it.

278. IF A MAN BUYS LAND TO BE CONVEYED BY SKEYTING[17]

If a man buys land to be conveyed by *skeyting* and gets the conveyance, the men who share the odal [with the seller] if they are in the fylki and wish to redeem the land, shall redeem it within the following twelvemonth; otherwise the purchaser shall keep it.

279. MORE ABOUT THE SAME SUBJECT

If a man buys land to be conveyed by skeyting, and the seller refuses to convey it, let him go before the thing and let him prove by witnesses that he has bought the land to be thus conveyed; and let him ask for a show of weapons[18] that the land may be conveyed to him by this show of weapons; then the conveyance is as valid as if the seller has made it, provided that he [the buyer] has taken earth in the right way.

[17] See below, pp. 186–87, and Glossary, "Skeyting."
[18] See Glossary, "Show of weapons."

280. CONCERNING REDEMPTION OF LAND[19]

If a man buys land and the [former] owner wants to redeem it, he may notify the purchaser on any day that he likes, one-half month before Thursday in Easter week, that he [the purchaser] may have the use of the [purchase] money that summer. If he redeems the land after the moving days, the tenant shall have both his purchase money and the year's rent.

281. IF A MAN WISHES TO REDEEM HIS ODAL

If a man wishes to redeem his odal and the one who is in possession of the land is outside our law or outside the kingdom, he shall go to find him and summon him before witnesses to the land. After that he shall proceed to the land and shall set his doom there and claim the land, as if the other man were present; and let him bring forward his odal witnesses and all his other witnesses as if the other man were present.

282. CONCERNING THE DIVISION OF ODAL RIGHTS BETWEEN BROTHERS

If two brothers are to divide odal rights between them, the odal shall pass to that branch of the family to which the lot gives it both with respect to the right of redemption and to actual occupation. It shall be offered to the other branch only in case this one comes to extreme want or in case there is no heir to the inheritance. Yet, the latter line does not lose its right [to the land], and the odal shall not pass from it until one in either line may marry a daughter in the other.

283. IF A MAN WISHES TO REDEEM LAND THAT HAS BEEN MORTGAGED

If a man wishes to redeem land that he has mortgaged, let him give the holder notice half a month [before] Thursday in Easter week. He shall then proceed to the land and shall set his doomsmen over against those of the other man and shall show by witnesses how much money the other man has in the land. He shall then pay that amount, unless witnesses allow him [the occupier] a

[19] This chapter appears to deal with land that has been pledged (or mortgaged) for a debt.

larger sum. Now if he redeems it in this wise, he has the land at his disposal. But if he redeems it at a later time, but before the plow is set into the ground, and if there is no fraud in it, he gets the rent, but the tenant retains the right to occupy the land. If he redeems it later still, he [the tenant] shall have both the money and the land without rent for that twelvemonth.

284. IF A MAN WISHES TO REDEEM LAND THAT HAS BEEN SOLD FOR A TERM OF YEARS

If a man wishes to redeem land that he has sold for a term of years, he shall give him [the occupier] notice in the autumn before two witnesses; if he likes, he may at the same time summon him to receive his payment on Thursday in Easter week on the land that is in dispute. When they have [both] arrived, the suitor shall place his doomsmen and show by witnesses how much money the other man has in the land; he shall then pay this [amount], unless the witnesses allow him [the occupier] a larger sum; in that case he [the occupier] shall have witnesses present at the moot where he [the owner] has the land that he wishes to redeem.

285. HOW LAND SHALL BE REDEEMED FROM A WOMAN

Now land shall be redeemed from a kinswoman in the same way and by one who is so near of kin that the odal right cannot be questioned. And she must reply in this wise: "This is by no means our odal, it is land acquired by our kinsmen; it goes by purchase right but not by odal right." Then the man shall produce witnesses at the doom through which he seeks to redeem the land that this land does go by odal right and not by purchase right. If the woman has any witnesses, she, too, shall bring them forward there.

286. CONCERNING LAND THAT HAS BEEN SOLD FOR A TERM OF YEARS

If a man wishes to redeem land that he has sold for a term of years, or land [that he has] mortgaged, and the one who has possession is outside our law or outside the kingdom, he shall redeem it from his agent; if there is no agent, he shall redeem it from the man's heir just as he would from the man himself. If he [the tenant] conveys land that is subject to redemption [to another] before the end of the term, he [the owner] may redeem the land from whom he will, from the one to whom he sold it or from the one who has come into possession. Land that is in mortgage [shall be dealt with] in the same way. If a man who has taken land that is in mortgage or subject to redemption [after a term of years] is outside our law or outside the kingdom and neither his heir nor his agent is within our law, the one who wishes to redeem [the land] shall go before the thing and issue a summons to the one who bought it to appear [at an appointed day]. And if he fails to come on that day, he [the suitor] shall proceed to the thing and shall show by witness what their agreement was; then he shall offer [redemption] money. But if the other man has authorized no one to receive the money, let the suitor have it and keep it till the other man comes to get it.

287. CONCERNING ODAL LAND

If a man wishes to sell his odal land, let him or some one to whom he has given power appear before the thing in the autumn and offer the land for sale to his fellow odalmen. Let him invite them to the land on Thursday in Easter week to buy the land for what others may offer. He shall do this in the thing district where the land is located. Now if they both come on Thursday in Easter week but disagree about the price, the one who wants to sell the land shall swear that he has been offered the price that he has set and that the offer is not a mere pretense. Then if another [odalman] shall also swear that "I will buy for the price [that is] now set," he shall have it if he wishes; otherwise he [the owner] may sell to whomever he likes. If the one who wishes to buy arrives but the one who offered the land does not come, the buyer shall have the land at a price set by impartial men, whether he [the owner] is willing or not. But if neither comes, the land remains as if no offer had been made. But an [earlier] purchaser has no legal title, if those who share in the odal come on Thursday in Easter week.

288. CONCERNING LAND THAT IS SOLD FOR A TERM OF YEARS

If a man wishes to dispose of land for a term of years or to give it in mortgage, he shall first offer it before witnesses to those who are nearest in the odal. He need not offer it to his son, unless he wishes to do so.

289. IF A MAN BUYS LAND THAT HAS NOT BEEN PUBLICLY OFFERED FOR SALE

If a man buys land that has not been publicly offered [for sale] and one who shares in the odal is within the fylki, this one may redeem it within the following twelvemonth. If he is outside the fylki, he shall have it redeemed within the twelvemonth following his return to the fylki. But if he does not redeem it in the way that I have now set forth, he has no right to renew his suit at a later time.

290. CONCERNING THE RIGHT TO REDEEM LAND

If a widow has the right to redeem land that has been sold, she shall find a man, whomever she may choose, to publish this fact at the thing within the following twelvemonth; and let her have [the land] redeemed within the first twelvemonth following her remarriage. But if she refuses to have a marriage arranged, let her select the man whom she wants to manage her lawsuit, only not a man [who might] prove too powerful for the man who bought the land.

291. MORE ABOUT THE RIGHT TO REDEEM LAND

If a maid has the right to redeem land, she shall find a man when she has completed her fifteenth winter to publish at the thing that she has the right to redeem certain lands which have been sold. And let her have [the lands] redeemed within the twelvemonth following her marriage. But if a maid or a widow fails to proceed after the manner set forth, they have no right to renew their suits at any later time.

292. CONCERNING THE CONVEYANCE OF LAND

If a man buys land in the presence of assembled men, it is the duty of the thingmen to convey the land to him. He shall summon the seller to be at home to receive a thing summons; and he shall bring forward his witnesses at the thing to show that he gave the seller a proper home summons and [that he summoned him] thence to the thing. He must take earth as the law prescribes; he shall take it from the four corners of the hearth and from under the highseat and from a place where the cornland meets the grassland and where the holt[20] touches the pasture; and let him have such witnesses at the thing [as can testify] that the earth was properly taken, along with those other men who witnessed the purchase. Now, if this witness is born to satisfaction, it is the duty of the thingmen to convey the land to him with the show of weapons. In every case when the buyer and the seller are agreed that the earth has been properly taken, the bargain shall be valid and the conveyance (skeyting) likewise.[21] [Whether it is made] at a church or at an alehouse or on a ship that is fully manned and large enough to have the benches counted, the conveyance shall be as valid as if it were made at the thing. Whenever the king conveys land his conveyance, too, shall hold.

293. IF A MAN WHO HAS SOLD HIS LAND COMES TO NEED

If dire need befalls a man who has sold his land for a term of years, he shall summon the tenant to be on the land that he has bought, giving half-a-month's notice. And he shall proceed to the place of summons and present witness there that dire need has broken their contract. And one of the men who share in the odal may have the land if he wishes, rather than the one who has it by purchase.

294. CONCERNING THE REDUCTION BY ONE-FIFTH

If there are two brothers and one of them dies before their father, but if a son survives him, this son may redeem from his uncle at a reduction of one-fifth [of its assessed value that part of] the odal land which his father would have had a right to from his father. But he shall not redeem it before the grandfather has passed away.

[20] See Glossary, "Holt."

[21] In such a case there would be no need to hear witnesses.

[THE LAW OF THE COAST DEFENSE]

295. HERE BEGINS THE LAW OF THE COAST DEFENSE

It is the king's right to command and to forbid and to determine our part in the coast defense. We cannot refuse to serve with the king's fleet [but must go] as far as the Land's End[1] if he orders it out in his need and to our profit. But all men shall serve in [the right] proportion according as the king has promised us.

296. CONCERNING THE COUNT OF MEN

When the levy is mustered, every man shall account for the men [of his household]; and no man shall refuse to allow another a new count [with a view] to a more equitable assessment. If a man shall demand a [new] enrollment from the men of his ship district, it is well if they all come to the numbering and to the oath taking. If some fail to come to the muster, those who do come shall assign such a reckoning to those who do not come as they wish to assign; and they shall do service for that number if they are informed of it. [Every man] shall include in his reckoning all those of his household for whom he is accountable in matters of the coast defense and also those of his freedmen who have not given their freedom ales. If a freedman has sufficient means he shall make his own contribution to the levy; otherwise his master shall do it. Every man shall include in his reckoning all those of his children who have seen three Holy Nights. If a man runs from fylki to fylki and from quarter to quarter to avoid the muster and performs his duty neither here nor there, and if he is accused of this and convicted, he shall be outlawed. If a man gives help to some member of his household to evade the oath, he shall, if he owns a thrall, forfeit the thrall to the king's bailiff; if he has more than one, the bailiff shall have the one that he chooses. But if he has no thrall, he shall pay a fine of three marks for every member of his household whom he has helped to evade the oath.

[1] In the twelfth century the "Land's End" meant the mouth of the Göta River on the southwest coast of modern Sweden.

297. MORE ABOUT THE MUSTER

When a general levy is ordered, every seventh man shall be called into service; but whenever the terms [of muster] are easier, all men shall have the benefit thereof. And in proportion to our numbers we shall provide in each fylki as many ships as we have agreed upon with the king.

298. CONCERNING THE MEN FOR WHOM NO DUES SHALL BE PAID

Now we shall tell what men there are for whom no dues shall be paid to the coast defense. A bishop shall pay no dues to the fleet for himself or for his priest or for his deacon. A mass priest shall pay no dues, nor shall his wife[2] or his cleric; but if there are others in the household, dues shall be paid for them. The king's bailiff shall contribute nothing to the fleet either for himself or for his wife or for his household.[3] No dues shall be paid for any leper. No contribution to the fleet shall be paid for a thrall who is in poor health; [let the owner] take him to the thing and offer to give him away; but if no one is willing to take him, and he is younger than forty [years], no fleet money shall be paid for him. There shall be no contributions paid by the men to whom we join in giving freedom here at Gula nor by those whom we manumit as shire men. There shall be no dues to the fleet for those whom poverty forces back upon the kindred, or for pauper freedmen, unless they are claimed [as thralls] because of debt. Though the number of children in a family shall increase, there shall be no contribution to the fleet [exacted for them], until there has been a new enrollment. If a member of your household, one for whom it is your duty to render dues [or service] to the levy, shall die, the payments shall continue till the next enrollment [is made]. If a man takes a wife or buys a thrall out of the muster list of another man and makes the purchase before the oaths are sworn, he shall add [that person] to his own list; but if the purchase is made after [the oaths were sworn], he shall deposit his next payment and then enter him on his own list. If a man fails to render

[2] Clerical celibacy was evidently not enforced in the twelfth century.

[3] This would include his thralls.

his dues to the fleet for a period of three winters and does not enroll himself in any muster group, he shall be outlawed. If a man enrolls himself in a muster group but does not pay his dues, the bailiff shall ask that he be fined for neglecting the coast defense to such an amount as the reckoning happens to show. Whenever there is a general enrollment of men, the levy groups shall be formed from the Land's End[4] forward, so that those who live near each other shall compose a separate group. No one shall pass ahead of another unless all the others have agreed to it. No one shall refuse to allow another man a new enrollment, and the freemen shall all attend the thing where the enrollment is made. Now if you wish to be enrolled in another eighth or in another quarter,[5] [you] shall state your request at the thing. But if the men refuse to enroll you there and refuse an adjustment [of the dues], you will have to charge the reduction to their account and do it on oath. If a man moves his household into another fylki or into another quarter, he shall not dispose of his ship or buy another, but let him enroll [in such a muster group] as he likes. If he joins a group which has to provide a ship, he shall pay such dues as other men [pay]. If a man leaves a muster group and moves into another jurisdiction, he shall leave money behind for the next payment. If a man leaves the kingdom, his dues must be paid for three winters; if they are not paid, let a fine be exacted when he returns home. If a man conveys his household out of our jurisdiction and into another fylki, let him leave money behind to meet the next payment where he formerly lived; after that he shall pay his dues where he locates.

299. CONCERNING THE COMMAND OF SHIPS

The man whom the king appoints shall command the ship; but if he refuses [to do so], he shall owe a fine of six marks. If another man deprives him of the steering gear, he shall owe a fine of six marks. Now, the shipmaster shall select the crew to sail with him, and all [those chosen] are in duty bound to sail or pay a fine of three marks. Now, it is well if there is a sufficient number of unmarried men; but if there is not a sufficient number, the farmers

[4] See above p. 188, note.

[5] The quarter division was limited to certain shires in the Gulathinglaw.

who have men to do the farm work shall join the crew; and it is well if there is a sufficient number [of such men]. But if there is not a sufficient number, men who have no helpers shall join [the crew]: one shall go forth, and two shall remain at home to care for the live stock, if a crew can be provided in this way; otherwise, let two go forth, and one remain at home.

300. CONCERNING THE COOK

Those men in a ship district who have thralls shall provide the cook; and [they shall] assign the duty by casting lots. The cook shall have the same wages as the sailors. The freeman who provides the cook shall remain at home unless [it be that] the ship is not fully manned. It shall be the duty of the freemen to appear at the muster, though the unmarried men [need appear] only if the shipmaster wishes it. The shipmaster shall send summons to all the men whose duty it is to equip or to launch a ship; and whoever fails to appear shall owe a fine of three oras. A sailor shall receive an ora per month in wages and two oras for two months. And the freemen shall find provisions of both kinds[6] for two months for each thwart, and an oar and a tent cover [for each].

301. IF A MAN FAILS TO APPEAR AT HIS OAR BENCH

If a man fails to appear at his oar bench when a ship is to be released from its moorings, his oar shall be raised up, and he shall be publicly charged with a fine of three marks. A widow who has no oarsman shall bring victuals and her other contributions to the ship and shall give them to the shipmaster. If there are five or more vacant benches on a twenty-bencher, the ship is not seaworthy. A baron or a bailiff, one who has [at least] an eighth part [of the fylki] in his stewardship shall send five oarsmen to the benches and not fewer. If a ship is not seaworthy, the freemen shall offer their force [of rowers] to another ship and if they are not accepted, they [the freemen] shall incur no penalty if they remain at home; but let them bring provisions to the bailiff for the king's support. When they come home, they shall call for a [new] enrollment, and if they do not find [a sufficient

[6] Meal and butter. See Glossary.

number], they shall shorten the keel and thus reduce the ship to a length corresponding to their number; but let it not be made so short that the benches need not be counted.[7] If they are too few to man a thirteen-bencher, they shall go to the thing and offer to join the levy with other men; but if they do not do this, they shall have the ship ready for the sea the following spring both with men and with meat. If a man contributes to the fleet elsewhere than where he owes the contribution, it is as if he has paid nothing. If a man boards another ship than the one that he ought to board, the result is that he not only rows with the expedition, but must also pay a fine [for neglect].

302. IF A MAN LEAVES THE SHIP WITHOUT PERMISSION FROM THE SHIPMASTER

If you are guiding the prow southward along the shore and a man deserts the ship while it is proceeding southward and the king is out to defend the land, he is an outlaw; but he may regain his rights with [a payment of] forty marks. But if the shipmaster deserts, he is an outlaw under all circumstances. The fleet must not be kept out at sea longer than that a man has victuals of both [kinds] left for half a month. If a shipmaster allows a man to leave the ship, he becomes responsible for the entire craft; and whoever leaves after that shall incur no penalty.

303. IF MEN SUFFER A SHORTAGE OF FOOD

If men while sailing northward on the return journey shall suffer a shortage of food, they shall display their provisions to [the men on] another ship and thus prove to them that they have no more than a month's provisions of each [kind] for two small troops [only]. They may then take two heads of a farmer's cattle and butcher them with impunity; but they shall make a payment of two oras for a cow, the same [amount] for a three-year-old ox, and two and one-half oras for a full-grown ox; and they shall leave the head, the hide, and the feet behind. If they butcher in this wise they have no guilt; but if they take away the head, the feet, or the hide, they are liable to punishment. If they butcher cattle belonging to a farmer who has [already] had cattle slaugh-

[7] See above, p. 92, note.

tered by others, but of which neither the head nor the feet are displayed, they butcher with impunity, if they pay for [the cattle], but if they butcher otherwise than is here set forth, the shipmaster shall owe a fine of forty marks and each member of the crew three marks. If they are accused of having butchered otherwise than is here set forth, the shipmaster shall enter a denial with a threefold oath for as many men as he wishes; but if he is unwilling to enter this denial for them, each one shall make his own denial with a threefold oath. If a man leaves his ship before it has been hauled up on the beams and [goes away] without permission from anyone [in charge], he shall owe a fine of three marks.

304. CONCERNING THE HOUSING OF SHIPS

When a ship comes home to the beams, it shall be hauled up and [all] the gear shall be put away. Let enough men be called in from each muster group so that the ship can be hauled up; but if some fail to come and the ship is hauled up [without them], each one of them shall owe a fine of three oras. But if the ship cannot be hauled up, those who failed to come shall be wholly responsible for the ship, if the summons came to [their] houses. Whenever the shipmaster sends forth the token, all are in duty bound to carry it, whether they belong to that ship district or not; and whoever fails to send the token forward shall owe a fine of three oras. If men come five nights too early or five [nights] too late, no one shall pay [fines for] another;[8] but if the difference in time is greater [than this], let those pay whose duty it is to pay and for the time that the reckoning shows.

305. CONCERNING THE CARING FOR SAILS

A sail must never be torn into more than two parts; but if one tears it into more, he shall owe a fine of three marks. The one to whom the lot gives the sail shall have the care of it, if he lives near the sea. If a sail is deposited in a church and the church burns down, the men shall be held to account for the sail, unless [the church] was purposely burned by [other] men. The men shall have a place to set up [the ship], just as they have had of old; but

[8] A parallel enactment in the later Common Law (*Landslov*, III, c. 14) would indicate that this may perhaps be translated: provide food for another.

if there is a lack of land, the king's land shall be used, if the king has land in that quarter. If he has no [such land], they shall buy a site, wherever they like, as men think most expedient.

306. CONCERNING SHIPBUILDING

If a ship is decayed with age and another has to be provided, let the men build it wherever they wish to build it, only so that no damage is done to cornland or meadow. Now, the duty lies with the king's land to provide [a site] for the building, if there is such land; if there is none, the builders may take [a site] in whosesoever forest they prefer. If there are several ships to be built, one man's forest must not be entirely stripped. Let the men whom the lot points out as the ones to provide the keel or the prow, the hull or the "neck,"[9] divide up the duty to fetch the timbers; if these are wanting, the fine shall be one-half mark. For every piece of timber that is needed for the gunwales of the prow and for each of the cross timbers in the prow, if they are wanting, the fine shall be three oras, and the timbers shall be provided, even if it [has to] be at a later time. For every missing rib that reaches athwart the ship inside there is a fine of three oras: one ora for every piece of knee timber;[10] one ora for every hook that is wanting, three oras for a plank and the same for a yard, as well as for all the longer pieces, even if they are for the inside of the ship. There shall be a fine of one ora for every missing board that the ship needs, an ora, even if the board be only an ell [in length], and let it be provided later on; one ora for every missing rivet and for the washer that belongs to it; one ora for every bucket of tar; one ora for every strip of oakum, an ora, though only an ell be wanting; one ora for every meal of food; one ora for every penny to be given in pay to the shipwrights. Now, [the builders] shall summon all the shipwrights who are in the quarter till the number is sufficient. Every prow builder who neglects to come shall owe a fine of six marks. If anyone runs away from the work, the prow builder or the deal hewer, after the keel has been laid on the stocks and the builders have begun the work, then such a prow builder or deal hewer shall be outlawed, since he hinders the king in his defense of the

[9] That part of the ship at the foot of the prow where the sides converge.
[10] Timber somewhat knee shaped and apparently serving as a rib.

land. The shipwrights shall be paid [as follows]: the prow builder shall have two oras, [each valued] at six ells [of wadmal] for the workdays between two Sundays, and the deal hewer, one ora. The [old] ship shall be neither burned nor broken up before the prow of the new ship is nailed to the keel. But if the men burn it or break it up before [that is done], they have failed in their duties to the coast defense, and they shall pay a fine of three marks for each oarlock.

307. CONCERNING THE BUILDING OF SHIP SHEDS

When a shed is to be built over [a ship], the shipmaster shall send forth the summons [for a time] so convenient that the men will be able to build the shed; but if they refuse to build it, they shall owe a fine of three marks to the king. Let them distribute the duty to bring materials; and they shall owe a fine of three oras for every corner post [that is not provided] and the same amount for every beam and for every rafter; and these must be provided even if it [has to] be at a later time. They shall owe a fine of three oras for every "turf holder,"[11] three oras for every "wind board,"[12] one ora for every "roof board,"[13] the same amount for every bundle of birch bark, and an ora for every [piece of] turf. And all these materials must be provided, even if it [has to] be at a later time.

308. CONCERNING A MOOT FOR SAIL MAKING

Now the shipmaster shall set a day and call the men to make a sail for the ship; and if it is not made at that moot, all those who have the duty to provide it shall suffer a penalty of three marks. If some go to work but others do not, [the latter shall suffer] a penalty of one ora for every ell; one ora for every boltrope, an ora, though an ell only be lacking; one ora for every ball of cord; one ora for every ring [in the tack]; and one ora for every hook [in the tack]. The length of rope shall be determined by the number of hides required. [There shall be a fine of] one ora for

[11] *Torfvǫlr:* a strip of wood laid along the eaves of a building to hold in place the turf which served as a covering to the roof.

[12] *Vindskeið:* a board nailed to the eaves on the gavel sides.

[13] *Tróða:* a board that was laid over the roof underneath the birch bark which was again covered with turf.

every hide that is not delivered, and let it be delivered, even if it [has to] be at a later time. If there is something lacking, the bailiff or the baron shall provide it so far as he has lands from the king; let him then sue [the delinquent one] for the penalty.

309. CONCERNING WEAPON THINGS

Whenever a weapon thing is to be held, the bailiff or the baron shall give due notice in the autumn and the thing shall be held in the spring. All free men of major age shall attend that thing; whoever fails owes a fine of three oras. Now the men shall display their weapons as the law demands. A man shall have a broadax or a sword, a spear, and a shield which at the worst must have three small plates of iron laid across it and shall have the hand grip fastened with iron nails. Now each of these three folk weapons, [if wanting], carries a fine of three oras. The freemen shall provide one bow and two dozen arrows for each thwart; they shall pay an ora for every arrowhead that is wanting and three oras for the bow.

310. WHETHER A SHIP SEEMS TO BE SEAWORTHY OR NOT

If the king sends his men into a fylki to inspect the vessels of his subjects and they or the shipmaster declare a ship to be unseaworthy, while the freemen call it seaworthy, men shall be summoned from another ship district, who are to declare on oath [whether it be] seaworthy or not. But if they refuse to swear, let the men launch their ship and test the craft [in that way]. Let it lie in water for five nights and then let them bail it out. Now if one man can manage the bailing out to the fareway, the ship is seaworthy. The anchor shall go with the ship; but if it is wanting, the men of the ship district shall pay three marks. And the shipmaster shall provide the steering oar[14] and the tiller.[15]

311. CONCERNING THE WATCH AT THE BEACONS

Whenever a hostile raid is feared, the men shall do service [as watchmen] at the beacons. The king's bailiff or the baron shall

[14] In the Northern "longships" the rudder usually took the form of an oar placed near the stern on the starboard side.

[15] *Stýrisdrengr:* the handle of the steering oar.

send forth the summons and whoever fails to come shall owe a fine of three marks. And if those who are appointed by the lot to keep the beacon fail to go [to the beacon], they shall be held accountable for the beacon. Now the men who keep the watch at the beacon shall take heed lest they sleep at the watch. If a man falls asleep, he shall pay twelve oras; but if the enemy comes in the meantime and the beacon is not lit, he shall be outlawed. He shall light the beacon on the appearance of five ships or more than five; but if he fails to light the beacon and the ships prove to be hostile, he shall be outlawed. If he lights the beacon on the appearance of fewer ships and thus causes the men to assemble in force, he shall owe a fine of forty marks. The one who is nearest the beacon that is farthest east shall be liable for forty marks; all others for three marks.

312. CONCERNING THE SENDING FORTH OF ARROWS

If a man who was once sent hence into outlawry returns to the land bringing true war tidings, he shall be allowed the right of habitation though he had formerly been outlawed. But if a man brings war tidings that are not true, he shall be outlawed even though he has already been allowed the right of habitation. If a man who has the right of habitation brings reliable war tidings, he shall have a mark from every fylki and three marks from the king. If a man brings war tidings, he shall send forth the iron arrow at the Land's End.[16] This arrow shall be carried from baron to baron and shall be conveyed on a ship with a full crew; it shall be carried forward by night and by day and shall travel the [common] fareway. All who fail to send the arrow forward shall be outlawed. Wooden arrows shall be sent from the fareway inward and up the fjords; they shall be sent out before witnesses, and each one shall carry it to the other; and whoever fails in this shall owe a fine of three marks. If the arrow comes to the home of an unmarried woman, she shall provide a ship and crew and provisions, if she has the means; but if she has none, the arrow shall go on past. But to all the men to whose homes the arrow comes, it brings a summons to [muster on] shipboard within

[16] See above, p. 188, note.

five days. But if anyone stays quietly at home, he shall be outlawed, for at such a time both thegn and thrall shall go forth. Every man must furnish provisions for himself and his companions. If they come upon a hostile force and a fight is joined and a thrall kills an enemy, he is a free man, though he was a thrall up to that time. If a hostile force invades the land and the king, fearing that men are likely to fail him, demands hostages from us, we have no right to refuse the demand. But whoever does refuse is [by that fact] guilty of treason. If men are given as hostages, the king shall keep them [as such] till the hostile fleet is five nights beyond the sight of land; then he shall send them back home. If the king charges a man with treason, let him refute the charge with a twelvefold oath; if the oath fails, the failure leads to outlawry.

313. IF MEN SAIL IN DEFIANCE OF A BAN

If men sail in defiance of a ban, the shipmaster shall owe a fine of forty marks and the sailors three marks each. One man shall be the master on every ship, the one who has his sleeping place nearest the gunwales on the starboard side. The action shall be brought against him; but all who own shares in a ship that sails in defiance of the ban shall pay fines in proportion to their holdings in it. There shall be no ban laid on the traffic in corn or [other] food between the shires; but if such [a ban] is laid, all the men of the fylki shall owe a fine of forty marks, one-half of which shall go to the king and one-half to the men of this jurisdiction.

314. CONCERNING THE THWART MONEY

If a man builds a longship out on the countryside but makes no announcement as to his plans or whither he intends to sail, then the bailiff or the baron shall go to him and ask him whither he intends to sail. If he refuses to tell, they shall demand that he give bail to the amount of forty marks. But if he refuses to give bail, they shall cut out a board five ells in length on either side of the keel. It they fail to do this, the freemen shall do it and also remove the sail, if there is one, and in this way prevent the sailing. But if they fail to do this, and the ship turns out to be a warship, they shall pay a mark for every thwart and three marks for the rudder strap; that is called the thwart money. If the men [who sail the ship] find their own provisions, the men of the herath shall pay the fines for those who live in that herath. If they renounce the peace and sail forth to harry those same shores, they are nithings; but if they harry elsewhere, they are outlaws but not nithings. If they sail forth without renouncing the peace, they are outlaws and nithings too and have forfeited their goods to the last penny, no matter where they harry. If they proceed to harry and the one who has suffered the foray is unable to find a force to pursue them, he may send forth the arrow, if he wishes. Now all shall gather where the arrow summons them to pursue the foeman. When they go forth in pursuit, all those who are present shall join in it. If one refuses to go, his property is liable to confiscation and the others may kill him, if they like, and divide his goods among them. If they come to the place where the man is who sent forth the arrows and [they find that] he has sent them with good right, then it is well. But if he sent them without right, no hostile band having visited his house, they may confiscate his property, and they may kill him if they like and divide his goods among them. But if he has sent the arrows with good right, they shall go with him as far as he desires. If they come upon a raiding party and they have to redden point or edge to recover the goods, the booty belongs to those who take it, and let them divide it among them. But if there is no need [to do this], the goods are his to whom they formerly belonged. If the raiders seize a merchant ship and break into the cargo with violence but after that bring [the merchandise] back to the herath and make peace with the king, the men who were plundered shall follow after them and swear to [the identity of] their property; and they [the raiders] shall restore everything, unless they can nullify the oaths with the hot iron. If those who are in the raid continue forward along the coast and a man buys something of value from them, the man to whom it belonged before shall have it, and shall recover possession by the witness of two men; but the one who trafficked with the vikings shall pay three marks to the king. But if the owner cannot bring witness against the one who has bought goods that were wrongfully acquired, he shall summon him before the thing; and it shall be the duty of the thingmen to award him the property or [to demand] a threefold oath. Now this oath like any other oath may be taken at any time within ten weeks of oath days; and any week in which there is one oath day is available for oath taking. The one [who demands the oath] shall summon the other [to appear] after five nights at whatever church door he wishes within the quarter. Now the oath must be taken before witnesses; two men shall be appointed to hear the oath, they shall [also] be the judges of the oath. If they disagree, one holding the oath [to have been] properly taken and the other, improperly, the one who is willing to swear to his opinion shall be upheld [in it]; but if both desire to swear, the one who wishes to help [the defense] has the best right to take the oath. If the oath is not sworn, [the defendant] must surrender his property to the claimant and pay three marks to the king.

We have now written down the laws governing the coast defense but we do not know whether the statement is right or wrong. But even though it be wrong, we shall keep the legal arrangements as to the levy that we had of old and which Atli[17] recited before the men at Gula, unless the king wishes to give us other [plans], and we shall all agree to them.

315. HOW MANY SHIPS FROM EACH FYLKI

It is the duty of the Vik-dwellers to provide sixty twenty-benchers and also a ship for [the men of] Grenland. The men of Agder shall build sixteen twenty-five benchers; those of Rogaland shall provide twenty-four twenty-five benchers; the Hords, the same number; the Sognings, sixteen twenty-five benchers; the Firthmen, twenty twenty-five benchers; the men from Möre, sixteen twenty-five benchers; the men of Raumdale, ten twenty-benchers; the men from North Möre twenty twenty-benchers; the Tronders, eighty twenty-benchers; the men of Naumdale, nine twenty-benchers; the men of Hálogaland, one thirty-bencher[18] and thirteen twenty-benchers, seven ships from the southern half and six from the northern half, inasmuch as they [the men of the north] keep the watch eastward.[19]

[17] Atli seems not otherwise to be known.

[18] The thirty-bencher was the ship that "kept the watch eastward."

[19] It is to be noted that the provisions of this chapter cover the entire coast area and not merely the Gula province. Hertzberg calculates the force needed to man this fleet (the watch ship not included) to number 27,040 men. See *Historisk tidsskrift*, Ser. V, Vol. I, 274–75.

[A LATER SYSTEM OF WERGELD]

316. HERE BEGINS THE NEW SCHEME OF MAN FINES WHICH WAS DRAWN UP BY BJARNI MARDSSON[1] AND IS CONCERNED WITH [THE FINE OF] SIX MARKS GOLD[2]

When the award for the life that was taken away is six marks gold, the money shall be paid to the son of the slain man, who is the [proper] person to receive the fine; and all the baugar and the fines, both greater and lesser, are included in the six marks gold. Now the son of the slain man shall receive twelve marks, weighed;[3] and the brother of the deceased [shall receive] six marks weighed. His paternal uncle, if he is living, [shall receive] four marks, weighed, and eight ertogs. If the paternal uncle has passed away but his sons, cousins of the slain man, survive, they shall have twenty oras, weighed, and four ertogs. If the paternal uncle is living but has no children, he shall have thirteen oras, weighed, and one ertog. If he has daughters but no sons and they are less than forty [years old] when the wergeld is paid, the paternal uncle shall take a mark, weighed, on behalf of his daughters' sons. If he has no children except a son by a free-born concubine, he [this son] shall have the mark that the sons of his daughters would [normally] receive. But if all these [classes] are present, daughters' sons of legitimate birth, sons of legitimate birth and a son by a free-born concubine, the son of the concubine shall be counted with his brothers in the matter of the man money and in addition to their share in the fines there shall be paid to him five oras less one ertog. If they die and leave no children these five oras less one ertog shall revert to the one who receives the wergeld. If the slain man's father is living and his son receives the wergeld, he [the father] shall have three marks weighed; but if he is not living, this fine reverts to the one who receives the

[1] Bjarni was a lawman who seems to have flourished about 1200.

[2] That is, if the entire wergeld is six marks gold (48 marks silver).

[3] Reckoned in silver.

wergeld. If there are a uterine paternal uncle and a uterine brother, this uterine brother shall receive twelve oras, and the uterine paternal uncle, six oras. If neither of these can be found or if one of them is wanting, his [or their] share in the fine shall revert to the one who receives the wergeld. And the total amount that these men receive is twenty-seven marks and two oras. If the man who was put to death had a stepson or a stepfather, the one who receives the wergeld shall pay out of the total just given twelve oras weighed to each one of them. If there are brothers-in-law, each one having the other's sister, the one who receives the wergeld shall pay them twelve oras; but if their kinship rests on one marriage only, the payment shall be six oras. If the slain man is survived by his maternal grandfather and his daughter's son, they shall receive of the wergeld four marks less two oras, or fifteen oras each; but if one of these is wanting or if both [are wanting], this fine shall revert to the one who receives the wergeld. If the slain man is survived by a maternal uncle and a sister's son, they shall receive twelve oras each. If he is survived by a son of his father's paternal uncle and by the son of a paternal uncle's son, they shall receive twenty-two oras, eleven oras each; but if one is wanting or if both [are wanting], this fine shall revert to the one who receives the wergeld. If the slain man is survived by a paternal aunt and she has sons, they shall receive nine oras and one ertog. And if the slain man is survived by a maternal uncle and he has sons, these sons shall receive nine oras, weighed, less one ertog; and the sons of his sister [shall receive] a mark. If the slain man is survived by a son of his brother's daughter, he shall receive thirteen oras; and those who are nearest in kinship after the slain man's brothers' sons shall also receive thirteen oras. And if the slain man is survived by women who are the children of his brothers and they have sons, these sons shall receive six oras and one ertog. But if the women who survive the deceased are the children of brothers and sisters[4] and they have sons, their sons shall receive five oras. And the men who are in the fourth degree of kinship on the masculine side, and those who are in the third

[4] *Systkinabǫrn;* see Glossary, "Sistkins." These "children of sistkins" will not be of the same sex and the father of the one must be a brother of the other cousin's mother.

[degree] on the feminine side, when one counts from the brothers and sisters, shall receive five oras and one ertog. In the fifth degree on the masculine side and in the fourth [degree] on the feminine side, each shall receive ten ertogs. In the sixth degree on the masculine side and in the fifth [degree] on the feminine side, each shall receive two oras; and in the sixth degree on the feminine side, [each shall receive] four ertogs. Such a sum shall each one receive from one [who is] in the same degree of kinship [to the slayer] and shall pay in the same way to one in the same degree of kinship [to the slain man]. Whenever money is paid to a father, it is also paid to his son; but the paternal uncle of the slain man and his sons and their sons shall each receive his own fine; and in the same way the paternal uncles of the slayer and their sons shall pay with him such amounts as are received by those [who are] in the same degree of kinship to the slain man. But if the paternal uncle has passed away, his sons shall receive a single fine and shall pay in the same way. And if the one who should receive or pay wergeld has daughters who survive him and they have sons, these sons shall pay or receive the amounts determined by the reckoning. And whoever withholds money that should be paid in wergeld or demands a larger fine than is owing him and gets into difficulties on that account, shall be called a pledge breaker.

317. HOW THE FIVE MARKS OF GOLD SHALL BE DIVIDED

When the award for the life that was taken away is five marks gold, the money shall be paid to the one who is known as the son of the slain man and is the [proper] person to receive the fine and all the baugar and the fines, both greater and lesser, are included in the five marks gold. Now the son of the slain man shall receive ten marks, weighed; and the brother of the deceased [shall receive] five marks, weighed. His paternal uncle, if he is living, and his sons [shall receive] three and one-half marks and one ora and six and one-third pence. If the paternal uncle has passed away but his sons, cousins of the slain man, survive, they shall have eighteen oras and seven pence. If a paternal uncle is living but has no children, he shall receive eleven oras and six and one-half pence. If he has daughters but no sons and they are less than forty [years old] when the wergeld is paid, the paternal uncle shall take seven oras less one ertog in behalf of his daughters' sons. If he has no children except a son by a free-born concubine, [this son] shall receive the seven oras less an ertog, which the sons of daughters would normally receive. But if all these classes are present, daughters' sons of legitimate birth, sons of legitimate birth, and a son by a free-born concubine, the son of the concubine shall be counted with his brothers in the matter of the man money and in addition to their share in the fines there shall be paid to him half a mark, weighed, less six and one-half pence. If they die and leave no children, this fine shall revert to the one who receives the wergeld. If the slain man's father is living and his son receives the wergeld, he [the father] shall have twenty oras; but if he is not living, this fine shall revert to the one who receives the wergeld. If there are a uterine paternal uncle and a uterine brother, this uterine brother shall receive ten oras and the uterine paternal uncle, five oras. If neither of these can be found, or if one of them is wanting, his [or their] share in the fine shall revert to the one who receives the wergeld. And the total amount that these men receive is twenty-two and one-half marks less one ertog. If the man who was put to death had a stepson or a stepfather, the one who receives the wergeld shall pay out of the total just given ten oras weighed to each one of them. If there are brothers-in-law, each one having the other's sister, the one who receives the wergeld shall pay them ten oras; but if their kinship rests on one marriage only, the payment shall be five oras. If the slain man is survived by his maternal grandfather and his daughter's son, they shall receive of the wergeld three marks, weighed, and one ora, or twelve and one-half oras each; but if one of them is wanting, or if both [are wanting], this fine shall revert to the one who receives the wergeld. If the slain man is survived by a maternal uncle and a sister's son, they shall have ten oras each. If the deceased is survived by a son of his father's paternal uncle and by the son of a paternal uncle's son, they shall receive eighteen oras and one ertog, or nine oras and one-half ertog each; but if one is wanting, or if both [are wanting], this fine shall revert to the one who receives the wergeld. If the deceased is survived by a paternal aunt and she has sons, they shall receive seven and one-half oras and three pence. If there is a maternal uncle living and he has sons, these sons shall receive seven and one-half oras less six and one-half pence; and the sons of his sisters shall receive seven oras less one ertog. If the slain man is survived by a son of his brother's daughter he shall receive ten oras and one-half ertog; and those who are nearest in kinship after the slain man's brothers' sons shall also receive ten oras and one-half ertog. If the slain man is survived by women who are the children of his brothers and they have sons, these sons shall receive five oras and three pence. But if the women who survive the deceased are the children of brothers and sisters[5] and they have sons, these sons shall receive one-half mark and one-half ertog. And the men who are fourth in the degree of kinship on the masculine side, and those who are in the third on the feminine side when one counts from the brothers and sisters, shall receive one-half mark and thirteen pence. In the fifth degree on the masculine side and in the fourth [degree] on the feminine [side], each shall receive not quite eight ertogs and seven pence. In the sixth degree on the masculine side and in the fifth [degree] on the feminine side, each shall receive five ertogs; and in the sixth degree on the feminine side [each shall receive] one ora and six and one-half pence. Such a sum shall each one receive from the one [who is] in the same degree of kinship [to the slayer] and shall pay in the same way to the one in the same degree of kinship [to the slain man]. Whenever money is paid to a father, it is also paid to his son; but the paternal uncle of the slain man and his sons and their sons shall each receive his own fine; and in the same way the paternal uncles of the slayer and their sons shall pay with him such amounts as are received by those [who are] in [the same degree of] kinship to the slain man. But as soon as the paternal uncle has passed away, his sons shall receive a single fine and shall pay in the same way. And if the one who should receive or pay the wergeld has daughters who survive him and they have sons, these sons shall pay or receive the amounts determined by the reckoning. And whoever withholds money that should be paid in wergeld or demands a larger fine

[5] See above, p. 202, note.

than is owing him and gets into difficulties on that account shall be called a pledge breaker.

318. HOW THE FOUR MARKS GOLD SHALL BE DIVIDED AMONG THE KINSMEN

When the award for the life that was taken away is four marks gold, the money shall be paid to the one who is known as the son of the slain man and is the [proper] person to receive the fine, and all the baugar and the fines, both greater and lesser, are included in the four marks gold. Now the son of the slain man shall receive eight marks, weighed, and the brother of the deceased [shall receive] four marks, weighed. His paternal uncle, if he is living, and his sons [shall receive] three marks less seven pence. If the paternal uncle has passed away but his sons, cousins of the slain man, survive, they shall have fifteen oras, weighed, less thirteen and one-half pence. If a paternal uncle is still living but has no children, he shall receive nine oras less one-half ertog. If he has daughters but no sons and they are less than forty [years old] when the wergeld is paid, the paternal uncle shall take five oras and one ertog in behalf of his daughters' sons. If he has no children except a son by a free-born concubine, he [this son] shall receive the five oras and the one ertog that the sons of daughters would [normally] receive. But if all these classes are present, daughters' sons of legitimate birth, sons of legitimate birth, and a son by a free-born concubine, the son of the concubine shall be counted with his brothers in the matter of the man money, and in addition to their share in the fines there shall be paid to him ten ertogs less one penny. If they die and leave no children, this fine shall revert to the one who receives the wergeld. If the slain man's father is living and his son receives the wergeld, he [the father] shall have two marks weighed; but if he is not living, this fine shall revert to the one who receives the wergeld. If there is a uterine paternal uncle and a uterine brother, the uterine brother shall receive one mark and the uterine paternal uncle, half a mark. If neither of these can be found, or if one of them is wanting, his [or their] share in the fine shall revert to the one who receives the wergeld. And the total amount that these men receive is eighteen marks less four pence. If the man who was put to death had a stepson or a stepfather, the one who receives the wergeld shall pay out of the total just given one mark to each one that is listed here. If there are brothers-in-law, each one having the other's sister, the one who receives the wergeld shall pay them one mark out of this fine; but if their kinship rests on one marriage only, the payment shall be one-half mark. If the slain man is survived by his maternal grandfather and his daughter's son, they shall receive twenty oras from the wergeld, or ten oras each; but if one of them is wanting, or if both [are wanting], this fine shall revert to the one who receives the wergeld. If the slain man is survived by a maternal uncle and a sister's son, they shall receive one mark each. If he is survived by a paternal uncle and by the son of a paternal uncle's son, they shall receive fifteen oras less one ertog, each one taking one-half; but if one is wanting, or if both [are wanting], this fine shall revert to the one who receives the wergeld. If the slain man is survived by a paternal aunt and she has sons, these sons shall receive six oras. If the deceased is survived by a maternal uncle and he has sons, these sons shall receive six oras less one penny or thereabouts; and the sons of the sisters [of the deceased shall receive] five oras and one ertog. If the deceased is survived by a son of his brother's daughter, he shall receive a mark and eight pence; and those who are nearest in kinship after the slain man's brother's sons shall also receive a mark and eight pence. If the slain man is survived by women who are the children of his brothers and they have sons, these sons shall receive one-half mark and one-half penny. But if the women who survive the deceased are the children of brothers and sisters and they have sons, these sons shall receive ten ertogs. And the men who are in the fourth degree of kinship on the masculine side and those who are in the third [degree] on the feminine side, when one counts from brothers and sisters, shall receive ten ertogs and one-half penny each. In the fifth degree on the masculine side and in the fourth [degree] on the feminine side, each shall receive six and one-half ertogs and three and one-half pence. In the sixth degree on the masculine side and in the fifth [degree] on the feminine side, each shall receive four ertogs and in the sixth degree on the feminine side, [each shall receive] two ertogs and nine pence. Such a sum shall each one receive from the one [who is] in the same degree of kinship [to the slayer] and shall pay in the same way to the one in the same degree of kinship [to the slain man]. Whenever money is paid to a father it is also paid to his son, but the paternal uncle of the slain man and his sons and their sons shall each receive his own fine; and in the same way the paternal uncles of the slayer and their sons shall pay with him such amounts as are received by those [who are] in the same degree of kinship to the slain man. But if the paternal uncle has passed away, his sons shall receive a single fine and shall pay in the same way. And if the one who should receive or pay the wergeld has daughters who survive him and they have sons, these sons shall pay or receive the amounts determined by the reckoning. And whoever withholds money that should be paid in wergeld or demands a larger fine than is owing him and gets into difficulties on that account shall be called a pledge breaker.

319. HOW THE THREE MARKS GOLD SHALL BE DIVIDED

When the award for the life that was taken away is three marks gold, the money shall be paid to the son of the slain man who is the [proper] person to receive the fine; and all the baugar and the fines, both greater and lesser, are included in the three marks gold. Now the son of the slain man [shall receive] six marks, weighed, and the brother of the deceased shall receive three marks, weighed. His paternal uncle, if he is living, [shall receive] two marks weighed, and four ertogs. If the paternal uncle has passed away but his sons, cousins of the slain man, survive, they shall have eleven oras less one ertog. If a paternal uncle is living but has no children, he shall receive seven oras, weighed, less one ertog. If he has daughters but no sons and they are less than forty [years old] when the wergeld is paid, the paternal uncle shall receive one-half mark in behalf of his daughters' sons. If he has no children except a son by a free-born concubine, he [this son] shall receive the one-half mark which the sons of daughters would [normally] receive. But if all these classes are present, daughters' sons of legitimate birth, sons of legitimate birth, and a son by a free-born concubine, the son of the concubine shall be counted with his brothers in the matter of the man money and in addition to their shares in the fines there shall be paid to him seven ertogs, weighed. If they die and leave no children these seven ertogs shall revert to the one who receives the wergeld. If the slain man's father is living and his son receives the wergeld, he [the father] shall have twelve oras weighed; but if he is not living, this fine shall revert to the one who receives the wergeld. If there is a uterine paternal uncle and a uterine brother, the uterine brother shall receive six oras and the uterine paternal uncle three oras. If neither of these can be found or if one of them is wanting, his [or their] share in the fine shall revert to the one who receives the wergeld. And the total amount that these men receive is thirteen and one-half marks and one ora. If the man who was put to death had a stepson or a stepfather, the one who receives the wergeld shall pay out of the total just given, six oras, weighed, to each one of them. If there are brothers-in-law, each one having the other's sister, the one who receives the wergeld shall pay them six oras; but if their kinship rests on one marriage only, the payment shall be three oras. If the deceased is survived by his maternal grandfather and his daughter's son, they shall receive from the wergeld fifteen oras, weighed, out of the wergeld, or seven and one-half oras each; but if one of them is wanting, or if both [are wanting], this fine shall revert to the one who receives the wergeld. If the slain man is survived by a maternal uncle and a sister's son, they shall receive six oras each. If the deceased is survived by a paternal uncle and by the son of a paternal uncle's son, they shall receive eleven oras, five and one-half oras each. But if one is wanting, or if both [are wanting], this fine shall revert to the one who receives the wergeld. If the deceased is survived by a paternal aunt and she has sons, they shall receive five oras less one ertog. If the deceased is survived by a maternal uncle and he has sons, these sons shall receive thirteen ertogs; and the sons of his sisters [shall receive] one-half mark. If the deceased is survived by a son of his brother's daughter, he shall receive six and one-half oras; and those who are nearest in kinship after the [slain man's] brothers' sons shall also receive six and one-half oras. If the slain man is survived by women who are the children of his brothers and they have sons, these sons shall receive nine and one-half ertogs. But if the women who survive the deceased are the children of brothers and sisters and they have sons, these sons shall receive two and one-half oras. And the men who are in the fourth degree of kinship on the masculine side and those who are in the third [degree] on the feminine side, when one counts from brother and sisters, shall receive eight ertogs each. In the fifth degree on the masculine side and in the fourth [degree] on the feminine side, each shall receive five ertogs. In the sixth degree on the masculine side and in the fifth [degree] on the feminine side, each shall receive one ora, and in the sixth degree on the feminine side, [each shall receive] two ertogs. Such a sum shall each one receive from the one [who is] in the same degree of kinship [to the slayer] and shall pay in the same way to the one in the same degree of kinship [to the slain man]. Whenever money is paid to the father, it is also paid to his son; but the paternal uncle of the slain man and his sons and their sons shall each receive his own fine; and in the same way the paternal uncles of the slayer and their sons shall pay with him such amounts as are received by those [who are] in the same degree of kinship to the slain man. But if the paternal uncle has passed away, his sons shall receive a single fine and shall pay in the same way. And if the one who should receive or pay the wergeld has daughters who survive him and they have sons, these sons shall pay or receive the amounts that are determined by the reckoning. And whoever withholds money that should be paid in wergeld or demands a larger fine than is owing him and gets into difficulties on that account shall be called a pledge breaker.

320. . . . FORM OF PEACE PLEDGE[6]

N. and N. were opponents in a lawsuit. Now that lawsuit has been terminated and compensation has been paid to the full amount into the hands of him who should have it, just as the doomsmen deemed it, the appraiser appraised it, the assessor assessed it, and the careful observer [thought] . . . .

[6] Inasmuch as this fragment is identical with the corresponding part of the peace pledge that had legal sanction in Iceland, it is believed that the terms and provisions of the two formulas were identical throughout. For a Norwegian version of the Icelandic peace pledge see Hertzberg, *Den ældste norske proces*, pp. 108–9. The translation is from Finsen's edition of the *Grágás*, cc. 114–15.

THE OLDER LAW OF THE FROSTATHING

NOREGR
FROSTATHINGLAW
Boundaries
Shires (Fylkir)
Jurisdictions (Lǫg)
Sandnes
Alost
Þjótta
Torgar
Leka
Njarðey
Byrða
Austrått
Rein
Agðir
Hitra
Nidaros
Solskel
Fræði
Stimr
Steinker
Stiklastaðir
Meðalhus
Selasjór
Lesjar
Bóreund
HÁLEYJA HALFFYLKI
NAUMDŒLAFYLKI
SPARBYGGJAFYLKI
VERDŒLAFYLKI
JAMTALAND
NORDMŒRAFYLKI
ORKDŒLAFYLKI
GAULDŒLAFYLKI
RAUMSDŒLAFYLKI
SUNNMŒRAFYLKI
HERJARDALR
EYSTRADALIR
GUDBRANDSDALIR

HERE BEGIN AND ARE SET FORTH THE LAWS THAT WERE ESTABLISHED BY HAKON THE KING, SON OF KING HAKON

[INTRODUCTION][1]

1. [CONCERNING MANSLAYING]

Hakon the king,[2] son of King Hakon and grandson of King Sverri, sends the greetings of God and his own [greetings] to clerks and barons, freemen and farmers, those now living and those to come, and to all God's friends and his own who now dwell in Norway. It must be quite generally known what great and manifold injuries have been suffered by the kindreds of most men in the realm through manslaying and the putting to death of the best men, which [evil] custom has been more prevalent here than in most other lands. And, whereas these doings are first of all doubtful and dangerous in the sight of God and to men a destruction of kinsmen and a loss of wealth, it is, moreover, disgraceful that it shall be told in those lands which have good customs that men practice such evil behavior more widely here than in any other land. Therefore, on the advice of the bishops and the archbishops, clerks and barons, lawmen and others of the most discreet men in the land, we have taken thought as to how [the frequency] of manslaying may be reduced. It seems to us most reasonable, to begin with, that the law of the holy King Olaf should be kept [exactly] as he established it, though men impelled by avarice have not hitherto complied with it, [namely], that whoever kills a man without cause shall have forfeited peace and property, and that wherever he is found he shall be deemed an outlaw for whom no atonement can be acceptable either to king or to kinsmen.

[1] Chapters 1 to 21 are new laws accepted by a council of the realm held in 1260.

[2] Hakon IV Hakonsson was king, 1217–63.

2. CONCERNING MANSLAYING

Although we might in all fairness award to the kingship all the movables belonging to a manslayer, as the book of the Frostathing testifies, we have tempered the laws with mercy, so that from whatever he leaves behind, either in movables or in landed property, the king shall take as thegn money[3] no more than was the custom of old, either of the movables or of the land. And if land is paid as thegn money, the kinsmen shall have the right to redeem it, if they wish to have it redeemed.

3. CONCERNING THE OUTLAWING OF A MANSLAYER

If a slayer who has been outlawed falls before the sword of the king or that of the slain man's kinsmen and leaves property behind, his kinsmen shall pay one-fourth of the wergeld out of that property, and let them in return receive pledges of peace and complete satisfaction from the kinsmen of the slain [man].

4. OUTLAWRY

If a slayer is in[4] Norway, his kinsmen shall pay one-fourth of the wergeld, and those who are nearest of kin, one on the father's side and one on the mother's, shall have charge, both when atonements are to be received from the kinsmen of the slayer and when atonements are to be paid to the kinsmen of the slain [man]. And if a banesman escapes while in the state of outlawry, his kinsmen shall pay half the wergeld according to the earlier schedule, if his property proves insufficient. An heir shall never sell the possessions which he inherits from an outlaw while the outlaw is still living. But let him pay all the lawful debts out of the landed property, if there are no movables.

5. CONCERNING OUTLAWRY

Now, it may come to pass that the king will give an outlaw permission to remain in the land on the request of important men or because of some other circumstance. In such a case he shall buy his peace from the king [on such terms] as the king's mercy may

[3] *Þegngildi:* a fine due the king when a subject was slain; it was due even if the slayer was outlawed.

[4] The text reads "outside Norway."

allow, and he shall pay that half [of the atonement] which remains unpaid and [shall pay it] in such installments as, in the opinion of discreet men, he is able [to meet]. But if he refuses to make atonement, the kinsmen of the slain man may take revenge upon him, even though he be at peace with the king, and they shall not incur outlawry, even though they kill him. And let those who had his property in their care while he was in outlawry restore to him what they took over both in land and in movables less the rent from the land.

6. IF A MAN WOUNDS ANOTHER

If a man wounds another without cause or does him an injury so serious that a full atonement must be forthcoming and revenge is taken by the injured men or his kinsmen before he [the offender] can offer a legal atonement with adequate security, he shall, as the one who first broke the peace, be deemed an outlaw, whether he be slain or [merely] injured, unless the king and other prudent men shall seem to find special circumstances in the case. But if he comes with an offer of atonement with adequate security, his life shall be inviolable, and whoever kills him after that shall be outlawed. And if a man who at one time did [an injury] to an innocent man comes to a settlement with him and then does such a deed a second time, trusting to his wealth or his kinsmen, and comes again to offer atonement, let him who was illtreated this second time accept the atonement, only if he is so inclined; and he shall remain in the king's peace and safe from outlawry, even though he takes revenge and whether the offender lives or dies. But all other deeds that lead to permanent outlawry shall be dealt with as the laws have decreed of old.

7. IF A MAN COMES UPON ANOTHER MAN

If a man comes upon another man while he is [in carnal union] with one of those seven women on whose account the law provides that one may take life without incurring guilt, let their case go forward as the law book directs. And if a man dishonors any one of these women and an action is brought against him and he refuses to make a defense, there shall be no outlawry, even if the injured man takes revenge for the dishonor. Now we have added these rules in [the matter of] manslaying and personal security, and they shall stand as long as they seem to us to be in accord with the counsel of our most judicious men and of those who may come after us.

8. CONCERNING THE KILLING OF MEN

It must be known to all men that a widespread and sinister custom has long persisted in this land, namely, that when a man is slain, the kinsmen of the dead prefer to remove from the slayer's kindred the one who is the most capable, though he was neither present at, nor consented to, nor had knowledge of the removal of the dead man, but they do not care to take revenge on the slayer, though they have that right. Thus the wicked one derives benefit from his base and baleful disposition, while the other man suffers innocently for his peaceful and manly behavior. And many a man has suffered great losses in his kindred by such doing and we have lost [some of] our best thegns in the realm. And for this reason we order the penalties of irrevocable outlawry and confiscation whenever anyone takes revenge on any other man than the one who committed or plotted the crime.

9. CONCERNING STOLEN PROPERTY

All the law books and the law of the land agree in this that whoever takes with thieving hands a cow or anything else that belongs to another man may be striken down and killed wherever one comes upon him.

10. CONCERNING [ADULTERERS]

It has also frequently occurred, though it is neither good nor decent, that wicked men have run away with the wives of other men; and many have atoned very little for that and some not at all. And inasmuch as we assume that discreet men will regard these matters as more important both before God and men than [many] other [crimes], it is our will that all men shall know that those who are convicted of such misdeeds shall be regarded as forever outside the law both in the sight of king and subject; [they may] be stricken down and slain wherever they are found, and [they shall] not be buried at church.

11. IF A MAN [HAS CARNAL DEALINGS WITH A BEAST]

If a man has carnal dealings with a farm beast and thus destroys his rights as a Christian, he shall be castrated, if the charge is proved, and after that let him go into outlawry.

12. CONCERNING OUTLAWS WHO HAVE BEEN HID IN THE SETTLEMENT

It has also frequently happened that outlawed men have come into a neighborhood to seek plunder, and that the freemen have paid fines to our officials for having given the outlaws house and shelter. This has been a source of income to the officials but a loss of money to the freemen; while those others who had done deeds worthy of punishment have escaped without chastisement. Therefore, it is our will that henceforth it shall be the duty of the king's officials with the help of the freemen to chastise those who commit such evil deeds as have just been described, not less than those who have been dealt with earlier in the laws. And every one, bailiff or other official, who persists in such trickery as has been specified, and will not punish evildoers, though able to do so, shall by that fact be deprived of the dignity that he holds from us; and shall, moreover, if he is a king's official, pay a fine of twelve marks, valued in burned silver. And the bailiff shall suffer in the same way, if he fails to punish; and the king shall have one-half [of the fine] and the freemen one-half.

13. CONCERNING FALSE OATHS

Men who swear false oaths, if the charge is proved against them beyond a doubt, shall not have the benefit of the oath or the testimony of any man, and none of them . . . [5]

14.

. . . that they know of a truth that it was unlawfully seized; but other and older [dues] remain as the book testifies.

15. IF A MAN OWES ANOTHER A DEBT

If a man has a debt owing him from another, let him demand the payment before witnesses and ask him to set a day [on which] to make payment. If he refuses, let him [the creditor] summon him before a thing, whether he is in the thing district or not,[6]

[5] The manuscripts are defective at this point; a page seems to be missing.

[6] See *Norges gamle love*, I, 124, n. 3.

and [let him have] a five-night warning. And let both bring forward their witnesses there at the thing. If the freemen award the man his money, it is their duty to go with him to collect the debt, unless he [the debtor] is able to provide a pledge with adequate security that payment will be made on a specified day. Let them go from the thing and take double the debt; and the suit shall not be taken from this thing to another.

16. CONCERNING PROPERTY IN LAND

In all [cases that involve] property in land or rents from land which men take to a five-day moot, the plaintiff shall call in two witnesses and then appoint the moot; and [the defendant] shall not be able to balk the moot. And if he does [try to] balk it, he shall pay twelve oras valued in burned silver; and the king shall have one-half of it and the plaintiff one-half. The witnesses shall testify in this wise: laying their hands on the [Gospel] book, [they shall] call God to witness that they were present when the moot was appointed; and [they shall] swear to nothing else. But if the doomsmen divide and cannot reach an agreement, let the one who is in error pay twelve oras valued in burned silver, unless he shall declare upon oath that he had before God no better knowledge. In every [such] lawsuit there may be one five-day moot but no more. We have frequently heard [it said] that some men, though justly accused, refuse to appear before the lawmen, even when summoned as the law directs; and many refuse to accept the lawman's opinion after he has declared the law. But it was our intention to employ lawmen and to endow them with grants out of our revenue and inheritance [to the end] that every man should be able to bring his suits to a conclusion according to the legislation of the holy King Olaf and the opinion of these lawmen; and therefore we have added a penalty of three marks to be due from every one who, when properly indicted and summoned, refuses to appear before the lawman, and the same from those who refuse to accept the lawman's decision.

17. CONCERNING UNTILLED LAND, IF ONE MOWS OR SOWS IT

With respect to untilled land which a man mows but does not sow, it shall be his duty as owner to forward all summonses and to convey indigent persons [from place to place]. And let the owner arrange [for these duties] with the one who lives nearest the untilled land, [on such terms] as competent men think right. But if the man not only mows, but also sows, the land, he shall [also] make such contribution to the coast defense as competent men shall agree upon at the muster thing.

18. CONCERNING UNTILLED LAND

In the matter of untilled land which men wish to make into a farm, it shall rest with the owner whether to provide the buildings and then rent the land for three winters to [any] one who will bring it into cultivation or to let the tenant have the land for six winters without rent if he puts up the buildings and brings into use the cornland as well as the meadow, unless the parties have agreed upon other terms. And the dues to the coast defense we have remitted for two persons and for so long a time as the farmer has the land without rent.

19. CONCERNING [PARCELS OF] LAND

As to [parcels of] land which are regarded as lying beyond [the limits of] the farm, having been carved out of the common, it is our will that such law and such arrangements shall hold between king and farmer as [prevail] in the southern and eastern parts of the realm, and that the subjects shall be held to such duties as the king has appointed there. It is also ordered that the freemen shall provide the king with riding horses according to his needs. The bailiff shall send out the call for horses, and all the farmers to whom the call comes shall join in providing the king with horses. Every horse that has borne harness or saddle shall go into the transport; and if the king finds the number deficient, they [the farmers] shall pay three oras valued in burned silver for each horse that is lacking.

20. CONCERNING LABOR

We have also been informed that nothing impairs our kingdom more than the fact that laborers are not to be had in the countryside;[7] for all now wish to go about as traders, and nobody cares to work for the farmers. It is our will, therefore, that any man who

[7] Due perhaps to the disappearance of thralldom. See Brandt, *Retshistorie*, I, 77.

has less than three marks worth of goods shall be strictly forbidden to go on a trading journey. This restriction shall remain in force from Easter to Michaelmas every year; but from Michaelmas on and through the winter let every one travel in peace with such [wares] as God has given him, whether they be more or less. And the ship masters who receive on their ships such men as have goods of less value than has just been specified shall pay six oras for every one who joins in trade with him.

21. CONCERNING THE KING'S RIGHTS

The following are cases in which it seems to most men that the kingship has long suffered an injustice; still, the law books testify that the king has no claim to fines [in such suits]. The first is that in which a man [merely] forbids an outlaw to partake of his provisions and thinks that his property is then sacred as against the king. The second is that in which men claim timber axes to be competent [weapons] and will not provide themselves with all the required folk weapons. The third is that in which men share their food with outlaws and refuse to answer [for it] to the king. The fourth is that in which men who have had a fight come to a private settlement so that the king can have no claim. The fifth is that in which a man catches a thief and gets his property back from him; in that case there is no fine to the king either from the thief or from the man who [caught and] released him. There are two other matters which do not concern you husbandmen any less than they concern the kingship: [first], if a summons is not properly delivered the legal decisions of men will fail, because the bailiff will be unable to look into [the case]; and second, that the men of the countryside do not have the right sort of weights and measures. Now we refuse to tolerate these wrongs any longer in any wise; and it is our will that such cases shall be dealt with in the way prescribed by all the law books of the land.

22. CONCERNING THEFT

At the time when these provisions were read and approved at the Eyrathing,[8] we allowed the men of Trondheim the following amendments to the law: namely, that if a man is outlawed for

[8] Chapters 22–24 of this title were published and accepted at the Eyrathing in 1260. See below, p. 224 and note.

thieving, the one from whom the goods were stolen shall claim his property with [the aid of] witnesses, and after that he shall take atonement according to his rank out of the thief's belongings, if any such remain.

23. CONCERNING ROBBERY

If a man robs another of his goods or his catch, let the one who was robbed take his property with [the aid of] witnesses and [let him take in addition] as much in expense money as his journey costs him and twelve oras as compensation for injury; and the king shall have a robber fine [of] such [amount] as is specified elsewhere in the laws. And it is our will that the freemen shall sue to enforce our rights as well as their own, either at the shire thing or at the thing held in the ship district, as seem most convenient.

24. CONCERNING WOMEN

If a women suffers a blow for no cause, an atonement shall be due both to the king and to her husband. The bailiff, too, shall have his compensation according to his rank.

25. HERE THE BOOK OF THE FROSTATHING BEGINS, AND IT IS TOLD HERE INTO HOW MANY PARTS THE BOOK IS DIVIDED

This book, in which the laws of the Frostathing are set forth, we have divided into sixteen parts, each part containing those laws which have some relationship to each other, so far as this plan has been feasible, since we also had to guard lest we should disturb the old plan according to which the book of the Frostathing had been arranged. And for [this reason] we have divided the book into several parts and have distinguished between the parts so far as possible on the basis of subject matter, that it might be easier for those to find what they want who have no earlier acquaintance with the plan of the book and do not know where each subject should be sought. But now there are headings at the beginning which indicate where the part dealing with each subject is to be found.[9] After that the laws as they follow each other show in their chapter headings what the subject and the order are in every part; This is found in the beginning as is shown here in chapter. . . .[10]

[9] This seems to refer to tables of contents at the beginning of each section; these have been omitted in this translation.

[10] A sheet is missing at this point.

I. [THE FROSTATHING]

1. CONCERNING ATTENDANCE AT THE THING

. . . [1] If any one neglects this, let him pay as large a part of two marks as the reckoning indicates. And the expense money for the journey to the thing shall be brought to the [man's] home three nights before [the day when] he is to set out on the journey. This applies to the region about the Fjord;[2] but beyond the mouth of the Fjord the one who is to make the journey shall decide [as to the time of delivery]. He who is to go shall pay nothing out of his own; he shall only make the journey. And let him who is to attend go forth with witnesses to inform the bailiff and to request the payment of his travel expenses. Now it is ordained that if the bailiff pays him the fee for attending the thing he shall collect fines from those who neglect to contribute, such as the law provides; the bailiff shall have one-half and the lawmen, all the shiremen,[3] one-half. Now if the bailiff fails to give the man the money, as the law provides, let him make the journey all the same. And the bailiff shall collect the fines and keep one-half and give one-half to the one who makes the journey. The bailiff shall give no one permission to remain at home who has been appointed to attend the Frostathing; even if he does give [permission], the man shall owe a fine all the same; but the bailiff has no [right to bring] action against one whom he has allowed to remain at home. But the freemen who go to the thing have the right to take action against them, and let them bring it up at the next thing; and let them demand that they [the wrongdoers] accept the obligation of payment. But if these refuse to accept the obligation, let them be summoned at that thing to another thing. If they still refuse to pay, the freemen shall go upon them and take a double [payment]. And whoever does not

[1] Three words are left untranslated, as the sentence is incomplete.

[2] The Trondheim Fjord.

[3] Taranger seems to hold that the fine was originally paid to the shiremen and that the law was later amended in the interest of the lawmen. *Trondheimens forfatningshistorie*, p. 17.

join in this distraint shall owe a fine of six oras to the king. If the bailiff remains at home without good cause, he shall pay a mark in current coin to the freemen who attended the thing; and the same [shall be due] from those who were appointed to attend the thing but remained at home.

2. CONCERNING THE ENCLOSURE THAT THE BAILIFFS SET UP

It is old law that a bailiff from each of the various shires shall set up an enclosure[4] here at the thingstead. And the enclosure shall have sufficient space so that all who are appointed to the law court shall have ample room to sit within it. The bailiffs shall appoint to the law court as many from each fylki as is stated [below]. From Inner Trondheim forty men shall be named from each fylki and from Outer Trondheim[5] sixty men from each fylki; and the men who are appointed to the law court shall be those who are oldest and most capable. No baron shall appear in the law court, unless the freemen give him permission to do so. It is further enacted that no man who is not appointed to the law court shall have a seat within the enclosure on pain of a fine of one mark. All those who are appointed to the law court shall sit in it as long as men wish the thing to remain [in session], except that one may leave for private needs; but if a man leaves the law court and goes elsewhere outside the enclosure, he shall be fined a mark in current coin. The men who are appointed to the law court shall declare the law in such cases as are brought to this thing and properly referred to it according to what is told in the law book; also in such cases as men agree with the handclasp in the presence of two witnesses [to refer to the law thing], and if these witnesses are produced. And in all cases that are not clearly determined by the law book, that is to be followed which the men of the law court are unanimously agreed upon and which seems most equitable before God.

3. MORE CONCERNING DECENT BEHAVIOR AT THE FROSTATHING

It is the counsel and the command of Archbishop Eystein,[6] to which the most discreet men have agreed, that all shall go fasting to the thing and shall appear at the thing when the sun is due east[7]

[4] *Vébǫnd:* sacred enclosure.
[5] See below, p. 279, note.
[6] See above, p. 35, note 2.
[7] About 6 A.M.

and shall remain at the thing till noon.[8] And the priest whose duty it is to interpret the law book shall have the great bell rung when he is about to go to the thingstead with the book; and while the thing remains in session that bell shall be rung for no other purpose. But if any one fills up with food or ale and thinks more of that than of the thing, he shall have no hearing for any of his complaints that year, whatever the case may be that he has to present at the Frostathing. Ale shall not be brought to the thing either to be sold or otherwise [disposed of]; but if ale is brought, it may be seized and shall belong to the thingmen.

4. CONCERNING THE EYRATHING[9]

Men from the eight shires shall [have the right to] hold the Eyrathing every twelvemonth a fortnight before Saint John's Day.[10] The bailiff in each fylki shall send forth the token for the summons and every freeman who has help with his farm work shall attend the thing; but whoever fails to attend shall pay a fine of one mark of full weight. And all the freemen shall be obliged to attend this thing, even if the bailiff neglects [the summons]. But the bailiff shall not be allowed to sue for that fine, if he has neglected to send forth the token.

5. CONCERNING PEACE AT THE FROSTATHING

Now it shall be told what peace those men shall enjoy who are chosen to attend the Frostathing. Those who are appointed [to attend] and all others who go to attend the thing shall be in each other's peace while on the journey to the Frostathing and until they have returned to their homes. And if any one shall violate this peace, he has forfeited his land, his chattels, and his right to peace among men; and let him never return to the kingdom.

6. OUR LAND SHALL BE BUILT UP BY LAW

Our land shall be built up by law, and let it not be laid waste by lawless behavior. And whoever will not allow another his legal rights shall not enjoy law.

[8] About 3 P.M.

[9] The Eyrathing was a court for the Trondheim area. It met on the sands near Trondheim at the mouth of the Nid River; it had the privilege of proclaiming a new sovereign. See above, pp. 9–10.

[10] June 10 or a few days later.

II. [THE CHURCH LAW][1]

1. EVERY CHILD THAT IS BORN SHALL BE BROUGHT UP AND CHRISTENED

This is the first command in our lawmaking that we shall be obedient to the faith and the church of Christ and to the king and the bishop, and that we shall live according to law and right behavior and the correct rules of the church. It is Christian law that every child that is born shall be nourished, brought to church, and baptized, if it has the head of a human being.[2] Every child has [a right to] a father. He whom the mother points out shall be [regarded as] the child's father, whether it is the child of a free woman or a bondwoman, unless his innocence shall be proved at the first doom to which he is summoned. But if the woman dies without having pointed out the father of her child, let him who has the right to atonement in her case take action both to secure his own atonement and to [force the accused] to acknowledge the child. And let the accused defend himself with his oath. If the woman assigns the fatherhood to one who is dead, let her prove [the charge] by the ordeal; [let her do] the same if she accuses a man who is outside the kingdom. If she succeeds at the ordeal, let the man's heir accept the child; but if she is [seriously] injured, let the child be her own care. If the woman who charges a dead man with fatherhood is also dead, the heir of the dead man has a choice of three [courses: he may] accept the child, or disprove the charge with the [hot] iron, or deny it with a threefold oath. If the woman refuses to name the father, let the king's bailiff summon her to a thing; and unless she names the father, let it be published that she has had a child by a thrall. A well-born woman shall owe the king a fine of three marks silver in such a case and the child shall go with

[1] The church law of this code (titles ii, iii) is based on Archbishop Eystein's church law, the so-called *Gullfjǫðr* (Gold Feather), a revision of the older laws in the direction of greater freedom for the church.

[2] Cf. *Gul.*, c. 21.

the mother. And if a woman gets no father for her child, it shall have such personal rights as his mother's father had.

2. CONCERNING THE EXPOSING OF A CHILD

If a man exposes his child, let him confess and do penance and pay a fine of three marks to the bishop. But if the man denies that the child was exposed, claiming that it was still-born, the woman who assisted [at the birth] shall testify; she must be a free woman, and if she [the mother] were alone [at the time of birth] she shall offer her own oath. But if the child was exposed on the householder's command, let him pay three marks to the bishop. If he denies the charge, he shall take an oath that it was not exposed on his orders; and let him pay six oras, if it was carried out by any one for whom he has to answer with pledge and promise; [if it is] otherwise he is free from guilt. If a thrall throws out his child on his own motion, let him pay six oras to the bishop or [let him] be flogged. And the bishop's bailiff shall find a man to flog him, unless his master is willing to redeem his skin with six oras. If a woman who goes [begging] from house to house dies and leaves a child, the householder shall take the child to church and have it baptized; and he shall offer it to anyone who is willing to bring it up in thanks to God. But if no one is willing to take it and have it as a thrall, let the householder take it home and keep it the following month; thereafter, the men of the fylki shall all join in having it brought up in thanks to God. And let the householder carry it to the nearest farm, bringing also the cup [from which it was fed]; and even if this farmer refuses to receive the child, he becomes responsible for it; and the one who brings it may lay it down with impunity, if there are witnesses present.

3. CONCERNING THE BAPTISM OF A CHILD

Archbishop Jon[3] has promised and ordained this, that if it shall happen that a woman is delivered of a child while all alone and the child is too weak to be brought to a priest and no man is near enough to give assistance in baptizing the child, the mother shall baptize it herself rather than let it die unbaptized. And she shall baptize it in water if there is water at hand; but if there is no water,

[3] Jón Birgisson, the first archbishop of Nidaros, was elected in 1152.

let her dip it three times in dew or snow or sea water. But if these are not available, let her take spittle and make the sign of the cross with it on the [child's] breast and shoulders, [at the same time] speaking the words that are ordered: I baptize thee in the name of the Father and of the Son and of the Holy Ghost; and let her give [the child] a name. The child may then be laid in hallowed earth and the woman may possess her husband as before.[4] A father, too, shall baptize his child rather than let it die unbaptized, and may possess his wife none the less. But if the child gains the necessary strength, let it be brought as soon as can be to a priest; and he shall anoint it with the chrism, using the words and the rite that belong to baptism. And if the priest doubts that the child has been baptized, let him who performed the baptism, or some one who was present, prove it with his own oath.

4. CONCERNING THE DUTY TO SHUN HEATHEN MEN

The next is this, that every man in the king's dominions must be a Christian. One may shelter a heathen man over night, if he is traveling toward a church where there is a priest; but if he comes from a church where there is a priest and he is still unbaptized, he must not be entertained. Let him keep to himself in his own booth and transact his business and leave the land as quickly as he can.

5. WHEN CHILDREN SHALL BE BAPTIZED AND IF ONE KEEPS AN UNBAPTIZED CHILD TWELVE MONTHS

Every child that is born between Michaelmas and Christmas shall be baptized before Christmas; and whoever has an unbaptized child in his house on Christmas night shall pay six oras to the bishop. All the children that are born between Christmas and Lent shall be baptized before Lent, or [the father] shall pay six oras to the bishop. Those that are born between Lent and midsummer shall all be baptized before midsummer, or [the father] shall pay six oras to the bishop. [Those that are born] between midsummer and Michaelmas shall be baptized before Michaelmas or [the father] shall pay six oras to the bishop. If a man harbors an unbaptized person for a twelvemonth, the bishop shall have every

[4] That is, the act of baptism in this case does not create any form of spiritual kinship. See *Gul.*, c. 26; *Frost.*, III, c. 8.

ora that the man possesses, but the wife shall keep what is hers. And both husband and wife shall go to confession and do penance. If there is fear of death, a child shall have baptism at once. If [a child] is not baptized as provided above, the householder who has it in his house shall owe a fine of six oras to the bishop, except in the case only that he is expecting the king, the bishop, or the jarl to come [to serve] as godfather, in which case he shall have the child marked with the cross; then let the matter rest for a twelvemonth. And every man in this country who remains a heathen but conceals the fact, has forfeited his right to peace among men and his chattels to the bishop as soon as the fact comes to light.

6. CONCERNING THE CHILD OF A BONDWOMAN

Every child of a bondwoman that is not acknowledged by the father shall be cared for by the woman's master till the father shall own it. And the child shall not be allowed to die [in passing] from hand to hand; but if it [is allowed to] die, let the master pay three marks [to the bishop].

7. CONCERNING THE BUILDING OF A SHIRE CHURCH

It shall be the duty of all the freemen of the fylki to build a church for the fylki and to have it completed within a twelvemonth; otherwise they shall pay fifteen marks to the bishop, if it is [to be] built of wood. But if the men wish to build the church of stone and some are unwilling and there is disagreement, the decision shall rest with those who are of the better will and a more knowing mind. If the men neglect to build [their stone church], the fine is the same as for neglecting to build a wooden church. If the men of a quarter or of a riding[5] neglect this, they shall pay such a part of fifteen marks as their number indicates. If the men who are charged with this duty neglect it, they shall pay six oras. Though only one piece of timber is lacking, the man whose duty it is to provide it shall be held for six oras; and [it shall be] the same for every load that is wanting, if the church is being built of stone; and let the stone be brought none the less. The shiremen shall all join in maintaining the fence about the church or pay a

[5] *Þriðjungr:* a third; in this case a third of a shire. Cf. the ridings of Yorkshire.

fine of three marks; [if one] neglects his whole duty, the fine is six oras, and one ora for each piece of timber that is wanting; and let it be furnished none the less. If the church is newly built and the duty to maintain it is neglected, or if one man neglects it, the fine is three oras. And thereafter the freemen shall cover the church thoroughly with tar every third winter.

8. CONCERNING THE CONSECRATION OF CHURCHES AND THE BUYING OF BELLS

The man who arranges for the consecration of a church shall provide suitable entertainment for the bishop; and the one who requests the [consecration] shall provide twelve candles and twelve ells of long linen cloth or wadmal [for the church]. The men of the fylki shall all join in buying a bell for the church at [a cost of] twelve oras; and if it is not purchased within a twelvemonth, they shall owe a fine of three marks to the bishop. But if they fail in this duty, every man who neglects it, shall pay three oras to the bishop.

9. WHAT CAN UNDO THE CONSECRATION OF A CHURCH

According to the laws of God a church retains its consecration as long as the altar stones are undisturbed and [the altar] itself remains unshaken; but [if a church is rebuilt], having been damaged by fire, the bishop shall sprinkle holy water on the new walls.

10. CONCERNING THE PEACE OF THE CHURCH

If a man strikes another with hostile intent, whatever it be that he strikes him with, or wounds him or kills him in Christ Church or in Saint Mary's Church, or in their [common] churchyard,[6] he who caused the strife has forfeited his peace and his property, his land and his chattels; and the property shall belong one-half to the holy King Olaf and one-half to the earthly king. And the one who was bruised or wounded shall first take his atonement out of that property, and [let him take] the double of what he would

[6] Archbishop Eystein (1161–88) began the building (or rebuilding) of Christ Church in Nidaros (Trondheim) toward the close of his pontificate. The high altar was placed over Saint Olaf's grave and the relics of the great king were translated to the new cathedral. An older church, Saint Mary's, occupied a part of the cathedral grounds but was moved away about 1178.

have taken in any other place. And wherever men are all pledged to keep the peace, the one who violates this peace shall pay a fine of forty marks silver to the king, and the atonement of those who suffer thereby shall be raised to the double, whether they suffer blows or wounds. The special peace that men have agreed to respect in the borough at Saint Olaf's Mass shall hold till [Saint] Lawrence's Day; and all private arrangements as to peace [and security] shall conform to the provisions of the law book. If a man commits the same [sort of evil] deed in a shire church or in the churchyard with hostile intent, he shall pay fifteen marks silver, one-half to the church and one-half to the bishop; and he shall never return to the land until he has atoned to the church. If such a deed is done in a private chapel or in a churchyard with hostile intent, let [the offender] pay seven and one-half marks, valued in burned silver, one-half to the church and one-half to the bishop, and [he shall] never return to the land until he has atoned to the church. This shall be [the rule] wherever the peace of the church is violated. If one strikes with hostile hands inside a church, the consecration is nullified, even though no blood is shed; on the other hand, bloodshed without hostile intent does not impair the consecration. The goods of the one who caused the strife shall be used in reconsecration before [any of] it shall pass to the king's or the bishop's garth. If a man leaps toward another in a threatening manner or wounds him with a weapon of a sort that one is forbidden to bear in church or churchyard, or strikes him dead, and is himself slain [in the fight], there shall be no atonement due in such a case for him or for his wounds, either to the king or to his kinsmen, even though he be slain, nor [shall he] be buried in the churchyard. And the same is enacted concerning those who support him with their weapons and come out with injuries. And if they are buried [in a churchyard] contrary to the wishes of those in charge, that church shall stand without services until the parish men shall have moved the bodies away. But it is further enacted that if this man had formerly been a decidedly peace-loving man and his kinsmen offer to honor the church where the peace was broken either with money from the wergeld, if such is [awarded], or [with gifts] from the property of the deceased, it shall be as the bishop thinks best.

11. THAT THE BISHOP SHALL GOVERN THE CHURCHES AND RULE IN MATTERS OF RELIGION

The bishop shall govern the churches and rule in all matters of religion. He shall appoint as priests whomever he will, but he has promised that we shall have such priests as are agreeable to us and [who] know the ritual correctly. That is old law.

12. CONCERNING THE BURNING OF A CHURCH

If a shire church or any other church shall burn down through the carelessness of the priest or his assistants, the priest shall have timbers hauled to the site for a church as good as the other. But if another man brings fire to the church, having no duty to bring it, he becomes responsible for the church and for all that is within it. But for all fire that is brought [to the church] on the orders of a priest, he becomes responsible, as if he had brought it himself.

13. IF A MAN REFUSES TO REBUILD A PRIVATE CHAPEL

If a man has his own private chapel and it falls down and lies [in ruins] for a twelvemonth, he shall pay three marks to the bishop. If it lies another twelvemonth and again a third, he shall once more pay three marks to the bishop [for each twelvemonth]; but after that he shall not pay. He shall build a fence around [the site], but he shall pay no more than nine marks to the bishop.

14. CONCERNING THE DUTIES OF A SHIRE PRIEST TO HIS PARISHIONERS

The shire priest or some one acting for him shall remain at home to render such services as men may need. But if he leaves without good cause and a man comes bringing the body of a near kinsman, or [comes] because he has some other great need and fails to find the priest at home, the priest has forfeited for that twelvemonth his income from the sixth or the eighth [of the fylki] where the man resides. Every priest shall carry with him the chrism and whatever else may be needed, if there are children to be baptized where his travels take him. But if he does not have [these things] and he is asked to baptize a child and the child dies unbaptized, he shall pay six oras to the child's father and three marks to the bishop.

15. CONCERNING INTERMENT AND BRINGING THE BODY TO THE CHURCH

Every Christian shall be buried at the church and his body must normally be brought to the church within five nights, unless he was by intent his own banesman or had cast aside his Christian faith while he was still living; but if he lost his life through negligence, he shall be buried at the church. If he is not buried at the church as the law demands, there shall be a fine of six oras to the bishop, and the body shall be brought to the church all the same. If a man wishes to convey a corpse out of his keeping but does not have sufficient help in his own house, let him call upon his nearest neighbors till he is one of five; but he shall make use of such capable men as he has at home before calling upon the others; and [he shall] find provisions for all. And whoever was chosen [but did not come] shall pay three oras, if he was properly summoned. If he denies [having received] the summons, his own oath shall suffice, unless the other can produce witnesses. If a pregnant woman dies, she shall be buried in the churchyard like any other person, but [the womb] shall not be opened or [the child] removed.

16. CONCERNING CORPSES THAT ARE FOUND AND [THE BODIES OF] BEGGARMEN

All corpses that are found and the bodies of beggarmen shall be taken to the nearest church that has a graveyard. But if the priest refuses [burial in] the churchyard or the patron [refuses the use of] the church, let him [who brings the body] declare the facts before two witnesses and convey the responsibility to them who refused [access to] the churchyard; and if the witnesses are sufficient, the man has no further duties in this case. And let him who forbade [the burial] take the corpse to the shire church, if he does not want it in his own; and he shall have the same duties [toward it] as the man had who brought it first.

17. CONCERNING UNCTION

If a man is in need of unction and the shire priest is unable to come, let the patron of the parish anoint the sick man with the aid of the priest's assistant, if no other help is available, or even without assistance rather than have the man die without unction. And if the sick man promises in the presence of his private chaplain to pay the greater tithe and the chaplain is with the shire priest at the unction, he [the chaplain] shall have one-third of the priest's share in this and the priest two-thirds. But if he is alone at the anointing, the shire priest not being present, let each of the two have one-half. And this rule is properly applied in cases where the priest's share would all go to the shire priest; in other cases the division shall be made according to circumstances. And the unction shall be without price in any other respect.

18. CONCERNING THE PAYMENT OF TITHES

Men have promised this to God, that they will give a tenth of all their crops and of all their rightful increase once every twelvemonth, [taking the tithe] out of the stack and making another stack. And if one fails to take the tithe from [the stack], he shall pay three oras valued in burned silver to the bishop and pay two bushels in each [of the four] tithe-lots,[7] as the tithe of the grain harvested from ten såld of seed grain, or let him pay what he prefers and defend [the payment] with his oath. If a tithe is demanded of a man and he fails to pay, he shall owe a fine of three marks the first year and a similar amount the second and the third year; but the fourth year he shall forfeit his right to peace and security, and his goods [shall go] to the bishop, whether he is a householder or a day laborer. Instead of paying a tithe of the increase among the farm animals, men shall make cheese of all the milk that is given on Friday before Saint John's Day; three parts of this shall be given to the church, the priest, and the bishop, and what remains shall be turned over to the poor.

19. CONCERNING THE TITHE OF THE COD FISHERY

For the tithe of the cod fishery one shall go to the drying frames and for that of the grain to the barn, whenever either is [to be] paid out. If a man lets out his land in lots [to several tenants], he shall pay tithe of the undivided increase, and let him have the care of it who occupies the land.

20. CONCERNING THE PETER'S PENCE

Peter's pence shall be paid every twelvemonth, a penny in current coin by every man who is reckoned [as having the value of]

[7] Hertzberg, *Glossarium*, *Såld*.

three marks, weapons and one suit of clothes not counted [in the reckoning]; and both men and women shall pay [this] or render an ora instead of a penny.

21. CONCERNING THE SAINT JOHN'S ALE

It is further enacted that every householder shall give an ale feast at Saint John's Eve, [brewed] from two measures [of malt]. And the archbishop has agreed that men may join together in larger or in smaller numbers as they prefer; but let every one give [a feast] or pay three oras to the bishop, if it is not celebrated before the Yuletide.

22. HOW TO PREPARE AND SEND FORTH THE CROSS[8]

Every priest who has a parish shall prepare a cross and let it go forth before each holy day or fast day and as many nights before as the men of the fylki have agreed upon. And he shall bring actions and receive fines just as the shire priest does. But if he fails to send the cross forth as directed, or if he does it at the wrong time and neglects to inform himself, he shall pay the bishop three oras for every cross that is not properly sent forth. But if he sends it forth correctly and it fails to arrive at the right nightstead, he shall follow it up to learn in whose hands it had stopped and [he shall] summon them to the thing. After that let him go or ride back, taking two witnesses with him and he shall notify them all to come to the thing that the priest shall summon to clear themselves with their oaths or pay the cross fine. But if a man will neither swear nor submit to a fine, the priest shall ask all the freemen to leave the thing with him and go upon that man to take from him a double [fine]; and let the freemen have one-half and the priest three oras. But if the freemen refuse to join in this distraint, each one of them shall owe a fine of three oras.

23. CONCERNING THE CROSS AND THE THING TOKEN

No person younger than twelve winters, whether man or woman, shall carry the cross or the thing token.[9] It shall be given into the hands of the husbandman, if he is willing to receive it; but if he refuses, he [the bearer] shall carry it to the house, set it

[8] Cf. *Gul.*, c. 19.

[9] Cf. *Gul.*, c. 131.

above the door, and go inside to notify the household. Anyone who has been admitted to a family may carry the cross or the token. If a thing token or any other summons is on the highway, the bailiff shall investigate at the first thing [whether it was properly delivered] and shall have sued for the fine before the third thing. Every token that comes to a house shall be carried to the nearest farmstead from which smoke arises, according as the freemen have agreed at the thing. And wherever a man sows and mows his ground and there are houses where men can abide, he shall have all the tokens forwarded. And that shall stand which the freemen and the shiremen shall agree upon at the thing respecting the bearing of summonses. And wherever several men share in cultivating a farm, they shall share in proportion according to their own wishes and agreement and not according to the size of their plots in the duty of forwarding summons and conveying paupers. And in case men divide their lands into two lots, or more than two, and do not themselves provide for the forwarding of summonses, the bailiff shall request the freemen at the thing to arrange for the forwarding. If he does not do this, the one who occupies the land is without guilt. But if there is newly cultivated land within the farm limits, let the owner of the land or his agent ask [the freemen at] the thing to assign the duty of forwarding the token.

24. CONCERNING HOLY DAYS

The festival of the Sunday begins at noon on Saturday and continues till daybreak on Monday. And there are sixteen days in the twelvemonth that shall be kept holy in the same way as Sunday.[10] The first is Candlemas. The second [is] Saint Mary's Day in Lent. The third [is] Holy Cross Day. The fourth [is] Saint Halvard's Day. The fifth [is] Saint John's Day. The sixth [is] Saint Peter's Day. The seventh [is] the Mass-day of the men of Selja. The eighth [is] Saint Olaf's Day. The ninth [is] the later Saint Olaf's Day. The tenth [is] Saint Lawrence's Day. The eleventh [is] Saint Mary's Day. The twelfth [is] the later Saint Mary's Day. The thirteenth [is] Michaelmas. The fourteenth [is] All Saints' Day. The fifteenth [is] Saint Andrew's Day. The sixteenth [is]

[10] See notes, pp. 45–46 (*Gul.*, c. 17).

Saint Nicholas' Day. These sixteen days are of equal rank with Sunday.

25. CONCERNING MASS-DAYS THAT DO NOT BEGIN AT THE PRECEDING NOON

These are the days that are not counted holy from the preceding noon.[11] The first is Saint Paul's Day. The second [is] Saint Matthias' Day. The third [is] Saint Gregory's Day.[12] The fourth [is] Saint Magnus' Day.[13] The fifth [is] the Mass-day of the Two Apostles that comes early in the summer. The sixth is Monday of Whitsun week. The seventh [is] Saint Botholf's Day. The eighth [is] Saint Swithun's Day. The ninth [is] Saint Margaret's Day.[14] The tenth [is] Saint James' Day. The eleventh [is] Saint Bartholomew's Day. The twelfth [is] Holy Cross Day in the autumn. The thirteenth [is] Saint Matthew's Day. The fourteenth [is] the Mass-day of the Two Apostles, Simon and Jude. The fifteenth [is] Martinmas. The sixteenth [is] Saint Clement's Day. The seventeenth [is] Saint Thomas' Day.

26. CONCERNING THE HERRING FISHERY

This is the favor and indulgence that Pope Alexander[15] promised and confirmed with respect to the herring fishery in Norway, namely, that one may fish at any time when the herring seeks the shore except on the days of the highest rank. These are the days that are excepted on the pope's behalf and on which there must be no fishing: the Exaltation of the Holy Cross, Michaelmas Day, All Saints' Day, Saint Andrew's Day, the first four days of the Yuletide, the eighth day of the Yuletide, the thirteenth day of the Yuletide, Annunciation Day, Easter Day, the [festival of the] Invention of the Holy Cross, Holy Thursday, Whitsunday, Saint John's Day, Saint Peter's Day, the earlier Saint Olaf's Day, and the two Mass-days of Saint Mary in the autumn. But both on Sundays and on all other days the herring may be fished for, if God sends it toward the land, and the catch and the nets may be brought to the shore, if they are in danger. But if fishing nets are

[11] See notes, pp. 46–47 (*Gul.*, c. 18).
[12] March 12.
[13] April 16.
[14] July 20.
[15] Alexander III (1159–81).

stretched across quiet creeks, let them remain there till work is permitted.

27. CONCERNING MEN WHO ROW OUT TO FISH

In the case of indigent men who row out to fish there shall be this indulgence, that men, who dwell in houses where there is want and who have fewer farm animals than two dependents can care for, a cow or the worth of a cow, and who, on days when the herring fishing is not allowed, fish for that which they later consume but do not keep or sell, shall suffer no penalty. But if those men fish who have more stock, or if men fish more extensively than is here allowed, they shall pay such fines as the law demands. And every man who fishes for herring with permission on these days shall pay as a tithe a basketful out of every "last,"[16] as has been ordered. And every shipmaster shall receive this and shall divide [it, giving] one-half to the poor and one-half to the church in the parish where the herring were caught; or let him [the fisherman] pay a fine as for any other labor performed on that day. In the intervening days in the Yuletide men may load herring on a ship or unload [a catch] or hang it up, if the poles are in place and other necessary gear. But [on those days] one may not cut poles or shape them or prepare the supports, unless one is willing to risk a fine. Such work shall, however, not be continued later than midday, though one may transport herring all day.

28. IF A MAN IS FOUND AT WORK ON A HOLY DAY

If a man is found at work on any one of those days that are counted holy from the preceding noon or on the preceding eve, he shall pay six oras. Likewise, if a man eats twice on the preceding day when he ought to fast, he shall pay six oras. [The fine is] the same for a bondman who works on his master's orders; but if he works on his own volition, his master shall pay three oras or have the thrall flogged. On the eve of all the other mass-days [one may] labor till night. But if a man works on those mass-days, he shall pay three oras, and there is a like [fine] if a free man eats twice on the day before, when fasting is commanded. And whoever eats

[16] *Lest:* a measure of weight equal to 12 "ship's pounds" or approximately two tons in modern reckoning. Lest is also used generally for a ship's lading.

twice when he ought to fast or does work at holy tide, no cross having come to his farm, may assert in his defense on his own oath that he really did not know that it was a holy day or a fast day; and let him either be held blameless or atone for his offense according to the rank of the day.

29. IF A PRIEST OR A BAILIFF COMES UPON A MAN AT WORK

If a priest or a bailiff claims to have found a man at work on one of those days that are holy, he may refute the charge with his own oath, if he denies it; otherwise he shall pay such a fine as is provided. Every priest shall sue for such fines and shall himself have that for which he sends forth the cross. But if neither priest nor bailiff has seen the man at work, witnesses to the fact of rumor shall be heard in such wise that one shall testify and two shall confirm his testimony, if the case involves three oras. But in cases involving six oras one shall testify and four shall confirm, and they must be men of that fylki. And this shall be the form of the oath: I call God to witness that I have heard this [rumor] and that it has floated about over three homesteads, or more than three; but I do not know whether it is true or not. And if the accused knows that he is lied about, let him make a denial with his own oath.

30. CONCERNING EASTER

On the first day of Easter no one shall do labor. But the bishop has agreed that on Monday men may scrape bark for their live stock and bring it home, if [the trees] have been felled earlier; but they must work no longer than till midday. They may bring straw for the cattle, and remove the dung from beneath them, and bring home hay, but not later than midday. But if one does other [work] on Monday or Tuesday, or [labors] longer than till midday, he shall pay three oras to the bishop. And if he labors on the first and the fourth days, he shall pay six oras.

31. CONCERNING THE GANG DAYS

On the lesser gang day[17] all men shall partake of dry food[18]

[17] April 25, a day dedicated to Saint Mark the Evangelist, though not the usual festival of Saint Mark.

[18] Fish and vegetables; milk was not allowed. See Maurer, "Nogle bemærkninger til Norges kirkehistorie," *Hist. tidsskrift*, Ser. III, Vol. III, p. 85.

[only] and shall keep [the day] holy after midday. On three gang days one is allowed to work till midday but must fast till noon; but the fourth is [to be kept] holy all day like a Sunday, for it is the day of our Lord's ascension. Whoever fails so to keep these days shall pay three oras to the bishop for Monday or Tuesday or Wednesday, but six oras for Holy Thursday, if he works on that day.

32. CONCERNING FASTING AND ALMSGIVING ABOUT SAINT MARY'S DAY

It is further enacted that on the eve of the earlier Saint Mary's Day and on the eve of All Saints' Day all persons who are twelve winters old, or older, shall partake of bread and salt only, that there may be good crops and peace and good health among men. And whoever does not fast shall pay the bishop six oras for each day. And the food that the husbandman and his wife would [regularly] eat on that day shall be given to the poor on the Mass-day or three oras shall be given to the bishop. Let them bring the food to the church and have it blessed and let those distribute it who are named for that [duty]. But if any one distributes food before these have given permission, it is as if he has given nothing. And the bishop's bailiff shall name as many men to assist him at the distribution as he sees are needed. And whoever is appointed [and fails to distribute properly] shall owe a fine as if he has distributed nothing. The bailiff shall be fined a like [amount] if he makes no appointments. If the bailiff is not at church, this duty falls to the priest. But if one has to travel over fjord or stream or mountain and therefore does not arrive on the appointed day, let him come on the first holy day after travel has become feasible; and let him prove with his own oath that he could not come because of bad weather; then he shall be counted guiltless; otherwise he shall pay the penalty whether he be a householder or a single man. And let the form of the oath be this, that he would not go hunting or fishing when the weather allows one to travel.

33. CONCERNING ALMSGIVING ON WHITSUNDAY

All men shall give alms on Whitsunday. A husbandman and his wife [shall give] a cake with relish upon it, and every unattached man shall give a penny; and [they shall do] the same on Saint

John's Day. All men who have a farm and stock shall give alms in corn on Michaelmas Day. Every farmer who keeps a helper shall give half a bushel,[19] and one who is alone about his work [shall give] one peck.[20] The priest [shall give] as other men [do] and shall carry his alms to the church as the farmers [do]. Every unattached man shall give a penny and bring it to church as the farmers [bring] their alms. Every man shall either give or receive [alms]. He who neglects [to do this] shall pay three oras to the bishop and an ora for every penny. The alms must be given on the risk of such a penalty as is set forth above. And a man incurs the same penalty if he fails to give the Olaf's corn.[21]

34. CONCERNING THE YULE FESTIVAL

During the Yule festival the first four days and [the first] four nights shall be kept holy; but on the fifth, the sixth, and the seventh [day] one may bring home fodder and remove the dung from beneath the cattle till midday; but the eighth [day] is holy like the first. The ninth, the tenth, the eleventh, and the twelfth [days shall be kept] like those between the fourth and the eighth; but the thirteenth, like the first. There are six days which carry a fine of six oras; in the case of the others it is three oras.

35. AS TO LOADING [HAY] OR FLOATING [TIMBER] ON HOLY DAYS

If a man has prepared a load of hay or wood before the day becomes holy, he may haul it [home], though it be on a holy day, but [he] shall bring under shelter only what the live stock or the household shall require during the festival. But a load of boards or timber shall be left standing where it is when the last third of the day begins; all other loads may be taken to shelter where one first finds it. Burdens borne on the back or in packs [on horses] shall be housed at the first opportunity. What is being floated across a lake shall be left lying where it was when the holy tide began; but if [it is being] drifted down a stream or a river, [one may] let it drift. In case wood, or a boat, or any other form of a man's property shall drift over upon the land of another, the man shall

[19] A *skjappa*, which is about half a bushel.

[20] Half a skjappa.

[21] Grain given in alms on St. Olaf's day.

have his own if he can identify it and has [the support of] two witnesses; but if he [the other man] has given care to it, let [the owner] support his claim with his own oath, if the property is worth three oras or less; if it is worth more, a threefold oath is required. If he refuses to give it up, he shall owe a baug and the action shall proceed as any other [suit for money].

36. WHEN SHIPS MAY BE UNLOADED

A merchant ship may be unloaded on a holy day only in case there is fear of wreckage or when it cannot be kept afloat by bailing; in such cases the lading may be carried up beyond the shore's edge. All such packages as a man can sit upon when in a sled or take with him on horseback when riding a horse, he may convey without guilt.

37. WHAT BURDENS ONE MAY CARRY AT HOLY-TIDE

It is ordered that when a man comes to the borough or is preparing to leave it, he may if he likes, carry his provisions to or from the ship: meal for a month, butter for the same [period], and a bundle of dried strips of halibut; and he may carry [his load] with impunity on his shoulder or in his hands, as he prefers. [He may] also [carry] with impunity any form of deck cargo, sails, and whatever belongs to a ship's gear if it is of the twelve-oar class or [of] a smaller [size].

38. CONCERNING LABOR ON SUNDAY AND THE EATING OF FLESH ON FAST DAYS

If a man eats flesh on Friday, but does it unwittingly, let him go to confession and do penance; but there are no dues to the bishop; but whoever eats thus with full intent shall pay six oras. If a man eats flesh on three successive Fridays, he has forfeited his right to peace among men and his chattels to the bishop. [It shall be] the same about all manner of work on Sunday: six oras for each day, if one works on two successive [Sundays]; but if he works also on the third, he forfeits his right to peace among men and his chattels to the bishop.

39. CONCERNING THE WATER FAST ON SAINT OLAF'S EVE

It is enacted that every man in good health who is fifteen

winters old [or more] shall, while within our jurisdiction, fast on Saint Olaf's eve, eating only bread and salt, or pay six oras.

40. CONCERNING HOUSEL TAKING ON EASTER DAY

Every person who is seven winters [old, or] older, shall on Easter Day in every twelvemonth receive the Lord's body, if he can get to church; otherwise he shall receive it as soon as he can get to church or find the priest. If one is fifteen winters old, or older, and his confessor has not forbidden him to partake of the housel and he lets a twelvemonth pass without receiving the housel or if he eats flesh just before he partakes of the housel, he shall owe a fine of three marks for the first year and the same amount for the second and the third; if he lets a longer time pass, he is outlawed. But if the priest refuses to give him the housel, alleging his evil behavior as the cause, then he who has been refused the housel shall appeal to the bishop or to the canons, if the bishop is not at home. But he may not east flesh without incurring guilt until his case is concluded.

41. IF A MAN EATS FLESH IN LENT

If a man of major age and of healthy mind eats flesh in Lent, he forfeits his right to peace among men everywhere and his chattels to the bishop. Every person who is twelve years old, or older, shall fast on Good Friday, eating only bread and water, or pay three oras to the bishop.

42. IF ANYTHING UNCLEAN DROPS INTO FOOD AND WHAT ONE MAY EAT

One may eat whatever is killed by a bear or [what] falls out over a cliff. And if a neat beast gores another, the dead neat may be eaten. A woman may kill cattle rather than let them die of themselves, and if she kills a beast because no man is at hand it may be eaten. If a neat beast is strangled in a manger, the flesh may be eaten. If a man castrates a beast and it dies, its flesh may be eaten; also, if a beast is bitten by a wolf or a dog, if it is the owner's own dog. But the hide shall be flayed off the neat and the skin off the sheep and all that which the teeth have rent shall be cut away and [shall be] sprinkled with holy water. If cattle jump into the sea or into a lake or fall into a well and are drowned, their flesh may be eaten. The flesh of a calf may be eaten if it is slain after it has taken food regularly for three nights. If anything [that is] defiling drops into the food of men or into the ale, one may partake of it after having sprinkled hallowed water upon it; and one shall share it with the needy on the priest's advice. In the same way [one shall deal] with beasts that fall into a heap of rocks or into a bog, and with all that of which the cause of death is known, though there has been no slaughtering. And any wild animal that one comes upon, or fish, or birds, one may eat if one wishes.

43. IF A MAN IS DELAYED BY BAD WEATHER ON AN OUTER ISLE

If a man is up on a mountain or out among the outer isles in Lent and is delayed by storms, he may eat, rather than perish, whatever is at hand, except only [the flesh of] man. But when he returns to the settlement, let him report to the priest whom he first meets; otherwise he shall owe a fine of six oras to the bishop and six oras in addition, if he passes by a second priest. But if he passes a third and keeps silent, he is an outlaw, and let the bishop have all his chattels. If the priest refuses to shrive him, he shall pay six oras to the bishop. If a man puts into another's food anything that is unclean or that one is forbidden to eat, let him offer a threefold oath if he denies the charge, or go into outlawry. But if he does it in the sight of men and with clear intent, let no man partake [of the food], and let him pay a double atonement to the one whose food it was, or deny his intent with a threefold oath, and pay six oras to the bishop. But out of the chattels of one who is outlawed in such a case the one whose food it was shall take a double compensation before the property is handed over to the bishop.

44. CONCERNING THE ARCHBISHOP'S PROGRESS AND HIS MEANS OF CONVEYANCE

The archbishop[22] shall visit each fylki every twelvemonth as a matter of duty to render service to the folk; otherwise he shall forfeit the payments that are due him there in that twelvemonth.

[22] The bishop of Nidaros (and the Frostathinglaw) was archbishop and primate of the Norwegian Church.

And wherever the [arch] bishop travels the freemen shall place at his disposal all the horses that have been broken to either saddle or harness, unless the bailiff gives other instructions. And whoever disregards this shall pay three oras for each horse and six oras for failing to forward the summons to provide conveyance. And if a man comes to the place where the duty to provide horses is to be assigned and conceals what he has in horses and does not allow them to come into the casting of the lots when the signal is sounded, it is as if he has done nothing.

45. CONCERNING THE ORDEAL OF THE IRON

The hot iron shall be borne in those cases only where the law demands it. If a man is the victim of violence and is not in position to submit a legal defense, the archbishop or the canons of Christ Church, if the archbishop is not in the neighborhood, shall arrange matters so that he shall have law or be allowed to carry the iron. And [the procedure shall be] the same if the man is lacking in oath helpers, though he has a proper defense.[23] In the country, the iron shall be carried at the shire church; in the borough, a church is assigned [for this purpose]. The priest who receives tithes from the man [concerned] shall bless the iron; but neither he nor the shire priest shall have a fee, except that the priest of a private chapel shall have what provisions he needs for the journey to the shire church.

46. CONCERNING PERJURY

A man who swears a false oath shall owe a fine of three marks to the bishop; and if he leads other men with him into the perjury, he shall pay six oras for each witness. If they knew that they swore falsely, they shall each pay a fine of three marks; but if they deny the guilt, let each one make his denial with his own oath. And the bishop's bailiff shall not bring such a charge against any man unless he has witnesses to common rumor or the guilt is evident. It is further ordered that if any person, man or woman, shall swear an oath that involves sin, whether it concerns treason plotted against the true king of the realm, or manslaying, or whoredom, or any other serious crime, he shall break that oath with impunity and shall confess [to a priest] that he swore an evil oath.

[23] Which means that he is innocent. See Hertzberg, *Glossarium*, *Vǫrn.*

III. [THE CHURCH LAW—CONTINUED]

1. THAT NO ONE SHALL TAKE A WIFE WITHIN THE KINDRED

It is enacted that no man shall take a wife within the kindred, except as the law provides and the bishop allowed at the Moster thing, to which all men have agreed. From two, brother and sister, six persons shall be counted on either side and one may wed the seventh. If a man wishes to marry a woman whom his kinsman has had, four persons shall be counted on either side from two, brother and sister, and let him take the fifth. There shall be a similar count if a man wishes to marry a woman of kin to the one whom he had earlier. And if a man takes a wife of nearer kin than we have now specified, he shall part from her at the next thing. The bishop's bailiff shall summon him before that thing on the bishop's behalf and bring action against him, and count up the kinship from the two, brother and sister, and let him name the intervening kinsmen, if he can. But if near kinsmen on the father's and the mother's side can show that the kinship is not so close that he may not have her, they have no guilt whatever. But in case no such near kinsmen on either side are to be found in the fylki, they shall be summoned to the next thing within our jurisdiction [after a time] sufficient to allow them to travel the road twice. But if there are none, either on the father's or on the mother's side the bishop or his bailiff shall appoint twelve freemen, the best in the fylki; and let him [the accused] have two of them at the second thing. And if he cannot enumerate the intervening kinsmen, let him part from the woman without penalty, if he was an unwitting offender. And if a quarrel shall arise between the two[1] before the wedding has been celebrated, the man has no right to bring suit either to secure the betrothed or to collect damages from the marriage man, until the case is concluded before the bishop according to law. But if he gives him [the woman],[2] the two shall each of them

[1] The fiancé and the marriage man; see Glossary, "Marriage man."
[2] Before the dispute has been legally terminated.

pay a fine of three marks, unless the woman has the right to decide for herself, in which case she shall be fined as her guardian would be [fined]. If he does not give up the woman at the first thing, as the law demands, the bishop's bailiff shall summon him to a second thing; and if he shall then be able to enumerate the intervening kinsmen, he shall possess the woman without guilt. But if he is still unable to enumerate the intervening kinsmen, he shall again owe a fine of three marks. And the bishop's bailiff shall summon him to a third thing, and let the man again enumerate the intervening kinsmen, if he can, and possess the woman without guilt. But if he still is unable to enumerate the intervening kinsmen, let him cease from the woman and pay three marks a third time. If he still refuses to give her up, he shall go into outlawry and the bishop shall have his chattels, but the woman shall keep what is hers. If a man takes the daughter of his paternal uncle or the daughter of his maternal aunt, the penalty is still three marks; but in passing toward the point where kinship ceases [to be a hindrance] two oras shall be dropped at each knee;[3] that will make one mark at the sixth knee. Kinship through marriage [shall be dealt with] in the same way.

2. WHAT FINES THE BISHOP SHALL HAVE

To prevent violation of church law the penalties in the following cases shall be levied [in weighed silver] like the fine for violating a freeman's personal right: sinful dealings with women, perjury, eating flesh before housel taking, non-payment of tithes, breaking the peace in church or churchyard, and failure to provide the bishop with horses or to forward the summons to make such provision. Fines for breaking the laws of the church shall be valued in burned silver; all other fines shall be reckoned in current coin.

3. FOR WHAT MARRIAGES A MAN IS OUTLAWED

There are eight women, who are not one's kin by blood, and three kinswomen for marrying whom a man is outlawed. The first is the one whom the man's father had. The second [is] the one whom the man's son had. The third [is] the one whom his brother had. The fourth is the mother of the wife whom the man had. The

[3] See Glossary, "Kinship."

fifth [is] the daughter of the wife whom the man had. The sixth is the sister of the wife whom the man had. The seventh is a woman at whose baptism you assisted or who assisted at yours. The eighth is a woman who has taken the veil and given herself to God. He is an outlaw who defiles her in her own place or entices her away or causes her to be enticed and then defiles her. But if this one ceases from her and another takes her afterwards, knowing her to be a nun, he shall pay the same penalty as if he had taken another man's wife. These are the others who are one's kinswomen: mother, sister, and daughter. Now if a man lies with any of these, they shall both be outlawed, and [the man's] chattels are all forfeited to the bishop, except only in case he breaks his bonds, or if men know of a truth that madness has afflicted him from time to time. Also, if the woman had been forced and has not willingly submitted to him since then, she shall owe no fine; still, let her do penance on the bishop's advice. If the man refuses to leave [the land], the bishop's bailiff shall summon him to a thing and bring witnesses with him [to testify] at the thing as to what is rumored. If he denies the charge, let him offer a threefold oath and this oath may be legally taken within ten oath weeks. But if the oath fails, he and all his possessions shall be outlawed, except his land, if he has any. And an action may be brought after this as after any other failure to take an oath. If he refuses to offer an oath, the bishop's bailiff shall give him a month [in which] to leave the land. Let the women, too, be outlawed unless she has been violated.

4. CONCERNING PUNISHMENT FOR FORNICATION

If a woman lies with a man whom she is not allowed to possess, she owes a fine of three marks, just as he does with whom she lies. And if he does not abstain and ignores three summonses to appear at a thing, he shall pay three marks for each summons, and she the same; that makes eighteen marks that they both pay. And let them cease [the relationship] or both go into outlawry. And the bishop shall have the man's property, but the woman [shall keep] what is hers.

5. CONCERNING ADULTERY

If a man keeps a woman in addition to his wife, or if a woman [entertains] a man in addition to her husband, each one of them shall owe a fine of three marks to the bishop, if they are convicted by the testimony of two witnesses or the woman is with child. And the facts must be brought to the notice of eyewitnesses; but if there are none such, the action may proceed with the testimony of men as to public rumor, and [the accused] may defend themselves with a threefold oath.

6. IF A MAN LIES WITH HIS MOTHER'S SISTER OR HIS [WIFE'S] DAUGHTER

If a man has his own wife but is still so lustful that he lies with his mother's sister or his wife's daughter or [with one] of such kinship to his wife that he may not possess her [his wife] after that, he has forfeited his right to live with his wife because of this lust; still, the holy bonds of their marriage remain intact on God's side, and the man shall owe a fine of three marks for every time that he goes to [another woman]. This rule applies to the wife the same as to the husband as long as they both remain alive. And let the bishop inquire according to the laws of God as to who caused the mischief. If it is his [the husband's] fault that they cannot live together, the wife shall have her husband's gift to her marriage portion, as if death has parted them.

7. CONCERNING WHOREDOM ON A WOMAN'S PART

If a woman is guilty of whoredom against her husband, she shall owe a fine of three marks to the bishop [to be paid] out of her own money and not her husband's, and it shall be counted out of her marriage portion. And the husband may still choose to possess her but [he may] not [possess] another woman as long as she lives.

8. CONCERNING ABSTENSION FROM SPIRITUAL KINSWOMEN[4]

No man shall take to wife a woman to whom he stands in spiritual kinship. And we shall honor this kinship with respect to the father or the mother as to the child itself. The one who holds the child when it receives the sign of the cross is the first in spiritual kinship. The one who brings the child to baptism is the second. The one who removes the white robe is the third. The one who leads [the child] to the bishop at confirmation is the fourth. The one who

[4] Cf. *Gul.*, c. 26.

loosens the chrism-band about the forehead is the fifth. All these are of equal rank in spiritual kinship. And the same fine is owing to the bishop and the same penance to God if a man takes a spiritual kinswoman [to wife] as if he takes a kinswoman [after the flesh], a paternal uncle's daughter or the daughter of a maternal aunt.

9. CONCERNING WEDDINGS

One must not take a wife in the three weeks before Yule or during the Yule festival or in the nine weeks before Easter or in Easter week or in Whitsunday week or in the three weeks before Saint John's eve or [in the three weeks] before Michaelmas; and no man shall go to a woman on the night before Friday or on any night that is followed the next morning by a fast day or a mass-day. Any man who weds a wife at any of those times owes a fine of six oras to the bishop. And any man who goes to a woman on the night before Sunday or before an ember day or in Lent shall owe a fine of three marks to the bishop, and the two shall both go to confession and do penance.

10. CONCERNING THE DISSOLUTION OF MARRIAGE

Every Christian shall have and possess one wife. But if one takes another while the lawfully wedded wife is still living, he shall forsake the later one and pay three marks to the bishop. And the children that he may have had with the later one shall not share in the inheritance. If two sons, each by a different mother and both rightly wedded according to the laws of God and the ancient laws of the land, claim to inherit from the father and the elder asserts that his father had not parted from his wife according to the laws of God when he took the later woman, he [the younger] is not obliged to produce witnesses [for a period] longer than ten winters.

11. IF A MAN GIVES MONEY TO A CONCUBINE

If a man weds a woman with whom he has earlier had children, those that are born after the marriage shall render those who were [born] earlier competent to inherit and the sons shall both share equally. In the same way, if there is a daughter but no son born after the marriage, she shall share equally in the inheritance with her brothers who were born before the marriage. But if both a son and a daughter are born after the marriage, she shall not share in the inheritance with her brothers; nevertheless, she will render legitimate such sisters as were born before the wedding and competent to share in the inheritance from the mother to such an extent as the law provides. And as soon as any child is born after the wedding, it makes legitimate heirs of all its brothers and sisters by the same father and of the same mother, who were born before the wedding, whether the one born after the wedding lives a long or a short time. However much a man may receive of his paternal inheritance by this rule, he continues with undiminished rights to all inheritances. And if any inheritance has been taken earlier in this manner, it shall remain intact.

12. WHEN A BETROTHED SHALL BE TAKEN AS WIFE

If a man pledges troth to a woman, he shall marry her within the twelvemonth unless circumstances prevent. And there is such a preventing circumstance, if he is ill or wounded or has to remain abroad over winter against his will; and let him give proof with his own oath and marry the woman within the next half year after his return home. It is further enacted that there shall be no penalty if the man and the guardian agree to a postponement. But if the man does not marry her according to these provisions, he shall owe a fine of three marks to the bishop; and the woman's guardian may sue him for damage fees, as the law provides. And the same rule shall apply to the guardian, if the delay is caused by him.

13. IF A MAN LIES WITH HIS BETROTHED

If a man lies with his betrothed, he shall pay the full atonement to her nearest kinsman. And if a child is begotten and the father dies within the twelvemonth and before the wedding can be held, the child shall take such an inheritance from his father as if his mother had been bought with the mund. But in no other case can a man come into an inheritance, only if his mother was bought with the mund, or he is brought into the kindred in legal manner. And if a man enters into betrothal with his concubine in order that by this arrangement his children may be made competent to inherit, or postpones his wedding that this end may be achieved,[5]

[5] That is, if the wedding was not held within the period set by law, which was ordinarily one year. The passage seems to mean that in such a case the

that arrangement shall not stand; for one shall not cheat in matters of inheritance or dishonor the marriage rite in this way.

14. CONCERNING THE CONSECRATION OF A NUN

If a woman desires to be consecrated a nun, the bishop shall consecrate her only if he has permission from her heir. But if at a later time she breaks her vow, she shall go to the bishop's garth [as a bondwoman] and he who seduced her shall be outlawed and the bishop shall have his property.

15. CONCERNING SACRIFICES TO HEATHEN GODS

If a man sacrifices to heathen gods or practices sooth-saying or sorcery, or if a man gives credence to such a one or harbors him for such purposes, he shall be outlawed like a banesman and the bishop shall have his property to the last penny. If he denies [the guilt], let him carry the hot iron, or, [if a woman], let her go to the hot kettle. And the one who accuses any man of this [and the man is cleared], shall be rated a slanderer, if witnesses are called to take note of it, unless he can produce witnesses to common rumor.

16. CONCERNING OATH BREAKING AND SHRIFT BREAKING

If any person, whether man or woman, defies the bishop, and becomes an oath breaker or a shrift breaker (and it is shrift breaking when a man returns to the sins that he had committed earlier and for which fines are levied and which had been brought into the confessional, or does not leave the land as had been ordered at the confessional), he shall pay three marks to the bishop and the same [amount] for a second and for a third offense. And if they [man and woman] commit such a sin more than once, the man shall be outlawed and the bishop shall have his property to the last penny. The woman, too, shall be outlawed, unless she has been violated, but let her keep her money.

17. WHAT A MAN MAY GIVE OF HIS WEALTH

It is the counsel and command of the good Cardinal Nicholas,[6]

man might think of postponing his marriage until there seemed to be assurance of further offspring.

[6] Nicholas Breakspeare, later Pope Adrian IV (1154–59), served as legate in the North on several occasions. This chapter dates from 1152. See Keyser, *Norges stats- og retsforfatning*, 337.

who later was made pope, and of Archbishop John on the approval of the most discreet men, that for the profit of all within our jurisdiction, we should adopt this amendment to the laws, that of all the wealth which men acquire in addition to their inheritance, one-fourth shall be given for the health of the giver's soul to whomever he wishes without asking the permission of his heirs, as [when one gives] a greater tithe. But a woman may give a tithe of her marriage portion and in addition [she may give] one-fourth of her husband's gift to the marriage portion.

18. CONCERNING CARNAL DEALINGS WITH FARM BEASTS

If a man is charged with having carnal dealings with cattle of any sort, which is forbidden to all Christians, the bailiff shall bring action against him with witnesses to [the fact of] common rumor; and let him carry the hot iron or go into outlawry.

19. CONCERNING THE IMPROVEMENT OF HIGHWAYS

On the working day just preceding Saint John's[7] eve all able-bodied men shall proceed to improve the highways, each in his fylki and ship district, wherever the need seems greatest. But if conditions prevent work on that day, let it be done before Saint Peter's Day.[8] And whoever neglects [this] shall pay the bishop an ora, valued in burned silver. If a householder fails to give his workmen leisure [to do this work], he shall pay fines for both himself and them. But if a workman, having received permission, refuses to go, let him answer for his own guilt. And over all streams that run across [the valleys] men shall build bridges, all in their respective heraths; and for this [work] let them use the day that is set aside for mending the roads during the twelvemonth in which the bridge is in building; but after that let them do as is ordered above. And the bishop's bailiff shall send summons to the men with tokens and with public notice given at church, and whoever fails to come shall pay an ora valued in burned silver. And the bishop's bailiff shall collect this on the bishop's behalf and shall pay one-half to the farmers to be used for bridge building, and let them furnish the labor. And this repairing of roads shall take the place of the manu-

[7] June 24.

[8] June 29.

missions[9] which are ordered in our laws and which all men have promised with thanks to God. And the bridge building shall be hurried forward as [fast as] the most discerning men in each herath think expedient.

20. AT WHAT TIMES A SUIT MAY BE BROUGHT

These are the times in the twelvemonth when no suit shall be brought, no thing shall be summoned, and no oaths taken, except in cases of theft and such as involve personal injuries, as are noted below: three weeks before the Yuletide; two [weeks] in the Yuletide; seven [weeks] in Lent; Easter week, and the week of the gang days; Whitsuntide and the three ember days before Michaelmas. But suits may be prosecuted on all other week days. And in cases involving church law and disputes about property the one into whose keeping the suit comes shall demand bail at this time to cover both chattels [and person], and let the defendant provide bail. If he has a farm in the country or a house in the borough, this will serve as security for him. If a suit is brought against one who is not a householder, let him find as surety for himself a man who has as much property as the suit involves. But if he offers no bail, he shall owe a fine of three marks silver, one-half to go to the king, and one-half to the prosecutor. And for the failure to give surety a fine [may be levied] as large as the amount involved in the suit. If the one who is sued is a poor man and he flees from the suit when it comes upon him, he is liable in that suit as soon as the day for the hearing arrives. If he withdraws his goods from the pledge and moves it into another fylki, he shall owe a fine of three marks as stated above. If the suit concerns the law of the church, the bishop's bailiff who has this duty shall sue [for the fine], and let each one have one-half, [the bailiff] and the one who brought the suit. But in all other disputes about property, let him who brought the suit prosecute it. If he [the defendant] sells property that he gave as security or otherwise withdraws it [from the pledge], let the prosecutor bring action for these chattels, [proceeding] with a formal demand and summons to the thing, and let him there produce witnesses [to the fact] that the chattels were given as bail; and let him demand judgment from the freemen [allowing him to

[9] Because thralldom had by this time disappeared in Norway.

go at once] to collect the debt and the fine in double amount, and let the freemen have the excess. And in cases of theft or personal injury there shall be suit and sworn oaths, only if the complainant conducts his case so as to bring the law into action and [if there are] six oaths. If oaths are promised, let the offer stand till there are oath days. No case shall be begun on a Tuesday, for then the fifth day will fall on Sunday; and whoever begins a suit on that day has ruined his case, unless he sets it[10] for the fourth or the sixth day after. If oaths are taken other than such as are here provided, the one [who swears] shall pay a fine of six oras in Lent and three oras at all other times, unless the day calls for six oras and the plaintiff can wait till the end of the term set by law. If a man needs to sue for his land rent at a time when suits are not allowed, he shall place a ban upon the crops and shall summon [his opponent] to a five-day moot, and let each one of them get his witnesses ready for the book and [let the case] stand till the oath days.

21. CONCERNING EXCOMMUNICATION

If the bishop excommunicates a man he shall have a respite of three months in which to order and conclude his affairs. And that a man may not be further tangled into misfortune, the bishop's bailiff shall summon him before a thing and declare him an outlaw, unless he brings his case to a proper conclusion there and at once. And let the bishop have all his chattels, but the king may sell him the right to remain in the land.

22. HOW A MARRIAGE SHALL BE ARRANGED

If a man wishes to give in marriage his daughter or another woman whose marriage he controls according to law, he shall take two witnesses [to act] on behalf of the one who wishes to marry her and go to inquire whether she is willing to accept the arrangement which he, as her legal guardian, places before her. And if she agrees or remains silent, the witnesses shall be asked to note the fact, and the woman is affianced by that [act]; but, if she refuses, she is not affianced. And if at any time she accepts the agreement, the man must betroth and marry her, if the facts are known to witnesses. And they shall be charged with the duty of bearing

[10] By agreement with his opponent.

this witness for a year and a day, and no longer. If she desires to break the engagement before the end of the twelvemonth, stating that she was bound against her will, the man shall oppose his witnesses to her statement and shall have the woman. But if he has no witnesses, let her deny upon oath that she was willingly [bound]; and let her father and her mother swear with her, or her nearest kinsmen, if there are no parents, and let her pay the man as much money as he was promised to get with her. After that let each one of them go his own way. But if this separation comes after the wedding, she loses her husband's gift to the marriage portion.

23. CONCERNING OUTLAWED PROPERTY

If a man is outlawed for violating church law, the bishop's bailiff shall give him a five-day respite at that thing to [pay] his debts, and shall demand security to cover his chattels. But if men shall attempt within the five-day period in summer or half a month in winter to defend property that has been awarded [by the court], they shall each owe a fine of three marks to the bishop, if the bailiff calls men to note the resistance. And those, who remove property or receive it or buy it from one who is outlawed for violating church law, shall also owe the bishop a fine of three marks; and the bailiff shall sue for that property with summons to a thing. But if men resist [in this way] or have dealings with the outlaw after the period of respite is past, they shall suffer the same form of outlawry as he suffers, and their property [goes] to the king as his [goes] to the bishop.

24. WHO MAY BE OUTLAWED BY CHURCH LAW

It is enacted in the secular laws that no one shall be outlawed unless a man summons him to a thing either by the arrow or by the horn, [which summons men] to the borough moot. And if a man is outlawed for breach of church law and he makes atonement before the outlawry becomes effective, there are no dues to the king. But if he is declared an outlaw at the thing, a payment is due the king for restoring his rights before he may return to peace and security. Fines are also due [the king] from those who associate with him, except that, when he is taken before the bishop to do penance, men may be with him without fear of penalty and also after the period has expired which the bishop set for him to atone for his guilt abroad. And the kingsmen shall not promise protection within the land to any one whom the bishop's bailiff has declared an outlaw for breach of church law. If he returns, having done the penance that he was to perform abroad, let him call a thing, and let him produce a writ from the bishop or from the chapter, if the bishop is absent or has passed away, and let him be restored to his personal rights; but first the king must be paid for annulling the outlawry. If action shall be brought on the king's behalf against a man charging that he was not restored to his rights after he had been outlawed, the man shall be obliged for a period of ten years to have witnesses who are ready to testify that he was restored to his rights; after that time he may prove with his own oath that the matter has passed out of the responsibility of witnesses; and no one shall bring action [against a man] for having had dealings [with an outlaw] after the passage of ten winters.

IV. [THE LAW OF PERSONAL RIGHTS]

1. [CONCERNING PERSONAL RIGHTS]

The first [provision] in our law of personal rights is that every one of our countrymen shall be inviolate in his rights and his person, both in the kingdom and outside the kingdom. And if a man slays another, he shall forfeit all that he owns except his land only, unless the slain man had brought the deed upon himself. If a man pursues an outlaw and slays him, he shall report on the same day to men of that same fylki that he has slain an outlawed man; if he does not report on the same day, he shall rightly be [considered] a murderer. But no one shall forfeit his land unless he commits a foul murder or a nithing deed.

2. CONCERNING FOUL KILLING

It is foul killing if one slays a man after peace pledges [have been given]; in such a case he forfeits both his land and his movables.

3. ANOTHER CASE OF FOUL KILLING

It is another case of foul killing if one slays a man to whom he has given grith.

4. CONCERNING MURDER

A third [case of foul killing] is murder; but the worst [form of] nithing crime is plotting to deprive the king of land and subjects. If the king charges a man with treason, he shall appoint from his household a man of equal rank with the one who has to answer the charge. If a freedman or a dependent has to answer such a charge, [the king] shall appoint the son of a freeman, if there is such a one in his household, and he shall have the king's writ and seal and shall prosecute the charge, when the king is absent from the fylki. A second [form of] nithing crime is the return of a man who was driven out of the land in times of unpeace in order to harry the land, without first renouncing peace; all who join in such doings are outlaws in the same degree. A third [form of] nithing crime is the breaking of the truce pledges which a man has himself given, if they are given according to law. A fourth [form of] nithing crime is that in which a man sets another man's homestead on fire and burns it down. The several kinds of foul killing and nithing crime which lead to forfeiture of land, if one is convicted of them, have now been enumerated. But no man can at any time forfeit more land than he actually owns.

5. ALL MEN SHALL ENJOY SECURITY IN THEIR HOMES

It is further enacted that all free men shall enjoy security in their homes and also in traveling to, or returning from, the more distant parts of the farm.[1] And if a freeman or a freeman's son is slain in his own home or while traveling to, or returning from, the outlying parts of the farm or while in the field or the meadow with his thralls, the one whom the members of the household point out and testify against shall be [regarded as] the banesman. In matters of house breaking a thrall or a bondwoman shall be as competent to testify as a free man and one who is eight years old, as an older person. And whoever is accused by witnesses of house breaking and does not seem able to clear himself with oaths, is to be [regarded as] the banesman clearly and without doubt, except only in case he was, on the day of the crime, so far away that he could not on that same day travel the road both ways, to the place of the killing and back again. If he were present at a thing or a church or a merrymaking or on board a ship of the twelve-oar class or larger, let the twelve thegns who were with him, free men and of full age, prove him guiltless of the charge. If he were not in any such place, let him defend himself with the hot iron, if he is unable to clear himself with oaths. If the men are unable to give this testimony at the thing, let two men give it and confirm their sayings with an oath on the Gospels. If a man is wounded but can [still] speak when men find him, the man whom he first accuses shall be the banesman, if he speaks with a rational mind and is able to recognize the man and his statement is sworn to at the next thing, unless the accused is able to clear himself with the hot iron.

[1] *Afheimr:* certain areas, meadows and the like, lying apart from the farm itself.

6. IF THREE MEN TRAVEL TOGETHER IN A BOAT

The next is this, that if three men travel together in a boat and matters turn out so ill that one slays another, the third man in the company, in his effort to stop the strife, shall lay up his oars. If it happens when they come to land that both send forth arrows and both come to the thing, their charges must be looked into with care. And let him whom the [slain man's] heir points out carry the iron first; but if both deny the guilt, let both carry the iron, and the one who is proved guilty shall go into outlawry.

7. IF A MAN IS STRICKEN DOWN AND KILLED

If a man is stricken down and killed, he shall be [counted] the banesman who reports the slaying as his own deed. And [he shall] report it on the same day within the fylki, giving his name, his night lodgings and the herath where he belongs; and he shall report it to a free man, one having full personal rights. Then at the arrow thing the slayer's lodgings shall be disclosed, and the householder who put him up for the night shall swear that he gave such and such a name, and the notice given by the slayer shall also be reported to the thing. But if a man refuses to testify to a slayer's report or as to his lodgings, let one of the slayer's paternal kinsmen come forward and give the man a summons to testify either for or against at a five-day moot. But if men refuse to testify either one way or the other, each one of them shall owe a fine of three marks, and let the prosecutor have one-half and the king one-half; and they shall lose the right to bear witness and to enjoy the benefit of witnesses, and they shall go away shorn of personal rights. And let other witnesses be dealt with in the same way as has been told in the law of personal rights; but in suits of this sort no man need give another a home summons. A thing shall be summoned at the five-day thing after [a space of] as many nights as men think proper in their thing circuit; and at that thing either the money shall be paid or distraint shall be allowed to the double amount. If the man who is reported to be the slayer is able to travel to the place where the deed was done and back again on the same day, no testimony as to his lodgings is necessary, seeing that his home is so near, [be it] within the fylki or without. On leaving the place where the slaying was, he shall not pass three homesteads without reporting his deed, unless the men who dwell there shall be near kinsmen, agnates or cognates. And if he does not report the slaying in this way, he is in the highest degree a murderer and has forfeited land and chattels; and he shall never return to the realm. And if the report of the crime and the statement of the wounded man are both presented at the next thing and the statement is made as provided above, the statement of the wounded man shall stand but not the report of the slayer; but it relieves him of the charge of murder though he will be outlawed. But if neither the statement of the wounded man nor witness as to common rumor[2] is presented at the next thing, but the slayer's report and the testimony of eyewitnesses are presented, the slayer's report, if given according to law, shall stand, but not the testimony of eye-witnesses. And the heir of the slain man shall proceed to the herath whence the man [who reported the slaying] claims to have come; and if, when he arrives, he happens to find the man outside our law, he shall bring action against him according to the laws as they are there; but if he finds him within our law, he shall summon him before a thing, and at that thing twelve free men not chosen by the court shall be competent to prove the [accused] man's innocence; and let him bring [them] forward at the thing to which he is summoned; but if that is not done, he is guilty as charged. And let the heir of the slain man return and [proceed to] prosecute two men to the twelvefold oath, and a third [only] in case he can prove him guilty; but, if he cannot convict him, he is himself outlawed with the same form of outlawry as [the other] would have suffered had he been found guilty.

8. CONCERNING THE TWELVEFOLD OATH

Whenever a twelvefold[3] oath is to be taken and by selected witnesses, the prosecutor shall select one-half of the witnesses and the defendant one-half; and let each name his witnesses as soon as the oath is agreed upon. And they shall name twelve holdar of the fylki or the best freemen, if holdar are wanting; neither kinsmen

[2] Hertzberg would emend *heimiliskviðarvitni*, witnesses to common rumor, to *heimsóknarvitni*, witnesses to an attack. *Den ældste norske proces*, p. 201.

[3] Cf. *Gul.*, c. 132.

by marriage nor enemies shall be named. He [the defendant] shall have two oath helpers of the twelve and his two nearest kinsmen; he [shall] himself [be] the fifth; thereafter [there shall be] seven free men of mature age, such as can answer for both pledge and promise. Holding the mass book in the hand and standing in front of the altar floor, the men shall swear the twelvefold oath; but if one witness fails [to swear], the entire oath fails. If any one of the witnesses has been refused access to the church, let him swear before the church door; if he may not have the book [to hold], let him place his hand on the door post; he can then swear as effectually as if he had the book. But if the priest refuses [to hand] him the book, he shall forfeit his income for the twelvemonth from that sixth or eighth [part of the fylki] where the man belongs. [Those who are to take the oath] shall in every case offer to take it at the home of him who is to hear it; and unless fjord or mountain forbid it, notice shall be given three nights before; but if fjord or mountain forbid, [notice shall be given] five nights before, whether the man is at home or not.

Whenever a man agrees to take an oath involving outlawry, the complainant shall specify a farm in the fylki where the defendant may offer a satisfactory oath. But if he does not specify how the oath may be offered, let it be taken within ten weeks of oath [days] and without further notice to him who is to hear it. But the bailiff shall be notified and it is sufficient if he is given notice the night before or the same day, whether he is at home or not. And every oath shall be taken there where men have taken oaths in former times, whether it is an oath involving outlawry or any other oath. Now if men doubt that action was brought against a certain man the first time, the witnesses of the plaintiff shall testify with him that he did bring action against a man who bore that name. In case a man agrees to take an oath involving outlawry and suffers a failure, the prosecutor shall summon a thing for the following month to which the one who gave him the trouble must come without further notice, and the prosecutor shall inquire how he fared in taking the oath. And if the prosecutor holds that the oath was not properly taken, the defendant shall call the two witnesses, whose attention he requested when he took the oath, [to testify] that he has taken the oath according to agreement. If a man agrees to take an oath involving outlawry and the prosecutor gives no care to his suit through the month next following the day set for the oath taking, he has forfeited his [right to bring] action, but nothing more. And as soon as the bailiff becomes aware of this, let him take action against the other man for failing to take the oath as agreed; but he must have brought the action within a month of days available for litigation or the case fails.

9. IF A MAN IS KILLED AT THE THING

If a man is killed at the thing, all men shall pursue [the slayer] into the woods; and whoever refuses to join in the pursuit shall owe a baug, and in this fine there are twelve oras. But near kinsmen, whether agnates or cognates, and near kinsmen by marriage are not required by law to join in the hue and cry unless they are willing to do so. And any man may render one kind of assistance to one who has committed manslaying, but let them give no other help than what has been accepted by all men: one may trip up a pursuer, if one wishes, and one may throw out an oar or a bailing dish [to the fugitive]; but of these three kinds of help only one shall be given. But if other kinds are given, the one who gives this other help shall be outlawed, unless he did it unwittingly; and let him offer his oath in defense. If the man leaves the land as an outlaw, his heir as a matter of course takes over the guardianship of his chattels and whatever he thinks should be in his care.

10. IF A MAN IS WOUNDED AT A THING

If a man is wounded at a thing and all join in pursuing the man who provoked the fight into the woods and he is run down, then if he wishes to present a legal defense, let him lay down his weapons and promise to conform to the law. As soon as he is seized or has laid down his weapons, he is entitled to security as long as the other man lives; and he must not be killed while the wounded man is living; but let him be bound and brought to the bailiff; and it shall be the duty of the bailiff, and also of the baron, to detain him. If the bailiff needs help in detaining him, he shall call upon the wounded man's kinsmen to keep the watch with him, or the freemen shall provide as many men as the bailiff requires. But if he [the prisoner] escapes from the bailiff and the wounded man dies, the bailiff shall be killed. If the bailiff is not at home, the man shall be left bound in his wife's keeping; and if neither is at home, he shall be left in the keeping of the foreman of the work rooms, and men [shall be appointed] to help him keep the prisoner. And the kinsmen of the wounded man have the right to detain the offender if they wish; but they shall not be held liable if he escapes from them. If the bailiff refuses to receive him, let the fact be noted by witnesses, and let the man be set down in bonds on the bailiff's floor; he shall then be responsible for him from that time on, unless the man is taken from him by violent force. And whenever a bailiff attaches the property of an outlaw, he shall find a man to strike the outlaw down, if he appears at the thing, unless the heir [of the slain man] is present. And the heir incurs no penalty if he allows him to escape; and the freemen incur no penalty even though the outlaw leaves the thing, if the slain man's heir allows him to escape. But if the slain man's heir does not allow him to escape, the bailiff shall slay the man as ordered above.

11. IF A MAN WHO HAS WOUNDED [ANOTHER FAILS TO] ESCAPE INTO THE WOODS

If a man receives a wound, and the one who wounded him fails to escape into the woods and is seized, and if he offers atonement according to law, the customary fines are due the king and the wounded man [shall have] the wound fine and the leech money.

12. CONCERNING THE LEECH MONEY

An ora shall be due as leech money for every month and also provisions of meal and butter for two months, and the same [amount] for every month till a scab has formed on the wound. And [the offender] shall offer these payments at the next thing, and his live stock and [other] movables shall be held as security until he has paid the customary fines to the king and the wound fine and the leech money to the wounded man. But if he offers nothing at the next thing, he shall be outlawed, he and his possessions, except what he carries with him into the woods. As soon as a scab has formed on the wound, the one who caused the wound shall have two men inspect it; but if the wounded man refuses to show his wound, the one who wounded him is no longer liable, even though the other man shall die. But if he does show it, they who view it shall bear witness concerning it. And he [the offender] shall summon a thing and offer to pay the fines to the king and the wound fine and the leech money to the wounded man, and he shall have paid [his fines] within half a month or go into outlawry. But if one asks to have a wound inspected[4] before a scab has formed on the wound, let him who makes the request pay the fine for evil intent to the wounded man according to the wounded man's rank.

13. IF A MAN IS WOUNDED BY ANOTHER

If a man is wounded by another, no matter where it is done, every free man shall join in pursuing [the offender], on pain of a baug, and in that baug there are twelve oras.

14. IF MEN GO TO AN ALE FEAST OR TO A MERRYMAKING

If men go to an ale feast or to a merrymaking (and a real merrymaking calls for [a brew from] three såld of malt, or more than three), it is ordered that no one shall gather men into bands when other men have gone to sleep. And it is ordered that, if a man is slain in a fight whether within the dwelling or in an outhouse, the men who are in his troop must know who the banesman is; if they cannot find the man, the member of the troop whom the slain man's heir accuses shall be [regarded as] the banesman. But if a man is slain in an alehouse after all the men have retired to sleep, they shall all arise and light a fire and each one shall take his own seat. If any one fails to occupy his seat, he shall be the banesman, unless he asked the men on either side to note the fact that all men were agreeable when he went away; and the testimony of two men shall clear him. If all the men are inside and no one misses a comrade and no one has assumed the liability for the slaying, the heir of the dead man may prosecute two men to the twelvefold oath, and a third man only if he can convict him; otherwise he shall suffer what these would [have suffered];[5] and let him bring his action as he likes, within the house or without. But if one has failed to ask [his benchmates] to note that the men were agree-

[4] *Sárbota,* the term used here, can have no meaning. Hertzberg would therefore emend it to *sársjonar*, inspection of a wound. See *Glossarium*, "Sárbœtr."

[5] The penalty would be outlawry.

able to his departure, and consequently has to face the suit, let him deny the guilt with a twelvefold oath and with selected oath helpers, if such can be secured, or let him carry the hot iron.

15. IF A MAN IS KILLED IN AN ALEHOUSE

If a man is killed in an alehouse, those who sat nearest to him shall testify one way or the other. But if they refuse to state whether he was killed or not, they shall each one of them owe the king a fine of three marks or swear a threefold oath that they knew not who the scatheman was. And the heir of the dead man may prosecute two men to the twelvefold oath as set forth above. And those who have knowledge but refuse to testify shall never more be competent to bear witness nor shall they enjoy testimony of any sort.

16. IF A MAN PUSHES ANOTHER INTO A FIRE

If a man pushes another into a fire with hostile intent, and if the man is burned and the injury is so serious that he must be bandaged, the customary fines shall be owing to the king and the injured man shall have the wound fine and the leech money, as provided above; also a half atonement and the largest [compensation allowed] for damage to clothes.

17. IF A MAN PUSHES [ANOTHER] INTO THE SEA

If a man pushes another into the sea with hostile intent, he shall pay him a half atonement; and if the man is injured by [the fall into] the water, he shall pay him the wound fine and the leech money and a full atonement, and [he shall pay] the customary fines to the king. If a man sits on the ship's edge attending to his needs and another pushes him into the sea with hostile intent, there shall be due him a full atonement and the fine for evil intent. If he is injured by [the fall into the] water, there shall be owing as provided above, the wound fine, the leech money, and the full atonement [to the man], and the customary fine to the king. And the same shall be owing if a man kicks another or jerks him away from his oar bench.

18. IF A MAN PUSHES ANOTHER AWAY

If a man pushes another away with hostile intent, a half atonement is due; but if the man both jerks and pushes, the full atonement is due. And if a man knocks another down and renders him helpless, he shall pay him a full atonement and the fine for evil intent; and [he shall pay] a baug to the king, if he [the injured man] has called upon men to note the facts. But if he has not called upon men to note the facts, he has the choice of demanding an atonement for himself and a baug for the king; and let him bring action with summons to a thing, and let him produce two witnesses who saw the deed, if such there are; and if there are none, [the accused] may make his denial with a threefold oath. But if he [the injured man] fails to make complaint, the rights of both the injured man and of the king fall. If a man leaps upon another but restrains himself, he shall pay a half atonement and a baug to the king if the man [who is attacked] calls witnesses to note the facts. But if he [the offender] is restrained [by others] and witnesses are asked to note the facts, a full atonement [is due] and a baug of twelve oras to the king. But if he restrains himself and witnesses are not asked to note the facts, the doings are a stupid game and there is no penalty.

19. THROWING MISSILES WITH HOSTILE INTENT

For the throwing of missiles of any sort with hostile intent a half atonement is due, if no blood is shed. But if blood is shed there shall be due the wound fine and the leech money and the customary fine to the king. If a man strikes at and maims another with an axhead[6] and then strikes at him again [with the edge], he shall be outlawed; but he may buy his release from outlawry with fifteen marks; and [he shall pay] a full atonement and the wound fine and the leech money to the man and the customary fine to the king.

20. IF A MAN STRIKES AT ANOTHER WITH AN AX AND HITS HIM WITH THE HANDLE

If a man strikes at another with an ax but aims too high and the handle [alone] touches him, that is a blow. And if a man strikes at another with an ax and tears his clothes and the other strikes in return, the one who struck first goes into outlawry, if the other man brings the matter to the attention of witnesses.

[6] The upper, blunt side of the ax.

21. IF A MAN THRUSTS AT ANOTHER WITH A SPEAR SHAFT

If a man thrust at another in hostile mood with a spear shaft or an ax handle or whatever [the weapon] that he uses but sheds no blood, a half atonement shall be due; but if blood is shed, there shall be owing the wound fine and the leech money and the customary fines to the king; but the half atonement falls away.

22. IF A MAN WOUNDS ANOTHER WITH HOSTILE INTENT

If a man wounds another with hostile intent, whatever [the weapon that] he wounds [him with], he shall be outlawed and shall forfeit all that he owns except his land alone and whatever he carries with him into the woods and is able to hide in bush and coppice and such money as has been paid out for land. But from the money and movables that remain the man who suffered the injury shall take his compensation without an increase, and the bailiff shall take what is left over. But if he [the outlaw] wishes to buy his release from outlawry, he shall pay fifteen marks; and [the injured man] shall take his compensation out of those fifteen marks and shall then give him pledges of peace. But his person shall never be wholly secure until he has paid compensation to the prosecutor and to the king's bailiff. If he offers atonement to both, he regains his rights whether they accept the offer or not. If a man by a single onset does injury to two men or more, he shall be outlawed to the same degree as if he had wounded only one; and let him pay the atonement due to each and fifteen marks to the king. And when a man does injury to two men or more by a single onset, he shall pay the wound fine to each one of them and one fine to the king.

23. CONCERNING ATTACKS BY BANDS OF MEN AND WOUNDS INFLICTED BY WEAPONS THAT ARE NOT ALL BORNE BY THE SAME MAN

If two bands meet, each counting five men or more than five and they come to blows and a man belonging to one of the bands is slain, he is the banesman who comes out of the fray and acknowledges the deed as his own; but if no one comes out [and assumes the guilt], they are all outlaws. And the dead man's heir shall have the right to name the best man in either band as the banesman, unless this one is able to clear himself with a threefold oath, or with the hot iron if he cannot find oath helpers. Let the deed be reported if there were not more than eight concerned in the fight, the dog being the ninth. Let it be reported if there were seven concerned, or fewer, unless eyewitnesses or the complainants were present; then the slayer shall not be held a murderer. If a man is slain with three weapons of a sort that are not borne together, the one a broadax, the second a timber ax, [the third] a spear and a sword, which are [borne together as] one man's weapon, the prosecutor may charge three men with the slaying. He shall call men to examine the wounds and shall have oaths taken on the [Gospel] book at the thing by men who are summoned to do so, as to how many weapons were employed in the slaying. But if there are five [men] in each of the two bands and a man is slain in either band, and if both sides send forth the arrow and charge each other with the guilt, and all come to the thing, the circumstances shall be examined with care, and that side shall [be judged to] have caused the slaying which had shown hostility at the beginning. If no specific action can be brought,[7] each one may clear himself with a twelvefold oath, unless the actual slayer shall be produced.

24. IF A MAN WOUNDS TWO MEN OUT ON THE HIGHWAY

If a man wounds two men out on the highway, each one shall testify for the other, and for each the wound shall serve as the second witness.

If a man comes upon a dead body in his forest or in the forest of another man, he shall send forth the arrow and send a message with the arrow, asking all to assemble where the body lies. If any one can identify the body, he has the choice, if he is the right man to bring the action, to prosecute two men to the twelvefold oath. But if it happens that no one can identify the man, the case shall rest, if the body shows the marks of a man's deed, till the prosecutor arrives, and he still has the right to prosecute two men to the twelvefold oath. If the prosecutor is in the fylki but does not arrive within seven nights, the bailiff shall summon him [to come]

[7] For lack of evidence against any particular man. See Hertzberg, *Glossarium*, *Sǫk.*

within half a month; a month, if he is outside the fylki, or two months, if he is outside this jurisdiction but within the land. Now if this one comes or does not come, and whether the bailiff has to prosecute the case or the proper prosecutor does come, two men shall be prosecuted with witnesses to common rumor to the twelvefold oath, and a third only if the guilt can be proved. But if the prosecutor refuses to bring action, he has lost his right in the case and after that it belongs to the bailiff. And the man who occupies the land where the body was found shall bring it to church or pay six oras to the archbishop. And he shall collect the expense from the landlord, unless the [slain man's] heir is accessible. In the same way, if a corpse drifts to land, the one who occupies the land shall take the body to church as is ordered in the church law or pay six oras to the archbishop.

25. IF A MAN DISAPPEARS SO THAT NO ONE KNOWS WHERE HE IS

If a man disappears so that no one knows where he is, he shall be sought after for a twelvemonth; after that, if he can be found nowhere, his heir has the right to prosecute two men to the twelvefold oath.

26. IF A MAN ACCIDENTALLY HURTS ANOTHER IN THE WOODS

If two men go into the woods together to fell trees and it turns out so ill that a tree falls on one of the two, [a tree] so large that one man [alone] cannot lift it off the one who lies underneath, a threefold oath shall be required in defense, if the heirs wish to bring suit and charges. But if one man can [lift the tree alone], he shall offer a twelvefold oath in his defense.

27. AGAIN CONCERNING TWO MEN IN THE WOODS

Again, if two men go into the woods to shape timbers and the ax used by one slips and strikes the other, and if men come to [the place] where he [the injured man] lies and he is still able to speak and states that the stroke was due to carelessness, the other man shall leave the land within five nights, if it is summer, and within half a month, if it is winter; but he shall keep all his property. But if the injured man is unable to speak when men find him, the other shall be outlawed and all that he owns, unless he can present a twelvefold oath in his defense.

28. IF A MAN SHOOTS OVER A HOUSE

If a man sends a shot over a house or a ship and hits another man, and if the wounded man is able to speak when men find him, or if men know that the wound was due to carelessness, the banesman shall depart from the land with all his [belongings]. And if an injury is due to chance or accident, there is nothing due to the king.

29. IF A MAN COMES BRUISED OR BLOODY TO THE THING

If a man comes bruised or bloody to the thing and one witness testifies with him, the man who gave him the injury shall be outlawed. If a man is hurt or wounded so [severely] that he cannot speak, let him send forth the arrow as soon as he is able to speak; and such an arrow thing shall be as valid as if the arrow had been sent forth the same day. But if the man dies, the arrow shall be sent forth by the one who occupies the land.

30. IF A MAN IS WOUNDED IN THE COUNTRY

If a man is wounded in the country, the arrow shall be sent forth on account of the wound and a thing shall be called. And if the one who wounded the man wishes to attend the thing, let him ask for grith, and the freemen shall give him grith for the journey to and from the thing, according to law, for five nights in the summer and half a month in the winter. It is further enacted that access to the thing shall be denied no man, except a banesman who slays a man at the thing and is caught in the hue and cry, and a thief [who is caught] with the stolen goods on his shoulder. And if a man is declared an outlaw at a shire thing or at an arrow thing held where the shire thing is properly held, and if he desires to go into that fylki to request a hearing at that thing, the freemen shall not grant the request. But every other man shall have access to the thing and shall defend his case as best he can. But if a man is refused access to the thing, he must not be outlawed at that thing but [sometime] after that thing. And the freemen cannot be held accountable, even though the injured man may die of his wounds, if the banesman is outlawed.

31. IF A FATHER BECOMES DEMENTED

If a father becomes demented to such a degree that he kills his son, or if a son [kills] his father, or a brother his brother, he shall leave the land as an outlaw and shall never return to the realm. And if he who was killed left a son or several [sons] or a daughter born in wedlock, they shall take such inheritance from their father as he would have taken if he were living. But if there are no such [children], the inheritance shall go to the one who is nearest to it, whether a man or a woman. If a father slays his son or a son his father or a brother his brother, the property of the slain man shall go as provided above. And the rule shall be the same in the case of women of the same kinship as [in the case of] men, unless he [the evildoer] shall break the bonds[8] that were laid upon him because of his madness or because [his sanity] was in doubt.

32. IF A DEMENTED MAN BREAKS HIS BONDS

If a man becomes so demented that he breaks his bonds and becomes a man's bane, he shall leave the land as soon as he is restored to reason, and he shall keep all his possessions. And he shall have grith for half a month in the summer and for a month in the winter. But if it appears that a man is insane, whoever will may bind him with impunity and bring him to the thing and turn him over to his kinsmen; let him release him there and disclaim all responsibility [for him]. It is the duty of men to watch over all madmen, and [they shall do it] without guilt. A demented man is the ward of his heir, but he does not come into this wardship until the heir knows that he is insane; and he may lay bonds upon him if he thinks best. If a man brings action charging the heir of a madman with failing to care for him, let him defend himself with his own oath. If a madman wounds another, [his heir] shall pay the wound fine and the leech money, but there is nothing due to the king. Only in case a man breaks out of his bonds and men know the circumstances are his doings to be regarded as those of a madman.

33. IF A WOMAN SLAYS A MAN

If a woman slays a man, his kinsmen have the right to kill her if they wish, if she does not leave the land within five days in the summer and half a month in the winter.

[8] This was regarded as unmistakable evidence of insanity.

34. IF A MINOR SLAYS A MAN

Every man is a minor till he is fifteen winters old. And if such a person slays a man, he shall leave the land by the fifth day in the summer and within two weeks in the winter; but he shall have all his chattels. If he remains beyond this reprieve, he is an outlaw, [he] and all his property. And his near kinsmen, agnate or cognate, may accompany the minor with impunity to some other part of the king's dominions to find home and keeps for him there.

35. IF A WOMAN KILLS HER HUSBAND

If a woman kills her husband or contrives [his death], being impelled by the wickedness of lying with another man or intending [to lie with him], the kinsmen of the slain man shall take no atonement in her case. Let them do as they prefer, maim her or kill her; and a full wergeld shall be taken out of her possessions if she did the killing and half a wergeld if she contrived it. And out of the property of him who did the killing the kinsmen of the dead man shall have a full wergeld; and the king shall have what remains both in land and in movables; and the man shall go into permanent outlawry. If she denies doing or having contrived the deed, let her clear herself with the hot iron. If a husband uses his wife ill without cause and the facts are known to eyewitnesses, and if anger overcomes her [to such a degree] that she does him injury, let her leave the land and abide abroad according as the archbishop shall advise and the circumstances of the case [shall demand]. And the husband's kinsmen shall have such compensation out of her property as seems right to good men. And if she returns on the advice of the archbishop, the king shall have payment for the release from outlawry.[9]

36. A FATHER IS ACCOUNTABLE FOR THE DEEDS OF HIS CHILD

A father is accountable for the deeds of his child till it is eight winters old; but a boy of eight winters shall be entitled to a half atonement, and shall pay atonement at the same rate, till he is fifteen winters old. Similarly, if a minor injures a man's property,

[9] *Skógarkaup:* payment for security outside the woods to which an outlaw would naturally flee.

let him pay a half compensation or offer a threefold oath, if the case is important enough to call for a threefold oath.

37. CONCERNING DAMAGE TO PROPERTY AND PLOTTING TO INJURE PROPERTY

It is further enacted that in cases of plotting to injure a man in his goods, he [the accused] shall support his denial with a threefold oath, if the plot has been carried out and is such as calls for a sixfold oath. If [the charge is] less [serious], a single oath [will suffice]; or let him pay a half atonement. If he refuses to pay, the plaintiff shall summon him to be at home to [receive] a thing summons and thereupon [he shall summon him] before a thing. And at that thing he shall pay a half atonement or go into outlawry.

38. IF A MAN OF MAJOR AGE CHARGES ANOTHER WITH HAVING USED HIM ILL

If a man of major age charges another with having used him ill in his youth to such a degree that an atonement can be claimed, but the man denies the charge, let him refute it with a threefold oath. But if he is found guilty and claims that the matter is already settled, let him produce witnesses who are able to state that he had come to a settlement with the guardian and the kinsmen [of the complainant]. If he can produce no witnesses to an agreement, let him prove his contention with a threefold oath or pay a half atonement. And whoever violates the agreement after such witness has been borne is a pledge breaker; [he is] also [a pledge breaker] if he has violated it earlier and his guilt is proved by witnesses.

39. CONCERNING THE SEVEN WOMEN ON WHOSE ACCOUNT A MAN MAY FIGHT AND KILL

Now, there are seven women on whose account a man may fight and kill[10] without fear of [action either by] king or kinsmen and with right to bring suit against the dead man. The first is the man's wife, the second his mother, the third his daughter, the fourth his sister, the fifth his stepdaughter, the sixth his daughter-in-law, the seventh his brother's wife. He shall send forth the arrow with this

[10] Cf. *Gul.*, c. 160.

message that he found the man in carnal union with the woman, whoever is named. As testimony [let him offer] the upper or the lower bed sheet or bloody clothes or such witnesses as were present, men or women.

40. IF A MAN DEPARTS FROM THE HIGHWAY

If a man departs from the highway [and travels] where there is neither horn path nor hoof path and men shout to him but he will not answer, and if they slay him, the action must be brought against the dead man; and the arrow shall summon [men] to the place where the slain man lies. And his heir shall have the choice of two courses, as he may prefer: he may let him be held unworthy of atonement as the suit implies, though no man finds any of his goods in the dead man's possession, or he may offer a sixfold oath in his defense; but the heir must make his claim good, if he wants to get atonement for his kinsman.

41. IF A MAN HARBORS AN OUTLAW

If a man gives food or shelter to an outlaw or conveys him or guides him, he shall lose all his rights and shall suffer the same form of outlawry as the other who did the deed. If a freeman is accused of having harbored an outlaw, let him clear himself with his own oath, if [the outlawry] has not been published in the fylki. But even though he harbors one whose outlawry has been published in the fylki, if he does not know him, he does it unwittingly and may defend himself with a threefold oath. If the king grants an outlaw permission to remain in the land, anyone may entertain him and consort with him with impunity; but to those whose duty it is to prosecute he remains an outlaw until he has made atonement and they have pledged peace to each other. A banesman shall not enter the land unless he has the king's token to show at the thing, or he has been restored to his rights by the king's official to whom he has shown the king's token at the thing where such action shall be taken, [authorizing] him [the official] to settle on the king's behalf all suits brought against the man in that fylki.

42. CONCERNING MUTILATION

If a man hews off another man's hand or foot or whatever the limb is that he cuts off, he shall be outlawed, he and all his possessions except his land or money paid out for land. He may buy his release from outlawry with fifteen marks and out of those fifteen marks the maimed [man] shall have three for the mutilation, the same kind of money as the king receives, and three marks additional from the man who maimed him. If the man has wounded him in several places, he shall owe the wound fine and the leech money [to the man] and the usual fine to the king, and he may remain in the land. And though there be but one severed limb, there shall be owing the wound fine and the leech money. And if men aid in the maiming by holding the man, everyone who is convicted of having held him shall pay a half wergeld, or let him deny with a threefold oath that he held him because he wanted him to get the hurt that he did get; and let the maimer pay a full wergeld. But if they are unwilling either to deny or to pay, let them all go into outlawry at the very next thing.

43. CONCERNING THE MAIMING OF A MAN

If a man castrates another who is free and entitled to peace and security, or cuts out his tongue, he is an outlaw and shall never be allowed in the land again. The arrow shall be sent forth and those who were maimed shall come to the thing. Three men shall suffer outlawry in such a case, the one who removed [the member] and and the two who held [the man]. The one whose tongue was cut away shall come forward at the thing to see if he can point out the man who did him ill; and if he recognizes him, he shall thrust his ax handle at the man, and the man shall be outlawed. But if he is not at the thing, the maimed one shall write his name, if he knows runes; if he does not know them, let him make such signs as will tell men what the truth is. Then the three who did the deed shall go into outlawry, the two who held the man and the one who did the cutting. But if he [the maimed one] accuses others of having shared in the deed, let them defend themselves with a threefold oath.

44. IF A MAN PUTS OUT ANOTHER MAN'S EYE

If a man puts out another man's eye, the deed shall send three men into outlawry, the one who put out [the eye] and the two who held [the man]. But if the man accuses more [than three], the other shall defend himself with a threefold oath. If they make an atonement, they shall stock a farm for him with twelve cows, two horses, and three thralls. If [any part of] this outfit perishes before the man dies, let them come forward with another like the first, and again a third time if the earlier one perishes but then the compensation shall be complete. They shall then give each other pledges of peace; but the king shall not take his fee for the release from outlawry before the first outfitting has been made.

45. IF A MAN CUTS OFF ANOTHER MAN'S NOSE

If a man cuts off another man's nose, he shall pay him an atonement of twelve oras valued in burned silver; for all atonements for violating the person of a free-born man, except in the case of dependents, shall be valued in burned silver. In case the upper lip is also cut away, three marks shall be due. If a man injures another in the nose, compensation shall be due for visible blemish, and it shall be thus wherever a blemish is not concealed by hair or by clothes. And the compensation for a visible blemish shall be rated by impartial men. If a man injures another in a joint, half a mark shall be due if the instep [is hurt] and six oras, if it is the knee or the hip. If a man knocks teeth out of a man's jaw, half a mark [shall be due] for each of the four in front; but there are four eyeteeth for each of which [the fine is] two oras; for each molar one ora. If a man knocks teeth out of another man's jaw with stroke or blow or thrust, they are to be paid for as specified above, and there shall be a full atonement in addition. If a man puts out another man's eye, there shall be due three marks and the leech money [to the man] and the customary fines to the king. If he [otherwise] wounds the man, he shall pay three marks and a full atonement. If he injures an eye, [the compensation] shall be six marks. If a man cuts off another man's ear, he shall atone with six oras.

46. THE VALUE OF A HAND IS STATED

The next is to state the value of a man's hand. If a man cuts off another man's thumb, he shall pay him twelve oras in compensation; half a mark for the next finger and the same amount for the long finger; three oras for the fourth finger and one ora for the little finger. But the toes shall be cheaper by half than the fingers, and one shall reckon in the same way from the largest toe as from the thumb.

47. CONCERNING THE EFFECTS OF WOUNDING A MAN

The next is what payments are to be made if a man wounds another. An ora is [due] if the flesh is touched; another, if the edge touches a bone; a third, if the edge cuts into the bone; a fourth, if the foot is wounded below the ankle. If a man injures another below the knee and the wound goes in as far as the marrow, he shall pay him half a mark in atonement for the wound; if it is above the knee and goes in as far as the marrow, he shall pay six oras. Flesh wounds shall be atoned for with one ora if the weapon enters; with a second, if it [goes through and] comes out. If a man is injured in the abdomen with a deep wound, he [the aggressor] shall atone with six oras; if the wound is in the chest and is deep, he shall pay four oras.

48. CONCERNING WOUNDS

If a man wounds another so that the covering of the brain is injured in front, the atonement is four oras; if it is injured in the back of the head, [the atonement is] six oras.

49. CONCERNING BONE MONEY, IF A BONE IS SEVERED IN THE WOUND

Now, bone money is due in every case where a bone has to be removed from a man's wound. If it is very small and [the coins] rattle on the shield,[11] an ora is due. An ora shall be due for every small bone till there are six. If the broken bone is so large that six holes can be bored into it, six oras shall be due, but bone money shall never exceed six oras. If it becomes necessary to burn a man's wound, an ora shall be due as compensation for the pain; this [shall be due] every time it needs to be burned. An ora shall be due every month as leech money and two months' supply of meal and butter; this shall be paid by him who caused the wound. If it shall be necessary to turn the [injured] man on his face, there shall be a fine for evil intent: six oras to a hauld, and as his rank rises above the

[11] The money is ready for payment.

hauld's rank, every man's compensation increases by one-third. And it shrinks in the same ratio: a free-born man's compensation is four oras; that of a reksthegn, three oras; and that of a freedman, two oras. All this shall be measured in burned silver.

50. NO MAN SHALL ATTACK ANOTHER IN HIS HOME

No man shall attack another in his home, neither the king nor any other man. If the king does this, the arrow shall be sent forth through all the shires;[12] and [men shall] go upon him and slay him, if they are able to seize him; and if he escapes he shall never be allowed to return to the land. And whoever refuses to join in pursuing him shall pay [a fine of] three marks, and a like amount shall be due for failing to forward the arrow.

51. IF A JARL ATTACKS A MAN IN HIS HOME

If a jarl goes upon a man in his home, the arrow shall be sent forth through four shires, and [men shall] go upon him and slay him; and if he escapes he shall never be allowed to return. And everyone who refuses to join in pursuing him shall suffer the penalty provided above; and for failing to send the arrow forward the fine is three marks silver.

52. IF A BARON ATTACKS A MAN IN HIS HOME

If a baron attacks a man in his home and slays him, the arrow shall be sent forth through two shires, and [men shall] go upon him and slay him. If he escapes he shall go into outlawry and let him never return to the land except in the train of a king who comes to conquer the land, or with a jarl, or if he returns with reliable tidings of hostile invasion. If any man fails to send the arrow forward, he owes a fine of twelve oras; and, if he fails to join in the hue and cry, he owes a baug. These [fines] shall all be valued in burned silver.

53. IF A HAULD WOUNDS A MAN

If a hauld wounds a man, he shall owe a fine of six baug fines to the king, and there are twelve oras in each baug. If a wellborn man wounds a man, he shall pay a fine of four baugar. If a reks-

[12] The eight shires about the Trondheim Fjord.

thegn wounds a man, he shall pay a fine of three baugar; and if a freedman wounds a man, he shall pay a fine of two baugar. If a baron wounds a man, he shall pay a fine of twelve baugar; and if a jarl wounds a man, he shall pay a fine of twenty-four baugar. If the king wounds a man, he shall pay a fine of forty-eight baugar. And there shall be twelve oras in each baug, and the fines shall be paid to all those who are of this jurisdiction.[13] And they shall all be valued in burned silver.

54. CONCERNING MEN FROM INNER, AND FROM OUTER, TRONDHEIM

If a man from Inner Trondheim[14] is slain in Outer Trondheim[15] or one from Outer Trondheim [is slain in Inner Trondheim], the arrow shall be sent forth. If the one who is the right man to prosecute the case is at the arrow thing, let him prosecute according to law; but if he [the prosecutor] is not at the first thing, the case may rest for a month. When he has learned [of the deed], let him summon the slayer wherever he comes upon him, to the thing; and it shall be the first thing to be held after his arrival. If he does not find him, let him summon him at that thing to a later thing. If he is the proper one to prosecute, he shall be allowed to produce his witnesses exactly as if he had been present at the first arrow thing; and the accused [shall be allowed] his defense in the same way. For no man may annul the suit of another during the month following the time when he learns of the deed. But if the one whose duty it is to prosecute denies [that he has learned of the deed], let him produce two witnesses at the thing [to testify] that he had not heard of this before. If the charge is against a freeman or the son of a freeman, one who occupies a farm, the law is that his homestead shall be held as security for him during the month when the other has the right to bring his action; after that it shall be released as a matter of course. If the one who has the suit has not destroyed it, let him bring the action as has been set forth above; and let him

[13] Apparently these fines were to be paid into a common treasury in which the king did not share.

[14] Inner Trondheim: the four shires lying about the inner stretches of the fjord.

[15] Outer Trondheim: the four shires bordering on the outer stretches of the fjord.

bring it within a twelvemonth if he is in the kingdom; otherwise he has destroyed his case.

55. TO RELEASE A THRALL

If a thrall is in the process of buying his release, let him not be given his freedom before he has paid one-half of the price. But if he receives his freedom before [he has done this], no one shall be outlawed for [his dealings with] him except the man only who gave him his freedom.

56. IF A MAN IS SLAIN IN THE COUNTRY AND IT IS NOT KNOWN WHETHER HE IS A FREE MAN OR A THRALL

If a man is slain in the country and no one knows whether he is a free man or a thrall, the arrow shall be sent forth none the less. Now if the man's master appears at the first thing, he shall be allowed to produce witness as to whether the man was a free man or a thrall. And if he proves him a free man, the banesman shall go into outlawry; but nothing shall be charged against the freemen, unless they harbor him after that. If the master does not appear at the first thing, the earliest thing to which he can come shall be counted his first thing, and he shall have his witnesses exactly as if it were his first thing. Then if he proves the slain a free man, the banesman shall go into outlawry; but if the [slain] man proves to be a thrall, his value shall be appraised and this amount shall be paid to the owner along with the fine for evil intent. If a man goes forth from the fylki in which he has his abiding place and kills or injures a man in another fylki, let the prosecutor come forward and summon him to a thing in the fylki where he [the prosecutor] suffered the injury and within half a month after the man's departure. And let him have as many men with him as he likes at the thing moot; and that thing shall be as competent as if it were held on the very day [of the offense]. If it is men from Outer Trondheim who have to deal with each other in that suit and both are outside their shires, let the prosecutor summon a thing after seven nights; also, if the men concerned in the suit are from Inner Trondheim, let the case proceed as stated above. If the men who have to deal with each other are from both Inner and Outer Trondheim, the thing shall be summoned [to meet] after half a month. And if men within the fjord area have to deal with men from beyond that area, but within our law, the thing shall be summoned [to meet] after a month. And if the men who have to deal with each other [in a suit] are from beyond the fjord area but each in his [own] fylki, the thing shall be summoned [to meet] after half a month. But if the men who have to deal with each other are both outside their shires and beyond the fjord area though within our law, however distant [they may be] from each other, the thing shall be summoned [to meet] after a month.

57. IF A BAILIFF IS WOUNDED OR SLAIN IN A CHURCH

If a bailiff is wounded or slain in a church or at a merrymaking or at a thing, the offender becomes an outlaw by [his attack on] him as on any other man. But [if the deed is committed] in any other place, he shall pay a fine of fifteen marks, and in any other place the [injured] man shall receive an atonement one-half less than that of a hauld. And all others who hold a bailiff's office, excepting the archbishop's bailiff, shall have their rights to atonement reduced below those of the king's bailiff as much as their lords' rights to atonement fall below [those of the king].

58. IN THREE PLACES ALL MEN SHALL ENJOY PEACE AND SECURITY

In three places, in church, at a thing, and at a merrymaking, all men shall be equally sacred [in their persons]; but nowhere else does a man incur outlawry on account of the place.

59. CONCERNING THE BISHOP'S BAILIFF

The bishop's bailiff shall enjoy such rights to atonement as belong to his rank and as he had when he entered upon the duties of bailiff.

60. CONCERNING THE KING'S TABLE SERVANTS

The king's table servants[16] shall have the same rights to atonement as the hauld in every respect, more and less. But his other servants, if one must atone [to the king] for them, shall have the hauld's right, [only] if they wear the ale cloth about the neck. Likewise, the man who steers the king's trading vessel from land

[16] See Glossary, "Seneschal."

to land shall have the hauld's right; the king's goldsmith, too, shall have the hauld's right. But the staller shall have a baron's right in every respect, more and less.

61. IF A THRALL ACCOMPANIES HIS MASTER TO CHURCH

If a thrall accompanies his master to church or to a merrymaking or to a thing, his person shall be sacred wherever the ship is moored or drawn up on land. If a man does him injury in any of these places, he shall pay the king a baug valued in burned silver; and the master shall have his atonement in burned silver. And whoever strikes a thrall shall be accountable for him, even though the thrall strikes back and does injury [in his turn]. If the master of the thrall proves the offense against anyone and the thrall dies, he shall have the value of the thrall from the man who struck first. And [the offender] shall remain responsible with respect to the thrall until he has atoned to the master.

62. IF EVILDOERS WEARING DISGUISES ARE KILLED AND HOW THEY SHALL BE ATONED FOR

If men put on disguises and go to a man's homestead to attack him and carry off his goods, the arrow shall be sent forth and the men shall be pursued and killed; but if they escape they escape as outlaws. If those of the household can identify the men who made the visit, whatever they testify to shall be regarded as truth. But if they [the evildoers] wish to make an atonement and return to the land, the leader shall pay a fine of forty marks and each one of the others three marks, and let them return to the fylki where they were outlawed. And [they shall] atone to the man whom they molested to such an amount as he can maintain on oath and for injuries to his livestock according to the award of impartial men; and [they shall pay] a full atonement for every blow up to three, and forty marks if there are more than three; and they shall not be restored to their rights until they have made these payments. They shall enjoy peace from all men in going to the thing to make this atonement, and one may entertain with impunity any man who is on the journey to this thing. But if they deny the guilt, the leader shall carry the hot iron, though for himself only; the others shall defend themselves each one with a threefold oath.

V. [MISCELLANEOUS PROVISIONS]

1. HOW A BEACON SHALL BE TENDED

It is enacted that if a man falls asleep while keeping watch at a beacon fire and the beacons burn to the south but not to the north, he shall owe a fine of three marks. A freeman or a freeman's son shall keep the watch at the beacon and shall keep [it] till midday. But if it is not kept in this way, each one of those [responsible] shall owe the king a fine of three marks valued in burned silver. Two shall keep the watch together. And if any hidden. . . . [1]

2–6. [CONCERNING LAW SUITS AND PLEDGES]

. . . the prosecutor shall have the right to sue for such an amount as the law indicates or as good men think right. Then this promise to abide by the law and this grith pledge shall be as completely valid for either side as if they had themselves accepted the promise and given the grith. And the chattels of those who did the deed [shall remain] in pledge, each for the other, but not the chattels of one who [merely] agrees to abide by the law, unless there is such an understanding. And if a man dies of his wounds, his heirs shall frame their suit according to the judgment of good men. A complete settlement can be attained by the man himself when he has been healed; but not by the one who took or offered the pledge unless he is the [deceased man's] heir.

7. CONCERNING ASSAULTS AND OTHER DEEDS OF VIOLENCE

Whenever men fight in hostile mood and two arrow things are summoned, each to its proper place, and the men come both to the five-day thing, the one who first sent forth the arrow shall call his witnesses first; and let him present all the witnesses that he has while the other listens to them. And the case shall remain undecided until both sides have presented their testimony, and the freemen shall weigh the evidence. But if either thing passes

[1] Lacuna in manuscript; a part of chapter 1 and chapters 2–5 are missing; chapter 6 is also missing in part.

judgment before this is done, thus thrusting aside the other man's thing and testimony, the one [who called it] has destroyed his case, and the one who declared the judgment shall owe a fine of three marks, and each one of the others who held up their weapons shall pay a baug. And let him have judgment who stands on the law.

8. CONCERNING PRIVATE HEARINGS

It is ordered concerning the five-day moot that the one who first laid the ban shall have his witnesses heard first. But if either one calls for a judgment before all the evidence on both sides has been heard and weighed, he who deals in this way has ruined his case. And nobody's suit shall be damaged by the character of the day on which he presents his witnesses, though it must not be on a day that becomes holy at noon.

9. CONCERNING NEAR KINSMEN, AGNATE AND COGNATE

Whenever near kinsmen, agnate and cognate, the four from either side who are authorized by law to give men grith [with a view] to settlement or to give pledges of peace and security, do give these in return for the wergeld, the grith [that is given] at the grith moot and the truce pledges shall be honored on both the father's and the mother's side, as if each [kinsman] had given them himself. But he who violates them is a trucebreaker and a grith nithing with respect to those pledges and guaranties which these near kinsmen have given, just as if he had himself held the [Gospel] book, if the case is dealt with as shall now be set forth. The money shall be paid before witnesses to the kinsmen [of the slain man] on the terms agreed upon at the peace moot. No one shall be allowed to offer any atonement other than that agreed upon and accepted by the kinsmen, agnate and cognate. If atonements are offered before witnesses, such [atonements] as he who should have them is willing to accept, but the man whose duty it is to collect the funds agreed upon to pay this fine is unable to provide for the [present] installment, the peace covenant shall not on this account be set aside. [The one who shall have the payment] shall appoint a man of his neighborhood to receive it, and it shall be delivered within three months; but if it is not delivered within that time, the grith is withdrawn as a matter of course. If a grith [pledge] or a [peace] pledge is violated, he is a grith nithing and a trucebreaker who is found guilty of doing this, whether it be done by counsel or by [actual] deed; his near kinsmen on both sides [are guilty] in the same way, if they themselves joined in the pledges. If the guilt is denied, the charge of instigating the crime shall be met with a sixfold oath and selected oath helpers; [a denial of] the deed itself [calls for] a twelvefold oath and selected oath helpers. And in any case in which a man has the right to demand compensation for violence against his own person or has such grievances as give him a right to atonement, he shall himself give the grith and the peace pledge and [set] the fine[2] in the presence of witnesses; and all his kinsmen are subject to these arrangements of grith and peace as completely as if each one of them had made the agreement himself. And if these arrangements are violated, the procedure shall be as set forth above. But if a man claims that he had no knowledge of the grith or the truce pledge that had been given and states that in violating an accepted settlement he was an unwitting offender, let him defend himself with a threefold oath; and if the oath fails, the failure leads to outlawry.

10. CONCERNING ATONEMENT MONEY AND WHO SHALL PAY IT

It is further enacted that if a man or men receive atonement [money] which they shall in turn pay to the kinsmen, let those who have shares in this present their claims before witnesses to such parts [of the payment] as are legally theirs. But if this is denied them and they make trouble on that account for those who paid the atonement, the one who withholds the money becomes a pledge breaker; and the same is true of him who demands a larger share of the money than is due him from the one who holds it and who makes trouble because he does not get what he demands in addition to what he ought to have. And let him who holds [the money] make the offer of payment before witnesses, if the other man refuses to accept [his share].

11. IF A MAN CLAIMS A SHARE IN THE ATONEMENT

If a man claims a share in the atonement, let him reckon up [the degree of] his kinship and let witness be borne if men have no

[2] *Sekt:* a fine to be paid to the authorities.

knowledge of it. But a man, who was born after the case had been settled and after the money had been paid into the atonement in which he would have shared had he been born earlier, does not share in the atonement.

12. CONCERNING A MAN'S WITNESSES, WHOEVER THEY MAY BE, WHO ARE TRAVELING TO THE THING

If a man's witnesses, whoever they may be, are traveling to the thing, [where they are] to testify as to the notice that one has given of a manslaying or to his night lodgings, and if they meet men who have been at the thing, they shall charge the men who have been at the thing with the duty to testify that they would have borne witness if they could have come to the thing. It shall then be satisfactory if they testify at the next thing. And if an arrow is sent forth when a thing token [only] is required, the freemen need pay no attention to it and the sender has forfeited his right to the help of men. Even though the freemen fail to attend that thing, they have nothing whatever to answer for, and the complainant has more than likely lost his suit, if men decide to take the matter up. No man shall suffer a conviction, unless he has been summoned to a thing by a man or an arrow. If a man is slain or stricken down or wounded before midday, an arrow thing may be held the same day, if the prosecutor wishes; but one held the next morning is also competent, if the prosecutor is present. And the arrow shall travel all the day when the thing is held and continue till sunset; and if the man is in condition to travel, the arrow thing [shall be held] at the nearest thingstead.

13. CONCERNING OUTLAWED PROPERTY

If a man's property is outlawed, the bailiff shall give a five-day summons at the thing to all those to whom the man who owned the property had debts to pay, [asking] them to come to the place where the chattels are; and let them all come to that place with their witnesses. Every man shall take away such payments as can be proved by witnesses, so long as the goods hold out. But if the goods do not hold out, the men shall all lose a proportional amount, and all [debts] of equal amount [shall be diminished] by as many oras as will be taken away when the sums are equalized.

But if the bailiff seizes the man's property before he has summoned the creditors, the men shall bring their witnesses forward at the next thing if they can get to it. If the bailiff refuses to hand [the chattels] over, they shall demand their goods; and if he still refuses to release [the property], they shall ask the freemen to join them in going upon him, and they shall take from him twice the amount that the witnesses have testified to. Let him [the creditor] have what is his and the freemen the remainder. But whatever has been paid to the man's wife in the presence of witnesses or given her in other forms of property, all that she shall keep; and if the bailiff takes away any of her belongings, he may be charged with plundering a homestead. And the aged and the minor dependents of an outlaw shall be dealt with in this wise: if the heir of an outlaw inherits land from him and the bailiff or other men in authority [take] all the outlawed goods, there shall be a five-day moot to which [the debtors] shall be summoned and men shall appraise [all] the encumbrances, those that rest on the land and those on the outlawed chattels; and the aged and the minor dependents shall be assigned to that part [the land or the chattels] as men think best. And the freemen shall appraise both the land and the outlawed chattels at the five-day moot to which men have been summoned and let them produce witness as to their claims in the outlawed chattels. But if the outlawed man owned no land and the bailiff attaches his movables, the aged dependents shall go with the movables. But if the outlawed man did own land and the bailiff takes nothing from his movables, he shall not be charged with his dependents. Well-born men shall not go begging in the king's garth;[3] money and maintenance shall be set aside for them out of the outlawed movables until the oldest has come of age. [The amount for] the support of each for a twelvemonth shall not exceed five oras, weighed and valued in burned silver; and thus [it shall be] whenever money is [set aside] for maintenance, that is, two and one-half oras, weighed.

14. PLUNDERING A HOMESTEAD

If men go upon a farmer to plunder his homestead and they take from him three cows, or more than three, or [chattels to] the

[3] See Glossary, "Garth."

value of three cows, it shall be called robbery, but only if so much is taken, unless it be that the farmer has only three cows, in which case it is robbery if one is carried off. And the arrow shall go forth and every man shall pass it into the hands of another or suffer the penalty of a baug. If men go in pursuit and find the robbers in possession of the stolen goods and they surrender, then the leader shall pay forty marks and each member of the crew, three marks. But if they resist they shall all be outlawed, no matter what happens, and they shall have no compensation for wounds; but the pursuers shall suffer no penalty and shall have compensation for all wounds.

15. IF A MAN LAYS BONDS ON A FREE MAN WITHOUT RIGHT

If a man lays bonds on a free man without right, he shall pay fifteen marks to the king and a full atonement to the man who was bound.

16. IF A HORSE DOES INJURY TO A MAN

If a horse does injury to a man or a dog bites [him] or a neat gores [him] or a boar wounds [him], let the owner of the beast renounce the ownership; but if he fails to do this, he has given support to a banesman, if the demand [for the beast] has been made upon him. But if no demand is made before the [close of the] fifth day, he [the injured man] has no claim in this matter; and the five-day period begins when he is able to take action. The one who is bitten shall go to the owner and demand the dog; and the owner shall put [a collar] on the dog, so that the other can take it away; [let him] push the dog from him, and hand him over to the one who was bitten. But if it is not done in this way, it is as if the owner of the dog had done [the injury]. If he [the owner] denies [responsibility], let him defend himself with a threefold oath in each one of the three cases. And if a horse does injury to a man or if a neat gores him, let him who is wounded bring action, and let him send forth such an arrow as he likes.[4] And if the owner does not surrender [the beast], it is as if he himself had done [the injury].

17. IF A MAN FEEDS [ANOTHER MAN'S] DOG

If a man feeds another man's dog longer than half a month, he becomes responsible for the dog's behavior as for his own dog.

[4] That is, take such a form of action as he prefers.

18. IF CHATTEL DESTROYS CHATTEL

If chattel destroys chattel, horn beast or hoof beast or thrall, half the value shall be paid [in reparation].

19. CONCERNING OATHS

If a man has offered an oath but later dies, and the oath is never sworn, his heir shall rid himself of that oath within the first ten weeks of oath days after he attains his majority, unless his guardians have given earlier satisfaction in that case.

20. IF A MAN KILLS A THRALL

If a man kills his thrall, he shall report the deed on the same day; he is then held answerable to no one but God; but if he fails to do this, he is a murderer.

21. IF A MAN DAMAGES ANOTHER MAN'S HORSE

If a man damages another man's horse, one that is rated at a mark or more in current coin [and he does it] with malice and hostile intent, and the guilt is proved against him, he shall be outlawed and all that he owns except his land, unless he acknowledges the deed and offers to pay the value [of the horse]. But if he denies the charge, a sixfold oath [is required], and if the oath fails he is outlawed. And [the value of] the horse shall be paid, even if [the damage is due to] chance or carelessness.

22. NO ONE SHALL SAY OF ANOTHER THAT HE SUBMITS TO DISHONOR

No one, neither a bailiff nor any other man, shall say of another that he has silently submitted to dishonor, unless ten men go with him to the thing to support the charge, as the secular laws provide. Two men shall swear and eight shall confirm the charge.

23–40.[5]

41. IF A MAN BUYS A THRALL FROM ANOTHER

If a man buys a thrall from another, the seller shall guarantee him for the time of the waxing of the next moon[6] against stitches

[5] Lacuna; several sheets missing. A fragment of five words is left untranslated.

[6] Literally, "for the following nine years," which looks like an impossible rendering. See *Gul.*, c. 57, a parallel enactment.

and fits and shall defend the sale throughout [the thrall's] life. And if he dies, let his heir assume the warrant.

42. CONCERNING DEBTS

In the matter of money debts that call for oaths, one oath can deny [a claim of] one [ora], two [oaths, one of] two [oras], and three [oaths, one of] three [oras]. But though the debt be more [than three oras], no greater oath than a threefold oath shall be demanded. And when men are bargaining in legal manner, let the reckoning be reduced if [it is] too high and increased if [it is] too low, until the right reckoning is found.

43. ALL HAVE A RIGHT TO ENJOY THE HARVEST

All who inhabit the land have a right to enjoy the harvest if God gives it. But if men place a ban in legal form on shipments from fylki to fylki but without the king's permission, it is ordered that, if barons counsel or join in placing such a ban, they shall owe a fine of forty marks to the king. If housecarles counsel or join in placing such a ban, they shall owe a fine of forty marks to the king. If a bailiff counsels and joins in placing such a ban, the same amount shall be due from him, if his wealth is sufficient; if it is not sufficient, the king shall determine his punishment.[7] And if the freemen place the ban on their own motion, all the men of the fylki who counseled and placed it shall owe the king a fine of forty marks.

44. CONCERNING NEW ORDINANCES

These new ordinances were adopted with the consent of King Magnus[8] and Archbishop Eystein and other bishops and the most prudent men of all the jurisdictions, namely, that all those who violate the pledges of peace and security which men give each other in cases of manslaying are to go into permanent outlawry and shall forfeit peace and property, land and movables, odal as well as other [land].

45. CONCERNING THEFT

Those who are killed because of thieving and banditry, whether they rob men on shipboard or on land, and [those who are killed]

[7] *Refsing:* probably corporal punishment in this case.
[8] Magnus Erlingsson.

for deeds of murder or witchcraft or for going abroad at night to call forth evil spirits or for seeking fortune tellers to promote heathendom thereby; and assassins who give aid in the slaying of men with whom they have no quarrel and take money for it (unless the king makes use [of them] to chastise and cleanse the land and thus to promote peace); and sorcerers and men who take women by violence or as booty in warfare contrary to the laws of God and men, whether they take their kinswomen or the wives of other men or take them without the consent of those who have the guardianship according to law or against the women's own will, no matter how their minds may change after they begin living together;[9] likewise those who take revenge for outlaws of this sort or demand money for them and the facts are known to witnesses—all such men are in permanent outlawry and have forfeited their right to peace and property. But those who defend their goods and their kinswomen against such men shall be in the protection of the law; and no fines shall be owing for the others either to king or kinsmen whether they be wounded or slain.

46. CONCERNING DOOMS[10]

All the dooms that are to be set to deal with cases of homicide or carnal dealings with those women on whose account a man has a legal right to kill shall be set according to law and [the defendant shall have] grith till the day set for the first payment.[11] And whoever disregards the legal decision of a doom without cause before the [day set for the] first payment or at the first payment violates his own grith and is a pledge breaker and has forfeited his right to peace and property. A man may be excused only if he is ill or wounded or has some other serious trouble which, as good men testify, prevents him from appearing [to make payment]; but the excuse must be presented on the appointed day. And the first [payment] shall be forthcoming within the same month and shall be brought to his [the plaintiff's] home and shall be proffered before

[9] Cf. *Gul.*, c. 32.

[10] Ordinance dating from the reign of Magnus Erlingsson, possibly published in 1164.

[11] This was a rather unusual form of the doom-institution which ordinarily did not deal with criminal cases.

two witnesses. And let him or his agent receive it there, unless the one who is to receive [the payment] wishes to ease the matter for the other. But in all [other] cases in which men join in appointing dooms, the one who disregards the decision shall owe a fine of eighteen oras to the plaintiff and the decision shall stand as before. And fifteen marks [shall be owing] to the king; and let the king or his officials bring action in behalf of both, but let him [the complainant] have his dues first according as the doomsmen have determined. The fines due to both [claimants][12] shall afterwards be apportioned according to the amount [of property] in dispute.[13] If the man still refuses to comply with the award, the [king's] officials shall summon him before the thing and declare him an outlaw, unless he shall pay [at the thing] such an amount as is here provided. The penalty is the same if a man disregards a decision that is reached at the Frostathing and confirmed with weapons both within the law court and without. And the eighteen oras which the prosecutor is to exact shall be divided in such a way that one-half goes to the men who were appointed to go from that fylki to the Frostathing in the year in which that judgment was reached. And let all [these] men sue for theirs along with the king's officials. But if either one shall utter dissatisfaction with his share, when the case returns to the herath, and asserts that it was not properly presented to the men of the law court, he may not disregard the decision without risk of penalty, but next year he may summon the man to the Frostathing who was in the suit against him and let both parties join in promoting the suit. And if the case is heard with the same outcome as before, the winner shall have his outlay paid in double by him who has annoyed him with a baseless lawsuit; and let him sue for this as in any other dispute about money.

[12] King and plaintiff.

[13] If there is not enough remaining to satisfy both fines.

VI. [THE WERGELD SYSTEM][1]

1. THE RECKONING OF THE WERGELD BEGINS AND IS DETAILED HERE AND ALSO HOW IT SHALL BE DIVIDED

Here a subject begins and is detailed which is dark to most men but which many have need to know; for there is a growing spirit of enmity among men and a lessening number of those who have the good will and the understanding [necessary] to distribute the prescribed fines, when they have been awarded. For at present it is more the custom to enumerate in the atonement how many marks of gold shall be owing for the one who was put to death; and the reason [for this] is that many do not know what a legal atonement should be, and even if they do know, few would now be satisfied with it. But the Frostathing book assigns a legal atonement to every man according to his rank and position and not such fines as may be screwed up or beaten down by those who sit in judgment and make the covenant.

2. CONCERNING THE SIX MARKS GOLD

Now it shall be told first of all how much each one shall receive from, or pay into, the baug or the atonement when a payment of six marks gold is awarded. The slayer or the slayer's son shall pay all the baugar unless there are *vísendr*. And since there have been inquiries as to who are called by this name, the term is now explained: if the slayer's father, son or brother, his father's brother, or his brother's son, the sons of his paternal uncles, or the sons of these sons are living, they are all called vísendr. And they are so called for the reason that each one of them is quite sure [*víss*][2] to pay that part of the atonement which is charged to him. And neither the slayer nor his son need pay the wergeld for these men, if there are such; but they shall pay the fines for all the *baugamenn*

[1] The editors of the Norwegian edition have suggested a number of emendations to the text of this section, most of which are to correct errors in numbers. These emendations have nearly all been incorporated in this version.

[2] This explanation is no doubt a conjecture merely.

that are wanting and [therefore do not join] in the payment, unless those who sat in the doom and made the award have agreed that the payment shall be dropped where the [corresponding] recipient is lacking; in that case such an amount is dropped for each one in the list as the others would receive if they were living.

3. MORE ABOUT THE SIX MARKS GOLD

The slayer or the slayer's son shall pay to the son of the slain man as a head baug five marks, weighed, out of the six marks gold. The father of the slayer shall pay a like amount to the father of the slain man. The brother of the slayer shall pay four marks, weighed, less two oras to the brother of the slain man. The paternal uncles of the slayer and the sons of his brothers shall pay twenty oras, weighed, to the paternal uncles of the slain man and to the sons of his brothers. And the sons of the slayer's [paternal] uncles and the sons of his "cousins"[3] shall pay thirteen oras, weighed, and an ertog to the sons of the slain man's paternal uncles and to the sons of his cousins. This money shall be divided into five parts and in such a way that the sons of uncles shall pay three parts and the sons of first cousins, two parts; and [they shall] receive [payments] in the same way

4. THE ONE MAIDEN WHO IS CALLED A BAUGRYGR[4]

Now, there is one maiden who is called a baugrygr; she both pays into the baug and receives payments from it, if she is an only child and has come into an inheritance, till she is seated in the bridal chair; then she throws the [right and the duty in the matter of the] fines back upon the knees of her kinsmen; after that she shall neither pay into, nor receive payments from, the baug. If there are two daughters or more, they shall have no right either to fines or to atonements. And the total amount that the baugamenn shall receive will be eighteen marks, weighed, less two ertogs.

5. CONCERNING THE GELD EKERS[5]

The men who are called geld ekers shall now be pointed out. A thrallborn son and a uterine brother are geld ekers, [also] a pater-

[3] See Glossary, "cousins."
[4] See *ibid.*, "Baugrygr."
[5] See *ibid.*, "Geld eker."

nal grandfather and a son's son, if both are living, which will rarely be. But even though both are living, the two shall receive [only] one man fine and they shall make payment in the same way. A thrallborn son of the slayer shall pay seventeen oras weighed to the thrallborn son of the slain man. A uterine brother of the slayer shall pay a like amount to the uterine brother of the slain man. The slayer's paternal grandfather and his son's son shall pay seventeen oras, weighed, to the slain man's paternal grandfather and to the son of his son. And to the sons of a geld eker there shall be paid eleven oras, weighed, and an ertog; and to the sons of the son of a geld eker a third less shall be paid.

6. CONCERNING THE SCHEDULE OF THE MAN FINES

There is one man whom we have not found in the schedule of man fines in the Frostathing Book; but he is none the less found in the kindred and is not farther away than a father's uterine brother. A complete conciliation is scarcely achieved if such a person is left outside, and the slayer remains in peril if this one has no share in the wergeld. Now this man fine is intended for him along with the son of a uterine brother; they shall divide twelve oras, weighed, and an ertog, if they are both among the living; but one shall take all, if there is only one; and they shall make payment in the same way. And the total amount that is paid to the geld ekers and to their sons and their sons' sons, will be thirteen and one-half marks, weighed, less one ertog.

7. THE MAJOR PAYMENTS TO COGNATES[6]

Here begins the [statement of the] major payments to cognates and is told how much each one shall receive from or pay to the others in this fine. The slayer's maternal grandfather and his daughter's son shall pay two marks, weighed, to the maternal grandfather of the slain man and to his daughter's son. The maternal uncle of the slayer and his sister's son shall pay twelve oras, weighed, to the maternal uncle of the slain man and to his sister's son. The sons of the slayer's "sistkins" shall pay a mark, weighed, to the sons of the sistkins of the slain man. The sons of the slayer's aunts shall pay five oras, weighed, and an ertog to the

[6] Paid to near kinsmen on the feminine side.

sons of the slain man's aunts. Now, the total amount that the men of the major cognate group receive will be five marks, weighed, and four ertogs, weighed.

8. THE LESSER PAYMENTS TO COGNATES[7]

Now it shall be told concerning the lesser payments to cognates how much each one is to pay to or receive from another [in this fine]. The son of the slayer's son's daughter shall pay nine oras, weighed, to the son of the slain man's son's daughter. The son of the slayer's daughter's daughter shall pay seven and one-half oras, weighed, to the son of the slain man's daughter's daughter. The son of the slayer's brother's daughter shall pay six oras, weighed, to the son of the slain man's brother's daughter. The son of the slayer's sister's daughter shall pay four and one-half oras, weighed, to the son of the slain man's sister's daughter. The sons of the slayer's sistkins' daughters shall pay three oras, weighed, to the sons of the slain man's sistkins' daughters. The sons of the daughters of the slayer's aunts shall pay one and one-half oras, weighed, to the sons of the daughters of the slain man's aunts. And the total amount that the men of the lesser cognate group shall receive will be four marks, weighed, less one-half ora.

9. MORE CONCERNING THE SCHEDULE OF THE MAN FINES

Now we shall speak of those men whom we have not found in the schedule of fines where the atonements are determined; for the Frostathing book does not distinguish clearly between those who are of the same mother and those by the same father. Still, they ought not all to share in the same fines, even though they be of equal kinship, if some are by the same father and others [only] of the same mother. One may take as example a man who is a uterine brother; he is not to be grouped in the matter of fines with one who is by the same father; the latter is a "baug man" while the former is a geld eker, and there is a fine intended for each. The payment provided for these in the new scale are as will now be set forth.

10. CONCERNING THE BROTHERS' SONS

Now, the sons of the slayer's uterine paternal uncles and the sons of his uterine cousins, shall pay ten oras, weighed, less an

[7] Paid to more distant kinsmen on the feminine side.

ertog to the sons of the slain man's uterine paternal uncles and to the sons of his uterine cousins. The uterine brother of the slayer's mother and the son of his uterine sister shall pay a mark, weighed, to the uterine brother of the slain man's mother and to the son of his uterine sister. The sons of the slayer's uterine sistkins[8] shall pay five oras, weighed, and an ertog to the sons of the slain man's uterine sistkins. The sons of the slayer's uterine aunts shall pay three and one-half oras, weighed, to the sons of the slain man's uterine aunts. A thrallborn brother of the slayer shall pay fifteen oras, weighed, to a thrallborn brother of the slain man. And this is the total received by these men.[9]

11. AND OUT OF THE SIX MARKS GOLD

And out of the six marks gold the total paid as lesser man money to the agnates amounts to thirteen oras, weighed, and an ertog. And this money shall be divided into five parts and in such a way that the men who are in the fourth degree of kinship to the slain man shall receive three of the five parts and the other two parts shall be set aside. And the total that the lot gives to those who are of this kinship and to be divided by them amounts to one mark, weighed. Now the remaining parts shall again be divided into five parts and the men who are in the fifth degree of kinship to the slain man shall take three of those five parts; and the amount will be three oras, weighed, and twelve pence, weighed. And the men who are in the sixth degree of kinship to the slain man shall take the two remaining parts; and the amount will be two oras, weighed, and eight pence, weighed. And we provide no fines farther out in the kindred for the reason that marriage is there allowed and kinship disappears. It is indeed very difficult to set a fine that will correspond exactly to [the degree of] kinship.

12. THE LESSER MAN FINES PAID TO COGNATES

The total of the lesser man fines paid to cognates amounts to five oras, weighed, and an ertog; and these fines shall be distributed like those discussed above. Let them be divided into five parts. Those who are in the fourth degree of kinship to the slain man shall

[8] See Glossary, "Sistkins." Cf. *Gul.*, c. 316.

[9] The total is not given; it will be five marks and one and one-half oras.

take three of the five parts, and these will amount to three oras, weighed, and twelve pence. Now the two remaining parts shall again be divided into five parts and those who are in the fifth degree of kinship to the slain man shall take three of these parts; and these will amount to one ora, weighed, and sixteen and one-half pence, weighed. And those who are in the sixth degree of kinship to the slain man shall take the two remaining parts; and these will amount to two and one-half ertogs, weighed, and one penny weighed.

13. CONCERNING THE SECOND [SCALE OF] FINES

Here begins the account of the second scale of fines and is told what each man shall receive or pay when a payment of five marks gold is awarded. The slayer or the slayer's son shall pay four marks, weighed, and four ertogs to the son of the slain man. The slayer's father shall pay a like amount to the father of the slain man. The slayer's brother shall pay three marks, weighed, and one ora, weighed, to the brother of the slain man. The slayer's paternal grandfather and his brother's son shall pay two marks, weighed, and two ertogs, weighed, to the slain man's paternal grandfather and to his brother's son. The sons of the slayer's paternal uncles and the sons of his cousins shall pay eleven oras, weighed, and six and one-half pence, weighed, to the sons of the slain man's paternal uncles and to the sons of his cousins. And the total amount received by the baugamenn will be fifteen marks, weighed, less one-half ora, weighed, and three pence, weighed.

14. CONCERNING THE GELD EKERS

Now it shall be told as to the fines allowed the geld ekers, how much each one shall pay to, or receive from, the other. The thrallborn son of the slayer shall pay fourteen oras, weighed, and ten pence, weighed, to the thrallborn son of the slain man. The slayer's uterine brother shall pay a like amount to the [uterine] brother of the slain man. The slayer's paternal grandfather and the son of his son shall pay fourteen oras, weighed, and ten pence, weighed, to the slain man's paternal grandfather and to the son of his son. And the sons of a geld eker shall receive nine and one-half oras, weighed, less three and one-half pence, weighed. And the sons of a geld eker's son shall receive a third less. And the total amount received by the geld ekers and their sons and sons' sons will be eleven marks, weighed, and five ertogs, weighed, and three and one-half pence, weighed.

15. CONCERNING THE MATERNAL GRANDFATHER AND THE DAUGHTER'S SON

The slayer's maternal grandfather and his daughter's son shall pay thirteen oras, weighed, and an ertog to the slain man's maternal grandfather and to his daughter's son. The slayer's maternal uncle and his sister's son shall pay ten oras, weighed, to the slain man's maternal uncle and to his sister's son. The sons of the slayer's sistkins shall pay seven oras, weighed, less an ertog to the sons of the slain man's sistkins. The sons of the slayer's aunts shall pay four and one-half oras, weighed, less three pence, weighed, to the sons of the slain man's aunts. And the total amount received by the major cognates will be four marks, weighed, and two and one-half oras, weighed, less three pence, weighed.

16. CONCERNING THE LESSER PAYMENTS TO COGNATES

Now it shall be told what each one shall pay to, or receive from, another, in the lesser payments to cognates. The son of the slayer's son's daughter shall pay seven and one-half oras, weighed, to the son of the slain man's son's daughter. The son of the slayer's daughter's daughter shall pay six oras, weighed, and fifteen pence, weighed, to the son of the slain man's daughter's daughter. The son of the slayer's brother's daughter shall pay five oras, weighed, to the son of the slain man's brother's daughter. The son of the slayer's sister's daughter shall pay one-half mark, weighed, less fifteen pence, weighed, to the son of the slain man's sister's daughter. The sons of the slayer's sistkins' daughters shall pay two and one-half oras to the sons of the slain man's sistkins' daughters. The sons of the daughters of the slayer's aunts shall pay four ertogs, weighed, less five pence to the sons of the daughters of the slain man's aunts. And the total amount received by the lesser cognates will be three marks, weighed, and two oras, weighed, and fifteen pence, weighed.

17. CONCERNING A THRALLBORN BROTHER

A thrallborn brother shall pay twelve and one-half oras, weighed, to the thrallborn brother of the slain man. The sons of the slayer's uterine paternal uncles and the sons of his [uterine] cousins, shall pay a mark, weighed, and four pence, weighed, to the sons of the slain man's uterine paternal uncles and to the sons of his uterine cousins. The uterine brother of the slayer's mother and the son of his uterine sister shall pay seven oras, weighed, less an ertog to the uterine brother of the slain man's mother and the son of his uterine sister. The sons of the slayer's uterine sistkins shall pay four and one-half oras, weighed, less four pence, weighed, to the sons of the slain man's uterine sistkins. The sons of the slayer's uterine aunts shall pay three oras, weighed, less five pence, weighed, to the sons of the slain man's uterine aunts. And the total amount received by these men will be four marks, weighed, and two and one-half oras, weighed, and five pence, weighed.

18. CONCERNING THE LESSER MAN FINES

And out of the five marks gold there shall be paid to the agnate kinsmen as lesser fines [a total of] eleven oras, weighed, and six, and one-half pence, weighed. This money shall be divided into five parts, and those who are in the fourth degree of kinship to the slain man shall have three of those five parts; and all those who are in the fourth degree of kinship to the slayer shall pay the fines. And the amount is seven oras, weighed, less an ertog, weighed. Now, the two remaining parts shall again be divided into five parts and the men who are in the fifth degree of kinship to the slain man shall take three parts; and this will amount to eight ertogs, weighed. And the men who are in the sixth degree of kinship to the slain man shall take the two parts; and this will amount to five ertogs, weighed, and six and one-half pence, weighed. And there is no need to pay atonements farther out in the kindred for there marriage is allowed and kinship disappears.

19. MORE ABOUT THE LESSER MAN FINES PAID TO COGNATES

The total of the man money paid to the lesser cognates amounts to four and one-half oras, weighed, less three pence, weighed. The money shall be divided into five parts, and the men who are in the fourth degree of kinship to the slain man shall take three of the five parts; and this will amount to eight ertogs, weighed, and three pence. Now the remaining two parts shall again be divided into five parts, and the men who are in the fifth degree of kinship to the slain man shall take three of the five parts; and this will amount to one ora, weighed, and three and one-half pence, weighed. And the men who are in the sixth degree of kinship to the slain man shall take the two remaining parts; and this will amount to two ertogs, weighed, and two and one-half pence, weighed. Now these fines are paid.

20. CONCERNING THE FOUR MARKS GOLD

Here begins the account of the third scale of fines and is told what each one shall pay to, or receive from, another when a payment of four marks gold is awarded. The slayer or his son shall pay three and one-half marks, weighed, less four ertogs to the son of the slain man. The slayer's father shall pay a like amount to the father of the slain man. The slayer's brother shall pay twenty oras, weighed, to the brother of the slain man. The son of the slayer's paternal uncle shall pay thirteen oras, weighed, and an ertog to the son of the slain man's paternal uncle. The sons of the slayer's paternal uncles and the sons of his cousins shall pay nine oras, weighed, less six and one-half pence, weighed, to the sons of the slain man's paternal uncles and to the sons of his cousins. Now the total amount received by the baugamenn will be twelve marks, weighed, less one ertog, weighed, and six and one-half pence, weighed.

21. THE GELD EKERS ARE DEALT WITH HERE

Now it shall be told as to the fines allowed the geld ekers how much each one shall pay to, or receive from, the other. The thrallborn son of the slayer shall pay eleven oras, weighed, and an ertog to the thrallborn son of the slain man. A uterine brother shall pay a like amount to a [uterine] brother of the slain man. The slayer's paternal grandfather and the son of his son shall pay eleven oras, weighed, and an ertog to the slain man's paternal grandfather and to his son's son. And seven and one-half oras, weighed, and three and one-half pence weighed [shall be paid] to the sons of the geld ekers and a third less to the sons of the geld ekers' sons; and the men who are the slayer's geld ekers shall pay the fines, if there are such men; if there are none, let those pay whose duty it is to compensate the geld ekers as the law provides. If the geld ekers are all among the living but none [can be found] to pay the fines on the slayer's behalf, the slayer shall compensate all the geld ekers; and if the slayer is no longer living, his son shall compensate all the geld ekers. But if neither the slayer nor his son is among the living, the slayer's father shall compensate two geld ekers: he shall pay eleven oras, weighed, and an ertog to the thrallborn son of the slain man and a like amount to the slain man's uterine brother. The slayer's brother shall pay eleven oras, weighed, and an ertog to the slain man's paternal grandfather and to his son's son. But if the slayer's father is not living, the slayer's brother shall compensate two geld ekers, and the slayer's paternal uncle and the son of his brother [shall compensate] one geld eker. Now, if the slayer's brother is not living, his paternal uncle and his brother's son shall compensate two geld ekers. The sons of the slayer's paternal uncles and the sons of his cousins shall compensate one geld eker. And each one of them shall demand pledges of peace and complete satisfaction in return for their payments. Now if all the geld ekers of the slain man are among the living but there is none living of the slayer's agnate kinsmen except those [who are] farthest out [in the kindred], these [latter] shall, nevertheless, compensate all the geld ekers. And the total amount received by the geld ekers and their sons and sons' sons will be nine marks, weighed, less thirteen pence, weighed.

22. CONCERNING THE MATERNAL GRANDFATHER

The slayer's maternal grandfather and the son of his daughter shall pay eleven oras, weighed, less an ertog, weighed, to the slain man's maternal grandfather and to the son of his daughter; and the slayer's maternal uncle and the son of his sister shall pay a mark, weighed, to the slain man's maternal uncle and to the son of his sister. The sons of the slayer's sistkins shall pay five oras, weighed, and an ertog to the sons of the slain man's sistkins. The sons of the slayer's aunts shall pay three and one-half oras and three pence, weighed, to the son of the slain man's aunts. And the total amount received by the major cognates will be three and one-half marks, weighed, less an ertog, weighed, and seven pence, weighed.

23. CONCERNING THE LESSER PAYMENTS TO COGNATES

Now it shall be told as to the lesser payments to cognates what each one shall pay to, or receive from, another. The son of the daughter of the slayer's son shall pay six oras, weighed, to the son of the daughter of the slain man's son. The son of the daughter of the slayer's daughter shall pay five oras, weighed, to the son of the daughter of the slain man's daughter. The son of the daughter of the slayer's brother shall pay four oras, weighed, to the son of the daughter of the slain man's brother. The son of the daughter of the slayer's sister shall pay three oras, weighed, to the son of the daughter of the slain man's sister. The sons of the daughters of the slayer's sistkins shall pay two oras, weighed, to the sons of the daughters of the slain man's sistkins. The sons of the daughters of the slayer's aunts shall pay one ora, weighed, to the sons of the daughters of the slain man's aunts. And the total amount that is received by the lesser cognates will be twenty-one oras, weighed.

24. CONCERNING A THRALLBORN BROTHER

A thrallborn brother of the slayer shall pay ten oras, weighed, to a thrallborn brother of the slain man. The uterine brother of the slayer's mother and the son of his uterine sister shall pay five oras, weighed, and an ertog to the uterine brother of the slain man's mother and the son of his uterine sister. The sons of the slayer's uterine sistkins shall pay three and one-half oras, weighed, and three pence, weighed, to the sons of the slain man's uterine sistkins. The sons of the slayer's uterine aunts shall pay seven ertogs, weighed, to the sons of the slain man's uterine aunts. The sons of the slayer's uterine paternal uncles and the sons of his uterine cousins shall pay six and one-half oras, weighed, less three and one-half pence, weighed, to the sons of the slain man's uterine paternal uncles and to the sons of his uterine cousins.[10] And the total amount that these men receive will be three and one-half marks, weighed, less an ertog, weighed.

[10] The fathers of uterine cousins would be uterine brothers.

25. ABOUT THE LESSER MAN FINES

Now there shall be told about the lesser man fines that are [paid] out of the four marks gold to the agnate kinsmen. They amount to nine oras, weighed, less six and one-half pence, weighed. The money shall be divided into five parts and the men who are in the fourth degree of kinship to the slain man shall take three of the five parts. And the men who are in the fourth degree of kinship to the slayer shall pay [the fines], and this amounts to five oras, weighed, and an ertog, weighed. Now the two remaining parts shall again be divided into five parts, and the men who are in the fifth degree of kinship to the slain man shall take three of the five parts. And the men who are in the fifth degree of kinship to the slayer shall pay [the fines]; and this will amount to two oras, weighed, and eight pence, weighed. And the men who are in the sixth degree of kinship to the slain man shall take the two remaining parts; and this will amount to four ertogs, weighed, and five pence, weighed.

26. THE LESSER MAN FINES PAID TO COGNATES

The amount of the lesser man fines paid to cognates is three and one-half oras, weighed, and three and one-third pence, weighed. This man fine shall be divided like that dealt with above, or into five parts. The men who are in the fourth degree of kinship to the slain man shall take three of the five parts; and this will amount to two oras, weighed, and eight pence, weighed. Now the two remaining parts shall again be divided into five parts, and the men who are in the fifth degree of kinship to the slain man shall take three parts, and this will amount to two ertogs, weighed, and eleven and one-fifth pence, weighed. And the men who are in the sixth degree of kinship to the slain man shall take the two remaining parts; and this will amount to one-half ora, weighed, and four pence, weighed.

27. CONCERNING THE THREE MARKS GOLD

Now it shall be told what each one shall receive as a fine or a baug, when a payment of three marks of gold is awarded. The slayer or his son shall pay twenty oras, weighed, to the son of the slain man. The slayer's father shall pay a like sum to the father of the slain man. The slayer's brother shall pay fifteen oras, weighed, to the brother of the slain man. The slayer's paternal uncle and the son of his brother shall pay ten oras, weighed, to the slain man's paternal uncle and to the son of his brother. The sons of the slayer's paternal uncle and the sons of his cousins shall pay seven oras, weighed, less an ertog to the sons of the slain man's paternal uncle and to the sons of his cousins. And the total amount received by these baugamenn will be nine marks, weighed, less an ertog, weighed.

28. WHAT THE GELD EKERS SHALL RECEIVE

Now it shall be told what [fines] the geld ekers shall pay. The thrallborn son of the slayer shall pay eight and one-half oras, weighed, to the thrallborn son of the slain man. The slayer's uterine brother shall pay a like amount to the uterine brother of the slain man. The slayer's paternal grandfather and his son's son shall pay eight and one-half oras, weighed, to the slain man's paternal grandfather and to his son's son. And to the sons of the geld ekers [there shall be paid] half a mark, weighed, less thirteen and one-half pence.[11] Now the total amount that is received by the geld ekers and their sons and sons' sons will be six and one-half marks, weighed, and five and one-half ertogs, weighed.

29. CONCERNING THE MATERNAL GRANDFATHER AND THE DAUGHTER'S SON

The slayer's maternal grandfather and his daughter's son shall pay a mark, weighed, to the slain man's maternal grandfather and to his daughter's son. The slayer's maternal uncle and his sister's son shall pay six oras, weighed, to the slain man's maternal uncle and to his sister's son. The sons of the slayer's sistkins shall pay half a mark, weighed, to the sons of the slain man's sistkins. The sons of the slayer's aunts shall pay three oras, weighed, less an ertog, weighed, to the sons of the slain man's aunts. Now the total amount that is received by the major cognates is twenty oras, weighed, and two ertogs, weighed.

[11] Something seems to have been omitted here. See the Norwegian edition of the *Laws*, I, 192, note.

30. CONCERNING THE LESSER PAYMENTS TO COGNATES

Now it shall be told how much each one shall pay into or receive from the lesser payments to cognates. The son of the slayer's son's daughter shall pay four and one-half oras, weighed, to the son of the slain man's son's daughter. The son of the slayer's daughter's daughter shall pay one-half mark, weighed, less fifteen pence, weighed, to the son of the slain man's daughter's daughter. The son of the slayer's brother's daughter shall pay three oras, weighed, to the son of the slain man's brother's daughter. The son of the slayer's sister's daughter shall pay two oras, weighed, and fifteen pence, weighed, to the son of the slain man's sister's daughter. The sons of the slayer's sistkins' daughters shall pay one and one-half oras, weighed, to the sons of the slain man's sistkins' daughters. The sons of the slayer's sisters' daughters shall pay two ertogs, weighed, and five pence, weighed, to the sons of the slain man's sisters' daughters. And the total amount received by the lesser cognate kinsmen will be two marks, weighed, less fifteen pence, weighed.

31. CONCERNING A THRALLBORN BROTHER

A thrallborn brother of the slayer shall pay seven and one-half oras, weighed, to a thrallborn brother [of the slain man]. The uterine brother of the slayer's mother and his uterine sister's son shall pay one-half mark, weighed, to the [uterine] brother of the slain man's mother and to his [uterine] sister's son. The sons of the slayer's uterine sistkins shall pay eight ertogs, weighed, to the sons of the uterine sistkins of the slain man. The sons of the slayer's uterine aunts [shall pay] five ertogs, weighed, and five pence, weighed, to the sons of the slain man's uterine aunts. The sons of the slayer's [uterine] paternal uncles and the sons of his uterine cousins shall pay five oras, weighed, less ten pence, weighed, to the sons of the slain man's [uterine] paternal uncles and to the sons of his uterine cousins. And the total amount received by these men will be twenty oras, weighed, and two ertogs, weighed, and five pence, weighed.

32. THE LESSER MAN FINES PAID TO AGNATES[12]

The part of the three marks gold paid in lesser man fines to agnates amounts to seven oras, weighed, less an ertog. This money shall be divided into five parts, and let two of these be set aside but let the three be taken up. And the men who are in the fourth degree of kinship to the slain man shall take these three parts, and those who are in the fourth degree of kinship to the slayer shall pay the fine. And the total amount of this will be one-half mark, weighed. Now the two remaining parts shall again be divided into five, and the men who are in the fifth degree of kinship to the slain man shall take three parts of the two [thus divided] and these [three] parts will amount to four and one-half ertogs, weighed, and six pence, weighed.[13] And the men who are in the sixth degree of kinship to the slain man shall take the two remaining parts, and these will amount to one ora, weighed, and four pence, weighed.

33. THE LESSER MAN FINES PAID TO COGNATES

Now, as to the man money paid out of the three marks gold to kinsmen on the cognatic side, one begins with eight ertogs, weighed; and this money shall be divided into five parts like that dealt with above. The men who are in the fourth degree of kinship to the slain man shall take three of these five parts, and those who are in the fourth degree of kinship to the slayer shall pay the fine. And the total amount will be one and one-half oras, weighed, and six pence, weighed. Now the two remaining parts shall be divided; they shall again be divided into five parts, and the men who are in the fifth degree of kinship to the slain man shall take three of these five parts. And this will amount to two ertogs, weighed, less one and one-half pence, weighed. And the men who are in the sixth degree of kinship to the slain man shall take the two remaining parts. And this will amount to one ertog, weighed, and five and one-half pence, weighed.

[12] See Glossary, "Agnates."

[13] As corrected by the editors of the Norwegian edition; the original is clearly incorrect.

34. THE TWENTY ORAS GOLD

Now it shall be told what each one shall pay to or receive from another when a payment of twenty oras gold by weight is awarded. The slayer or his son shall pay two marks, weighed, and two ertogs, weighed, to the son of the slain man. The slayer's father shall pay a like amount to the father of the slain man. The slayer's brother shall pay twelve and one-half oras, weighed, to the brother of the slain man. The slayer's paternal uncle and his brother's son [shall pay] one mark, weighed, and an ertog to the slain man's paternal uncle and to his brother's son. The sons of the slayer's paternal uncles and the sons of his cousins shall pay five and one-half oras, weighed, and three and one-half pence, weighed, to the sons of the slain man's paternal uncles and to the sons of his cousins. And the total amount received by the baugamenn will be seven and one-half marks less sixteen and one-half pence weighed.

35. A THRALLBORN SON

A thrallborn son of the slayer shall pay seven oras, weighed, and five pence, weighed, to a thrallborn son of the slain man. A thrallborn uterine brother of the slayer shall pay a like amount to a thrallborn uterine brother of the slain man. The slayer's paternal grandfather and his son's son shall pay seven oras, weighed, and five pence, weighed, to the slain man's paternal grandfather and to his son's son. The sons of the geld eker shall receive five oras, weighed, less seventeen pence; and the sons of a geld eker's sons [shall receive] a third less. And the total amount received by the geld ekers and their sons and their sons' sons will be five and one-half marks, weighed, and two ertogs, weighed, and twelve pence, weighed.

36. THE MOTHER'S FATHER AND THE DAUGHTER'S SON

The slayer's maternal grandfather and the son of his daughter shall pay seven oras, weighed, less an ertog, weighed, to the slain man's maternal grandfather and to the son of his daughter. The slayer's maternal uncle and his sister's son shall pay five oras, weighed, to the slain man's maternal uncle and to his sister's son. The sons of the slayer's sistkins shall pay ten ertogs, weighed, to the sons of the slain man's sistkins. The sons of the slayer's aunts shall pay two oras, weighed, and thirteen and one-half pence, weighed, to the sons of the slain man's aunts. And the total amount that these men receive will be seventeen oras, weighed, and thirteen and one-half pence, weighed.

37. CONCERNING THE LESSER PAYMENTS TO COGNATES

Now begins the account of the fine which men call the lesser payments to cognates.[14] The son of the slayer's son's daughter shall pay one-half mark, weighed, less fifteen pence to the son of the slain man's son's daughter. The son of the slayer's daughter's daughter shall pay three oras, weighed, and seven and one-half pence to the son of the slain man's daughter's daughter. The son of the slayer's brother's daughter shall pay two and one-half oras, weighed, to the son of the slain man's brother's daughter. The son of the slayer's sister's daughter shall pay two oras, weighed, less seven and one-half pence, weighed, to the son of the slain man's sister's daughter. The sons of the slayer's sistkins' daughters shall pay one ora, weighed, and fifteen pence, weighed, to the sons of the slain man's sistkins' daughters. The sons of the daughters of the slayer's aunts shall pay two ertogs, weighed, less two and one-half pence, weighed, to the sons of the daughters of the slain man's aunts. And the total amount received by the lesser cognates will be thirteen oras, weighed, and seven and one-half pence, weighed.

38. CONCERNING A THRALLBORN BROTHER

A thrallborn brother of the slayer shall pay six oras, weighed, and fifteen pence to the thrallborn brother of the slain man. The sons of the slayer's uterine paternal uncles and the sons of his uterine cousins shall pay one-half mark, weighed, and two pence to the sons of the slain man's [uterine] paternal uncles and to the sons of his [uterine] cousins. The uterine brother of the slayer's mother and the son of his uterine sister shall pay ten ertogs, weighed, to the uterine brother of the slain man's mother and to the son of his uterine sister. The sons of the slayer's uterine sistkins shall pay two oras, weighed, and thirteen pence, weighed, to the

[14] See Glossary, "Cognates."

sons of the slain man's uterine sistkins. The sons of the slayer's uterine aunts shall pay one and one-half oras, weighed, less two and one-half pence, weighed, to the sons of the slain man's uterine aunts. And the total amount received by these men will be seventeen oras, weighed, and seventeen and one-half pence, weighed.

39. MORE CONCERNING THE LESSER MAN FINES PAID TO AGNATES

The total amount of the lesser man fines [paid] to agnates out of the twenty oras gold will be five and one-half oras, weighed, and three pence, weighed. This money shall be divided into five parts. The men who are in the fourth degree of kinship to the slain man shall take three parts, and the men who are in the fourth degree of kinship to the slayer shall pay the fines; and the amount will be three oras, weighed, and an ertog. Now the two remaining parts shall again be divided into five parts, and the men who are in the fifth degree of kinship to the slain man shall take three of these five parts, and the amount will be four ertogs, weighed, less two and one-half pence.[15] And the men who are in the sixth degree of kinship to the slain man shall take what remains, and the amount will be two and one-half ertogs, weighed, and three pence, weighed.

40. THE LESSER MAN FINES PAID TO COGNATES

The total amount of the lesser man fines paid to cognates will be two oras and thirteen and one-half pence, weighed, and it shall be divided into five parts. The men who are in the fourth degree of kinship to the slain man shall take three parts, and those who are in the fourth degree of kinship to the slayer shall pay the fines; and the amount will be an ertog, weighed, and three pence, weighed.[16] Now the two remaining parts shall again be divided into five parts and the men who are in the fifth degree of kinship to the slain man shall take three of those five parts; and the amount will be an ertog, weighed, and a penny, weighed.[17]

[15] The editors of the Norwegian edition would omit the words "less two and one-half pence." (I, 195, note.)

[16] For a possible emendation see *ibid.*, note 5.

[17] See *ibid.*, note 6, for a necessary emendation; no provision is made for kinsmen in the sixth degree.

41. WHERE TWO MARKS GOLD ARE AWARDED [AS MAN MONEY]

Now it shall be told what each one shall pay to, or receive from, another when a payment of two marks gold is awarded. The slayer or his son shall pay thirteen oras, weighed, and an ertog, weighed, as a head baug to the son of the slain man. The slayer's father shall pay a like amount to the father of the slain man. The slayer's brother shall pay ten oras, weighed, to the brother of the slain man. The slayer's paternal uncle and his brother's son shall pay seven oras, weighed, less an ertog to the slain man's paternal uncle and to his brother's son. The sons of the slayer's paternal uncles and the sons of his cousins shall pay four and one-half oras, weighed, less three and one-half pence to the sons of the slain man's paternal uncles and to the sons of his cousins. And the total amount received by the baugamenn will be six marks, weighed, less twelve and one-half pence, weighed.

42. CONCERNING A THRALLBORN SON

A thrallborn son of the slayer shall pay six oras, weighed, less an ertog, weighed, to a thrallborn son of the slain man. The slayer's uterine brother shall pay a like amount to the uterine brother of the slain man. The slayer's paternal grandfather and the son of his son shall pay six oras, weighed, less an ertog, weighed, to the slain man's paternal grandfather and to the son of his son. And one-half mark, weighed, less thirteen and one-half pence [shall be paid] to the sons of a geld eker and one-third less to the sons of a geld eker's sons. And the total amount that a geld eker and his sons and sons' sons receive will be four and one-half marks, weighed, less six and one-half pence, weighed.

43. CONCERNING THE MATERNAL GRANDFATHER AND THE DAUGHTER'S SON

The slayer's maternal grandfather and his daughter's son shall pay five oras, weighed, and an ertog to the slain man's maternal grandfather and to his daughter's son. The slayer's maternal uncle and his sister's son shall pay one-half mark, weighed, to the slain man's maternal uncle and to his sister's son. The sons of the slayer's sistkins shall pay eight ertogs, weighed, to the sons of the slain man's sistkins. The sons of the slayer's aunts shall pay five ertogs, weighed, and six and one-half pence, weighed, to the sons of the slain man's aunts. The total received by the major cognates will be fourteen oras, weighed, less thirteen and one-half pence, weighed.

44. THE SON OF A SON'S DAUGHTER

The son of the daughter of the slayer's son shall pay three oras, weighed, to the son of the daughter of the slain man's son. The son of the daughter of the slayer's daughter shall pay two and one-half oras, weighed, to the son of the daughter of the slain man's daughter. The son of the daughter of the slayer's brother shall pay two oras, weighed, to the son of the daughter of the slain man's brother. The son of the daughter of the slayer's sister shall pay one and one-half oras, weighed, to the son of the daughter of the slain man's sister. The sons of the daughters of the slayer's sistkins shall pay an ora, weighed, to the sons of the daughters of the slain man's sistkins. The sons of the daughters of the slayer's aunts shall pay one-half ora, weighed, to the sons of the daughters of the slain man's aunts. And the total amount received by the lesser cognate kinsmen will be ten and one-half oras, weighed.

45. CONCERNING A THRALLBORN BROTHER OF THE SLAYER

A thrallborn brother of the slayer shall pay five oras, weighed, to a thrallborn brother of the slain man. The sons of the slayer's uterine paternal uncles and the sons of his uterine cousins shall pay three oras, weighed, and thirteen pence, weighed, to the sons of the slain man's uterine paternal uncles and to the uterine sons of his cousins. The uterine brother of the slayer's mother and the son of his uterine sister shall pay eight ertogs, weighed, to the uterine brother of the slain man's mother and to the son of his uterine sister. The sons of the slayer's uterine sistkins shall pay an ertog, weighed, and seven and one-half pence, weighed, to the sons of the slain man's uterine sistkins. The sons of the slayer's uterine aunts shall pay five ertogs, weighed, and six and one-half pence, weighed,[18] to the sons of the slain man's uterine aunts. And the total amount received by these men will be fourteen oras, weighed, less ten pence, weighed.

[18] As corrected by the editors of the Norwegian edition (I, 196).

46. THE LESSER MAN FINES PAID TO AGNATES

The total amount of the lesser man fines paid to agnates out of the two marks gold will be four and one-half oras, weighed, less three and one-half pence, and the money shall be divided into five parts. The men who are in the fourth degree of kinship to the slain man shall take three parts, and those who are in the fourth degree of kinship to the slayer shall pay the fines; and this will be eight ertogs, weighed. Now the two remaining parts shall again be divided into five parts and the men who are in the fifth degree of kinship to the slain man shall take three of the five parts, and those who are in the fifth degree of kinship to the slayer shall pay the fines; and that will be three ertogs, weighed, and four pence, weighed. And the men who are in the sixth degree of kinship to the slain man shall take the two remaining parts; and that will be two ertogs, weighed, and two and one-half pence, weighed.

47. CONCERNING THE LESSER MAN FINES PAID TO COGNATES

The lesser man fines paid to cognates out of the two marks gold will amount to five ertogs, weighed, and seven pence, weighed. This part of the wergeld shall be divided into five parts as were the earlier amounts that were paid to cognates. And the men who are in the fourth degree of kinship to the slain man shall take three of these five parts, and that will be one ora, weighed, and four pence, weighed. Now the two remaining parts shall again be divided into five parts, and the men who are in the fifth degree of kinship to the slain man shall take one ertog, weighed, and five and one-half pence, weighed. And the men who are in the sixth degree of kinship to the slain man shall take seventeen pence, weighed.

VII. [THE LAW OF THE COAST DEFENSE]

1. HERE THE LAW OF THE COAST DEFENSE IS SET FORTH

It is the king's right to command and to forbid, but [he must] rule according to law. If there is no ship fitted out in a fylki, the fine is three marks for each rowlock. If a ship is to be built for the coast defense and [materials] are to be provided, there is a fine of six oras for each piece of timber that is wanting, or if the entire undertaking fails. If nails are to be provided for the building and one nail is wanting, the one who is to provide the nails shall pay a fine of one ora; and the penalty for every nail that is wanting is an ora till the number of nails is six; then six oras shall be due; and [he shall] provide a sufficiency of nails besides. But the nail fine shall never exceed six oras, weighed, in any one undertaking, whether one fails in his duty or the whole undertaking fails. A ship must be coated with tar as soon as it is built; and if a bucket of tar is lacking, the penalty is six oras. And whether one man is neglectful or the whole contribution fails, the fine shall be six oras; and whoever is delinquent shall pay six oras only, even if the whole contribution fails; and the [fine is the] same though one man only neglects his duty.

2. HIRING SHIPWRIGHTS

If the freemen have ordered the building of a ship and have hired shipwrights, and if they have appointed a moot when the hire is to be paid and the one who is to receive payment has come to this moot, it shall be the duty of all those who dwell in the ship district to join in this payment. But if anyone moves away, he shall not be called upon to leave a payment behind. But whoever comes into the district before the moot is held shall join in the payment. Likewise, when the freemen are buying a ship, they shall proceed as has now been set forth in [the matter of] building a ship. But if anyone refuses to contribute at the moot referred to, the freemen, who belong to this ship district, with the king's bailiff shall go upon him and take from him such [a part of the] ship's value as is due from him and a like amount in addition. The added amount shall go to the freemen, but the bailiff shall have the fine, if there is one, and if he is willing to join in the distraint; but if he does not join, he shall have nothing and the freemen may proceed alone without fear of penalty. When freemen undertake to build a ship and the building has begun, those who are willing to pay their dues shall direct the work, but the others who refuse to pay shall pay the penalties due.

3. CONCERNING THE BUILDING OF SHIP SHEDS

If a ship shed is to be built and a piece of timber is wanting, the penalty is three oras; moreover, the fine remains though the whole undertaking fails. If a man demolishes a ship shed that was built to house a ship belonging to the coast defense, he shall owe a fine of three marks if the charge is proven, and [he] shall build another ship shed as good [as the first]. But if he denies the charge, a threefold oath is required.

4. CONCERNING THE EQUIPMENT OF A SHIP[1]

The freemen shall provide tackle for their ships. If a stay is wanting, the penalty is twelve oras. For every halyard [it is] half a mark; for every missing brace, half a mark; for every shroud, three oras; and for each missing back-stay, three oras. For a missing sheet [the penalty is] two oras; for every clew that is lacking [it is] one ora, and an ora for each reefing rope to the number of six ropes. And the payments for the rings [that are wanting] in the sails shall never be more than six oras in a single outfit; but for the reefing rope the fine is an ora in each case.

5. CONCERNING THE SAILS

If there is no sail provided at the moot referred to above, a fine of six oras shall be added to each contribution to the levy. If there is lack of sail cloth, the man [concerned] shall owe a fine of six oras; and he owes the six oras even though the entire undertaking fails. For a mast that is missing, the fine is three oras; for a yard, three oras; and for a boom, three oras. [The penalty is] three oras,

[1] The translation of this chapter is an approximation only; English terms exactly equivalent to those used in the original text cannot always be found.

if a man fails to take his share in the cost of the anchor, and twelve oras, if the anchor is not provided. The ship shall be left to soak for five nights before the water is bailed out of it and victuals are brought on board. But if the freemen's ship is in such condition when the provisions and the sailors' baggage are brought on board that men have to bail half of the time [only], it is seaworthy; but, if it leaks more than that, it is not seaworthy, and the crew shall incur no penalty if they leave it.

6. CONCERNING ATTENDANCE AT THE THING

If a freeman fails to attend a thing that is called to provide for the building of ships, the penalty is six oras; if he fails to attend a thing called to provide for the building of ship sheds, the penalty is three oras.

7. THE KING SHALL APPOINT THE SHIPMASTER

The king shall appoint shipmasters for all the ships. And if one who is appointed shipmaster refuses to sail, he shall owe a fine of six marks. The shipmaster shall select the crew, and if a sailor is chosen at the next thing, the fine [for failing to serve] is three marks. He shall first name such men as are not householders, and when every capable unattached man has been chosen, he shall appoint farmers, but only such as have help with their labor. If these do not suffice, two farmers who have no helpers shall join the crew while a third remains at home; but all who can go out to sea shall have their names on the muster roll, those who work alone, the same as other men.

8. CONCERNING A MUSTER THING

When men hold a thing to prepare the muster roll, all the freemen shall attend and also the bailiffs and the barons and such [unmarried] women as maintain a household, unless they have good excuses; but, if a woman must be excused, let her send a man to the thing to swear the muster oath for those of her household. And if anyone is found concealed in that person's house after that, the penalty is the same as if he had taken the oath on his own behalf. If a man fails to appear at the thing to swear the muster oath and no one comes on his behalf, let the freemen score the tallies to his account for as many men as they like, and he shall meet the dues of those men during the following twelvemonth. If a man fails to come to the muster thing, having no good excuse, he shall owe a fine of six oras; and the same [shall be owing] for every thing called to fit out ships for the fleet and until they are ready to sail. These fines [for nonattendance] are all reckoned in burned silver. If a baron or a bailiff fails to appear at the muster thing and no one comes to swear the muster oath in his behalf, the freemen shall score the tallies to his account for as many services [to the fleet] as they like; and he shall meet those dues during the twelvemonth following. If men have assessed the contributions but a man dies before he has paid it, no one shall need to pay his dues for him. When the provisions are in the chest and the meal is in the leather bag, all the equipment shall be put on board. If a man neglects to contribute to the fleet or to serve with it, the bailiff shall have action brought [against him] before the ship has been replaced on the beams, if the crew has served the required term; [if he delays the action] he ruins the suit. And the bailiff shall take action at the thing [to make sure] that the man has rendered his service [to the fleet] and not neglected it; then he is responsible in that suit. And if the bailiff or the *gjaldkeri*[2] shall charge a man with not having rendered a single service to the coast defense, let him give satisfaction with his own oath; but if the oath fails, let him make such payment as the law demands.

9. EVERY MAN SHALL PAY HIS DUES TO THE FLEET WHERE HE IS ENROLLED

Every man shall render service to the fleet in the place where he was the night before the morning when the enrollment was made or where he has his home; and he shall go forth from that place if he is called. But if he fails to do this or does not go forth as the call indicates, it is as if he has left the duty undone and has not gone forth, even though he has gone forth from another place; let him pay the prescribed fine in both cases.

10. EVERY MAN SHALL PAY DUES TO THE FLEET FOR HIS DEPENDENTS

Every man shall render service to the levy for his dependents in the place where he abides; if he neglects this, the responsibility

[2] See Glossary, "Gjaldkeri."

is with him and not with the freemen. But those men, free men of major age, to whom a man gives house and home shall themselves be liable for dues [or duty], and not the freemen. However, in the presence of the bailiff the householder shall score a mark on the tally stick for all those of his household who are present at the ground end of the gangplank. And for his thralls every man shall render service where he serves for his own person.

11. IF A MAN OWNS A HOUSE IN THE BOROUGH

If a man owns a house in the borough and a homestead in the country and travels back and forth between these, staying in each by turns, he shall pay one-half of his dues to the levy in the country and one-half in the borough. For all those who travel with him and for those who are continuously in the country he shall render dues in the country, and in the borough for those who are continuously there. Likewise, if a man has two homesteads in the country, he shall make such arrangements there as have just been outlined. And if a man who is not a householder travels back and forth between borough and countryside buying and selling, and if he is in the country at Yuletide but binds and loosens his leather bag[3] in the borough the rest of the winter, he shall perform his duties to the levy in the borough. Every man who is born in the borough but travels about in the country as a trader and has no home either in the country or in the borough shall perform his duties to the levy in the borough; but one who is born in the country and travels about in the manner described shall perform his duties in the country. If a man breaks up his household in the country and moves to the borough before the enrollment [is made] but returns later to the country, the freemen have a right to his contribution. If a boroughman has a thrall in the country [at the time] when the fleet sails out from the borough, he shall pay dues for him in the borough; but if the fleet is mustered in the country and not in the borough, he shall pay dues for him in the country. If a man departs from the land, he shall leave behind one contribution to the levy and shall pay his dues the following twelvemonth and provide for service if the fleet sails out in that period, but not for a longer time. All our countrymen who abide among

[3] That is, lives, eats, and sleeps.

us shall serve with us in the fleet; but aliens shall have been domiciled here for a twelvemonth before they shall have to pay dues to the levy. All who have lived a year in the country shall. pay all their dues to the levy and all that is owing to the general defense there and until they have lived continuously in the borough for three winters, unless they own houses in the borough. All those who move [to the borough] shall be counted as belonging to the ship district where they were born, and each one shall be accountable for his dues; and let the king have action brought against them, if they neglect them.

12. IF MAN OR MEAT IS WANTING AT THE OAR BENCH

If a man fails to place food at the oar bench when his turn comes, he shall owe a baug and a like amount if he fails to provide a man. But if both the man and the victuals are lacking, the penalty is three marks; likewise, if a man conceals another man or several men, the penalty is three marks, and they must perform the fleet service none the less. If a man has received notice but fails to perform his service to the levy, he shall pay such part of the penalty as the reckoning shows, that is, twelve oras. If a tent covering [is missing] the penalty is three oras, and for an oar it is one ora.

13. CONCERNING THE BOW

There shall be a bow lying at each thwart. The two bench mates who row together shall provide the bow and shall find a string for it or pay an ora and shall have to provide the bow besides. [There shall be] two dozen shafted arrows or square-pointed arrows; these the freemen shall provide, and for every one that is missing [the fine is] half an ora and six oras for the two dozen arrows. Every man who is unmarried shall have a shield, a spear, and a sword or an ax. But only such axes as have handles and spears that are shafted are satisfactory. And if a man fails to provide himself with any one of these three weapons, he owes a fine of three oras; and if all [three] are wanting, the penalty is nine oras; and he shall enjoy no atonement rights until he has provided himself with these weapons.

14. WHEN A SHIP IS TO BE FITTED OUT

When a ship is to be fitted out, all the men [concerned] shall come [to the ship]; but if the duty is neglected, the tallies shall be turned over to the bailiff, and all who have scores on the tallies shall assemble at the ground end of the gangplank. And every bailiff in the fylki shall place victuals and money and all the required equipment at each end of three thwarts. For this he shall have the right to all the fines for neglecting the levy; but if the bailiff refuses to do as is told, he shall have no claim in such cases.

15. CONCERNING A SATISFACTORY SHIELD

Every wooden shield shall be regarded as properly made if three iron bands are laid across it and the grip is [fastened] on the inner side.

16. CONCERNING DUES TO THE LEVY

Every man shall render service to the levy for his minor son [or dependent] unless [the boy] is a leper.

17. A PRIEST PAYS NO DUES TO THE LEVY

A priest who has duties at the shire church shall pay no dues to the levy either for himself or his wife[4] or his deacon or for his priest if he has one with him.

18. THE BARONS SHALL CONTRIBUTE TO THE LEVY

Barons shall contribute to the levy just as other freemen do and shall have such a share in the levy ships as [the rule] was in Olaf's day; and they shall pay dues for every male person who is six winters old or older than seven[5] winters.

19. IF A SHIP BECOMES UNSEAWORTHY

If a ship becomes unseaworthy after the men have sailed from home, they shall set it up on land and burn it, and let them bring the nails home to the freemen. But if they do not burn it, they shall pay the value of the nails, every sailor half an ora, and an ora if the money has to be sued for. If a ship of the levy becomes

[4] Cf. *Gul.*, c. 298.

[5] Evidently a scribal error, but all the manuscript copies have "seven winters."

unseaworthy after the men have come on board and provisions have been placed upon it, and it is so far to the rear of the fleet that the men cannot be taken on board another ship, let them put the provisions in a safe place and with them the wage money that they have not yet earned, and let them send a message to the nearest bailiff, [asking him] to take the food and the money. But the shipmaster and the crew shall go to the king's [garth], if they can find conveyance; and they shall render such service [or dues] to the levy there as they owed at home. But those who turn back homeward shall take no more of the provisions than is needed for the journey home; and they shall bring home the sail and all the ship's gear. But if they can get no conveyance to the king's [garth], they shall owe no fines.

20. EVERY MAN SHALL BRING HOME HIS ROWLOCK

Every man who had a rowlock[6] on the journey out from home shall bring it back, unless he provides the shipmaster with another man whom he is willing to accept. But if he deserts the ship while men are on the journey home, he shall owe a fine of three marks and his responsibility to the ship continues like [that of] the other men. When the men have returned home, their responsibility for the ship shall cease after three nights. The shipmaster shall send forth the summons and the freemen shall gather to set their ship up; and any freeman who refuses to join in this shall owe a fine of six oras. And a man may build a ship shed on the king's land wherever he likes.

21. THE CREW AND THE FREEMEN SHALL SHARE THE EXPENSE EQUALLY

The members of the crew shall restore to the freemen the provisions and as much of the wages as the reckoning shows that they have not earned. But if they were kept out longer than the time [for which] they have received food and wages, the freemen shall [add what is lacking]; but if they are out [only] five nights longer or [five nights] less than was estimated, there shall be no change in what either side has received or paid.

[6] *Hamla;* see Glossary, "Oar bench."

22. THE RESPONSIBILITY OF THE FREEMEN, IF THE SHIP IS SEAWORTHY

If the ship provided by the freemen is seaworthy according to prescription, their responsibility ceases as soon as the stern comes to [the place] where the prow was; and their duties to the coast defense are all performed and all their responsibility is ended.

23. WHAT MAY BE SLAUGHTERED, IF THE CREW IS SHORT OF FOOD

If the men of the coast defense in sailing homeward find themselves in need of provisions, they may kill with impunity two head of a farmer's cattle, each to the value of one cow; and let them leave behind the head and the hide and two oras of silver in current coin. And if other men come following these and they, too, wish to slaughter cattle, let the husbandmen produce the hide and the head and tell [what has been done]. And if those who came last do any slaughtering after that, they shall owe fines for cattle killing. The same fine shall be due from those who slaughtered first, if they killed more than is allowed, [that is], three beasts or more than three.

24. IF A FREE MAN PREPARES THE FOOD

If a free man undertakes to prepare the food on board a ship, he shall have no claim to atonement from any person on board if he shall suffer bodily injury because he fails to prepare such food for the master and the crew as the agreement calls for; but if he shall suffer [bodily] injury for any other cause, let him take such atonement as his rank demands.

25. IF A MAN SAILS FORTH AS AN ENEMY

If a man sails forth as an enemy and returns to harry the land or [to trouble] those who are in the king's peace, natives or men of alien birth, he has forfeited his land and his movables; but if he is willing to make an atonement, the shipmaster shall pay a compensation of forty marks to the king and each member of the crew shall pay three marks; and to all those whom they have harried they shall pay as much as those who were ravaged can claim upon oath.

26. IF TIMBER IS TO BE CUT FOR A SHIRE CHURCH

If timber is to be cut for a shire church or for a ship of the levy, one may cut as one likes in any man's forest; but it is more proper to ask [permission], though the owner has no right to refuse. [If there is need] of a hillside [on the shore] on which to build a ship for the coast defense, one may build it wherever one likes and on any man's land, only not where [the work will damage] cornland or grassland; but it is more proper to ask [permission], though the owner has no right to refuse. And if stone [of the sort] that is needed for a church is found on any man's land, a man may break what is needed; but it is more proper to ask [permission], though the owner has no right to refuse. But if a man forbids any of these things to be done, either with a "law ban"[7] or with illegal action, he shall owe a fine of three marks. . . .[8] And let the one who works there continue his labor with impunity just as before; but if cornland or grassland suffers damage, let the freemen assess the loss.

27. CONCERNING FORBIDDEN SAILING ABROAD

It is stated in the old laws that if men sail abroad in defiance of the king's ban, the shipmaster shall owe a fine of forty marks to the king and each member of the crew three marks. If the king places a ban on traffic abroad in meal or in wares of any sort, anyone who carries on such trade, shipmaster or sailor, shall owe a fine of three marks to the king; for no one [in the crew] shall be fined on account of another man's wares. But if men journey to Fressey[9] or to some other market with the king's permission and the king's enemies approach them, they shall incur no guilt if they bargain with them as with those who are in the king's peace.

[7] See Glossary, "Ban."

[8] This sentence is incomplete in all the manuscripts.

[9] Fressey (Fress Isle) is east of Trondheim in Jemtland, now Swedish territory.

VIII. [THE INHERITANCE LAW]

1. [THE FIRST INHERITANCE]

A son shall inherit from his father when nature takes its proper course, the one who is taken into the kindred, as well as the one who is born to freedom and family. But when matters go ill, the father inherits from the son, if the son has no heirs born to him.

2. THE SECOND INHERITANCE

The second inheritance is that which a daughter and a son's son take, the son's son [inheriting only], if he and his father are both of legitimate birth.

3. CONCERNING A SON'S SON

If there are two sons of sons, both legitimate, who are in line for an inheritance and the father of the one is of legitimate birth but the other's is not, the one whose father is legitimate shall have the inheritance. But if there is no such [person] and [there is] no daughter, the other shall divide the inheritance with the son's daughter; and let him share it as a son's son ought to share with a daughter; and thus it shall be in all the degrees of kinship from that point on. The same rule applies to a brother's sons begotten in the same way. And if there is a daughter she shall share equally in the inheritance [with the son's sons], though they be quite numerous; and, if there are many daughters and only one son's son, they shall share equally none the less. If there is odal land [included] in the division, the brothers shall redeem it for themselves with such forms of payment as are generally approved by men; [they shall redeem it] with gold or burned silver, or [with thralls, but no such thrall] shall be younger than fifteen winters nor older than thirty winters.[1] And, if there is no daughter or son's son, the son's daughter shall inherit in preference to a brother.

[1] See Gjessing, *Annaler for Nordisk Oldkyndighed* (1862), p. 101. Cf. the Norwegian edition of the *Laws*, I, 205, note 5.

4. CONCERNING THE THIRD INHERITANCE

Now, the third inheritance is that which a brother takes from a brother, if they are by the same father; but, if a brother is wanting, the inheritance goes to a sister by the same father.

5. CONCERNING THE FOURTH INHERITANCE

Now, the fourth inheritance is that which is taken by the paternal grandfather, a paternal uncle, and a brother's son, each taking one-third. But if there is one paternal uncle and several sons of brothers, the paternal uncle shall halve the inheritance with them. If there is one brother's son and several paternal uncles, the one shall again halve their inheritance with the others. If there is [only] one in this group, it is his right to take the entire inheritance. If there is no paternal grandfather or paternal uncle or brother's son, the paternal grandmother shall have the entire inheritance. But if she is wanting, then a paternal aunt of legitimate birth, the mother, if legally married, and a brother's daughter of legitimate birth shall take the inheritance; and the mother shall halve the inheritance with the others. If there is only one of the others, either a paternal aunt or a brother's daughter, the mother takes one-half of the inheritance as before. If there is only one paternal aunt but there are several daughters of a brother, the paternal aunt takes one-half of the inheritance as before. But if there is only one brother's daughter but several paternal aunts, the brother's daughter shall halve the inheritance with the others as before. But if there is no paternal aunt and no brother's daughter, the mother does not share in the fourth inheritance.

6. CONCERNING THE FIFTH INHERITANCE

Now, the fifth inheritance is that which is taken in common by a uterine brother and by sons of brothers.[2] But if there is no uterine brother, the brothers' sons shall have the entire inheritance; and if there are no brothers' sons, a uterine brother shall have the entire inheritance. If there are no uterine brothers and no brothers' sons, a uterine sister and the daughters of brothers[3]

[2] Brandt seems to read "paternal uncle" instead of "brother," *Retshistorie*, I, 146.

[3] "Paternal uncles" according to Brandt. *Ibid.*

shall have the inheritance and shall share it as the others would have shared it, had they existed.

7. CONCERNING THE SIXTH INHERITANCE

Now, the sixth inheritance is that which is taken by a mother of legitimate birth, when she inherits from a son, and by a paternal aunt of legitimate birth.

8. CONCERNING THE SEVENTH INHERITANCE

Now, the seventh inheritance is that which is taken by a bush lad and a corner lad and a thrallborn son, if they have been given their freedom. They all share in the same inheritance and each becomes the other's heir. And if there are no living heirs in advance of the seventh inheritance [group] on the agnatic [side], except one brother of legitimate birth and he shall die and leave no children, let his baseborn brother in the sixth inheritance take the inheritance rather than have it go into the eighth inheritance [group]. But if there is no such person, let a thrallborn daughter and baseborn daughters begotten in bush or corner have [the inheritance]. They shall all share in the same inheritance and each becomes the other's heir.

9. CONCERNING THE EIGHTH INHERITANCE

Now, the eighth inheritance is that which is taken by the sons of first cousins and by those in the third degree of kinship on either side. But if these are wanting, the inheritance shall pass to the women who are daughters of first cousins.

10. CONCERNING THE NINTH INHERITANCE

Now, the ninth inheritance is that which is taken by a maternal grandfather and a daughter's son. They both share in the same inheritance, and each becomes the other's heir. But if these are wanting, the maternal grandmother and a daughter's daughter shall have [the inheritance], each one becoming the other's heir, if either is wanting.

11. THE TENTH INHERITANCE

Now, the tenth inheritance is that which is taken by a maternal uncle and a sister's son. They both share in the same inheritance, and each becomes the other's heir. If these are wanting, a maternal aunt and a sister's daughter shall have the inheritance. They both share in the same inheritance, and each becomes the other's heir.

12. CONCERNING THE ELEVENTH INHERITANCE

The eleventh inheritance is that which is taken by the sons of two sistkins, a man and a woman. They both share in the same inheritance, and each becomes the other's heir. But if they are wanting, the sons of the daughters of two sistkins, a man and a woman, shall have the inheritance. They both share the same inheritance, and each becomes the other's heir.

13. CONCERNING THE TWELFTH INHERITANCE

The twelfth inheritance is that which is taken by the two sons of maternal aunts. They both share the same inheritance, and each becomes the other's heir. But if they are wanting, the inheritance goes to the women who are the daughters of maternal aunts. They both share the same inheritance, and each becomes the other's heir. It is further provided that every one shall inherit with the group to which he is counted [as belonging] and that he shall not inherit in preference to others.

14. CONCERNING THE THIRTEENTH INHERITANCE AND [THE LAW] THAT NO MAN SHALL SLAY ANOTHER TO GET AN INHERITANCE

It is also ordained and told in the secular laws that if a man becomes the victim of such madness that he kills a man to get an inheritance, he forfeits and destroys his right to that inheritance. And let the inheritance travel its proper course, as if the man who committed manslaying to get the inheritance no longer exists.

15. CONCERNING THE FOURTEENTH INHERITANCE WHICH THE KINGS HAVE GRANTED

Now, this is the fourteenth inheritance which was granted by the sons of Magnus, Sigurd, Eystein, and Olaf,[4] and which is to be taken by the father's baseborn brothers and by the baseborn

[4] Magnus Bareleg died in 1103 and left the kingdom to his three young sons, Olaf, Eystein, and Sigurd. Olaf died in 1116; Eystein, in 1122; and Sigurd (the Crusader), in 1130.

sons of brothers, if they are all by free-born mothers, and also by another uterine brother of the father and by the son of a uterine brother, if [the brothers] are both of legitimate birth; and let them share according to number. But if these are wanting, let the women in the corresponding degrees of kinship have the inheritance and divide it as provided above. But if these, too, are wanting, let it pass to the father's uterine brother of illegitimate birth and to the sons of a uterine brother, whether of legitimate birth or not; and let them divide according to their number. But if these are wanting, let the women of the corresponding degree of kinship have the inheritance and divide it as provided above. And if all these are wanting, those who are [nearest] within the fifth degree of kinship shall take the inheritance, unless nearer kinsmen are found, rather than have it escheat to the king.

16. CONCERNING AN INHERITANCE BELONGING TO ONE WHO IS BEGOTTEN ABROAD

If a man is begotten abroad and has no ale feast witnesses [to support his claim] but does have the tokens of the king, a bishop, or a jarl, let him bring those tokens to the ordeal. If he succeeds at the ordeal, let him put forth a formal demand for the inheritance and let him appoint a five-day moot; and at this moot let him produce witnesses to the fact that he has successfully carried the [hot] iron for his inheritance.

17. CONCERNING SUITS FOR INHERITANCES AND CLAIMS TO INHERITANCES ALREADY ASSUMED

It is ordained that, if the rightful heir is not at hand when the inheritance becomes available and the one who is nearest in kinship takes possession, the one who is nearest to the inheritance shall proceed to sue the other out of it at a five-day moot. But when the rightful heir has come into possession, no one shall venture to sue him out of it.

18. HOW ATONEMENTS SHALL BE PAID OR RECEIVED AND ALSO HOW INHERITANCES SHALL BE RECEIVED

[Kinsmen related to the slain man or to the slayer in a double degree shall have the right to] man money as of the nearer degree but shall make payment as of the more distant degree;[5] inheritances [shall] pass by the same rule.

19. CONCERNING A THING FOR UTEY

The kings[6] have given the men of Utey the right to have a thing of their own at Jorulfstead[7] to be of equal competence with [those of] the other fylkismen.

[5] See Hertzberg, *Glossarium*, "kné."

[6] See above, p. 327, note.

[7] Now Jörstad on Ytteröy in the inner part of Trondheim Fjord. Hertzberg argues for "outer isles." *Den ældste norske proces*, p. 146.

IX. [THE INHERITANCE LAW—CONTINUED]

1. CONCERNING LEGITIMATION[1]

A man is fully legitimated if his father brings him into the kindred with the consent of those who are the nearest heirs to the one who brings him into the kindred. [The father] shall give a feast [with as much ale as can be] brewed from three sáld of malt; and he shall butcher a three-year-old ox and flay the skin off the right hind leg above the knee joint and make it into a shoe. Then the father shall order the one who is to be legitimated to put that shoe on; at the same time he shall have on his knees the sons who are still minors, but those who are of age shall [also] put on the shoe. If he has no sons who are legal heirs, the men who stand nearest to the inheritance shall put on the shoe, and they shall lead the man [who is] to be legitimated to the knees of the father and his wife. Women may testify for a man on the same terms as men as to the completeness of his legitimation, as may the shoe which the men have put on, if it is preserved. A thrallborn son shall be brought into the kindred by the one who gave him his freedom; and let it be given by the father or by a brother or by the man who is the nearest heir, whether he be young or old; and let them give their consent who are the nearest heirs to the one who wishes to bring a man into the kindred. The son of a free woman shall be legitimated in the same way as the son of a bondwoman. And after this manner shall the free-born agnatic kinsmen bring a man into the kindred, if there is no father or brother living.

2. CONCERNING THE INHERITANCE OF MEN WHO ALL DIE AT THE SAME TIME

If men fall in a battle from which none escape, or if they all drown, or perish in a fire, their inheritances shall pass as if they had all yielded their lives at the same time.

[1] Cf. *Gul.*, c. 58.

3. ANY ONE MAY DISPOSE OF HIS INHERITANCE [AS A GIFT]

Those who are guests in the houses of others may dispose of their belongings by gift, whether they be men or women. A man may will his property, if he is in good health, and he may take the gift back, but he may not take a gift back a second time.

4. HOW A WOMAN MAY DISPOSE [OF HER PROPERTY]

A woman may dispose of her property [by will][2] three times and the third time the gift holds; but she may not make such a will unless she is in good health. One who makes a will may cancel it in three places: at the church, at the thing, or at an ale feast. If the gifts are to be in land, they shall be given with warranty; if in other forms of property, let [the terms] be as witnesses know them [to be], even when there is no final transfer (skeyting) but the gift is a capital tithe and witnesses can testify to it. Likewise, if a man gives a fourth of a [certain] acquired property and there is land involved in [the gift], the gift shall hold if witnesses have knowledge of it, though there be no final transfer.[3]

5. CONCERNING THE INHERITANCE OF A GUEST KINSMAN[4] IN CASE HE SHALL DIE

If a man [occupies] another man's land as a guest and dies there, let the owner of the land have his belongings, if their value is six oras or less; [let him] also [have] his farm implements and his live stock, all the corn and grass that are still standing, and every piece of timber that is set in the earth. But if [the value] is more than six oras, the king shall have one-half of what is over and above and the owner of the land, one-half. But if a guest kinsman shall die on [another] man's ship and the value of his belongings is not more than six oras, the shipmaster shall have it all; but if it is more, the king shall have one-half of what is over and above and the shipmaster, one-half. If a man lies ill and is cared for on another man's land and dies there, his belongings shall pass as

[2] The right to make a will probably could not be exercised if there were legal heirs, except when the testator wished to make certain gifts to the church. See above, III, c. 17. Later the right was extended to gifts of many sorts.

[3] Skeyting.

[4] See Glossary, "Guest kinsman."

provided above. If a guest kinsman enjoys the rights of a home in a freeman's house, the host shall publish the fact that he [the guest] ties and unties his skin bag[5] at his house; and if he dies, the host shall take the inheritance from him, unless he shall have willed it to some one else. A man is properly a guest kinsman if he is a Norwegian from within the realm and all those of his kindred are dead who are counted in his inheritance group. If a guest kinsman dies on the homestead of the man with whom he dwells, let the owner of the land keep the inheritance for a twelvemonth to determine whether or not there is an heir, and let him pay all such debts as are confirmed by witnesses. If a man dies on shipboard or where he enjoys the rights of a home, the same procedure shall be followed. If a married woman who is in guest kinship shall die, let the host keep [her belongings] for a twelvemonth and give adequate security that the property will be preserved.

6. ON ASSUMING AN INHERITANCE IN CASE A MAN DIES WEST OR EAST OF THE MIDDLE [OF THE NORTH] SEA

If a man dies west of the middle [of the North] Sea or in Iceland, his heir shall assume the inheritance according to the laws of those who live in that land; but if he dies east of the midsea, his property shall pass according to the rules of the Frostathing law.

7. CONCERNING PATERNITY WHEN MEN ARE IN DOUBT

If a man demands the inheritance from his father, and the other [claimant] concedes that he is the son of the man whom he names and [is born] of a free woman and is in line for the inheritance, and if he is begotten within the realm, he shall have his paternal inheritance; and he shall oust with witnesses and with testimony the one who denied that he was the rightful heir. But if this one denies that he is the son of the man whom he names, or that he was born of a free mother, the claimant shall make a formal demand upon him and upon the keeper of the property and shall have a doom before which he shall present his evidence that he is the son of the man whom he names. If he is begotten abroad, he shall make a formal demand for his paternal inheritance or the

[5] Cf. *Gul.*, c. 109.

inheritance that he claims, and he shall [be allowed to] call witnesses to testify that he is entitled to the inheritance; and let him proceed with all the dooms, unless his opponent shall yield earlier.

8. CONCERNING MEN WHO ARE EQUALLY NEAR TO AN INHERITANCE

Whenever a man and a woman are equally near in kinship to one deceased, the man shall have the inheritance and the woman shall yield it, if both are agnates or both are cognates. But if the woman is nearer in kinship, she has the prior right to the inheritance; for the agnatic kinsmen are preferred to the cognates in matters of heritage, whether they be men or women.

9. CONCERNING WHAT A DAUGHTER SHALL INHERIT FROM HER MOTHER

These things a daughter shall inherit from her mother; if there is a brother living: all her clothes except velvet cloaks and cloth that is uncut, these the brother shall have; and if the brother wishes to do so, he may remove all the gold lace from the clothing. All the mantles of fine woven stuff, all the bed curtains, and all the clothes that are fringed, embroidered, or tapestried, these the daughter shall have; also the bedclothes stuffed with feathers or down. If a web is in the loom the son shall have what is woven and the daughter what is not yet woven. The son shall have all the covers and cushions that are used on seats and benches and all the rugs and tapestries; but the daughter shall have the bed covers, if they belonged to her mother; if they belonged to the father, the son shall have them. The daughter shall have five sheep and five fleeces, all the flax and yarn, and the geese; the son shall have what there is in addition. The daughter shall have the wardrobe, if it belonged to her mother. The daughter shall have her mother's cross or brooch, as she prefers, or her best breast jewel, if it is not made of gold but of silver, and all the dress fastenings, if they weigh an ounce or less and are made of silver, and her beads, too, even though there be silver in them. All the cups from which women drink to each other across the floor at home in the house, the daughters shall have; also the decorated cups, though there be silver in [the decoration]; but the silver vessels shall go to the son. The daughter shall have one hand bowl, unless it is fastened [to another] with a chain, in which case she shall have both.

10. CONCERNING SUIT AND DEFENSE IN A CASE BETWEEN MASTER AND FREEDMAN

Every freedman shall continue in dependence upon him who gave him his freedom, if it was given by one who had the right to give it. But if tongues speak dubiously as to whether he was released by the one who is now called his lawful master and [the freedman] himself denies it, let him who claims to be his master proceed to the thing and call two witnesses to prove that the freedman was released by him; then he [the freedman] is this man's [dependent], unless he can find two witnesses, free-born and reliable men, to testify that his freedom ale has been given, or that he has been released from the obligation to give it. Then, if he produces such evidence, he is freed from dependence on that man. And if one who gets into [such] a controversy claims to be a free-born man, let him enumerate his four ancestors, free-born men, he being himself the fifth [in line], and let him have two free-born householders as witnesses to this. But if he is lacking in support so that he cannot find witnesses though he does set up this claim, let him prove his free-born kinship with the ordeal. And if he is cleared by testimony or by the hot iron, [his opponent] shall pay him a full atonement and a fine for perjury to the bishop. But if he is not cleared, he has forfeited all his movables to his master and is liable to a fine of three marks valued in burned silver, unless he pays the price of his freedom. Freedmen of the higher class[6] [shall be dealt with] in the same way. If more than one man lays claim [to a freedman], he shall present the same defense.

11. CONCERNING THE STATUS OF A FREEDMAN AS TO INHERITANCE AND DEPENDENCY

The family of a freedman shall remain in dependency for four generations but the fifth is out of it, even though there has been

[6] *Vánarmenn:* men from whom other men outside the kindred may expect to inherit. The term (*vánarmaðr*) was applied only to the higher class of freedmen who, except for this defect in right to inherit, enjoyed what was practically complete freedom.

no payment. But the freedman who has given his freedom ale or has bought his freedom and received a warranty shall inherit from his son, his daughter, and from his freedman grandson. The sons of a freedman shall inherit from six persons: father and mother, son and daughter, brother and sister, and from their own freedman as the seventh [person]. In this way the son of a freedman shall inherit and the son's son, and the son of this [last] one, all who inherit in this way; also the daughter and the sister just as the son or the brother [would inherit], if these did not exist. Moreover, each one shall look after the needs of the other. But when these six are no more, the right to all the inheritance to the ninth knee reverts to the master; and let him care for those who need care. If a freedman takes a wife, whether a freedwoman or one who is well-born, two-thirds of the children shall fall to the father and to his master, both with respect to support and to inheritance, and one-third to the mother [and to her master]; the children that go with the mother shall be rid of dependency, if she is well-born.

12. CONCERNING THE FREEDOM ALE[7]

If a thrall takes up land or sets up a home, he shall give his freedom ale, [serving the brew of] nine measures [of malt]. And he shall kill a wether; a free-born man shall cut off the wether's head; and his master shall take the thrall's neck ransom[8] off the wether's neck. Now if the owner seems willing to let him give his freedom ale, he shall ask him before two witnesses whether he may give his ale and he shall invite him with five others to the feast that he plans to give as his freedom ale.[9] He shall give it whether or no, and let the highseats of the master and his wife be left vacant. And if the master has doubts as to how the ale was given, he [the freedman] shall bring forward the witnesses who were present and drank of the ale, and let the witness be borne at the thing. If they bear such witness that the law is satisfied, the matter shall remain in that way. And after that time the fact shall be published every tenth winter, and let him [the freedman] have the benefit of this testimony whenever he needs it; and it remains valid even though

[7] Cf. *Gul.*, c. 62. [8] See Glossary, "Neck ransom."

[9] The editors of the Norwegian edition believe this sentence to be incomplete. See I, 212, note 5.

the facts be not published every tenth winter, if witness is borne by men who heard [the testimony] at the thing.

13. CONCERNING A BONDMAN WHO IS LIBERATED BY A FARMER OR BY MERCHANTS AT SEA

If a farmer or merchants at sea wish to buy a man to liberate him, that man shall not be [regarded as] dependent on anyone. If he dies before he has given his freedom ale, his [former] master shall inherit from him; let him also look after his needs while he lives, if he should come to want. But if he wishes to give his freedom ale, let it be done as provided above.

14. IF A MAN WISHES TO RID HIMSELF OF DEPENDENCE BY A MONEY PAYMENT

If a man wishes to rid himself of dependence and of a defect in his right to inherit by a money payment rather than by giving his freedom ale, that may be [done], if his [lawful] master makes the sale with proper warranty. And the agreement shall never be broken after that.

15. IF A MAN IS BORN BETWEEN LAPS

If a man is born between laps, he shall have such personal rights as his father had; and a man who is born between laps [shall enjoy] such a degree of freedom as was given to his father. If he [the father] had taken a wife before he gave his freedom ale and has a son by that wife, such a son is born between laps;[10] he shall have no man's inheritance.

16. IF A MAN CARRIES ANOTHER MAN'S FREEDWOMAN FROM THE LAND OR IF SHE LIES WITH HIM

If a man carries from the land a woman from whom another man has the right to inherit, or who is his freedwoman, the shipmaster shall pay a fine of twelve oras and shall hand over all the property that witnesses award to the master as having belonged to the freedwoman. But if the shipmaster took her unwittingly,

[10] This term is applied to the child of a freedman whose manumission is still somewhat imperfect. The child can, therefore, not be received on any knee that can guarantee a legal protection. The master has surrendered what right he had, and the father has not yet acquired such a right.

let him prove his assertion with a threefold oath. If a man's freedwoman commits fornication, she shall pay three marks to her master; and let any man who wants to do so make the payment. But if she wishes at a later time to rid herself of dependence [by a money payment], she shall go to her master in the care of a keeper [like a thrall]. And if a free-born man takes [another] man's freedwoman [to wife], she shall owe a fine of three marks to her master; but their children shall be free from dependence.

17. WHAT A FOSTER FATHER MAY GIVE TO HIS FOSTER SON

A hauld may give his thrallborn son and his foster son each twelve oras valued in burned silver, if he likes, without [asking] his heir's consent; but even though there is [only] one such person, he shall give no more than twelve oras without his heir's consent. In the same way other men may give money to their foster sons, if they like; a free-born man [may give] a mark and others as much as their rank allows.

18. CONCERNING HOW MUCH A MAN MAY GIVE WITHOUT HIS HEIR'S CONSENT AND CONCERNING THE TITHE OF THE ONE-FOURTH

Any man who wants to do so may give tithe of his property and may dispose [of his tithe] as he likes, whether he be in good health or not, [only] so that the one to whom he entrusts it shall use it for the giver's soul; [he may] also [give] one-fourth of his income [as a tithe]. But no man shall take more out of his goods than is here allowed, except the tithe of the one-fourth, without his heir's consent.

19. CONCERNING THE VIOLATION OF PEACE PLEDGES THAT DO NOT CONFORM TO THE LAWS; AND CONCERNING THE GIFT TO THE MARRIAGE PORTION, IF A MAN LOSES HIS WIFE

If a man breaks a peace pledge, he is a pledge breaker; but if he breaks pledges that are not expressly demanded by law, though they are [among those] enumerated in our law book, he shall not be held accountable. If a man makes a formal transfer of land to his wife as his gift to her marriage portion and his wife passes away, he becomes himself the heir to that land; for it is our law that every husband shall pay over the marriage portion and as much money as he has received [in addition]. But if the husband dies first, the wife shall keep her husband's gift to her marriage portion, if she has not forfeited it.

20. HOW LONG ONE SHALL HAVE THE DISPOSAL OF HIS PROPERTY

Every one shall have the disposal of his property, woman as well as man, as long as he is able to sit in his high seat. But if a man becomes so feeble mentally that it seems to the nearer kinsmen on both sides [of the house] that he is no longer able to look after his property, let the care [of it] be given to the one who is the nearest heir. But the property must not be sold away from him who owns it; but he shall be given so much of his money for his maintenance that neither shall suffer dishonor.

21. WHO MAY BRING [A PERSON] INTO THE KINDRED

A man may never bring a woman into the kindred, nor may a woman [bring in] a man.

22. CONCERNING GUARDIANSHIP

The property of a minor shall be in the keeping of the one who is nearest to the inheritance. And [let him] pay off all debts that are known to witnesses with the advice of the [ward's] kinsmen, both cognates and agnates, and let him pay in land and give warranty if there is no other property. And the minor, if he disregards this warranty, becomes a pledge breaker just as much as if he had given it himself. And whatever is left over shall be assessed to the last ora in the presence of kinsmen on both the father's and the mother's side; after that the guardian shall have the increase or suffer the shrinkage, and he shall return to the ward the [exact] amount that he received. But if he takes a minor's property that has not been appraised, he [the ward], when he is fifteen winters old and reaches his majority, has the right to charge him on oath with as large an amount as he likes; and he [the keeper] shall then pay over every penny that the ward swore to. But if he has taken it as the law directs, the ward shall have all the increase except [from] land that has been mortgaged for a debt. And if there is a dispute between the ward and the guardian about the land rents, the guardian shall state on oath how much he has received and shall pay it all. The guardian shall provide the minor with clothes out of his [own] money and shall render payment and service for him in and to the coast defense; but the other minors shall all be clothed at their own expense and their maintenance shall be taken from the maintenance money.

23. CONCERNING THE GUARDIANSHIP OF A SISTER'S PROPERTY

When she is fifteen winters old a sister has the same right to manage her property as a brother. If [a guardian] has wasted the property of a minor, he shall repay as best he can while his money lasts; and he shall [then] state on oath that he has nothing more with which to pay. And after that, whenever he [the ward] finds property which he recognizes as his own or as having belonged to his father or to any [other] man from whom he was to inherit, and if he has [further] evidence that he lost this through his guardian and that he had pressed him to the utmost, let him take what is his wherever he sees it. But if he [the guardian] tries to hold on to it, let the claimant charge him with robbery in the presence of witnesses; and let him summon him to be at home to receive a thing summons, and let him thereupon summon him to [appear before] the thing [to answer] for the robbery. If a man receives a minor's property into his keeping and it has been appraised, he shall produce witnesses at the next thing [to testify as] to how much he took over and he shall repay the minor every penny according to their testimony. If he refuses to do so, let the minor make a formal demand for his property, and let him summon him to be at home after three nights to receive a thing summons, and let him then summon him to the thing on the charge of robbery. The minor shall present his case at the thing in legal form and, if his claim proves to be valid, he shall ask the freemen to go upon him [the defendant] to collect the debt and to take an equal sum [in addition] together with a fine of three marks for the king. And the defendant shall proceed to recall what he has disposed of in this case, [going] wherever he is able to get what is his. And to the same end that he has brought suit against his property guardian the minor may bring suits against other men to recover property wherever he finds it, if the guardian has paid to the utmost, as has been said, and the facts are known to men.

24. CONCERNING THE MISMANAGEMENT OF A MINOR'S PROPERTY BY HIS GUARDIAN

If a man has been appointed a property guardian and will not give care to what he is given to keep, the minor shall [none the less] as soon as he is fifteen winters old make such claim to his property as if the man had been a proper guardian.

25. CONCERNING THE DUTY TO PROVIDE FOR MINORS TILL THE OLDEST IS FIFTEEN WINTERS OLD

If a man at his death leaves minors but no property, he [the guardian] shall take the minors all the same and rear them till one of them is fifteen winters old. Then let him call in witnesses and let him speak in this wise: "I am no longer able to provide for them." After that he has no responsibility whatever, even though they be reduced to begging.

26. IF A MAN DEMANDS HIS PROPERTY BEFORE HIS GUARDIAN WILL ALLOW THAT HE IS ENTITLED TO IT

If a man demands his property before his guardian will allow that he is entitled to it, his mother, if she is living, shall take an oath that he is fifteen winters [old]; but if the mother is not living, the nearest kinsman on the mother's side may take the oath; after that the man shall have his property.

27. IF AN INHERITANCE COMES INTO THE HANDS OF A MINOR

If a man who seems to be the heir receives an inheritance and men present the claims of a minor and he [the minor] asserts that the one who has the inheritance in his possession is not the right heir, his claim shall rest till he is fifteen winters old, when he shall himself prosecute his suit; but no man shall press his claim earlier.

28. NO MAN SHALL CARRY THE PROPERTY OF A MINOR FROM THE LAND

No man shall carry the property of a minor from the land or outside our law, unless [it be that] the one who is the rightful guardian is outside our law but owns land within our law which he believes will be adequate to secure the minor, who remains within our law, to the amount that he carries away. And if there is more than this, let the man within our law who is nearest to the guardianship have the care of it. And no man shall sell any part of a minor's land that has been put in pledge until the minor has come into his property and has made a settlement with his guardian. And if it has been sold, let the minor as soon as he comes of age, proceed to annul the transfer and serve a summons to a five-day moot; and at that moot let him show by witnesses that the land was pledged on his account; and it shall be awarded to him to have and to hold from that time on till he comes into his own. If the property is carried off in some other way, the man who is nearest to the guardianship of the property shall come forward and demand security from the one who tries to carry it away. If he fails to do this, he shall pay the minor every penny that was due him from the other man; or let him swear a threefold oath that he did not know that the other intended to leave [the land]. But if this one runs away with the minor's property, he shall, if he returns, pay one-half more than that which he carried away.

29. CONCERNING THE PERIOD OF LIMITATION IN INHERITANCE SUITS

If a man has to take legal action to secure an inheritance, he shall have taken it within ten winters after he has reached his majority. But if he remains in the realm till he is twenty-five without initiating any action, he can raise no claim at any later time. If a man succeeds to an inheritance, he shall have claimed it within ten winters from the time when it became available, if he is within the realm; but if he fails to act within that time, he has forfeited his right to bring suit; and the same [rule] shall hold in all actions to enforce property rights that men have to bring. But if he is outside the realm, let him sue for his property in the ten winters following his return; and the winters that he spent in Norway before he went abroad shall be included in the reckoning.

30. CONCERNING AN INHERITANCE

If a man has to sue for the possession of land which he should have received as an inheritance, he shall bring his action with the law billet[11] and produce witness at the five-day moot that the man whose heir he is owned the land and that he had neither given it away nor conveyed it by sale nor handed it over in lawful payment to other men. He shall bring his suit for the land in this way within the ten winters from the time when he comes of age. One shall also take action with the law billet if a harvest or live stock make a part of the inheritance; but all the movables shall be sued for with a formal demand as set forth above.

[11] See Glossary, "Law billet."

X. [THE MERCHANT LAW]

1. NO ONE SHALL TAKE [ANOTHER MAN'S GOODS]

We have stated in the secular laws that no one shall take an ertog from another or more than an ertog. But if [so much] is taken, the man whose goods were taken shall go after them with witnesses and shall demand his own within a month after he has learned [where they are]. If he [the accused] yields the property, he has nullified his own claim; but if he holds on [to what he has taken] and will not surrender it, he is guilty of robbery and has lost his case the same as before.

2. CONCERNING A HOME SUMMONS

A freeman shall be summoned to be at home and [the suitor] shall go to his house. If he finds him within the [enclosure of] the home fields, let him summon him to be inside the house in his highseat and let it be done before his witnesses to his demand [for restitution]; for they are the proper persons to bear witness both to the summons and to the demand.

3. IF A MAN OWES THE DUTY TO TESTIFY WITH OTHERS AS TO A LEGAL EXCUSE

If a man is a witness to a home summons or to a thing summons or to a demand [for restitution] and after that a ban is placed on his harvest, and if the summoning is all for the same day, to thing and to doom and to five-day moot, he shall demand of the man who has enjoined him from harvesting the choice of [having a moot at the end of] four or six nights; if he will choose neither, it shall be [set for] six nights, unless the day [appointed shall] be a holy day, in which case it shall be [set for] five nights. If both are called for the same day, an arrow thing and a weapon thing, all the freemen to whose homesteads the arrow comes shall proceed to the arrow thing and shall bring their weapons, for the inspection there shall be as competent as at the shire thing. If the bailiff has a deputy there, the freemen may attend with impunity.

If both are called for the same day, an arrow thing and a thing to hear a lawsuit, and each is to meet in its own place, he [the plaintiff] may summon him [his opponent] to a later thing, and the suit shall remain in force on either side. But if he fails to find him [the defendant] at home and [the men] of his household state that "we do not know where he has gone, a long or a short distance," he shall summon him to be at home at his abiding place after five nights. But if the household states that the man has traveled over the mountain or [has gone] out beyond Agdaness[1] or north across the Isthmus[2] or some distance into the country, the suitor shall summon him to be at home at his abiding place after two months. But if the household speaks in this wise: "We do not know whither he went, but it was somewhere this side Agdaness or [this side] the high mountains or [on this side] the Isthmus," the man shall be given a home summons and his household shall send a man after him and he shall count the length of the journey in days both coming and going. But if the case belongs somewhere in the four shires beyond Agdaness and the household states that he is in the fylki, he shall be summoned to be at home after half a month. And if the household states that he has gone outside the fylki but is within the realm, he shall be summoned to be at his abiding place after two months.

4. HERE IT IS TOLD HOW A MAN SHALL BE SERVED WITH A HOME SUMMONS

A man shall be served with a home summons in this wise. [Let the suitor] call the man by name and speak as follows: "I summon you to be at home on the farm that you till or on the farm where you reside (and here I name the farm), [I summon you to be] by the fire and the fireplace and in the house where covers are spread on the benches to hear my demand or to be summoned to the thing"; and let him name a day from sunrise to sunset and take witness to this.

[1] Agdaness: a headland at the mouth of Trondheim Fjord. It was regarded as the outer limit of Trondheim.

[2] The Isthmus: a neck of land lying north of Nidaros [Trondheim] between Trondheim Fjord and Folden Fjord.

5. IF THE MAN WHO WAS SUMMONED FAILS TO COME

He shall now be obliged to come home unless he has a good excuse. But if he does not come and no excuse [is pleaded], the suitor shall proceed to state his claim none the less, and the defendant shall owe a fine of three oras in current coin.

6. HERE IT IS TOLD HOW A DEMAND [FOR RESTITUTION] SHALL BE SET FORTH

A man shall set forth his demand [for restitution] in this wise. He shall address the other man by name and shall demand the return of the chattels that are owing him, naming each article. And let him make his request in legal manner and in legal terms, and he shall name his witnesses [at the same time]. Not more than four men shall enter the house; if there are more than four, they shall be counted a band, and the defendant need not propose a doom, unless he desires to do so.

7. CONCERNING THE HOME SUMMONS AND THE [FORMAL] DEMAND

One may serve a man with a summons to be at home on any day that one likes. And let him [the summoner] have free men present, whomever he likes, but competent to testify, to be witnesses to the thing summons. But to witness his demand [for restitution] he shall take freemen residing in the fylki where the defendant has his home. But if a man refuses to serve as witness to a home summons, to a thing summons, or to a demand [for restitution], he shall owe a fine of three oras in current coin, or support his refusal with his own oath. And one may summon a man [to be at home] to receive a thing summons after three nights or after five nights, if there is fjord or mountain to cross. But if neither of these is to hinder, let the claimant summon as he prefers, for three nights or five.

8. IF A MAN WHO WAS NOTIFIED TO BE AT HOME HAS RETURNED TO HIS HIGHSEAT

If a man who was notified [to be at home] has returned to his highseat, the suitor shall present his request in legal terms. Then the one to whom the demand is directed shall ask for the judgment of a doom; whoever proposes a doom shall inquire about the witnesses, and the plaintiff shall name them, if he is asked [to do so]. And he shall have such witnesses as are willing to take the oath with him.

9. CONCERNING A MAN'S HOME IN [THE CASE OF] A HOME SUMMONS

No man shall move his residence within a baron's garth or a bailiff's garth. If a man has a father or a mother living, he [the suitor] shall summon him to that [parent's] house; and if one or both of these have a farm in the fylki, there shall be no need to inquire after the home of the man against whom the action is directed. But if he does hired labor on a farm and the fact is commonly known, he shall be summoned to that place.

10. CONCERNING FREE LABORERS AND IF TWO MEN HIRE THE SAME MAN

If a free laborer leaves his service, let him pay the man who hired him the same amount as was promised him [in hire]; and the man who [now] hires him shall owe an equal amount to the one who hired him first, if he knew [the facts]. And let him[3] summon him[4] to a thing where they may settle their dispute, if they like; if they fail to do so, the freemen shall go upon the offender and take double the amount; and whoever refuses to join [in this] shall pay to the king six oras valued in burned silver. If two men hire the same workman, the one who hired him first shall have him. But if a freeman dismisses a workman from [house and] service, he shall have a legal award like the one provided above.

11. HOW ONE SHALL PROPOSE A DOOM AND [CONCERNING THE COURSE OF] THE ACTION

A man who is served with a formal demand may throw down the law billet and request the judgment of a doom. And the one who made the demand shall accept the offer and appoint a doom [to be held] after an interval of five nights at the doomstead which

[3] The farmer who hired the man first.
[4] The man who last hired him.

the men have used before, and the one who appoints the doom [also] names the farm. The men who witnessed the serving of the demand are competent to bear witness for both plaintiff and defendant. Now the [two], plaintiff and defendant, shall go to the doomstead and each shall wait for the other till midday. If either fails to appear, the other shall set the doom none the less with six men from either side. And if anyone who was to sit in the doom for one of the parties fails to serve, that side has lost its case.

12. IF THE PLAINTIFF FAILS TO COME TO THE DOOM

If the plaintiff fails to come to the doom, his suit is void. Now the defendant shall bring forward his own witnesses to the plaintiff's demand, and in that way make him a defaulter.[5] But if the defendant fails to come to the doom, he shall owe a fine of three oras; and let the plaintiff set the doom none the less and bring forward his witnesses to his demand and after that his other witnesses. When adequate witness has been borne for the plaintiff, the doomsmen shall give the decision that he has made his contention good. Then the plaintiff shall appoint [another] doom for the same place after five nights. If the plaintiff comes to the second doom but the defendant does not come, the latter has lost his case and shall owe a fine of three oras. But if he does come to the second doom, he shall [be allowed to] present all his witnesses at this doom. And a third doom shall be appointed for the same place after five nights, and the plaintiff shall appoint it.

13. CONCERNING THE REFUSAL TO ACCEPT THE DECISION OF A DOOM

If a man breaks up a twelve-man doom and does it by his own act, he shall owe a fine of eighteen oras valued in burned silver, which is twelve oras, weighed, and let the doom remain intact as before. His heir incurs the same penalty if he breaks a doom that has been accepted on his behalf and [does it] after the witnesses have been heard. The prosecutor shall summon him to be at home to [receive] a thing summons and then [he shall summon him] before the thing. And at that thing let him produce testi-

[5] See Glossary, "Dómflogi."

mony that his opponent has rejected a decision agreed to by twelve men. And the bailiff shall have one-half of the money and the prosecutor one-half.

14. CONCERNING THE SETTING OF A THIRD DOOM

If both parties come to the third doom, each one bringing doomsmen with him, the doomsmen shall be placed in two rows. Near kinsmen on the father's or on the mother's side shall have no places in that doom, nor shall foster fathers, dependents, and men who are closely related by marriage.

15. CONCERNING THE WAGER DOOM

When the number in the doom is complete for both sides, the plaintiff's doomsmen shall offer to wager and then remain quiet. If those [on the opposite side] are not able to [reach across and] take the others by the hand, they shall move forward in sitting position toward those who propose the wager. If a man on either side rises [and leaves the doom], the doom is void. If there are eleven on one side and twelve on the other, those who are twelve in number shall present their witnesses. These are called "doom stakes" and shall be standing about on the outside but near enough so that their voices can be heard. Then they shall testify against those who are eleven in number that they failed to present a case. If there is disagreement about the decision, the lot shall fall to those who have two witnesses more than the others, both sides having wagered. Each doomsman shall wager two oras of silver and both sides shall have the silver there and shall place it in a neutral hand; and if [either side is] lacking in a single ora, its case is void. When the wager is made, the plaintiff shall serve the defendant with a home summons and thereupon he shall summon him before a shire thing. All the dooms shall then be declared of no effect and both sides shall be allowed to present their witnesses there.

16. A BARON SHALL NOT BE APPOINTED

A baron shall not come to a doom or to a farm where a doom is sitting, except he be traveling on the highway; but if he does come, let them both go forth, plaintiff and defendant, and order him to leave. And if either side has appointed him, that side has destroyed its case. Nor shall a baron be present at a five-day moot any more than at a doom, unless he has a suit to prosecute or to defend.

17. CONCERNING THE HOME SUMMONS AND THE APPEAL TO A DOOM

If a freeman has been served with a home summons and the suitor fails to find anyone at home who can propose a doom, he [the defendant] owes a fine of three oras in current coin. Now let the suitor summon him before the same witnesses to be at home, and let him come there early in the morning when the specified number of days have passed. When he arrives he shall make his formal demand and shall agree to accept a doom, if a grithman[6] proposes a doom before he [the suitor] comes from under the roof. If the offer is made after he [the suitor] has come from under the roof, he [the defendant] shall owe a fine of three oras in current coin. If there is no one [at home] who can make the offer of a doom, he [the defendant] shall owe a fine of three oras. If he suffers three formal demands [and does nothing], the plaintiff shall summon him before a thing and shall bring forward at that thing all his testimony both as to the home summons and to the formal demand. Having now carried forward his suit as the law directs, let him wait for his opponent to pay him what is his; but if he does not pay, he shall ask for a force of men to go upon him and take from him the double amount. Let the suitor first have what is his, then [let] the bailiff [have] nine oras from the property on the farm, and let the farmers have what is left over. If they [the defendant and his household] offer resistance, they are outlaws, while those who come to collect remain in the protection of the law. But if the men at the thing refuse to give him this force, every one who fails to join in going upon the defendant owes a fine of six oras, and those who fail to come to the thing shall owe six oras in addition; that is, twelve oras are owing from every one who fails to attend the thing and does not join in going upon the defendant.

[6] See Glossary, "Grith."

18. CONCERNING THE THIRD DOOM

Every man may keep his suit [valid] till the third doom, but after that he shall either agree to make payment or to [accept] a wager.[7]

19. CONCERNING NOTORIOUS PROPERTY[8]

Chattels that have been pledged before witnesses shall be [regarded as] notorious property.

20. A SECOND [FORM OF] NOTORIOUS PROPERTY

A second [form of] notorious property is that which a man has acknowledged before witnesses.

21. CONCERNING A THIRD [FORM OF] NOTORIOUS PROPERTY

A third [form of] notorious property is created when men clasp hands [at an agreement] and there are six men on either side.

22. CONCERNING A FOURTH [FORM OF] NOTORIOUS PROPERTY

Whatever a doom awards a man he holds as notorious property; [the same is true] if a man summons another before a thing and men there at the thing order the defendant to pay the suitor's claim.

23. CONCERNING A FIFTH [FORM OF] NOTORIOUS PROPERTY

No one shall ask the payment of a debt at the homestead of a deceased unless he has witnesses [to the debt]; and no one shall swear to what the deceased alone can know, except as is provided in our book.

24. HOW ONE SHALL SUE FOR NOTORIOUS PROPERTY

Notorious property shall be sued for like any other debt. Let it be demanded formally three times, though one demand shall be sufficient; and let robbery be charged, if the accused holds on [to the property]. And he [the defendant] shall be summoned to

[7] The translation here is tentative, the sentence being apparently incomplete.

[8] *Vitafé:* property the title to which can be established by witnesses, or is a matter of common knowledge.

a thing, unless he appoints a day [for settlement], after three nights but within the five-day period. If an agreement is then reached, it is well; otherwise let the plaintiff summon him [his opponent] before a thing, and let him produce all his witnesses there. But if he [the defendant] fails in his defense, he shall be liable for the debt and for such fines to the king as the case assigns to him: three marks for each demand, whether the demands were made at one time or not, or [let him] suffer distraint; and it is the duty of the freemen to join in the distraint. But in all suits to recover property that cannot be brought with the law billet, though witnesses are available, the formal demand shall be made and the fine for robbery shall be threatened; and if [the accused] holds on [to the property], the plaintiff shall summon him before the thing and [let him] produce all his witnesses there. If the defendant still refuses to pay, the freemen shall go upon him and take from him double the amount and the robber fine for the king. But in suits for debts in which witnesses are [not][9] available, [the claimant] shall summon [the defendant] to be at home to receive a thing summons, and thereupon [he shall summon him] before a thing. He then has two choices: to pay the debt or to take such oaths as the law demands. And let the freemen go upon him and take double the amount. And in cases of injury done to a man's live stock, and likewise when chattel injures chattel, the one [who has suffered the damage] shall summon [the other] to receive a thing summons and thereupon [summon him] before a thing, and let him prove there that it was a man's deed; likewise, when chattel injures chattel, [let the owner of the offending chattel] be summoned to be at home to receive a thing summons. If he is allowed to deny the guilt, let him take the oaths demanded by law; otherwise he shall pay compensation according to the award of men. But if he will do neither, the freemen shall go upon him and take from him double the amount [claimed]; and whoever refuses to join in this shall owe a fine of one baug.

[9] Hertzberg argues that "not" belongs in the sentence. *Den ældste norske proces*, pp. 30–31.

25. CONCERNING THE SETTING OF A DOOM AND THE FAILURE OF THE WITNESSES TO THE DEMAND TO APPEAR

If men have set their doom and a witness to the plaintiff's demand fails to appear, he [the plaintiff] shall wait till midday; and after that let him set his doom. But if the other party [to the suit] does not set an opposing doom, he shall owe a payment of three oras; and the other witness to the demand shall make such a statement as he is willing to swear to on the book at a second doom. If both witnesses to the demand appear at the second doom and they testify adequately for the one who made the demand, the two dooms shall both be held valid. Now the third doom is the one in which the wager is to be made, unless [the one side] drops the suit. In every case in which a man claims a warrantor, an appeal shall be made to a doom.

26. CONCERNING SUITS AGAINST ONE WHO IS NOT A HOUSEHOLDER

If a man wants to bring a suit against one who is not a householder and finds him in the fylki, he shall inquire about his residence, and the man shall tell him where his home is. But if he deceives him as to his home, the plaintiff shall call in witnesses and assign him a home in the fylki, and he shall bring the action against him there. He may take him home with him and keep him in such durance as he likes, [only] he must not injure him. [And he] shall summon a thing and bring him before the thing, and he shall have the benefit of such testimony as his witnesses bear. If he refuses to pay, the claimant shall request his kinsmen to release him [with] such an amount of money as he owes and as witnesses know that he ought to pay. But if they refuse to release him, he [the claimant] shall assess the value of his limbs for the [payment of the] debt, and the smaller the debt, the easier the penalty. And his kinsmen can claim no compensation if he has been offered to them. But if he finds a home for himself, the suitor shall ask him to give surety that he will be found at home, and the surety shall be given. The plaintiff shall go with him to the place where he expects to get bail, and if he fails to get it there, he shall go with him to the two nearest householders and ask them to give bail for him; and if they refuse, he shall take him home with him and shall deal with him as directed above.

27. CONCERNING BAIL IF A MAN GIVES IT

If he [the defendant] gives bail that he will be found at home, he [the plaintiff] shall bring up his suit against him there; but if he fails to find him at home, let him bring action against the one who gave bail for him.

28. CONCERNING AGREEMENTS CONCLUDED WITH A HANDCLASP AND BARGAINS MADE IN THE PRESENCE OF SURETY WITNESSES

Whenever men conclude [a dispute] by clasping hands, six men being present for each side,[10] everything shall stand as the doomsmen have decided. And if it is known to witnesses that [a payment of] money is pledged, the pledge shall be valid. If a witness to warranty is [also] a witness to the conveyance of land, he shall be held to account for twenty winters; after that he may state on a threefold oath that the business is now so old that a witness to warranty can no longer be held responsible. But in all other cases of buying and selling the witness shall be held to account for ten winters; after that he may state on his own oath that the business is now so old that a witness can no longer be held responsible.

29. HOW A MAN MAY [ACT] FOR ANOTHER

No man shall give power of attorney to any man of higher rank or birth than the one with whom he is in litigation either as plaintiff or defendant, except in cases that concern the king or the archbishop. But if he does otherwise, he loses his case, whether his part is suit or defense. If he feels the need of a deputy, let him get one at once, whether he be ill or in good health and whatever his occupation or his needs may be, within the fylki or without.

30. WHAT THE SHIREMEN MAY DETERMINE

Every decision in which the shiremen are all agreed [shall stand], and when they have declared the law in any case which they

[10] At a *sættarstefna*, a private meeting of the litigants to seek a satisfactory settlement.

have a right to determine, their decision must by no means be ignored, even though the near kinsmen, on both sides of the house and those of near kin by marriage dissent and withdraw [from the thing].[11] If one-fourth or more of the thingmen, proper, withdraw [from the thing], he [the loser] shall return to the thing and call upon the assembled men to testify to a mistrial and demand that the case be sent to a two-shire thing. But even though none of them return to the thing to claim a mistrial, no freeman shall suffer a penalty for going away with them. And if men reach no agreement at the two-shire thing, [the case] shall be referred to a four-shire thing. If no decision is reached there it may be referred to an eight-shire thing; and let the men be satisfied with what is there agreed upon and with what comes before the law court. If the fylki is divided [into several court areas], it is ordained that a decision reached in any one of these shall have the same effect as [one agreed to] by all the men of the fylki.

31. A FREEMAN SHALL DEFEND HIS LAWSUITS AT HOME

A freeman shall defend all his lawsuits as to property at home on his farm, except only in case he has property in the borough. If a freeman is ordered to give bail in the borough let him give surety [only] that he will appear on the borough moot floor, though he be [also] ordered to give bail to appear at a doom. And if there is then a disagreement as to whether the case originated in the borough or in the country, let the freeman call God to witness that the case did originate in the country, and let him present his defense in the country. And he shall give security that he will proceed to his home to receive summons, and let his live stock be used as security. But the hire of thralls and the rent for land shall be sued for according to the law of the Frostathing.

32. WHERE A LAWSUIT SHALL BE BROUGHT UP

If a case that originated in the borough shall be tried in the country, let it be tried according to the law of the Frostathing and decided according to the Birch Isle law. If a case that originated in the country is to be tried in the borough, it shall be tried

[11] Dissent from the opinion of the majority.

according to the Birch Isle law and decided according to the Frostathings law, if it comes to a judgment. If a suit which must be decided according to the Birch Isle law is being prosecuted according to the law of the Frostathing and one witness at the hearing supports the plaintiff in his claim that the defendant owes the debt, the defendant may deny the claim with a sixfold oath and selected oath helpers. There shall be named four freemen who live near his [the defendant's] home and in the fylki and of these four let him select the two whom he can get to take the oath with him and let the man himself be the third. If he cannot get oath helpers from among those chosen, he shall pay ten ertogs for every oath helper of his own selection;[12] and if he is not himself [among them] he is guilty of the charge that he offered to refute with oaths. If the plaintiff has no evidence to support his contention at the hearing, the defendant may reply with a sixfold oath, [the oath helpers to be] of his own selection, if the amount [involved] is more than three oras, valued in burned silver. And the plaintiff shall have all the fines that the defendant has to pay for the oath helpers that fail him.

33. EVERY KING'S BAILIFF SHALL PROSECUTE HIS OWN SHIREMEN

Whenever men commit offenses that make them liable to pay fines to the king, each bailiff shall prosecute his [own] shiremen. But if a man has himself an action to bring up, let him prosecute as he likes; and he may prosecute a bailiff as any other freeman, if he deals unjustly with a freeman or any other man; for a bailiff shall not deprive a freeman of as much as an ertog or more than an ertog. If he seizes [property], let the one from whom it is taken come forward and demand that the bailiff restore the goods; and if he refuses to restore it, let the freeman summon him to be at home to receive a thing summons, and then [let him summon him] before the thing. If he still refuses to restore it, [the complainant] shall ask the freemen to go upon him and take the goods from him, and let them add three marks; and that money shall all belong to the freemen. The complainant shall

[12] Brandt believes that this fine was paid to the plaintiff. *Retshistorie*, II, 268.

bring suit against the bailiff to enforce the penalty that is provided, and the freemen shall aid him and shall have the fines. But if the freemen refuse to help, they shall each owe a fine of six oras in current coin. And let the complainant and all the [other] freemen bring suit against them to enforce the penalties and let them have the fines that are provided.

34. CONCERNING THE RIGHTS OF MEN TO ATONEMENT

The hauld shall receive three marks as his full atonement. Now the amount of the atonement money shall be increased by one-third from the hauld upward and decreased by one-third the other way.

35. CONCERNING TERMS OF ABUSE, [SUCH AS] LIKENING A MAN TO A FOUR-FOOTED BEAST, AND THE PENALTY FOR SUCH

If a man likens another to a female beast of whatever sort, it is abuse that calls for a full atonement, if the injured man secures his witnesses. If one speaks [in this wise] of a hauld, he shall pay three marks; of a well-born man, two marks; of a reksthegn,[13] twelve oras; of the son of a freedman, one mark; his son's son too, takes a mark. A full atonement shall be valued in burned silver in every case except that of a dependent; and there shall be thirty pence in every ora, whether the money be counted or weighed. A freedman's [atonement] shall be six oras, if his freedom ale has been given; if not given, it shall be one-half mark. If a man says of another that he has been used as a woman, he shall pay him a full atonement. If a man likens another to a horse or to an ox or to any other beast of this sort, a half atonement shall be forthcoming. But if men wrangle and abuse each other, let the one word revenge the other.

36. CONCERNING AN ACTION BROUGHT AGAINST AN UNMARRIED WOMAN

If a man wants to bring action against an unmarried woman, let him summon her and her defender to be at her home, and let him make his demand there. And let her select as her defender a man of equal rank to the one who had her just before; but if

[13] Cf. IV, c. 49; see Glossary, "Reksthegn."

she appoints a man of higher rank, she has spoiled her case. If she is a maid and has neither father nor brother living, she shall appoint a man of equal rank to her father; [she shall proceed in] the same way, if her father or a brother is living but pays no heed to her affairs; let her appoint a man of equal rank to them.

37. CONCERNING THE RIGHT OF A WOMAN TO COMPENSATION FOR INJURY

This deals with a woman's right to atonement. Every man has the right to a full atonement with respect to his wife. A hauld can demand three marks, if his wife suffers injury. A widow shall have the atonement herself; and, if she likes, she may sue for such atonement as he could claim who had her last. If a maid is injured, the man who is nearest of kin shall take such atonement in her case as he can demand in his own. And if she is to have the atonement herself, let the one who is the right man to prosecute summon the thing.

38. IF A WOMAN WOUNDS A MAN OR [ANOTHER] WOMAN

If a man's wife wounds another woman, he shall render atonement equal to one-half of what might be claimed by the injured woman's husband or by her father for his own person; and the payment shall be taken out of her money. The same [rule shall hold] if she steals and the case is closed by agreement. If a man's wife wounds a man, her husband shall pay a full atonement out of her money. One man shall receive all the atonement due for any free-born woman except a man's betrothed; in her case her father and her betrothed shall receive such atonement as is due the rank of each.

39. CONCERNING ABLE-BODIED VAGABONDS

All able-bodied persons who refuse to work and go [begging] from house to house shall, [each one], unless they are rated as dependants, owe a fine of three marks, women as well as men. And the bailiff or any other man shall arrest such a person before witnesses and take him before the thing. Let his kinsmen release him with [a payment of] three marks, or let the one who brought him before the thing make such use of his labor as he likes.

40. WHAT RESPONSIBILITY ONE HAS FOR A THRALL

Let everyone maintain for his thrall, if native born, his pledge and promise, or whatever comes up in word or deed. But if he runs away from his master, the master shall have him flogged by the fifth [day], if he recovers him. If he will not do so, the bailiff shall take him and have him flogged by the fifth [day] and have the use of his labor. But the master has the right to redeem the thrall's skin with six oras in current coin and to have him himself. If the bailiff refuses to flog him, the freeman shall have his thrall. If the thrall is an alien and a charge is raised against him, the master shall give him into the hands of the prosecutor, who may torture him till he speaks the truth, but only so that he shall be none the worse for work or in value; and if he is cleared, the freeman shall take his thrall and have the use of him. If an alien thrall runs away from his master and is caught later on, the bailiff shall have him castrated before the fifth [day] or let the freeman have his thrall. And if a thrall runs away from his master and out of the fylki but remains within our law, let his master redeem him from those who took him with two oras, valued in burned silver, as the finder's reward, and with half a mark if it was outside our law.

41. IF A MAN WOUNDS A HORSE BENEATH ANOTHER

If a man is sitting on horseback and another man wounds the horse beneath him, let him pay a fine of six oras, if the horse is wounded in front of the saddle, and half a mark if [the wound is] behind the saddle. If the man falls off the horse, a full atonement shall be due. If he is bruised, it is as if the other man had done it himself, if he [the injured man] wishes [to have it so]; but if he disregards it, there is nothing due to the king. If one wounds a horse that a woman is riding, the penalty is the same as if the horse were wounded beneath a man; and if she falls off the horse, [the man shall] pay her a half atonement and her husband the fine for evil intent. If [a man] strikes a horse that is bound to a fence, let him pay an ora to the owner. If [a man] takes a horse at any place where it is bound and rides away from the owner with it, he shall pay six oras valued in burned silver to [the owner, if] a hauld, half a mark to a well-born man, three oras to a reks-thegn, and two oras to a freedman.

42. CONCERNING A SECOND [FORM OF] CONVERSION

A second [form of] conversion is when a man takes another man's boat with oars and with thwarts; and the risk and the fine are the same whether the owner sees it or not. And whether a man takes a horse or a boat, he shall be held to account for it till he has returned it.

43. CONCERNING A THIRD [FORM OF] CONVERSION

A third [form of] conversion is when a man takes another man's conveyance when he goes to the thing or to the church or when he travels the highway; in these cases the fines are the same. If a man takes a horse from the pasture or a boat from the boat shed without permission from the owner, he shall pay no more than two oras, valued in burned silver, [as a fine] for the conversion. And in all cases of unauthorized use of property everyone shall pay the full penalty, no matter how many shared in [the guilt].

44. CONCERNING FINES FOR CONVERSION

The king can collect no fines for unauthorized use of the ships or the horses that belong to his court; nor has a thrall any such rights with respect to his belongings. If a man comes upon [another] man's thrall on his horse or in his boat, he can demand no compensation, though he may have the thrall flogged; for a master shall pay no fine for conversion, whether his thrall takes a man's horse or boat.

45. CONCERNING CONVERSION WHEN A MAN LENDS ANOTHER A HORSE OR A BOAT

If a man lends another a horse or a boat and the one to whom the loan was made wishes to have the use of it for his own needs but the lender comes and takes the loan from him, the owner of the horse or the boat shall pay the fine for conversion; but if he [the borrower] keeps [what he borrowed] longer than it was lent for, let him pay a fine for conversion.

46. IF A MAN MAIMS A HORSE

If a man cuts the tail hairs off another man's horse, he shall pay three oras. If he cuts the tail off, [the value of] the horse shall be appraised and he shall pay the owner what the horse is worth and the fine for evil intent in addition: six oras to a hauld, half a mark to a well-born man, three oras to a reksthegn, two oras to the son of a freedman, and one ora to a freedman. The money [paid] to well-born men shall be valued in burned silver; that [paid] to dependents shall be current coin. And if a man strikes the teeth out of [the jaws of] another man's horse, let the one who injured the horse have him, and let the owner have the value [of the horse] and the fine for evil intent in addition. The same [rule shall hold] if he cuts the tail off the horse so that the rump goes with [the hairs]. If horses go to fighting, let the owners bear the consequences; but if a horse is attacked without cause and injured, [the owner of the offending horse] shall pay the owner of the injured horse the fine for evil intent according to his rank. If a man removes a halter from a horse without the owner's permission, [he shall] pay the owner three oras, and [he shall] be accountable for the horse and for whatever the beast may do till it is returned into the hands of the owner, and let him defend himself with an oath. If a man cuts the forelock off a horse, he shall owe a fine of two oras. If a horse comes running after a rider, he shall give him into the keeping [of some one] before he has ridden past three farmsteads; otherwise the responsibility remains with him. If [a man] cuts the tail off another man's cow or ox, he shall pay one-half ora, valued in burned silver, and the fine for evil intent, as shall be done in every case when one does injury to another man's beasts.

47. CONCERNING A CORNER LAD OR A BUSH LAD

If a man lies with a free woman in the woods and begets a son with her, he [the son] is called a bush lad; he shall have the same personal right as his father had. But if the man lies with a free woman at home in one of the farm houses and begets a son with her, he [the son] shall be called a corner lad. He, too, shall have the same personal right as his father had. But a thrallborn son, if he has been given his freedom from the corner and the cup, is not older than three winters, and has not labored with rope and spade, shall have a right to atonement one-third less than that of his father, and he shall be no man's dependent. If the son of a well-born man and a bondwoman is given his freedom, whether the father gives it or one of the well-born agnatic kinsmen he shall owe dependence to no man. If he gets a well-born woman to wife and [marries her] in a proper and legal way and begets children with her, they shall be regarded as of the kindred in matters of atonement, and they shall inherit the right of the paternal grandfather to ownership and heirship of every sort; and such children are called *betrfeðrungar*.[14]

48. IF MEN BARGAIN ABOUT A HORSE

When men bargain about a horse, the sale shall be valid if it is made according to law, but the buyer may return the horse within five days, if latent defects come to light. Latent defects are such as these: deafness and blindness, impaired breathing and lameness, spasms and a balky disposition. But the bargain cannot be broken unless the horse is returned within five days. If a man is on a journey with a horse that he has bought and he finds a defect in him within five days, let him prove with his own oath that the blemish was discovered within five days; and let that day be [counted as] his fifth on which he comes back to return the horse. And let him declare on his own oath what circumstances hindered him from returning the horse within five days; and his payment shall then be returned to him and the seller shall take back his horse. But if another defect has come upon the horse through the fault of him who traveled with the horse, let it be rated by discerning men and let him who had the horse make proper compensation. If he refuses to take back the horse, he shall offer it to him in the presence of two witnesses and shall renounce all responsibility [for the horse]. But if he still refuses to return the payment, let him [the purchaser] charge him with robbery, demand a fine for the king, and summon him before the thing.

[14] *Betrfeðrungr:* a son whose status with respect to personal rights is "better" than that of his father.

XI. [THE MERCHANT LAW—CONTINUED]

1. IF A MAN CARRIES OFF ANOTHER MAN'S BETROTHED

If a man carries off another man's betrothed, he shall pay a full atonement to the one who had betrothed her, [but only] if [the deed is done] within the twelvemonth after the man had betrothed her, unless the marriage had been postponed for good reasons as provided in the church law. [He shall] also [pay] a full atonement to her father; but if her father or her guardian is accused of having consented to her departure, let him take the threefold oath or pay as much as her marriage portion would have been.

2. CONCERNING THE GUARDIANSHIP OF UNMARRIED WOMEN

The father and the mother shall arrange for the marriage of their daughters or [the decision shall rest with] the marriage man. And the heir of a marriage man must never withhold a marriage portion, unless the amount exceeds what is promised. If daughters come to inherit from the father or the mother or a brother or whomever it may happen to be, and some are married and others unmarried, the unmarried ones shall first receive as large a share of the undivided inheritance as the married ones received on leaving the home.

3. CONCERNING AN EQUITABLE DIVISION OF AN INHERITANCE

If all the daughters have left the home as wives but the marriage portions given to them have not been of equal amount, let [those who received the lesser portions] take out of the undivided inheritance as much as the one received who took the most away from home, so far as the inheritance allows.

4. CONCERNING [MONEY OR] CHATTELS LENT FOR A [MARRIAGE] PORTION

All such money or chattels as are lent for a marriage portion and have been assessed and paid into the hands of the one who receives the bride shall belong to him as securely as if the father or the mother had given them as a marriage portion. And if the man asserts that he did not lend these things for that purpose, let him confirm his statement with his own oath, a woman as well as a man, and let him bring action for an equal amount against the woman's marriage man. But the husband's gift to the marriage portion need not cover this amount.[1] And if a widow goes from her home into marriage and allows the chattels of another person to be counted as part of her marriage portion, the owner having lent them for that [purpose], the husband shall possess them with the same right as that which the widow owned. But if the man denies that he lent them for that [purpose], let him confirm his statement with his own oath, and the marriage portion shall be reduced by such [an amount].

5. CONCERNING THE RELATIONS OF WIFE AND HUSBAND WITH RESPECT TO PROPERTY

The husband shall have the management of his wife's property so long as they continue in married life and their household remains unbroken, except only such moneys as were set aside at the betrothal or at the nuptials; these the wife shall have in her own control and be accountable for. If a married woman comes into an inheritance and there are minors in [that inheritance] but [there is] no money, her husband shall provide for them and shall perform their duties to the coast defense; and her marriage portion shall not be drawn on for this purpose till notice is given at the inheritance ale. But if there is money in the inheritance, the land and all the movables shall be [properly] appraised, and he [the husband] shall be responsible for the property and shall have the increase; and he shall pay back [later] such an amount as he received, excepting the land rents which he received after [the appraisal].

6. CONCERNING PROPERTY THAT HAS NOT BEEN APPRAISED

But if a husband takes over property that has not been appraised, the wife shall herself swear to [the value of] her property.

[1] In determining his gift the husband need not take disputed amounts in account. He merely adds one-half to the portion so far as the title is undisputed. See Glossary, "Husband's gift."

If he survives her, he shall pay to her heirs as much as he received, and let him swear that he received no more. If a wife loses her husband after they have lived together a twelvemonth, she shall have one-third of the stock and the movables on the farm and her clothes in addition.

7. CONCERNING THE DEBTS OF EACH

The wife shall pay the land rent to [the extent of] one-third but no other debts. If married people have their home on land belonging to one of them, neither one shall pay rent to the other. If a widow claims that all her property has not come to her, let her authorize a man, one of equal rank to the one who had her last, to look after her lawsuits and her defense, and to sue for her money. But if the heirs of the deceased hold that she has more [than is hers], let them bring action against her. But if the husband and the wife did not live together as long as a twelve-month, let her demand such property as she claims is wanting.

8. WHEN THE PROPERTY OF MARRIED FOLKS IS FORMED BY LAW INTO A JOINT HOLDING

If a man marries a maid or a widow who has her own homestead he shall have no property rights in this homestead until they have lived together a twelvemonth; then their possessions are formed by law into a community holding. If two indigent persons marry in legal manner and they acquire property, the husband shall have two-thirds and the wife one-third of both the land and the movables. And if one of the two shall die and the witnesses at the nuptials[2] cannot be produced, the survivor shall take an oath as to his property and let two upright men who enjoy full atonement rights confirm his or her oath, and let the money be paid over according to law. If [a man] uses his wife's property, cattle, or movables, for the purchase of land, and she survives him, the heir shall deliver to her only the land that she brought as a marriage portion and her husband's gift to the marriage portion, even though he [the husband] brought her to the oath-taking to receive the conveyance, for the law breaks such an arrangement;

[2] Or possibly some later ale feast given to secure publicity for certain financial arrangements.

and [she shall have] the chattels that the heirs hand over to her. But if she comes into an inheritance after marriage and it is paid out for her in land, that land shall be hers.

9. IF A MAID WHO IS THE KEEPER OF HER BROTHER'S PROPERTY IS TO MARRY

If a maid is the keeper of her brother's property, let the boy's kinsmen on his father's and on his mother's side allow her as much from the boy's property as a marriage portion as seems proper to the more judicious ones; but if they disagree, the decision shall rest with the agnate kinsmen who are next in the line of heirs, if they are men of good sense. And if the heir when he comes of age charges them with having taken [his] money to promote his sister's marriage, let those who have to meet the charge defend themselves with their own oaths. And if anyone is convicted of the charge that he has taken a bribe to this end, let him return to the boy whatever he took as bribe-money, and let him be known as a base fellow. And the sister shall not be allowed to take more for her marriage portion than is permitted by the men who have now been pointed out. But if she takes [such money] by other means than those now indicated, let her keep it only at the will of her brother when he comes of age.

10. CONCERNING THE MARRIAGE OF A SISTER

If there are brothers of whom some are minors and the oldest gives a sister in marriage with the consent of the kinsmen, the contract shall be as valid as if they were all of major age.

11. CONCERNING A SUIT FOR COMPENSATION THAT REMAINS UNFINISHED ON THE DEATH OF THE ACCUSED

If a man dishonors the daughter or the wife of another or is guilty of some other misdeed for which the latter has a right to atonement and the facts are current in the common talk of men and if the offender dies before the suit is ended, the injured man may bring action against his heir, if he [the heir] has inherited property from the deceased. But if an award had not been agreed to,[3]

[3] By the defendant; in this case because the action had not reached completion before the defendant's death.

the heir shall make payment only in case the property of the deceased shows a surplus over and above what has been set aside for the maintenance of minors and for the payment of debts, whether this amounts to a full, or to a half, atonement.

12. WHAT RIGHT A MAN HAS TO ATONEMENT IN THE CASE OF HIS DAUGHTER

Every man has the right to a full atonement in the case of his betrothed as in the case of his wedded wife for a time as long as the law determines. But if she remains at her father's or her brother's house, they, too, have the right to a full atonement in her case, the same as her betrothed.

13. IF EITHER ONE OF A MARRIED COUPLE COMMITS WHOREDOM

If a man has a wedded wife and goes to lie with another woman, whether it be inside the house or without, let him pay his wife three marks for every time.

14. IF A WOMAN LIES WITH A MAN

If a woman lies with a man other than her husband or leaves him [her husband] without cause and contrary to the laws of God, she has forfeited her mund and her husband's gift to her marriage portion. But if her husband offers to continue the married life and she refuses, the husband shall keep and care for all her property as long as she lives; after her death the one who is her nearest heir shall receive her marriage portion but not the husband's gift. If they come to an understanding and he takes her [again], their relations as to property shall remain as if their original contract has suffered no breach. If she falls again into this sin and her husband refuses to live with her, he shall, nevertheless, have the care for her property as long as she[4] lives; after [her death] it shall be dealt with as stated above. But if she has never been charged with having sinned in this way [before] and promises atonement to God and to her husband and offers to cohabit with him but he refuses to possess her, she shall have her marriage portion but not her husband's gift. If the husband tries to deprive her of her

[4] The text has: as long as he lives.

marriage portion and accuses her of having been guilty of such misdoing at an earlier time but, so far as men are aware, he has never raised this charge against her before, let her refute the charge with her own oath; and if he refuses to take her again, she shall have her marriage portion but not her husband's gift. If because of some physical hindrance a marriage is annulled by the authority of him who is allowed by the laws of God to annul a marriage, let each one have his or her property. If a man comes to a settlement with one who has lain with his wife, he whose wife she is shall give pledges of peace and safety. And if he receives his wife once more into wedded life, and if, while they are living together, the other man lies with her a second time, he is a pledge breaker just as the husband would be if he should attack him while the pledge were still intact. And if the woman's husband sets upon him after that, he attacks [him as] a pledge breaker for whom there is no atonement due either to king or kinsmen.

15. CONCERNING THE COLLECTION OF LAND RENTS AFTER THE DEATH OF A WIFE OR A HUSBAND

If death comes to either the husband or the wife and the wife dies after the Mass-day of the Two Apostles, the one that comes early in the summer,[5] the husband shall collect the rent for her land in the following autumn but he shall pay no part of this rent to her heirs. When a husband passes away, the wife shall collect whatever is due her and still unpaid and shall also have her husband's gift to the marriage portion. Likewise, if a man has made a contract for land and the landlord or his agent dies before that same Mass-day, the tenant has the right to a year's contract. But if the landlord dies after the Mass-day, the tenant has the right to a two years' contract, namely, [the right to] the crop [of the year] in which the landlord dies and that of the following year.

16. THERE SHALL BE NO GIFT IF THE MARRIAGE PORTION IS NOT VALID

Every marriage man who deals rightly with a woman will see to it that the marriage portion is entirely valid. And in case any part of the marriage portion has to be collected by litigation,

[5] May 1: Philip and James.

[that part] shall not be taken into account in determining the husband's gift.

17. WOMEN WHO SUFFER NEGLECT SHALL HAVE CONTROL OF THEIR OWN AFFAIRS

If kinsmen neglect the affairs of the women who are in their care and these [have to] find their own maintenance, they shall be allowed to manage their own affairs as they like. And the kinsmen shall have no right to compensation in such cases, unless the woman lies with a man; in that case her nearest kinsman shall take atonement for her, whether he is on the agnatic or the cognatic side. But if two or more [men] are equally near to the woman in kinship, some on the father's and some on the mother's side, they shall take one atonement in common and divide it into equal parts according to their number. If a son comes at the first birth, he shall not share in the first atonement, but shall look forward to such atonements as may be assessed later. And let him who is nearest of kin on the mother's side claim compensation on the child's behalf, if it is to be collected from the child's father; but if it is to be collected from another, the child's father shall claim it on its behalf and have the keeping of it till the child comes of age. And if the child dies, let the atonement [money] remain with him who has it [in his keeping].

18. CONCERNING A MAID WHO INHERITS FROM A MAN

A maid who has received an inheritance, whoever [the man be] from whom she inherited, may give herself in marriage to whomever she will when she is fifteen winters old, [though only] with the advice of the kinsmen who are the most prudent and the nearest of kin both on the father's and on the mother's side.

19. WHAT A MAN CAN BE HELD FOR WHO IGNORES A WARRANTY[6]

If a man ignores a warranty that was given by one whose heir he is, he shall not be held [to account] as a pledge breaker, for a greater amount [of money] than that which he received as heir from the man whose warranty he ignores.

[6] This chapter has in view pledges or warranties given on the conveyance of land.

20. A THRALL SHALL NOT BE SOLD FROM THE LAND

No man shall sell a thrall or a bondwoman from the land; but if he does [this], he shall pay the king three marks, unless [the thrall] is an evildoer, and the fact is known to men.

21. CONCERNING THE RIGHT OF A HAULD TO ATONEMENT FOR HIS CHIEF BONDMAN

A hauld shall receive three oras in current coin [as atonement] for his chief bondman, his personal servant, his chief bondwoman,[7] and his housemaid, and two oras for all his other thralls. And a thrall shall receive a compensation for personal injury two-thirds less than that due to his master. If a thrall does injury to another thrall, there shall be a like compensation, but there is nothing due to the master.

22. A HAULD'S WIFE MAY BUY WARES TO THE VALUE OF AN ORA

A hauld's wife may buy [wares] to the value of an ora but no more. If she buys to a greater amount, the purchase shall not be valid unless the husband approves it; but all such purchases as the husband approves shall remain valid.

23. CONCERNING THE BUSINESS AFFAIRS OF A FREEDMAN

If a freedman has not yet bought his freedom from dependence, his business affairs shall be conducted in this way: of land he may rent as much as he needs; in addition he may buy seed corn for six oras in current coin. But all his other transactions shall be valid only if his master approves them. A farmer's wife may in no case make larger purchases in the borough than in the country.

24. CONCERNING THE KILLING OF A LAP DOG

If a man kills another man's lap dog, he shall pay twelve oras (and it is a lap dog if one can place his hand about the dog's neck so that the fingers meet). For a greyhound [the fine is] six oras; one-half mark for a dog used in hunting and the same for a cattle dog, if it is bound when the last animal [comes in] and released

[7] Apparently a bondwoman in charge of the housekeeping. See Glossary, "Housekeeper."

when the first [leaves]; it shall be the same for bitches. If a watch-dog is killed [the fine shall be] one ora.

25. IF [A MAN] KILLS A HAWK

If a man kills a hawk in another man's possession, he shall pay a mark in current coin, but valued in burned silver, and a fine for evil intent. If he kills it elsewhere [the fine is] one-half mark. All this shall be valued in burned silver.

26. IF A DOG BITES A SHEEP

If a dog bites a sheep, the owner of the dog has no claim to compensation[8] but shall pay one-half of the value [of the sheep], unless the dog was with him, in which case he shall pay the entire value; [if the dog bites] a second time, the entire value shall be paid.

[8] If the owner of the sheep kills the dog.

XII. [THE REDEMPTION OF ODAL LAND]

1. CONCERNING THE PURCHASE OF LAND

Every contract [for land] shall be as witnesses know it to be. If a man buys land from another, he shall, for a period of twenty years, have the benefit of witnesses to the [terms of] warranty that followed the agreement; after that let him transfer the responsibility of these witnesses [to others], whether [the land] is within or without the enclosure. And if the one who sold the land claims the right to redeem it, he shall have witnesses, two of the men who were present at the transfer (skeyting) or four who have taken over the duty of the two, to testify as the law provides. And he shall have the land redeemed within twenty winters in accordance with this testimony. If the one who claims the right of redemption shall die and his heir is still a minor, or if there is a son, or [if there are] several [sons] or daughters, the oldest shall bring action to redeem the land in behalf of all within ten winters after he has attained his majority; after that there is no [right of] redemption. And this shall be the form of the oath [to be taken] by those who are to swear to the right of redemption, namely, that it was a condition in the purchase and the conveyance and the warranty that the one who sold the land should have the right to redeem it, and that in the agreement there was no attempt to deceive the purchaser. And if silver is in greater or less value when the land is redeemed than when it was bought, men shall recall what the rate was when the purchase was made and the price shall be made equal in value to that which was determined by the rate at that time. If the purchaser has built or repaired houses on the land, an estimate shall be made as to how far the land is better now when it is being redeemed than when it was sold. And the occupier shall receive compensation in such property as passes for payment, unless it is agreed to use a part of the land. This applies to such legal actions as have been made after this law book was accepted; but those [that were initiated] earlier shall be dealt with according to the statement of witnesses.

2. CONCERNING LAND THAT HAS BEEN MORTGAGED

If a man wishes to give his land in mortgage,[1] the right terms of such a transaction are that he shall receive the same amount as [the value of] that which he transfers [to the other]. If the owner wishes to redeem his land, he shall offer him [the holder] his money after Michaelmas and before Holy Night and shall make his payment in the pre-Lenten fast on the Saturday preceding Sexagesima. And he shall pay in burned silver or gold an amount equal to that which the holder could buy for the goods with which he acquired the land and as gold and burned silver were rated at the time. And if he [the occupier] wishes to have his money[2] he shall demand it before Holy Night in the presence of witnesses. If a woman has the keeping of the property and she has a husband, the money shall be offered to both, if both are near at hand, and to one, if only one is available; and demands shall be made in the same way. But if he does not get his money, he shall add an ora to every five oras, and he shall [continue to] receive the rent.[3] And for the following twelvemonth he shall add the legal interest; and legal interest is an ora for every five oras. Now if the one who holds the mortgage wants his money, let him make a formal demand for his money after Lent, and let him have what advantages come to him at the doom. And if he is unable to produce witnesses who were present when he gave money for the land, let him find witnesses to prove that he rented the land and received rent for the following twelvemonth. If there is disagreement as to the amount owing and the terms of payment and the one who gave the money for [the land] has no witnesses, let him who pays the money prove with his own oath that what he is now offering is just as much and just as good [money] as he received for [the land]. And if he [the mortgagor] refuses to settle accounts with him [the mortgagee], he shall summon him to be at home on the land on which he has the mortgage to receive summons to a thing; and let him state [that he has given] full value for the land. And he shall present all his evidence at the thing, and he shall ask the

[1] See Glossary, "Mortgage."
[2] The money originally paid for the use of the land.
[3] Because men who took land as security for a debt usually rented it to others.

freemen to confirm with a show of weapons that there is conveyed to him as much of that land as he received rent for, unless he [the debtor] shall pay him his money. And if the money remains unpaid for a twelvemonth, he shall proceed after Yule in the following spring with a claim that he has paid the full value of the land, if he cares to do so. And he shall summon him [the debtor] to be at home on the land to receive a thing summons, and let him demand a conveyance. But if he [the debtor] refuses to convey the land to him, he shall summon him before a thing and shall bring forward all his evidence at the thing [to show] that all has occurred as he asserts. Now if he has sufficient testimony to support his claim, the thingmen shall all allow him the show of weapons; and the land shall then be his as completely as his own odal land is: namely, so much of the land as he paid money for and took rent from; or let him [the original owner] pay the money.

3. CONCERNING LAND THAT IS IN MORTGAGE

Everyone shall restore such land as he received it; if it is in better condition, he has a credit; if it is worse, he shall make good the loss according as men deem it to be.

4. IF A MAN WANTS TO SELL HIS ODAL LAND

If a man wants to sell his odal land, he shall offer it to his agnate kinsmen at the thing in the fylki where the land is located. The nearest kinsmen have the first right to purchase the land; still, all these kinsmen have the right to make an offer. He shall then give them a month's notice to pay the value of the land. If there is disagreement as to its value, the one who wants to sell shall take an oath that he has been offered a certain price and that someone offered this who was willing to pay it. The witnesses to such an offer have no obligations longer than ten winters. If the man [who has been summoned] has secured the money for [the purchase], but the odal-man is now unwilling to sell according to summons, he who wished to sell shall redeem the land [from the would-be purchaser] with a fine of an ora for every ten oras in the price for breaking the bargain. And if the one who wants to sell has doubts as to whose is the money that the other offers to give for the land, let the one who wishes to buy take an oath that his intention is to buy the land for himself as an odal and not to bring it by fraud into another's control. And let him buy as much as he has money [to pay for], and let there be no further bidding on this. And the fine for breaking a bargain is levied in such cases only. And if the odal land that he bought shall be demanded of him or [shall be] offered for sale, he shall offer it again to him from whom he bought it, if it was his odal. And let him sell the land for what is offered him, if he is willing to swear that such an offer was made. Land does not become any man's odal until three of his ancestors have owned it and it comes to the fourth in unbroken descent. If the king conveys land to a man, he need not offer that land to any man, if he should want to sell it, no matter who the earlier owner may have been, if the king had it later with full warranty. No man shall offer [to sell] the land to the king, or the king to any other man. If a man buys odal land that has not been publicly offered, his offer shall be as valid as that of an odal-man and shall be made on the same terms; but if the odal-men fail to redeem it on the day appointed for making the payment, he shall have the land with the same title as if an odal-man had offered it [to him]. If the man offers to restore the price or has paid money before witnesses to the one who sold it, but he [the seller] refuses to accept it, let him demand a conveyance (skeyting) from him. And if he refuses, he shall give him a thing summons to the shire thing where the land is located and after as many nights as will fit the distance that he has to travel. And let him present his testimony and offer to deliver the purchase money and demand a conveyance. If he refuses to give this or fails to come, he [the buyer] shall ask the freemen to make the conveyance with the show of weapons. If the freemen refuse they shall owe a baug, each one [a baug] of twelve oras. And if he [the earlier owner] shall violate this transfer, he is [as much] a pledge breaker as if he had himself made the transfer.

5. A SISTER SHALL OFFER LAND TO A SISTER

A woman shall not offer [odal] land to a man nor a man to a woman; but a sister shall offer land to her sister, if they are the heirs to the odal.

6. CONCERNING THE REDEMPTION OF LAND

If a man has land [that he wishes] to redeem, he shall begin the process in the autumn after Michaelmas, and he shall have had one doom before the Yuletide, though he may have more than one. If a man occupies a farm of which he owns a part and other men the rest, and [another] man proceeds to redeem the farm, he [the occupier] shall call for a doom and shall meet the formal request with the name of his warrantor.[4] Then the one who made the demand shall choose whether to redeem the part that he owns or to bide the time when they can be present who share the ownership with him.

7. CONCERNING REDEMPTION

Every man who proceeds to redeem land shall have his case brought up within twelve months without fail, else his suit is worthless. And he [his opponent] shall hold to his defense during the twelvemonth just as the plaintiff [holds] to his claim. It is ordered that the right to redeem land shall be published within twenty winters and [that it shall be] published in the fylki where the land is located. But if the man remains in the kingdom for twenty years without publishing such right, he has forfeited his right to redeem the land, and [can demand] no more from the one who bought the land than a threefold oath; and the terms of this shall be that he is now released from the obligation to produce witnesses to the warranty. And the other man can raise no suit after that.

8. MORE ABOUT THE REDEMPTION OF LAND

A formal request shall be served on the one who occupies the land and he shall ask a hearing before a doom; and he shall inquire about witnesses and shall name his own warrantor. And the claimant shall name his witnesses when he makes his formal demand, if he is asked [to do so], and he shall present his evidence at the first doom; but if he is asked about witnesses and names none, he shall be allowed to present no witnesses. And he shall produce evidence at the doom that he had given legal notice and witnesses to testify that he is without doubt the one who has the

[4] Fellow-owner or landlord.

right to redeem the land and that the odal is his. The defendant shall name his witnesses at the first doom and shall present all his testimony at the second doom. And if the doomsmen are all at one in the matter, they shall order the tenant to fetch his warrantor[5] and [shall allow him] what time he needs to travel both ways, going and returning; and let him summon his landlord to defend his land. But if the landlord is out beyond Agdaness or over the mountain or north of the Isthmus, he shall be given a summons to come home within two months to defend his land, if he is anywhere within the realm. If he is abroad, his return shall be awaited for a twelvemonth; and a man's witness shall be waited for the same [length of time] if he is abroad. Now the claimant shall demand the land from the tenant when he returns, though the landlord remains at home. If the landlord shall offer to submit the case to a doom, the tenant is relieved of the duty to defend; but if the landlord refuses to submit the case to a doom, the tenant shall make the offer and the plaintiff shall appoint a doom after five days at the proper doomstead. They shall then proceed to that doom. Then if the landlord is there and wants to name his doomsmen, the tenant is relieved of the duty to defend; but if he refuses to name the doom, the tenant shall name the doomsmen for his landlord, whether he [the landlord] is present or not, and shall produce witness that he summoned his landlord to come; then the tenant is relieved of the duty to defend. And the plaintiff shall set his doom over against [that of] the defendant after a space of five nights at the proper doomstead, whether he [the defendant] is there or not; and let the doom be set and held and let the men wait till midday. And when the midday is past, the plaintiff shall summon the defendant to a wager doom[6] at the proper doomstead after a space of five nights. And the plaintiff shall appoint men to that doom too, and each side shall have twelve doomsmen and the doomstakes[7] shall be present, and [let them] wait once more till midday. If the defendant does not come to the doom, the plaintiff's doomsmen shall make the wager; they shall extend their hands and name witnesses to testify that the plaintiff has come into [possession of] the land that he has redeemed.

[5] The landlord.

[6] Cf. *Gul.*, c. 266; *Frost.*, X, c. 15.

[7] See Glossary, "Doomstakes"; cf. *Gul.*, c. 269.

XIII. [THE LAW OF TENANCY]

1. CONCERNING LEASEHOLDS, THE TERMS OF TENANCY, AND THE LEASE CONTRACT IF THE TENANT DIES, AND CONCERNING THE BUILDINGS AND THE PAYMENT OF RENT; AND THE LANDLORD'S STATEMENT SHALL STAND UNLESS IT IS REFUTED BY WITNESSES

Land shall be leased and the rent paid in the presence of witnesses. Actual occupation validates the terms of the lease; but the payment of rent secures the crops and the other fruits of his labor [to the tenant]. The earliest moving day is the first lesser holy day after the thirteenth day of the Yule season. When a man hauls the first load of his belongings into the garth, let him have two witnesses present, and let him notify the man who occupies the farm. But if this one claims to have the lease, let him place a ban and appoint a five-day moot in the presence of the same witnesses, unless he calls in others; but if he does not appoint a five-day moot, the one who brought the load shall have the land. If the man who occupies the land is not at home, let the other man go with witnesses as soon as he can to give him notice or wait for him at his home; then let him proceed as stated above. The occupier shall vacate one-half of the houses to the new tenant and shall remain until he has secured land; and let him have one-half of the houses for a month after he has secured land. If he has not been able to get a lease elsewhere, he shall have one-half of the houses till summer day[1] and one-fourth of the grassland, if he is a homeless man. The farmer shall let one-fourth lie fallow, and the one-fourth of the fallow [he may sow] to rye if he likes. If he places a fence around [this field], he shall have the entire crop in the autumn, even though he leaves the land; but if he does not build a fence, he shall have compensation for the seed sown only. For every sáld of grain that he sows he shall keep a neat beast or pay half an ora for every one that is wanting. Five and one-third measures of land

[1] April 14.

for horsefodder, that is, ten summer loads,[2] the tenant may transfer to another for separate cultivation without risk of penalty and he may allow him five loads of wood and three of scraped bark. The tenant shall haul all the winter manure out upon the fallow where there has been no fertilizing, except only [what is produced in] the night before the morning when he leaves the place. If the fallow has [already] been fertilized, the manure shall be hauled where it is most needed; and let the tenant defend his doings with an oath, if the landlord desires it. He shall be allowed a site for one building, if he wants it, and he shall pay the fine for trespass if he takes several. The rent shall be paid on summer day; otherwise the tenant sows and mows for the owner of the land. Houses shall be built according to agreement, and if that is not done, the landlord shall have such a part of the crop as each house is worth, and an equal part of the rent shall be [regarded] as not having been paid. If the houses are not built as well as agreed, they shall be appraised, and the tenant shall make amends according to this appraisal. If a building falls down, the lumber shall not be used for fuel, and if it is so used, [the tenant shall] replace it with new timbers, or pay the fine for trespass, or deny the guilt with his own oath, [swearing also for] all those for whom he is responsible. If an old house is to be rebuilt but [the tenant] does not rebuild it, he shall pay such compensation as men think right; and if he refuses [to pay], the landlord shall appoint a five-day moot and shall place a ban upon his crops. And the landlord shall have such a part of the crops as men estimate the work of rebuilding to be worth, unless he [the tenant] can show by witnesses at the five-day moot that the contract gives him no duties with respect to the house. The statement of the landlord as to the terms of tenancy and occupation shall stand unless the tenant can refute it with witnesses. The statement of the landlord shall stand for a twelvemonth after the tenant has left the land, unless the one who had the land has witnesses who have better knowledge. If a man who has leased a farm shall die and the landlord asserts that the rent was not paid, let the heir of the deceased produce testimony that

[2] As great a load as can be hauled in the summer. A "measure" of land was as much as could be sown with a measure of grain. See Glossary, "Measure."

it was paid; and the terms of tenancy [shall all be determined] in the same way. But if there are not witnesses, the landlord shall confirm his statement with an oath. And [the procedure shall be the same] if the tenant is outlawed.

2. IF A MAN BURNS A HOUSE ON ANOTHER MAN'S LAND

If a man [tenant] burns a house on another man's land, he shall have a new one built within the next twelvemonth, if he has leased the land for a term of years. But if he has taken no [such] lease, he shall haul sufficient timber to the site for a house as good as the other, and all that is needed except the turf; and he shall have it hauled in before the following midsummer. And if it is not hauled, the landlord shall demand of him all that is not provided and the fine for trespass in addition. If a man allows the hearth fire on another man's land to go out, that is, if he moves off the land before Holy Night, he shall pay three marks, and the landlord shall have whatever he leaves behind [on the farm]. The tenant shall not allow any one to make a garden on the land except his son, his thralls, or the free man who works with him, unless the landlord gives permission, and only where the plot will add to the cornland or the meadow. If two men cultivate the same farm, each one shall be held to account for his own buildings with respect to fire and also for his forest, even though the fire comes from the other man's [buildings]. If a tenant departing from another man's farm leaves a fence torn down, he shall haul in rails and posts for the fence. If he leaves the land before he has done this hauling, let him do it later and pay the fine for trespass. Nor shall he tear down the fences about the fallow, but if he does tear them down, he shall pay the fine for trespass. If he makes a garden for angelicas or onions, let him take away one-half of each [crop], and let him gather onions till midsummer. If a man takes a lease [for a term of years], it shall hold as far and as fully as can be determined by witnesses, even though the landlord shall sell the land. If the landlord finds himself deprived of a homestead and wishes to move in upon his own land, he shall redeem his land with one year's rent, and he shall inform him [the tenant] before Holy Night that he has no homestead, and let him confirm his statement with an oath.

3. IF A MAN HAS PAID HIS LAND RENT IN ADVANCE

If a man has paid his land rent in advance, he shall have the land [for as long a time] as witnesses can vouch for; and if he dies, his heir shall have it on the same [terms]. But if a man dies and his land rent is not paid, his heir shall have the following harvest, even where the lease is given by a priest. If a man has not surrendered his lease before Holy Night, he shall have the land for the rent that was last paid, if the landlord is willing to convey it to him with the handclasp. But after Holy Night the landlord shall offer him the land [to rent]; and if he does not want it, the landlord shall have his land again and the rent with it from the one who has just left it, as agreed before.

4. WHAT ONE MAY CUT IN THE WOODLAND

If a man has a lease he may cut enough [timber on the land] for a ship of twelve oars or less, but not for a larger one, and not for more than one ship unless the landlord consents. If he cuts more during the term of his lease, [he shall pay] the fine for trespass. He may, during the same term, gather birch bark and other bark to use for roofing the houses and to buy salt for his stock and his household; but if he lives by the sea he shall make [his own] salt. [Let him make] as much as he needs to buy birch bark[3] and other bark and as much as he needs for his own use, but not any more.

5. CONCERNING GOSHAWKS

All goshawks that are taken from the nest while [they are] still unable to fly [are taken from] the owner of the land to whom they belong; and the one who takes them shall return them and pay the fine for trespass.

6. THE MAN WHO KILLS A BEAR SHALL HAVE THE CARCASS

The man who kills a bear shall have [the carcass], unless the lair was barred; in that case it belongs to the one who barred the lair.

7. CONCERNING TRAPS FOR WILD BEASTS

No man shall set traps in another man's forest for any beast except wolves, foxes, and otters; and no man shall dig into another

[3] For roofing.

man's ground or break into heaps of rocks unless the owner gives permission.

8. WHAT A TENANT MAY PERMIT

A tenant shall not permit [anyone] to set up [and leave] a ship on his land for longer than five nights if there is a favorable wind and good sailing weather.

9. THAT EVERY MAN SHALL POSSESS THE WATERCOURSE AND THE FISHING GROUNDS THAT FRONT HIS LAND

Every man shall possess the watercourse and the fishing grounds that front his land, unless they have been alienated in legal manner. If a stream eats away a man's land, a measure shall be drawn from the greensward on either side, or from the farther edge of the matgrass[4] and [the distance] shall be divided at the middle, and each shall have what falls to him. But if there is firm land or rock on either side and no land has been worn away, the measure shall be drawn from the green grass and the firm sod. If a shoal is formed in the midst of the stream or nearer the one side, or if the current has torn away the sod on both sides and formed an eyot which is covered with grass or matgrass, and if [the shoal or the eyot] falls to the share of one and not to the other, the one to whom the grass falls shall have it. From that point let a measure be drawn to the shore of the other man who shares in the ownership of the stream, unless both are satisfied with what earlier measurements have shown. But if there is disagreement, the measure shall be drawn from this point across the stream, the line stretching straight across from shore to shore. If a solid piece of turf has been torn away from either shore but grass grows on it [where it is lodged], the measure must be drawn from this grass. If a man owns the land on both sides of a stream that cannot be used for floating timbers, he may throw a fence across it, if he wishes to do so; but if those who live higher up the stream shall protest that this was not done in the days of Saint Olaf, let them proceed to place a ban and to appoint a five-day moot; and let the man who built the fence be allowed to present his witnesses.

[4] *Nardus stricta*. See Hertzberg, *Glossarium*, "Hærbua."

10. IF A MAN TAKES ANOTHER MAN'S PUNT

If a man takes another man's punt out of its enclosure and uses it either upstream or down, he shall be held to account for it till it is returned, and he shall pay the fine for conversion to the one who owns it. But whoever wants to use a punt to cross a stream that cuts [the valley] may take it with impunity. One must pull up or make fast another man's punt; otherwise, if it drifts away he becomes responsible for it; and let the owner provide a rope [for his punt]. If a man has had a mooring place on another man's land for ten winters or longer, no one shall forbid him to use it, and the same [rule shall hold] as to roads to the sea and to salt water, to the forest, and through the length of the countryside. But if a man forbids another to use the road, the latter shall demand [the use] of it before witnesses. But if the man still refuses to let him use the road, he shall summon a thing and present his testimony at the thing that he had [the use of] that road in earlier times. Then he shall have the road, but if they [his opponents] resist, they shall be outlawed whatever may happen to them, while those who raised the claim shall remain in peace and security. The matter of mooring places, if their use is forbidden, [shall be dealt with] in the same way. If a man [goes out to] cut wood in another man's forest without permission, the owner shall take men to the stumpage to see what has been cut; after that let him bring suit for trespass and for the value of the wood; and the value shall be assessed in the forest where the cutting was done. And no man shall fell timber in another man's forest except to repair his means of travel, his sled or his ship or whatever it be that needs repairs, or to use for fuel, if he camps out in the open; in other cases he shall pay the fine for trespass.

11. IF A MAN PLACES A BAN ON THE USE OF HIS PASTURE LAND

If a man places a ban on the use of his wood pasture and some one makes use of it after that, he [the latter], if the guilt is proven, shall owe the robber fine to the king and the fine for trespass, valued in burned silver, to the owner of the land. If the owner has not come upon the man in the act, he shall lead men to the stumpage and show them what has been done; let him have the damage assessed and let him accuse whomever he will. He shall summon him to be at home to receive a thing summons, and [let him] then summon him before a thing; and the accused may clear himself with a threefold oath, if he cares [to do so]. If the oath fails, he shall pay the fine for trespass, valued in burned silver, the value of the wood, and the robber fine to the king. But if he will neither take the oath nor offer payment, the complainant shall ask the freemen to go upon him to seize as much as is due and a like amount in addition, and the freemen shall have the money.[5] But if he offers to take an oath and it fails, the complainant shall summon a thing after a month's respite, and men shall come to this thing without further summons. The plaintiff shall then ask the freemen to go upon [the offender] as stated above and take such an amount of money as has been indicated above. No one shall go into another man's nut grove, but, if he does, let him give over the nuts and pay the fine for trespass. In the case of apples and hops, the value shall be paid and the fine for trespass in addition.

12. CONCERNING FINES FOR TRESPASS

If a landlord allows a man to do some sort of labor for his own needs in his forest and the man's fire leads to a wider damage than was allowed, the man shall clear himself of evil intent with a threefold oath and shall make the damage good according to the award of [neighbor] farmers. But if the oath fails or the man admits his guilt, let him pay the fine for trespass in addition to the damage money and three marks to the king. But if he denies the guilt, let him deny it with a threefold oath.

13. IF A MAN SETS FIRE TO ANOTHER MAN'S CROPS

If a man sets fire to another man's crops, or to his fence posts or his fence rails, or to the garth that he has to keep in repair, or to the mountain pasture that has been fenced off and does not belong to the common, let him make good the damage to the extent that men think right; and [let him pay] the fines for trespass and for evil intent to the owner. But if he denies the guilt, let him deny it with a threefold oath.

[5] The text has the word *eið* (oath); Hertzberg corrects this to *féit* (the money, or the goods). *Den ældste norske proces*, pp. 84–85.

14. IF A MAN PLACES A BAN

If a man places a ban on [the use of] a wood lot or a pasture or a fishing ground, he shall publish the ban at the church or at the thing [in the district] where the land is located. And if the ban is published by the owner or his agent, it shall remain valid during the following twelvemonth.

15. CONCERNING TRESPASS

For trespass on land a hauld shall have [a fine of] six oras; a baron, nine oras, all in current coin unless [the trespass is] in defiance of a ban. A bishop [shall have] two marks; a jarl, two marks; and the king, three marks. The archbishop [shall have] twenty oras; an abbot, twelve oras; and an abbess, the same [amount]. A well-born man [shall have] four oras; a reksthegn, three oras; the son of a freedman, two oras; and a freedman, four ertogs.

16. IF SEVERAL MEN HAVE LAND IN COMMON

If several men have land in common, they shall all receive such fines for trespass as would be due the man of highest rank who has a share in the land. A maiden shall take such a fine for trespass as would be due her father, and a widow such as [would be due] the one who had her last. If some allow other men to use the forest but some do not, the one who gave no permission shall take his fine for trespass in full and [shall have] such parts of the fine for unauthorized labor[6] as his share in the land [would give him]. If several have refused permission, they shall all take the fine for trespass.

17. CONCERNING DISPUTED RIGHTS TO LEASED LAND

If two men [claim to] have leased the same land and the one who leased it first declares that his witnesses are abroad, he shall have the land for twelve months, if men know the facts. But if after a period of twelve months those witnesses fail him, then the one who leased it before witnesses shall have that part of the crop that has not been consumed and the value of that which has been consumed. And there shall be a mark in current coin for every

[6] Or of the fruits of the labor done.

sáld of sown grain and the hay shall go with [the grain]. And the landlord shall have the rent from him who gets the crop and the fine for trespass valued in burned silver from the one who tilled [the land]. If two men make contracts for the same land and both lay a ban [against tillage], they shall have a five-day moot and the one who leased it first shall produce his witnesses, and the one who leased it last shall surrender [his contract]; and he shall be reimbursed with a [year's] rent by the landlord or [be given] land equally good within the fylki. But if he proves defiant and will not leave [the land], the other man shall proceed to the land with witnesses and let him turn his cattle loose and outside his keeping. If the man offers resistance, he shall be charged with robbery and [his opponent] shall summon him to be at home to receive a thing summons and after that [he shall summon him] before the thing. And [let him] produce his testimony at the thing that they had a five-day moot and that it was proved by witnesses that he had leased the land first. He shall then ask the freemen to go upon the man and to oust him from the land and take the robber fine for the king. If a man mows grass in another man's meadow, the owner shall proceed to place a ban upon the meadow, whether the hay lies on it or not. Then let the one who seems to be most in need [of a decision] appoint a five-day moot and at this moot let witness be produced by each one who was in possession the year before. [The procedure shall be] the same with respect to cornland if another man cuts [the grain]. And if the meadow or the cornland is awarded to the one who laid the ban first, he shall demand restitution [and ask] that everything be restored within five days, and let him add a fine for trespass, valued in burned silver. But if he [the guilty man] makes no restitution, the suitor shall summon him before the thing [to answer] for the robbery and demand the fine for trespass valued in burned silver; and let him summon him to be at home to [receive] a thing summons and after that let him summon him before the thing.

18. IF TWO MEN OCCUPY THE SAME FARM

If two men occupy the same farm and they disagree about the fencing, and the one wishes to build the fence where it was formerly built, then he[7] shall go to him and make his request in the matter of the fence. But if he refuses to accede to this, let the other man drive home to him the cattle belonging to both and pass the responsibility for them into his hands. [The latter] shall also make good all the damage that may be done by the cattle belonging to both and shall pay for all [the cattle] that may be killed. Neither one shall forbid the other to use an undivided pasture.

19. CONCERNING JOINT OCCUPATION

Wherever a boundary furrow is drawn between [the lands] of men, a man's cattle may be forbidden to cross, if there is a herdsman, and a ban has been laid. And if they cross the line later on, or if the owner drives them in that direction, the fine for trespass shall be due and also the robber fine to the king, if a ban has been laid. But if he [the one who occupies the land] drives them away, there is no fine due. If there is no herdsman the entering cannot be forbidden. But if he [an occupier] wishes to forbid the use of his grassland, let him set up a fence where [the lands] meet, and let him set it on his own ground or pay the fine for trespass.

20. IF TWO MEN LIVE ON THE SAME FARM

If two men occupy the same farm and both sow [grain] in the same [divided] field, and if the one has reaped earlier and has stacked his harvest and wants to pasture his stock in his part of the field, he shall herd his cattle in such a way that they do not come into his neighbor's field; otherwise he shall pay the fine for trespass and [pay] for the corn that may be destroyed. After the one who reaped last has stacked his grain, the former shall continue to herd his stock in such a way that they do not get to graze in his neighbor's pasture before both parts have been grazed equally; otherwise he shall pay the fine for trespass. The same rule shall hold if a man's cattle enter a cornfield or a meadow where there is a competent fence.

21. CONCERNING A COMPETENT FENCE

A fence is competent if there is [the space of] an ell between the palings, if every third paling is a support, and if all are fastened

[7] Literally "the other"; but the context seems to require the translation given above.

to the top rail, so that no hog wearing a collar shall be able to crawl through; and the collar must be two thumb ells[8] [long]. Cattle [that break through a fence] shall be sent home to the owner with a warning. But if he [the offender] does not herd his cattle any better than before, the other man may with impunity kill two beasts to the value of a cow. If he still does not look after [his stock], the other man may send them home with a warning a second time, or kill with impunity two beasts to the value of a cow. And [he may] send the cattle home with a warning the third time or kill two heads. Now six heads have been killed for which no compensation is due. But if one fails to send cattle home with a warning from a poorly fenced field and kills the cattle or other stock, half their value shall be owing, if a thrall has killed them, and the owner of the beasts shall have the hide and the carcass. But if a free man has killed them, the full value shall be owing and the owner shall have the hide and the carcass. If a horse strays into a man's field or meadow, he shall take the horse and shut him up; and he shall go with witnesses to the owner of the horse and demand compensation for damages; he shall show the men what damage has been done and shall place a ban against [allowing] the horse [to graze there]. But if the owner takes his horse away without paying compensation, he shall pay the robber fine to the king and the fine for trespass to the owner of the land in addition to compensation for damages.

22. IF A MAN LAYS HIS FALLOW ALONGSIDE ANOTHER MAN'S MEADOW OR CORNFIELD

If a man lays his fallow alongside another man's meadow or cornfield, he shall enclose it with a competent fence.[9]

23. CONCERNING HOLT AND PASTURE

Whenever men disagree about the use of holt or pasture, cornfield or meadow, there shall be a ban placed. And let him who feels most aggrieved appoint a five-day moot; and at a five-day moot six men shall be named for each side as in a doom. And if neither one appoints a five-day moot but both place a ban, or if one alone [does it], then, if [either one] goes out to labor there in defiance of

[8] See Glossary, "Thumb ell."

[9] The fallow was usually fenced in and used as a cattle pen.

the law billet, but does [not][10] appoint a five-day moot, he has ruined his case and shall pay the robber fine to the king and the fine for trespass, valued in burned silver, to the owner of the land. But for the work that a man does in field or meadow before the five-day moot, if he does not bring [the fruits of] it away in defiance of the law billet, he shall incur no penalty. And let each one produce his witnesses at the five-day moot. The one who placed the ban first shall have his witnesses heard first; but if the one produces testimony as to ownership and the other as to [actual] occupation, the one who has witnesses to [prove] ownership shall have his suit. And every man shall have what is his according to the testimony of witnesses.

24. IF MEN COMPETE IN PRESENTING WITNESSES

If men compete in presenting witnesses for the love of strife or [to please] their supporters, whatever the dispute may be, and the one has two witnesses more [than the other], there shall be appointed at once at the hearing twelve of the oldest and most worthy freemen in the fylki, six for either side, men who have had no interest in the controversy. And whoever refuses to name [such men] loses his case. And the twelve who have thus been appointed shall estimate the worth of the testimony as seems to them to be most right before God. If they are all agreed, let him have his suit who seems to have the better right; but if they disagree, let the side which is the more numerous have its suit; if there is an equal division, let that side have its suit which [can get] a man from the other group for the sake of agreement to call God to witness that this side seems to us before God to have the better right. But if they disagree, both [sides] claiming to be right and both sides appealing to God, the matter in dispute shall be divided into halves. Such a decision is allowed because false witness is often presented in vain pride and from love of contention; and often a man who is without proper support loses his case though he may have the better right.

25. CONCERNING THOSE WHO TESTIFY TO AN UNTRUTH

Men who have testified to an untruth shall, each one of them,

[10] This word is required by the context; without it the sentence has no meaning. See Hertzberg, *Glossarium*, "Fimtarstefna," 2, d.

owe a fine of three marks to the king; and they shall never be capable of giving testimony after that, nor [shall they] enjoy witnesses [in their own behalf] or have any right to claim atonements. If both [parties to an action] have witnesses to possession [of land] but neither [side] has witnesses to odal right, and if one [of the litigants] is an odal-man while the other has his land by purchase, the odal-man shall take his own oath to as large a claim as he put forth when he laid his ban. But if the odal-man refuses to swear, let the one who has his land by purchase swear, if he is willing, to as large a claim as he put forth when he laid his ban. If neither is willing to swear, let the [matter in dispute] be divided into halves. If one is willing to swear but the other is not, the one who swears shall have the decision. If both swear, [the matter in dispute shall] be divided into halves. And the testimony of a man who has land by purchase shall stand, if the one who testifies with him has the odal right to the land in dispute. If the one has witness to possession and the other has no witnesses, the one who has this witness shall be allowed to swear, and let him who has no witness proceed with a lawsuit. Concerning holt and pasture, the testimony of two is as competent as that of ten; and no man shall do labor in holt or pasture before the five-day moot, if a ban has been published against it. If a man places a ban upon another man's harvest or upon his movables on a Tuesday, if he has the right to place such a ban, he shall serve his opponent with a summons for Saturday or Monday, as the latter may prefer; if he makes no choice, it shall be for Monday, unless that be a holy day, in which case the five-day moot shall be set for Saturday. But if the fifth day is a Mass-day, the other day shall [be appointed].

26. PLACING A BAN UPON A HARVEST [FIELD]

One may place a ban upon a harvest [field] or against unauthorized labor on a farm wherever one finds, within the fylki, the man who did the work. But if he does not find him, let him go to the harvest [field] or to [the place] where the work was done and place a ban upon it; after that let him serve notice on him, or on his household if he cannot be found. And if the landlord is so far distant that he cannot come to a five-day moot, he shall be given a summons at the thing as to a doom; meanwhile he [the occupier] may use of the harvest as much as he needs. And if the one who placed the ban comes into possession of the crop, an estimate shall be made by impartial men as to how much the other man had [harvested and] consumed up to the time of the thing summons.

XIV. [THE LAW OF TENANCY—CONCLUDED. THE LAW AS TO THEFT]

1. THERE SHALL BE AN AGENT FOR EVERY ESTATE IN THE FYLKI

Every man who has land within our law shall have an agent in the fylki where the land is located. And the one who has this stewardship may bring action in all cases of trespass and unauthorized labor, as if he were himself the owner; he shall have one-half [of the fine] and [pay] one-half to the landlord. [He shall] lease the land but not to himself and he shall collect the rent, if the landlord wishes it; but if an agent collects rent and refuses to let the landlord have it, the landlord shall demand the money and sue for it with a thing summons. And if an agent denies that he has accepted the stewardship, the statement of the landlord shall stand, unless the other man denies it with his own oath. The term of an agent's appointment is for three winters; after that his duties expire without further action.

2. IF A MAN IS OUTSIDE OUR LAW

If a man who owns land is in the kingdom but outside our law, the agent may hold his stewardship as long as he [the owner] wishes. But if he wants to take it from him, he may authorize whomever he will to take it from him; and this person shall have witness [to the fact] that the landlord authorized him to take the stewardship from the one who had it before. [And he may] then assign the agency to whomever he will and by the same authority as the landlord has himself. If the landlord asserts that the agent has taken a part of his land for his own use, whether from within the garth or from without, and good men have clear knowledge of this, and if the man who is found in possession [of this property] claims to have bought it from a man who had the title to it when he claims to have bought it, his witnesses shall be held accountable for as long a time as other witnesses to bargains and conveyances [are usually held]. But if these witnesses fail him, let fair-minded men estimate what he [the owner] has lost, and let him bring action with a formal demand; let him claim the fine for trespass in addition; and the fact that the right is somewhat old shall not invalidate the action. Let him sue the one who took the [land] or his heir;[1] but to obtain ownership [let him sue] the one who is in [actual] possession. But if the one who took [the property] from the land is in possession of the land, it is as if he is in possession of land that he has not leased; but if another is in possession, this one is accountable for the rent only. And the landlord has the right to take the stewardship from his agent whenever he wishes; but the lease remains valid for the terms that the steward had power to grant it, that is, for three harvests. The agent shall not give a new lease before the old lease has expired. But if the landlord or his agent shall die, the lease shall remain valid after that for one harvest. Also, if the landlord goes abroad, the stewardship remains valid for three winters, unless the landlord shall die before [the end of the term]; in that case the stewardship expires without further action. But if the agent doubts that the landlord is deceased, his heir shall produce a witness who is willing to swear that he believes the decease to be a fact.

3. THE AGENT MUST NOT HIMSELF DO OR ALLOW LABOR

The agent must not himself do labor or allow [anyone to] labor in holt or pasture more than twice as much as the tenant may permit, unless the landlord consents. The lands in the herath or in the parish that belong to a church shall be placed in the care of the most reliable man; and the archbishop will appoint the patron [of the Church as his agent], if there is such [a man]. And let every tenant get his warrant from each successive priest, whether the stewardship of the lands is held by the patron or not. And the Church must not suffer loss in its domain because of the lapse of rights or the carelessness of the priest or the covetousness of the steward. And the Church acquires odal right [to land] after having held it for thirty winters, if the men of the parish bear witness to such [possession].

[1] For damages and the fine for trespass.

4. CONCERNING THE DIVISION OF LAND

When [the use of] land [that is held in joint tenancy] is to be divided, an agent may act on the landlord's behalf. And the one who wishes to have such land divided shall give notice at the thing that he wants to have the arable divided [for use and occupation]. But if the one who owns the land with him refuses to appear, his agent shall call in freemen, and, joining with the other owner, he shall divide the arable [for occupation]. He shall cast an unmarked lot [for the owner who is present], but his own shall be marked; and let him [the absent owner] use the parcels of land [that fell to him] till both allotments have been utilized to the same extent.[2] If men wish to parcel out odal land and some of them are outside our law though within the kingdom, they shall be summoned to appear on the land after two months. If they do not come to that appointment, the one who sent out the summons shall parcel out the land with the [help of] freemen; and let him carry his lot in his coat lap, as stated above. But if the others do not appear and refuse to convey the land to him,[3] he shall inform the thing and produce his witnesses, and let him ask the freemen to give assent by the show of weapons; and the land is conveyed to him by that action. And by such a conveyance the other [man], [if he resists], becomes a pledge breaker as much as if he had himself made the transfer. If the landlord is abroad, the one who wants a division shall give him a twelvemonth summons to appear for such division; and if he fails to come, let the act of division proceed as set forth above. If one of the two has made improvements on the land, and these have been appraised, land shall be given [in return, as much] as men are willing to award on their oaths, [which is] to be [held] in pledge [but not in ownership]. Odal land shall be divided in the autumn and the summons shall be for the fifth day and within the fylki; but if the joint owners are so many that they cannot all get together by the fifth day, all those [who are] in the fylki shall be given a five-day summons at the thing; while those

[2] The chapter down to this point deals with division for purposes of cultivation only, the title remaining undisturbed. The rest of the chapter has to do with the division of land into parcels which will be owned separately.

[3] By skeyting.

who are outside the fylki but within our jurisdiction shall be given a month's notice.

5. IF A MAN LEAVES THE COUNTRY

If a man leaves the country and he has debts to pay or creates [debts] after his departure, his agent shall provide for them as long as he has the stewardship, if payment is demanded in legal form; and the man's heir [shall do this] when the term of the agent's appointment has expired; [let him pay] according to the testimony of witnesses and as long as the property of the one who made the debt holds out. But the heir need not pay his own money till it is definitely known by the testimony of two witnesses that he [the debtor] is dead.

6. IF A MAN LEAVES THE COUNTRY

If a man leaves the country and his heir learns of his death, and witness is produced at the five-day moot and is borne by men who either were with the deceased on his journey or have been reliably informed by those who were with him on the journey, and they state that they know before God what is most true in this case, the heir shall enter into the inheritance and his heir likewise, if he shall pass away, [and shall have it] till it shall be more correctly known that the owner of the property was living at the time when the first heir took over the inheritance. But in every case that was concluded before the subject was covered by a new law, the settlement shall stand as it had been accepted.

7. CONCERNING THE COMMONS

The commons shall remain as they have been of old, both the upper[4] and the outer commons.[5] But if men come to a disagreement, the one claiming for his own what the other calls common land, let the one who claims it for his own place a ban upon [the use of] it and then appeal to the thing where such a case can be decided, whether it be the shire thing or a thing for half [a fylki]; and let him have the thing summons sent forth within the five-day period. But if he fails to do so, his ban is worthless for the time being. And at the thing there shall be chosen twelve holdar or the

[4] The mountain pasture.

[5] The fjords and the sea.

best freemen, if holdar are lacking, each litigant [naming] six from his own thing district. And [the claimant] shall have any two of the twelve whom he can get and who are able to swear whether the land belongs to him or is common land. And at that thing the one who claims the land shall appoint a five-day moot; and at that moot he shall be allowed to present such witnesses as were named at the thing. If the fifth day falls on a holy day, the moot shall be held on the earliest lesser holy day following; for the evidence may be presented as completely on such a day as at a five-day moot. And the oath shall be sworn in this wise: "I have heard that this line marks the boundary between the commons and the farmers' [own] land and I know nothing more nearly true in this case." Then the five-day moot shall be set, and this body shall determine what each one shall have. But if the bailiff or the king's agent charges a man with having land in his possession that has been cleared in the common without the king's permission, and if he replies that this land was cleared before the time of three kings, none of whom was in the land less than ten winters, and if the bailiff or the king's agent doubts this statement, the man who is in possession shall, as stated above, be allowed to present such testimony as one is allowed to present [in disputes] as to the boundaries between the commons and private land.

8. THE KING MAY LEASE THE COMMON

The king may lease the common[6] to whomever he wishes. And the one who takes the lease shall enclose the land during the first twelvemonth and shall have no right to move the fence afterwards. He shall have [the right to gather materials] for his fence within a knife's[7] throw in all directions. Any parcel of meadow that one finds in the common shall belong during the twelvemonth to the one who first puts his scythe to the grass. Whoever desires to do so may set up a shieling [on the upper common] and may remain there through the summer if he chooses. If any one sows seed in the common, but has no lease from the king's agent, the harvested grain and the hay that is mown there shall both belong to the king. If a man sets fire to a shieling hut on the common or to a smithy

[6] See Glossary, "Common."

[7] See above, p. 124, note.

or to hunting shacks or to a tar kiln or to other materials whatever they be, he shall owe the king a fine of fifteen marks, unless the fire was due to carelessness; in any case he must compensate the owner for the damages done. If two men go out at the same time to mow grass, let each one have what he mows; but if they disagree as to who began the labor first, he shall have his claim who proves it with his own oath, unless the other man has witnesses to the contrary. Fishing grounds in the common belong equally to all. Timbers and boards may lie in the common for a twelvemonth, if need be; but as for other [wood], only so much may be hewn as can be removed before nightfall; otherwise [hewn wood] is common property. But if such wood as might be allowed to lie in the common, as stated above, is carried away before the end of twelve months, the one who takes it shall owe three marks to the king, and the owner of the wood shall have the worth of it.

9. CONCERNING TRAPS[8]

Whoever wishes to set traps for wild animals in the common shall set them so as not to spoil another man's chances to get game. No man shall set [a trap] so near to one already set that the stroke of his ax can be heard in that place; but he may place [his own contrivances] quite close to [the end of] his neighbor's game hedge, if he chooses. If a game pit is left unused longer than twenty winters, whoever will may repair it and use it as long as he keeps it in shape. A spear hedge shall be allowed to stand no longer than ten winters; if it is left to stand [longer], it shall be dealt with as set forth above.

10. CONCERNING THE FINDING OF WHALES[9]

A hauld has the finder's right to an entire raven whale. But if a well-born man comes upon such a whale, he has the finder's right to one-half. Lesser whales belong to the freemen who find them; but if a thrall comes upon one, his master owns it. If the bailiff fails to come [to inspect the find], let the finder bring the dorsal fin to the thing and let it testify for him. If the whale is of a sort that any free man may cut up, the bailiff and the freemen shall be summoned for the fifth day; and if they fail to come, there is

[8] Cf. *Gul.*, c. 95. [9] Cf. *ibid.*, c. 149.

no penalty for the finder, if the rope shall break. If a whale drifts away before the fifth day and no [part of the] rope remains fast on the land, the one who found it shall pay fifteen marks, unless the rope proves to be broken; then there is no penalty, if a part of the rope remains on the land. The finder shall secure the whale [with ropes] and he shall have the finder's share of the blubber. He shall have what can be loaded on a boat that is nine ells along the keel and has four planks on each side from the keel up; and he may load it as full as he likes, [only] so that it does not sink. But if it sinks before the stern has traveled to where the prow was, he has nothing to claim. The finder's blubber shall be cut from the dorsal fin outward and backward along the sides and in to the bones. There shall be one man in the boat; he shall have an oar, a bailing dish, and one bottom board. And if a whale drifts in upon the fishing grounds of a man who has the right to cut it up, he shall have all that part that lies inside his grounds; but the king and the freemen shall have the part that lies beyond the grounds.

11. CONCERNING SEALING GROUNDS

It is enacted concerning the individual sealing grounds that from three weeks before Saint John's Day to six weeks before Christmas all the sealing grounds are inviolable and that no man shall enter the sealing grounds of another in that period without permission. And if a man is found on the sealing grounds of another in those weeks and is taking seals on those grounds, he shall be guilty of theft as much as if he were caught stealing in another man's store house. At other times let men secure their sealing grounds as they secure their possessions on land, namely, by using the law billet.[10] Anyone who enters [the grounds] after that [has been done shall owe] the robber fine and the fine for trespass, valued in burned silver; and [he must surrender] all the seals that he took on those grounds.

12. IF A MAN STEALS AN ERTOG

If a man steals an ertog or more than an ertog, he is a thief. And a thief is convicted by [the testimony of] a bloody carcass, unless it be a dog's [carcass]. If a man goes into a field and brings

[10] By placing a formal ban upon and about the grounds.

away one or more tethered horses, he is a thief. If a thief is caught in a man's storehouse or in some other place, the stolen goods shall be bound upon his shoulder in the fylki where he was taken and he shall be brought in bonds to the bailiff. And the bailiff shall take him to the thing and from the thing to the beach; and the bailiff shall find a man to slay him; all thieves [shall be dealt with] in this way. It is the duty of the freemen to accompany the thief to his execution and then their obligation ends. But if they refuse to accompany him, they owe such a penalty as for failing [to attend] the thing. All the goods that are taken from a thief shall belong to him who took him, unless witnesses give the goods to another; and all his other chattels [belong] to the king. The one who binds a thief shall be held accountable to the king to the amount of fifteen marks until he places him fettered and in the presence of witnesses on the floor of the bailiff's house. If a thief tries to resist, he shall go into outlawry. Whoever releases a thief shall owe fifteen marks to the king, a bailiff the same as any other man. But if a man steals less than an ertog, he shall be [called] a "turf-and-tar man";[11] let him run the gauntlet and let anyone throw at him whatever he chooses and let him get away as best he can; but thereafter he shall have no right to atonement. If a man steals less than a farthing, he shall be called a pilferer forever after that and shall have no right to atonement.

13. CONCERNING THE SUCKING OF COWS

If a man lies down under another man's cow to suck her, he shall lose his right to atonement.

14. IF A MAN ENTERS AN ONION PATCH

If a man enters [another] man's onion patch or angelica patch, he shall have no claim [to compensation] though men strike him and beat him and take away all that he wears and carries.

15. CONCERNING THE TAKING OF MOWN GRASS

If a man travels the highway with a horse and there is grass near the road, he may, if he has need [for it], take as much as his horse requires to eat; but if he takes [hay] with him and is found in possession of it, he is a thief.

[11] "His head was shaved, smeared with tar, and given a cap of downy feathers"; after that he had to run the gauntlet. Keyser, *op. cit.*, p. 382.

XV. [THE LAW AS TO THEFT—CONTINUED]

1. THE TWELVEFOLD OATH IN CASES OF TREASON

The twelvefold oath shall be required if the king accuses a man of plotting to deprive him of land and subjects. And whenever a man is accused of treason, the king shall select a man from his household, one of equal rank with the one who has to answer the charge. If the accused are freedmen or dependents, the king shall select from his household the son of a freeman and authorize him with writ and seal to prosecute the charges when he [the king] is not in that fylki. And he [the accused] shall offer to take the oath at the king's garth in the fylki within three nights, unless he prefers to take it earlier.

2. CONCERNING THE TWELVEFOLD OATH

The twelvefold oath shall be [required] if a man accuses another of having set fire to his house or to his crops within the garth and thus placed the entire homestead in peril of fire.

3. CONCERNING THE TWELVEFOLD OATH

A twelvefold oath is also [required] if one is accused of killing a man after having given him pledges of peace and security.

4. THE TWELVEFOLD OATH IN CASE OF MURDER

A twelvefold oath is also [required] if a man, having failed to report a homicide, is accused of murder. The arrow shall go forth with summons to a thing in the fylki after three nights or after five nights if the fjord is impassable. He [the accused] shall then pledge himself to refute the charge with an oath at the next thing or go into outlawry, if the thingmen are all agreed.

5. CONCERNING THE HERRING FISHERY

It is enacted that, when men go out to fish for herring, they may throw [and leave] the fish wherever they like, on cornland or on meadow; but they must have everything removed by Easter.

If all is not removed, the owner of the land may claim, as he prefers, either a fine for trespass or the herrings that still lie on the ground. And even though the bailiff has forbidden [the men to do this], they have no liability until Easter.

6. CONCERNING THE HERRING FISHERY

If men dip herrings out of the nets of [other] men, and they are neither beggars nor attached to the households of the owners [of the nets], let the owners call men to view the deed and let them have all the herrings that the others had dipped out of the nets without permission and had carried away. If a man intentionally tears another man's net or slashes it to get the herrings out, he has forfeited his right to atonement, no matter how he is molested later on. And he shall owe three marks to the king and repair the damage to the net; [and he shall] pay the fine for evil intent to the owner of the net, if this one has called the deed to the attention of witnesses.

7. CONCERNING THE SIXFOLD OATH

A sixfold oath is [required] in the first place if a neat beast is stolen from a man. Let the owner go out to look for it till he suspects [some one]. Let him then go to this man's house, taking with him the farmers who live nearest to him, and let him call the head of the house out. When he comes out he [the visitor] shall state his errand, saying that he has lost a beast. "Now the color is such as I report, and I have inquired and heard that you have stolen the beast, and I want permission to search your homestead." If he refuses to allow the search, he is the thief. But if he replies in this wise, "You are not doing right just now, you saw the beast I have [just] killed and you are giving your own beast the color that you saw that mine had," and if they then go inside and find the head and the hide bearing such marks as he [the accuser] described, then a sixfold oath shall be required.

8. THE SECOND SIXFOLD OATH

The second [case that requires a] sixfold oath is that in which a man's goods[1] have been taken away. He shall take the men of

[1] *Fǫt.* This frequently means wares wrapped up in a package. The scribe in this case seems to have clothing in mind. Cf. *Gul.*, c. 255.

his household and proceed to the place that seems most likely to him and call the farmer out and demand a search. Then the owner of the house shall reply in this wise: "Remain where you are and do not enter until you have been searched, for I must go to my neighbors and ask them to be present." But if you go in without having been searched, then [it is a case of] goods hidden there by others; and the householder is not liable, but if they make a search, they shall ask the farmer: "Does anyone carry keys except you and your wife?" If he then replies, "My thrall and my bondwoman," and if the windows in the storehouse are so [placed] that materials can be shoved in from the outside, the fivefold oath shall be required. But if one cannot throw anything in from the outside, the thrall is the thief, if the [stolen] goods are for a man's use; but if they are for women, the bondwoman is the thief. But if neither the thrall nor the bondwoman have access [to the storehouse] and one cannot throw anything in from the outside, the sixfold oath shall be required. And even though the stolen goods be found in a chest or in a locked coffer, the demands [of the law] go no further.

9. THE THIRD SIXFOLD OATH

The third [case that requires a] sixfold oath is that in which a man has lost silver. And let him from whom it was stolen go forth and search for it. If he finds it in another man's purse and the man replies in this wise: "If this is your silver you have yourself put it in my purse," then the one who searched and from whom it was stolen shall have the silver. But if he speaks in this wise: "You paid me that silver," then the accused shall have the silver but he shall swear the sixfold oath.

10. THE FOURTH SIXFOLD OATH

The fourth [case that requires a] sixfold oath is that in which a horse worth a mark or more is injured or slain, or cattle to the value of three cows or more than three are injured or slain.

11. THE FIFTH SIXFOLD OATH

The fifth [case that requires a] sixfold oath is that in which a man burns another man's boathouse or a ship of six oars or more, or if he breaks the timbers or hews into them with an ax, wherever the ship may be. And if he owns that he has done this burning or cutting or breaking, let him offer to restore the value to the owner or go into outlawry. If a man damages a ship of the coast defense to the extent of one mark, and if he denies the charge, a threefold oath is required; if he is convicted he is outlawed. If the damage amounts to more than a mark, the sixfold oath is required; and if the man is convicted he is outlawed. And the sixfold oath shall be taken in this wise: the accused shall stand with a kinsman in the church holding the Psalter in his hand, and there he shall take the oath. And for the sixfold oath there shall be chosen six holdar or the best freemen, if holdar are wanting. The plaintiff shall name one-half of these witnesses and the defendant shall name one-half; he shall select one of the six, the second shall be one of his nearest kinsmen, he himself shall be the third, and the other three shall be free men who are able to give account for both pledge and promise.

12. THE SIXTH SIXFOLD OATH

The sixth [case that requires a] sixfold oath is that in which a man burns another man's haystack outside the enclosure or destroys a load or more than a load, though there is no likelihood that the entire homestead may be destroyed.

13. THE SEVENTH SIXFOLD OATH

The seventh [case that requires a] sixfold oath is that in which a man cuts down another man's crop in a field sown with five measures of grain or more than five. If the accused is convicted [of this deed] he shall be outlawed, or he shall restore the value to the owner according as men estimate [the loss]. But if he denies the charge, let him refute it with a sixfold oath or go into outlawry.

14. THE EIGHTH SIXFOLD OATH

The eighth [case that requires a] sixfold oath is that in which a man is charged with having contrived the murder of a man, or one [to whom he had] given grith.

15. CONCERNING GOODS THAT ARE CONCEALED OR NOT CONCEALED

If a man finds a bundle of his belongings[2] outside [another man's] door, or wherever he finds it, in the house or without, if [it is] not concealed, or if [he finds it] inside or outside the garth but not concealed, the threefold oath is [required], if the owner decides to bring charges. But if it is buried under the floor of the kitchen or is [otherwise] concealed, a thrall shall be the thief, unless his master is willing to swear a threefold oath in his behalf.

16. IF A MAN FINDS A BUNDLE OF HIS BELONGINGS

If a man finds a bundle of his belongings in a haymow or in a stack of straw or in a heap of wood where one can insert if from the outside, the threefold oath is [required]. But if it is under the heap, either in the stack or under the wood where a hand cannot reach, the one who stacked the heap shall be the thief, whether he be a thrall or a freeman.

The kings have given the men of Utey the right to have a thing of their own at Jorulfstead[3] to be of equal competence with [those of] the other shiremen.

[2] Most probably clothing.
[3] See page 329, note.

XVI. [LATER ENACTMENTS]

1. CONCERNING NEW LAWS THAT THE KINGS HAVE AUTHORIZED

Here begin the new enactment which the kings, Sigurd, Eystein, and Olaf,[1] have given to the men who live within this jurisdiction. The first is that all gifts, new and old, the malt measure and other dues in kind, customs dues in every form, and all the harbor dues have been remitted to all men who serve with us in the coast defense. If a man is outlawed and leaves the land, and an inheritance to which he has a right becomes available, the nearest kinsman who is counted in the line of heirs shall receive the inheritance, and not the king. But if he returns and make his peace with the king, he shall have the inheritance himself. Every man is at liberty to leave the land when the king has brought peace to the realm. Every man who leaves the land shall be allowed to reside wherever he wishes; no summons shall be sent to him and on his return he shall have all that is his, unless he returns deliberately with a hostile shield. Buried goods shall belong to the one who finds them; but a fine for trespass is due the landowner from those who dig without permission. The bailiff, and not the freemen, shall provide lodgings for the king, unless they [the freemen] volunteer to do so.

2. CONCERNING NEW ENACTMENTS

This new enactment the kings have given to the men of Hálogaland:[2] [they have remitted] the fish tribute both from the headlands and from the fishingsteads, except the five fishes that men have given the king; this gift shall be rendered by every man who catches fish in the Bays.[3] [They have also remitted] the malt meas-

[1] Sons of Magnus Bareleg; see page 327, note.

[2] The coast lands of northern Norway: Hálogaland began approximately at the sixty-fifth parallel and extended to the limit of the Norwegian settlement somewhere near the sixty-ninth.

[3] Certain fishingsteads in the Lofoten Islands.

ure, the spindle gift, and the butter pail.[4] Moreover, they have allowed them to have the commons as they had them in the days of the holy King Olaf, both the outer and the upper [common] to the south and to the north. And all the pelts of savage beasts [taken] north of Vinjar Sound[5] the king has the sole right to purchase. But if the [king's] bailiff accuses any one of having bought pelts here, the threefold oath shall be required; and if he has bought [pelts], he shall surrender them and owe a fine of three marks to the king. No man shall search the house of a native in Hálogaland, unless he is a baron or a bailiff who has the right to bring a legal action, except only in case a man flees from suit and surety; in that case the gjaldkeri[6] shall demand bail from the man that he will be found at his home; and no one shall have the right to prosecute farther than is here allowed.

3. CONCERNING THE BUTTER PAIL

The king has relieved the men of Naumdale[7] of [the following dues]: the butter pail[8] the spindle gift, and the malt measure. And they shall pay these no more than do the other men of Trondheim.

4. CONCERNING NEW ENACTMENTS

This amendment to the law was given by King Harald[9] and King Magnus[10] to the men of Trondheim and to all the others who are in their law. All the laws that were given and established by the holy King Olaf and all the amendments that have since been allowed by those of his kinsmen who have sat as kings in the land shall be loyally kept.

[4] *Vinjarspann*, which the editors of the Norwegian edition have emended to *smiọrspann*. Cf. Taranger, *De norske fokelovböker*, p. 81: Taranger regards the vinjarspann as a corn tribute.

[5] At the southern limit of Hálogaland.

[6] See Glossary, "Gjalkeri."

[7] The northernmost fylki in the Frostathinglaw.

[8] See above, note 4. The word here is written "syniarspọnn."

[9] Harald Gillecrist (1130–36).

[10] Magnus the Blind (1130–35).

GLOSSARY

GLOSSARY[1]

Agent: *umboðsmaðr*. One who has the *umboð*, or the power to act for another. *Frost.*, XI, c. 15, *et passim*.

Agnate, agnatic kinsman: *bauggildismaðr*. A near kinsman on the father's side and in the male line. The bauggildismenn received (and paid) the larger payments in the wergeld. In the Gulathing law the outer limit of this circle was the first cousin; in the Frostathing law the son of a first cousin was also included among the agnates. *Gul.*, cc. 37, 59, 135, 156; *Frost.*, IV, cc. 9, 34; V, c. 9; IX, cc. 8, 20.

Ale, ale feast: *ǫl*. A social gathering so called because the ale was the most necessary provision in Old Norwegian festivities. Ale (also called *mungát*) was a native brew; a stronger beverage, *bjórr* (beer) was imported from Germany. *Gul.*, cc. 6, 58; *Frost.*, I, c. 3; IX, c. 12.

Alehouse: *ǫldrhús*. Any house, usually a private home, where a feast was in progress. *Gul.*, cc. 71, 187, 292; *Frost.*, XI, cc. 5, 8.

Ancestor: *afi*. One in a regular and continuous series of ancestors. *Gul.*, c. 270.

Appraise, assess, estimate: *meta, virða*. To make an estimate of values, losses, etc. Such an estimate was usually made by neighbors called in by the person, or persons, concerned. *Gul.*, cc. 266, 274, 320, *et passim*.

Arrow: *ǫr*. A token shaped like an arrow, which was sent forth through the community to summon the farmers to a moot or a thing, especially when cases of homicide were reported or when there was news of hostile raids. The arrow was usually made of wood (*skera ǫr*, to cut or carve the arrow, was the term often used); but iron arrows (*járnǫrvar*) were employed to summon the host or the fleet. A verbal message was sometimes sent with the arrow; whoever received the token was obliged to carry it to his neighbor. The term *þingboð* was also used. *Gul.*, cc. 32, 151, 160, *et passim*. *See* Cross; Thing token.

Arrow thing: *ǫrvarþing*. A thing called to deal with a case of homicide or of serious personal injury. *Gul.*, c. 156; *Frost.*, IV, cc. 7, 29, 54.

[1] The references to chapters in the "laws" are added to illustrate the use of the word. The list is in no sense inclusive.

Assassin: *flugumaðr.* A hired assistant in crime; literally a "fly-man," one who is like a fly, an insect which to the Northmen symbolized cajolery and seduction. *Frost.*, V, c. 45.

Atonement: *réttr.* Money, goods, or land received as compensation for injuries suffered at the hands of another. The amount due in such cases varied with the rank of the person aggrieved; hence "réttr" in its many gradations came to be used to indicate rank and social position. The gravity of the offense was also considered: some wrongs might demand a double or even a triple compensation; others might be satisfied with a half atonement (*halfrétti*) or even less. *Gul.*, cc. 195, 200; *Frost.*, XIV, c. 18; *et passim.*

Atonement right: *réttr.* The right to claim and to receive compensation for injuries in person and in property. *Gul.*, cc. 71, 190, 216; *Frost.*, XI, c. 12.

Aunt. *See Frost.*, cc. 7, 8, 10 and elsewhere, where the term "sisers" is evidently used for mother's sisters.

Bail: *tak.* Money, or its equivalent, delivered to a claimant to make sure that his opponent in a lawsuit would proceed home to receive summons (*brautartak*), that he would be present when the suit came to a hearing, and that he would comply with the decision of thing or doom (*lagatak*). Various other forms of tak might be listed. The amount of the security that might be demanded would in a rough way correspond to the amount involved in the action. If bail was not forthcoming, the defendant's own person might be seized and held as security. *Gul.*, cc. 102, 254; *Frost.*, III, cc. 20, 23; IV, c. 12. *See* Amira, *Vollstreckungsverfahren*, pp. 329–45.

Bailiff: *ármaðr.* Steward, deputy, or servant. The king's ármaðr had charge of the royal lands in a given locality and he also served as his master's executive official in that same area; as such he looked after the royal revenues, especially the fines due the king, he provided entertainment for the king when he came into that part of the country, he had the keeping of prisoners, he prosecuted certain lawsuits, and in many other ways promoted the king's business. *See* "ármaðr," in Hertzberg, *Glossarium.*

Ban, to place a: *lǫgfesta.* An action by which the person against whom it was directed was forbidden to make use of certain lands or other property claimed by the one who takes the action, or was forbidden to proceed in such a way as to impair the claimant's rights in these properties. Bans were laid at church, at the thing, or at the place where the property in dispute was located. *Frost.*, XIII, cc. 14, 15, 19.

Band of men: *flokkr*. Five men constituted a band or a gang. *Gul.*, cc. 142, 154, 183.

Banesman: *bani*. A manslayer. But the laws distinguish clearly between secret killing, which was murder, and manslaying, in which the element of secrecy or concealment was wanting. *Gul.*, cc. 156, 174–76.

Baptize: *hefja ór heiðnumdóme*. "To lift out of heathendom." *Gul.*, cc. 21–22. The term *skira*, to cleanse, is also used. *Frost.*, II, cc. 2, 3, 5.

Bark, scraped: *skaf*. Bark scraped or shaved off trees was often used for cattle fodder. *Gul.*, c. 75; *Frost.*, XIII, c. 1.

Baron: *lendr maðr*. A man of the chieftain class who held land from the king by a quasi feudal tenure and in return for the royal favor assisted in the local administration, particularly in such business as was of interest to the king. In 1277 the lendr maðr was given the European title of "baron," though he was not at any time a magnate like the Anglo-Norman baron of the same age. *See* Gjerset, *History of the Norwegian People*, I, 387–88.

Baug: *baugr*. A payment; literally, a ring. A baug might be (1) a fine paid to the king, the amount of which was apparently twelve oras in every case; (2) the more important fines paid as man money to the family of a slain man. The laws recognize three baugar in the wergeld: the head baug (*hǫfuðbaugr*), which was paid to the son or to the father of the slain man; the *bróðurbaugr* (brother baug), which was paid to his brother; and the *brœðrungsbaugr* (cousin baug), which was paid to his cousins on the paternal side. *Gul.*, cc. 243–45, 316–19; *Frost.*, IV, cc. 9, 13, 18, 53.

Baugamenn: the men who receive baug fines. *Gul.*, cc. 243–44, 249; *Frost.*, VI, cc. 2, 4, 9, 13, 20.

Baugrygr. A woman who receives (or pays) a baug; she must be an unmarried daughter or sister who has, in the absence of male heirs, the right to inherit property, including odal land. *Frost.*, VI, c. 4.

Benefice: *veizlujǫrð*. Land held by a subject from the king on terms that somewhat resembled those of the land tenure in early feudal times. A man who had such land was a *veizlumaðr*. *Gul.*, c. 206. *See Germanistische Abhandlungen zum LXX Geburtstag Konrad Maurers*, 312 ff. (Hertzberg).

Birch Isle law: *Bjarkeyjarréttr*. Borough law; markets and fairs (so far as these existed) were under this law. The word seems to be derived from Bjarkey, Birka, the name of an important early commercial center in Lake Mælar, not far from the modern Stockholm. *Frost.*, X, c. 32.

Bone money: *beingjǫld*. Compensation for a broken bone or joint. *Frost.*, IV, c. 49.

Borough: *kaupangr*. A town that enjoyed trading privileges and was governed largely by borough law. The borough referred to in the Frostathing law was in most cases Nidaros (Trondheim). In the Gulathing area, the chief (perhaps the only) borough was Bjǫrgvin (Bergen). *Frost.*, II, cc. 10, 45; VII, c. 11.

Bryti. The foreman among the thralls. *Gul.*, c. 198.

Burned silver, valued in: *silfrmetinn*. *See* Silver.

Bushel (half): *skjappa*. *Frost.*, Introd., c. 21; II, c. 33.

Bush lad: *rísungr*, *hrísungr* (*hrís*, bushes, shrubbery). An illegitimate son of a free man by a free woman, but begotten in secret. *Gul.*, c. 58; *Frost.*, VIII, c. 8; X, c. 47.

Butter pail: *smjǫrspann*. A tribute paid in butter. With certain other unpopular taxes it was attributed to Sweyn Knutsson who ruled in Norway 1030–35. *Frost.*, XVI, cc. 2, 3.

Capital tithe: *hǫfuðtíund*. A tithe given once for one's entire wealth and not merely the natural increase. *Frost.*, II, c. 17; III, c. 17.

Chattels: *fé*. *See* Movables.

Christman gifts: *jólagjafir*. A tribute said to have been levied first by Sweyn Knutsson (*see* Butter pail) and abolished by Sweyn's successor, Magnus the Good. *Gul.*, c. 148.

Coast defense: *leiðangr*. *See* Levy.

Cognate, cognatic kinsman: *nefgildismaðr*. A near kinsman on the feminine side. In the Gulathing law the circle of *nefgildismenn* extended to and included kinsmen of the second degree; in the Frostathing law the outer limit was the third degree. *Gul.*, cc. 37, 59, 156; *Frost.*, IX, cc. 8, 20.

Common: *almenningr*. All that part of the country, including the water front and the plateau lands, which was not private property was regarded as a common possession. To all this the king held the title, but the subjects were allowed to make such use of the common as custom permitted. *Gul.*, cc. 145, 150; *Frost.*, XIV, c. 7.

Community: *félag*. Common ownership or control of property. The term is used particularly of the union of properties within the family, when the wife's possessions were merged with those of the husband. *Gul.*, c. 53; *Frost.*, XI, cc. 5, 8, 15.

Concubine: *friðla*. A free-born woman whose relationship to the man concerned seems usually to have been a matter of common knowledge. *Gul.*, c. 125; *Frost.*, III, cc. 11, 13.

Conversion: *áfang*, *fornæmi*. Unauthorized use of another man's property and the fines for such trepass. "Afang" is the more general term; "fornæmi" seems to be limited in its application to the unpermitted use of a sled, a horse, or some other means of conveyance. *Gul.*, cc. 71, 92; *Frost.*, X, cc. 42–45.

Conveyance of land. *See* Skeyting.

Corner lad: *hornungr* (*horn*, corner). The illegitimate son of a free man by a free-born concubine (friðla). *Gul.*, cc. 58, 104; *Frost.*, VIII, c. 8; X, c. 47.

Corner post (of a church): *hornstafr*. The early churches in Norway were often built of timbers set upright; in such structures the corner posts formed very important parts of the framework. *Gul.*, cc. 10, 12.

Cousin: *brœðrungr*, Son of a paternal uncle. *Gul.* 224–26. In *Frost.*, VI, the term *brœðrasynir*, literally sons of brothers, must be taken to mean sons of a father's brothers.

Cow: *kýr*. The Norwegian cow was the ultimate standard of value (*kúgildi*, the money value of a cow). In the payment of man money ten marks were counted as the equivalent of 32 cows. A cow, therefore, had the value (in law) of about two and one-half oras. *Gul.*, cc. 219, 223; *Frost.*, II, c. 27.

Crew, member of ship's: *skipari*, *háseti*. On merchant ships the crew was frequently made up of those who had taken passage or were shipping freight on the ship. The oarsmen on a ship of the coast defense were usually called *hásetar*. *Gul.*, cc. 102, 299, 300; *Frost.*, V, c. 14; VII, cc. 21, 24.

Cross: *kross*. A token in the form of a cross sent forth by a priest to inform his parishioners when fast days or holy days were imminent. *Gul.*, c. 19; *Frost.*, II, cc. 22–23, 28–29.

Cross: *krossa*. To mark with a cross. The term is used with reference to bans or the placing of bans on grain fields. *Gul.*, c. 72.

Cross payment: *þversǫk*. A part of the wergeld payments which according to the Gulathing law was paid by a certain group in the slayer's kindred to two others but not exactly corresponding groups in the kindred of the slain man. *Gul.*, cc. 224, 250–52.

Current (or counted, *talenn*) coin. The value of coined silver in the twelfth and thirteenth centuries appears to have been only about half that of the weighed metal in the same denomination. Thus a mark, *talenn*, was worth only half as much as a mark, weighed.

Defaulter: *dómflogi*. A man might default either by failing to attend the hearing of his case or by violating the accepted rules of court procedure. A dómflogi is one who flees from the doom. *Gul.*, c. 269; *Frost.*, X, c. 12.

Demand, formal, for restitution: *kvaða, kvǫð*. Literally, a greeting. When the merits of a dispute were not generally known, the claimant proceeded with a kvaða, or request that he do right in the matter. The defendant must then either comply with the request or agree to have the complaint heard and considered by a doom. *See* Doom. *Gul.*, cc. 37, 267.

Doom: *dómr, skiladómr*. A tribunal of twelve men called in by the parties to a suit to hear the contention and, if possible, to pass judgment. The doom was usually employed in cases that were not entirely clear and could, therefore, not be taken immediately to a thing. *Gul.*, cc. 37, 40, 78, *et passim*.

Dómflogi. *See* Defaulter.

Doomsman: *dómandi*. One who sits in a doom. *Gul.*, c. 86; *Frost.*, X, cc. 12, 14, 15.

Doomstakes: *dómstaurar, heyrendr*. Witnesses called to testify before a doom. They stood outside and around the doom circle. *Gul.*, c. 269; *Frost.*, X, c. 15.

Door, principal: *karldyrr*. The men's door. This was the principal door in a dwelling house and was ordinarily placed in the west end. When there was a door in the east end, it was called the women's door. *Gul.*, c. 266.

Double amount: *halfu meira*. Literally, one-half more; but the scribes had in mind not a half added to the original sum but one-half of the total after the addition had been made. *Gul.*, cc. 3, 35.

Eighth (of a fylki): *áttungr*. The term was sometimes loosely used for a limited area within the fylki. *Gul.*, cc. 11, 298; *Frost.*, II, c. 14.

Ell: *ǫln, alin*. A measure of length. *See* Thumb ell.

Enrollment thing: *manntalsþing*. A moot held to number the available men and to prepare the muster lists. *Gul.*, c. 298; *Frost.*, VII, c. 8.

Ertog: *ertog, ertogr, ǫrtug*. Unit of weight and value. As a unit of value the ertog was equal to ten pence, or to one-third of an ora. *Passim*. *See* Monetary system.

Evil intent, fine for: *ǫfundarbót*. A fine additional to the compensation for loss or injury by which the offender was made to suffer for his evil intentions. *Frost.*, IV, cc. 12, 17, 18.

Fallow: *trǫð*. Trodden ground, so called because the fallow was frequently enclosed and used as a cattle pen. *Frost.*, XIII, cc. 1, 22.

Farm, outlying parts of: *afheimr*. Cultivated plots or meadow land not contiguous to the home farm and usually some distance away. *Frost.*, IV, c. 5.

Fence: *garðr*. Fences were sometimes built of felled trees (*Gul.*, 82); but the approved "garth" was built of strong poles set upright and held in place by a horizontal top rail. *Frost.*, XIII, c. 21.

Fine: *bót, sekt*. The general distinction between "bót" and "sekt" is that the former term was used for the fines paid to private persons, while the latter was used for such as were paid to the public authorities (king, bishop, commonalty, etc.); but the rule is not without its exceptions. *Passim*.

Fine, customary: *lǫgbaugr*. A fine paid to the public authorities, but usually to the king; it was often a large fine. *Frost.*, IV, cc. 11, 12, 16, 17, 19, 21, 22.

Fire wolf: *brennuvargr*. One who is outlawed for the crime of arson. *Gul.*, 98.

Fish tribute: *fiskigjafir*. A tax on the fishing industry. *Frost.*, XVI, c. 2.

Five-day moot: *fimtarstefna*. A moot called to meet after five days; also a five-day notice or warning. *Gul.*, c. 162; *Frost.*, XIII, c. 23, *et passim*.

Five-day week: *fimt*. The Old Germanic week. After the introduction of Christianity into the North this had to give place to the new week of seven days; but the change was not complete for a long time. In matters of law and public business the five-day week continued in use. *Gul.*, cc. 22, 159; *Frost.*, IV, cc. 33–34.

Forest: *mǫrk*. Wooded land attached to a farm though not necessarily contiguous to it. *Gul.*, cc. 75, 91, 95, 161.

Foster inheritance: *branderfð*. The foster father inherited from the foster son, but the right was not reciprocal. *Gul.*, cc. 108, 270.

Free-born: *ættborinn*. Born of a family whose freedom was not qualified by any form of dependency. *See* Well-born. *Gul.*, cc. 62, 71; *Frost.*, IX, c. 1.

Freedman: *frjálsgjafi, leysingi, leysingja* (feminine form). One whose freedom was limited or imperfect. The "frjálsgjafi" was one whose manumission had been published at a freedom ale. The "leysingi" was one who had attained a practically free status either by giving his freedom ale or by other means. The freedman was not entirely free from dependence and his disability was inherited by his descendants for several generations. *Gul.*, cc. 62–63; *Frost.*, IX, cc. 11, 16.

Freedom ale: *frelsisǫl*. An ale feast celebrated to give sanction and publicity to the emancipation of a thrall. *Gul.*, c. 62; *Frost.*, IX, c. 12.

Freeman: *búandi, bóndi*. A general term for any free householder who was not attached to the service of the king, a bishop, or any other man, but applied more specifically to the free farmer (not of the hauld class) who held land by right of lease or purchase. *Passim.*

Fylki. A local administrative and judicial district, roughly the equivalent of the English shire, though, in the Gulathinglaw, somewhat more extensive in area. Each fylki had its thing which all the farmers who were not excused from thing duties were expected to attend. After the introduction of Christianity each fylki had a church which ranked above the other churches in the same area and was maintained by the fylki as a whole. *Passim.*

Gains (in a suit): *gagn*. Such advantages as might come to either party in the course of a lawsuit. These might arise from various contingencies, but chiefly from error or neglect on the part of the opposing litigant. *Gul.*, cc. 59, 121, 268–69.

Gang, gang fight: *flokkr, flokksvíg*. *See* Band. *Gul.*, cc. 152, 167, 183, 189.

Garth: *garðr*. Primarily, a fence or enclosure. Later the term was extended to include the area enclosed, such as a churchyard, a homestead, and the arable, meadow, pastures, etc., of a farm. The term is, therefore, used most generally for the homestead and the lands attached to it in so far as they lie within the outer fences. *Gul.*, cc. 37, 255, 268.

Garth, king's: *konungsgarðr*. A farm owned by the king and sometimes used as his residence. However, the king had many estates and most of them could scarcely have been used for residential purposes except on rare occasions. *Frost.*, V, c. 13.

Geld eker: *sakauki*. One who increases the wergeld. The geld ekers were certain more distant members of the kindred who did not originally share in the man fines; when they were allowed to do so it naturally became necessary to eke the geld. *Gul.*, cc. 236–37; *Frost.*, VI, cc. 5–6, 14, 21.

Gift of God: *guðsgæfi*. Fish and game which at times appeared in large numbers and in extensive shoals to the great profit of men. The herring which approached the shores at intervals in this manner were eminently gifts of God. *Gul.*, c. 85.

Gifts to the women: *gjafir*, *kvenngjafir*. Additions to the wergeld which were paid by the near kinswomen of the slayer to the wife and near kinswomen of the slain man. *Gul.*, cc. 221, 245.

Gjaldkeri. A borough official with financial and other functions. He was of great importance in the later centuries of the Middle Ages, but in the period of the older law his office was exceptional only. *Frost.*, VII, c. 8; XVI, c. 2.

Grim oath: *grímueiðr*. An oath sworn by the accused and six oath helpers in the selection of whom he had no part. *Gul.*, 134.

Grith: *grið*. A limited period of peace and security granted a law breaker to enable him to put his affairs in order (*Frost.*, I, c. 5; IV, c. 30). The term is also used for the peace and security that was enforced at certain times and in certain places (*Frost.*, II, c. 10) and for the peace and security that one finds and enjoys in a home. Thus a "grithman" (*griðmaðr*) is one who, though not of the family, has been admitted into its circle and shares in all its rights and activities. *Gul.*, c. 255.

Guest kinsmann: *gestfeðra*, *gestfeðri*. A man, or woman, who dies in the house of another or on his land. For purposes of inheritances such a person was regarded as a kinsman, if no relative appeared to claim his goods. For the derivation of the term *see* Hertzberg, *Glossarium*, 858. *Gul.*, cc. 109–13.

Hand sold: *handsalað*. Concluded with a handclasp in the presence of witnesses. Agreements made in this way acquired a peculiar sanction. *Gul.*, cc. 40, 70.

Hauld: *hauldr*, *hauldsmaðr*. A landowner of a class just above that of the common freemen. The hauld in the greater part of the kingdom had his land by odal right; he was born to this right (*óðalborinn maðr*). *Gul.*, cc. 149, 185.

Herath: *herað*. In general, the countryside; more specifically, the term was applied to a local area corresponding to the English hundred, though much larger in extent. The herath had its own thing. In the Frostathinglaw, where the shires were small, the herath-institution was wanting. *Passim.*

Highseat: *andvegi.* The most prominent seat in the house and occupied by the head of the family. In certain cases a legal action could be brought against a man only when he was at home and in his highseat. *Gul.*, c. 35; *Frost.*, X, cc. 2, 8.

Hird: *hirð.* The king's household, especially his military guard. *Gul.*, c. 2; *Frost.*, IV, c. 4; XV, c. 1.

Holdar. Plural form of hauld, which see.

Holt. A parcel of stony ground overgrown with bushes and small trees. *Gul.*, c. 292.

Holy day, lesser: *rúmheilagr dagr.* A day which the church regarded as holy, though the laws did not demand that it be observed in the same strict manner as the greater days of the church. *Frost.*, XIII, c. 1; XIV, c. 7.

Home summons: *heimstefna.* A legal action by which a man is notified to be at home and in his highseat on a certain day to hear the plaintiff's claim or demand and to learn what witnesses will be heard, in case witnesses are available. *Gul.*, cc. 37, 46, 266; *Frost.*, X, cc. 2, 7, 9.

Hospitality, gift in return for: *drekkulaun*, "Reward for drink". A gift presented by the king to one who had entertained him. *Gul.*, 270.

Housebreaking: *heimsókn.* An attack on a man in his own house. *Gul.*, cc. 178, 242.

Housekeeper: *deigja.* The ranking bondwoman in a household. She seems to have had a general supervision of the work about the house. *Gul.*, c. 198; *Frost.*, XI, c. 21.

Housemaid: *seta.* A bondwoman ranking second in the household. It is the belief that her work was principally within the house. *Gul.*, c. 198; *Frost.*, XI, c. 21.

Husband's gift (to the marriage portion): *gagngjald, tilgjǫf, þriðjungsauki.* The last term is used in the Frostathing law only, and means "the addition of a third," though actually it was one-half (*see* Double amount). Except under abnormal circumstances the husband's gift remained the property of the wife. The laws also take note of another gift, the *línfé* (linengift), which the husband presented to the bride the morning following the nuptials, if she had come to him as a virgin; but this does not seem to have been necessary to a valid marriage contract. *See* Lehmann, *Verlobung und Hochzeit. Gul.*, cc. 104, 115; *Frost.*, III, cc. 6, 17, 22.

Interest (for use of money): *lagaleiga.* The legal rate of interest in Old Norway seems to have been 20 percent. *Frost.*, XII, c. 2.

Jarl. An ancient official, the highest dignitary in the kingdom next to the king. The title still lives in the English word "earl." *Gul.*, cc. 178, 200; *Frost.*, II, c. 5.

Jurisdiction. *See* Law.

Kettle: *ketill. Frost.*, III, c. 15. *See* Ordeal.

Kindred: *ætt.* The circle of kinsmen, usually counted on the masculine side. *See* Phillpotts, *Kindred and Clan*, pp. 47 ff. *Gul.*, c. 58; *Frost.*, IX, c. 21.

Kinship: *frændsemi.* Two systems of reckoning and determining the degrees of kinship were in vogue in medieval Norway: one derived from canon law, and the other from heathen custom. The canonists spoke of "degrees" and began with brothers and sisters who were then in the first degree with respect to the ancestor (in their case the father) from whom the reckoning proceeds. In the native system, on the other hand, the count began with first cousins, who were then said to be in the first "knee." *Gul.*, c. 24; *Frost.*, III, c. 1.

Knee: *knê. See* Kinship.

Land pledged for a loan. *See* Mortgage.

Law: *lǫg.* One of the four large jurisdictions into which the Norwegian shires were grouped in the Middle Ages. These were the Gulathinglaw, the Frostathinglaw, the Borgarthinglaw, and the Eidsivathinglaw. The last two were in the south and southeast. Each of these "provinces" had its own representative assembly which met annually. *See* pp. 6 ff. *Gul.*, c. 3, *Frost.*, II, c. 39.

Law billet: *lagakefli.* A small stick of wood that was used in connection with certain legal actions. It seems to have been necessary to given legal force to bans and injunctions, especially when they concerned the use of land or growing crops. The law billet seems also to have been used when a defendant met a "formal demand" with an appeal to a doom. The one who made use of the billet apparently threw it on the ground as he spoke the closing words of the required legal formula, or of the formal statement that he had to make. *Frost.*, IX, c. 30; X, c. 11; XIII, c. 23; XIV, c. 11. *See* Hertzberg, *Den ældste norske proces*, pp. 55–56; Amira, *Nordgermanisches Obligationenrecht*, I, 268, 319–20.

Law court: *lǫgrétta*. A committee of presumably thirty-six men (though the number is in dispute) appointed from the law thing, the duty of which was to discuss the business that was to come up before the thing and to report its findings to the larger body. Technically the law court had no judicial power; but, since one of its functions was to interpret the law, its opinions in specific cases (lawsuits) could not lightly be set aside. *Frost.*, I, c. 2; V, c. 46; X, c. 30.

Lawman: *lǫgmaðr*. A judicial functionary of great importance in the later Middle Ages, but scarcely mentioned in the older laws. *Frost.*, Introd., c. 16.

Law thing: *lǫgþingi*. The annual court of the great provincial jurisdictions. *See* Law.

Lease: *arðarmáli, máli*. A contract for land. The arðarmáli ran for one year only; the máli was a longer lease. *Frost.*, XIII, c. 3; XIV, c. 2.

Leech money: *læknisfé*. The fee for healing. The money was due from the man who caused the wound. *Frost.*, IV, cc. 11, 12, 16.

Legitimation: *ættleiðing*. The act and ceremony of bringing a person, usually of illegitimate birth, into the kindred. The ceremony, which is doubtless of ancient origin, is described in *Gul.*, c. 58, and *Frost.*, IX, c. 1.

Levy (naval): *leiðangr*. Service with the coast defense and the dues and taxes that the subjects owed to this service. *Gul.*, cc. 295–315; *Frost.*, VII.

Live stock: *bú*. Cattle and other animals needed on a farm, including thralls. The word "bú" may also mean a landed estate with everything necessary to its complete economy. *Gul.*, c. 3; *Frost.*, IV, c. 44, *et passim*.

Major age, of: *fulltíða*. A man or woman became a major on completing the fifteenth year (*Frost.*, IX, c. 22). In the legislation of Magnus Lawmender (1263–80) the age was set at twenty years.

Malt measure: *reykmælir*. A tribute of a measure of malt due the king from every house where smoke rises from the fireplace. This tax, too, was ascribed to King Sweyn (*see* Christmas gift), it was abolished by the sons of Magnus Bareleg. *Frost.*, XVI, cc. 1–3.

Man fines, lesser: *frændbœtr*. A term used in the Frostathing law for certain fines paid to the more distant kinsmen of a slain man. The payments began at the fourth (canonical) degree. *Frost.*, VI, cc. 11–12, 18–19. *See* Geld eker.

Man fines, schedule of: *saktal*. *See* Wergeld.

Man money: *manngjǫld, mannsgjǫld*. *See* Wergeld.

Mark: *mǫrk*. A measure of weight and value. As a measure of weight the mark was equal to 215.8 grams, somewhat less than an English pound sterling, which contains 349. 7 grams. As money of account, a mark was equal to 8 oras, to 24 ertogs, and to 240 pence. Except where gold is indicated, the mark may be taken to mean so much silver. *See* Monetary system.

Marriage man: *giptingarmaðr*. One who has authority to arrange the marriage of an unmarried woman. The marriage man was usually the woman's father; but he might be a brother or other near kinsman, or even a guardian if near kinsmen were wanting. *Frost.*, III, 1; XI, cc. 2, 4.

Marriage portion: *heimanfylgja*. Money, goods, or land that a bride brings with her from her home to the new household. Under ordinary circumstances the marriage portion remains the property of the wife. *Frost.*, III, cc. 7, 17.

Meal and butter. Apparently a technical term for provisions.

Measure: *mælir*. A measure of capacity approximately equal in content to one-half bushel. *Gul.*, cc. 6, 58; *Frost.*, II, c. 21.

Messenger: *erendreki*. One who goes on the king's (or bishop's) errand. The term seems applicable to any one who has authority to act for the king (or the bishop) in any specific case. *Gul.*, cc. 9, 11, 33; *Frost.*, XIV, c. 7.

Mile: *rǫst*. Literally, rest, or the distance between resting places. Hertzberg believes that the *rǫst* was equivalent to about 24,000 feet or about four and one-half English miles. *See Glossarium, rǫst; Gul.*, c. 266.

Minor, minority: *úmagi, úmegð*. The term *úmagi* was also used for pauper dependents. *Frost.*, IV, cc. 32, 34. *See* Major age.

Minor fasts. *See* Preparatory fasts.

Monetary system. The Old Norwegian laws recognize a monetary system of four units: mark, ora, ertog, and penny, in the following ratio: one mark = 8 oras = 24 ertogs = 240 pence. Most of these were units of account, as it seems that the silver penny was the only coin in actual circulation. Gold is also mentioned as having monetary functions, but there was probably no gold coinage. The ratio between the two metals (silver and gold) seems to have been eight to one. *See Gul.*, cc. 316–19. These units were units of weight as well as of value. In the earlier history of Norwegian coinage the minted silver was, it is believed, of approximately full weight; but in Norway, as elsewhere, there came to be a progressive debasement of the coinage, till in the twelfth century a penny, coined, was worth only about half as much as a penny, weighed. The same, of course, would be true of the ertog, the ora, and the mark. *See* Hertzberg, *Glossarium*, "ertog," "eyrir," "mǫrk," "penning"; Holmboe, *Das älteste Münzwesen Norwegens*.

Mortgage: *máli, forsǫlumáli*. A pledge to secure a loan. The Norwegian mortgage in the Middle Ages resembled the English mortgage of the same period in that the land or the chattel that was pledged was given into the possession of the mortgagee and remained in his keeping till the mortgagor had repaid the loan. If he failed to make this payment the mortgagee became the actual owner of what he had up to that time held only in pledge. "Máli" and "málajǫrð" are the terms used by the scribes of the Gulathing law for the mortgage contract and the mortgaged land. The corresponding terms in the Frostathing law are "forsǫlumáli" and "forsǫlujǫrð." *Gul.*, cc. 283, 286, 288; *Frost.*, IX, c. 22; XII, cc. 2, 3.

Movables: *fé, lausir aurar*. "Fé" is the broader term and is used for money and the value of money whatever it is; usually, however, fé can be translated chattels or movables. "Lausir aurar" can mean movables only. *Frost.*, V, c. 18; XIV, c. 12, *et passim*.

Moving day: *fardagr*. The day when the tenant's right to remain on the land expires. In the Gulathinglaw, this was nine days after "summer day," or April 23. In the Frostathinglaw, it was the lesser holy day after Epiphany. *Gul.*, cc. 72–73, 82; *Frost.*, XIII, c. 1.

Mund: *mundr*. A sum of money, or its equivalent in chattels or land, that was paid at the nuptials by the bridegroom when he received the bride. According to the laws as we have them the mund was paid to the bride herself. The amount to be delivered was a matter of contract, though custom and convention must often have been the determining factors. The smallest amount that could be accepted as mund was twelve oras, the value of five cows or a little less. Without the payment of mund there could be no legal marriage. *Gul.*, cc. 25, 58, 124; *Frost.*, III, 13. c. *See* Lehmann, *Verlobung und Hochzeit*, pp. 58 ff.

Murder, murderer: *morð, morðingi*. Homicide committed in secret or not properly reported. The punishment for murder was more severe than for ordinary manslaying. *Gul.*, cc. 22, 32, 132; *Frost.*, IV, c. 7. *See* Slayer's report.

Muster group: *manngerð*. A group of men who coöperated in fitting out ships and providing sailors for the coast defense. Usually a small group of neighbors would find equipment for one man; hence such a group would be called a "manngerð." *Gul.*, cc. 298, 304.

Mynda, mynding. "Mynda" (v) seems to mean to attain a certain control of the property of one's wife through the payment of the mund. The control may have meant practical ownership, though on that point scholars are in disagreement. *Gul.*, c. 54; *Frost.*, XI, 4.

Neat, neat beast: *naut.* A cow or an ox. Smaller farm beasts including young cattle were *smali. Gul.*, cc. 43, 82; *Frost.*, XIII, cc. 1, 18–20.

Neck ransom: *halslausn.* Money or goods given to liberate the neck of a thrall (a free man is a "free necked" man). At the freedom ale the ransom fee was put in a purse which was then hung on the neck of a wether. *Frost.*, IX, c. 12; for a different procedure *see Gul.*, c. 62.

Neighbor farmer: *granni.* A farmer who lives in the same house or on the same farm with another. In the latter case the homesteads would be separate, though quite near each other. On a large farm there might be several such occupiers. Men who occupied separate farms but whose homesteads were not far apart might also think of each other as grannar. *Gul.*, cc. 9, 33, 81–82.

Neighborhood ale: *samburðarǫl.* An ale feast to which several families contributed their brewing. Such a feast was required by law. *Gul.*, c. 6.

Nithing crime: *níðingsvíg.* A crime, usually murder, committed under such circumstances and by such methods as to give the criminal the character of a nithing (a mean, infamous, treacherous person). Nithing deeds usually led to permanent outlawry. *Gul.*, c. 178.

Noon: *nón.* The ninth hour of the day or approximately three o'clock in the afternoon. The major saints' days and other prominent holy days normally began at nón on the preceding day. In the language of the laws such a day was *nónheilagr*, or "noon-holy." *Gul.*, cc. 16, 18; *Frost.*, II, cc. 24, 25, 35.

Norway: *Noregr.*

Notorious property: *vitafé.* Property the title and ownership of which are known to men and can be established by witnesses. *Gul.*, c. 49; *Frost.*, X, cc. 19–23.

Oar bench: *sess, hamla, halfrými.* The place of a rower on a ship. The sess is the oar bench, but the word also refers to the place of the bench in the ship. The size of a ship is indicated by the number of benches; thus, a twenty-bencher (tvítugsessa) would have seats for twenty pairs of oarsmen. The hamla was a rope or strap which held the oar in place; the word was also used to point out that part of the ship where the rower sat, though the more correct term would be "halfrými" (half room). *Gul.*, cc. 223, 300–301; *Frost.*, VII, cc. 1, 12, 20.

Oath: *eiðr*. *See* Hertzberg, *Glossarium*, "eiðr."

Oath, failure of: *eiðfall*. A failure to clear the accused, either because the forms of law were not strictly observed or because some one in the group of oath helpers refused to swear. *Passim.*

Oath day: *særr dagr*. Any day on which oath taking was permitted. *Gul.*, cc. 30, 57, 98, 135; *Frost.*, III, c. 3.

Oath helper: *váttr*. One who helps a man to clear himself of a charge by joining with him in an oath. In the selection of oath helpers both parties to an action usually had some share. Those chosen, or secured, by the principal in the oath taking were called *fangaváttar;* those selected for him by his opponent or by the court were known as *nefndarvitni*. If any one of the men chosen to share in the oath should refuse to swear, the entire oath would fail. The term váttr is also used for witness generally. *See Haskins Anniversary Essays*, pp. 133–56 (Larson).

Odal, odal right: *óðal*. Odal is usually defined as (1) land and the right to own it; (2) "family ownership of land and also the land as the object of such ownership." The significance of family ownership lay in the fact that the title to land was conceived as remaining not wholly with the individual owner, but with the kindred to which the owner belonged. Odal right was not exercised, however, until the owner took steps to dispose of his holdings by sale; in that case the other odalmen had the first right to buy it. If the land should actually be transferred to a purchaser from another kindred, it was possible for the odalmen to redeem it from him, provided that they took action according to legal prescription. It is Taranger's opinion that odal right extended only to the fenced fields of the home farm; the outlying forest and the mountain pasture were dealt with according to other principles. Vinogradov, *Essays in Legal History*, pp. 159–73 (Taranger). *See* Skeyting.

Odal land, redemption of: *óðalsbrigði*. While it was possible to convey odal land with odal right to a purchaser in another kindred, ordinary sales were conditional and would allow redemption. But an odalman who wished to keep his right active would have to publish, at the thing or in some other place where men come together and some time before the close of the twenty-year period, the fact that he had the odal right to some specified farm or to a part of it. *Gul.*, c. 265.

Odal witness: *óðalvitni, árofi.* A witness who can testify to one's odal right, particularly in cases of redemption. For the qualifications of such witnesses *see Gul.*, cc. 266, 268, 272.

Official, king's: *sýslumaðr.* A royal functionary in charge of the king's business in a fylki or in a considerable part of a fylki. In the later Middle Ages the "sysselman's" office was of outstanding importance; but in the period of the earlier laws it seems exceptional and undeveloped. *Gul.*, cc. 32, 37; *Frost.*, III, c. 24; IV, c. 41.

Ora: *eyrir.* A unit of weight and value. As a measure of weight it was the Norse form of the ounce. As money of account the ora was more widely used than any other monetary denomination. It contained three ertogs and was the equivalent of one-eighth of a mark. *See* Monetary system.

Ordeal: *járnburðr, ketiltak.* Men who had to appeal to the judgment of God usually had to carry the hot iron or walk over hot plowshares. Women might also be required to deal with the hot iron, but more commonly they had to plunge an arm into boiling water. *Gul.*, cc. 32, 158; *Frost.*, III, c. 15.

Outlawed (man), outlawry: *útlagr, útlegð.* Outlawry was a common form of punishment in the Middle Ages. In Norway it was of two kinds: (1) common outlawry, which meant much the same as honorable exile and from which the outlaw could be released by making certain payments to the king and to the family that had the blood feud; (2) permanent or irrevocable outlawry, from which there was no escape. One who was sent into permanent outlawry was an *úbótamaðr*, one from whom, or for whom, no fine could be received. *Passim.*

Outlawry, release from: *friðkaup, landkaup, skógarkaup.* In most cases the outlaw had no choice but immediate flight to the neighboring woods (*skógr*); release from outlawry therefore meant release from the woods and was called *skógarkaup*, though it might also be called *friðkaup* (purchase of peace), or *landkaup* (purchase of the right to remain in the land). The king alone could annul a sentence of outlawry. One who was allowed to return from exile was said to be *ílendr* (from *ílenda*, to allow a man the right of habitation). *Frost.*, III, c. 24; IV, cc. 44, 62.

Patron of church: *upphaldsmaðr kirkju.* One who builds and undertakes to maintain a private church or chapel of ease (*hœgendiskirkja*). *Frost.*, II, c. 16; XIV, c. 3.

Pauper freedman: *grafgangsmaðr.* A freedman who has come to want and is allowed to starve to death in the barbarous fashion described in *Gul.*, c. 63.

Peace pledge, truce pledge: *trygð*. A solemn assurance and pledge given in cases of homicide (or injuries that might lead to homicide) that the person in need of such assurance should be allowed to live among men in peace and security. Such pledges were a part of all settlements that involved the payment of atonement or man money. The fine exacted for the pledge was called *trygðakaup* or *tryggvakaup*. *Frost.*, V, cc. 9, 44; IX, cc. 19, 22.

Penny: *penningr*, *peningr*. A silver coin. *See* Monetary system.

Personal rights: *réttr*. The rights that every one enjoyed as members of the social body, particularly the right to be compensated for wrongs and injuries to oneself or to one's kindred. To be deprived of "right" was equivalent to exile. *Gul.*, c. 200, *et passim*.

Personal servant: *þjónn*. One of the ranking thralls; usually found in wealthy and prominent families only. *Gul.*, c. 198; *Frost.*, XI, c. 21.

Plaintiff, suitor: *sóknari*, *sækjandi*. One who brings legal action against another. *Gul.*, cc. 35, 37, 86, 266; *Frost.*, IV, cc. 8, 24; X, cc. 11, 15–16, 24, 26, 32.

Pledge and promise: *orð ok eiðr*. Literally, "word and oath." Persons of major age were said to be responsible for word and oath. *Gul.*, c. 24; *Frost.*, IV, c. 8.

Preparatory fast: *gagnfasta*. Periods of fasting of which the clergy (and cloister folk) alone were required to take account. They were the three weeks preceding each of the following festivals: Saint John's Day, Michaelmas, and Christmas. The two weeks before Lent comprised also a period of preparatory fasting. For the clergy, Lent was, therefore, a nine-week fast. *Gul.*, c. 27; *Frost.*, XII, c. 2.

Prosecutor in criminal actions: *sakaráberi*. One who has the right to prosecute was called *eptirmælandi*. *Gul.*, c. 32; *Frost.*, IV, cc. 24, 54, 56.

Public notice, publication: *lýsing* (v. *lýsa*). To call certain facts to the attention of assembled men, usually at church, at an ale feast, or at the thing. Such notice (lýsing) had to be given to validate certain acts and to keep alive certain rights, such as the right to redeem odal land. *Gul.*, cc. 53, 94, 127; *Frost.*, III, c. 19.

Purchase right, land held by: *kaupajǫrð*. The title to land held by purchase right was regarded as imperfect, since it was, in most cases, at least, subject to odal right. *Gul.*, 223. *Frost.*, XIII, c. 25 (*Kauplendingr*, the owner of such land).

Quarter (of a fylki): *fjórðungr*. Because of their great extent the shires of the Gulathinglaw were sometimes divided into quarters, each of which might have its own thing and its own church. *Gul.*, cc. 9, 12, 19, 46, 68, 102, 267.

Reksthegn: *reksþegn.* A descendant of a freedman who had almost attained the status of complete freedom. The term is found in the Frostathing law only. *Frost.*, IV, cc. 49, 53; X, cc. 35, 41, 46.

Riding: *þriðjungr* (thrithing). The third part of a fylki.

Robbery: *rán.* A very clear distinction was drawn in the old laws between robbery and theft. The thief works in secret or under the cover of night, while the robber (*ránsmaðr*) commits his depredations by daylight and often uses violent methods, which were, however, regarded as less reprehensible than those of a sneak thief. Rán entailed compensation for the one who had suffered the robbery and the payment of a *ránbaugr* to the king. *Gul.*, cc. 32, 77, 81; *Frost.*, X, cc. 24, 48.

Sáld. A measure of grain equivalent to approximately three bushels. *Gul.*, cc. 3, 58, 62.

Salt, black: *svartasalt.* Dark salt produced by burning sea weed (tang). It was used for live stock only. *Gul.*, c. 75.

Seneschal: *skutilsveinn* (dish servant). A functionary at the royal court whose duty was to serve food at the royal tables. *Gul.*, c. 200; *Frost.*, IV, c. 60.

Seventh-day ale: *sjaund.* An ale feast given by the heir of one deceased on the seventh day after the decease. It might also be given on the thirtieth. At this feast the heir seated himself in the highseat, entered formally into his inheritance and heard all the claims against the estate. *Gul.*, cc. 23, 115, 119.

Shieling: *sætr.* The mountain pasture and the huts provided for those who had charge of the cattle in the grazing season. *Gul.*, cc. 84, 86, 131; *Frost.*, XIV, c. 8.

Ship district: *skipreiða.* A district, the inhabitants of which had the duty to provide crew and equipment for one ship of the coast defense. *Gul.*, cc. 300, 304, 310.

Show of weapons: *vápnatak.* Approval of an act, a proposal, or a decision, shown by uplifted weapons. Decisions taken in this way had the highest sanction. *Gul.*, c. 267; *Frost.*, V, c. 46.

Silver, burned. Silver that was held to be pure, or nearly pure. Whatever was valued in burned silver (*silfrmetinn*) was worth about twice as much as the same thing would be if valued and paid for in current coin.

Sistkins: *systkin*. Brothers and sisters; two of the same sex may be brothers or sisters but cannot be sistkins. In the wergeld provisions "sistkins" appears to be used for cousins, sons of brother and sister. Uterine sons of sistkins are sons of sistkins who have the same mother but not the same father. *Gul.*, cc. 316–19; *Frost.*, VI.

Sixfold oath: *séttareidr*. An oath taken by the accused and five oath helpers to deny and refute an allegation. *Gul.*, cc. 30, 57, 96, *et passim*.

Skeyting (v. *skeyta*). An ancient ceremony by which land was conveyed to a purchaser. The essential act was the "earth taking": the seller took earth from various places in the house and on the land and emptied it into the coat lap (*skaut*) of the buyer. *See Gul.*, c. 292. Taranger believes that the ceremony of skeyting was used only when land was conveyed to a purchaser from another kindred and that it was the odal right rather than the land that was transferred in this way. Vinogradov, *Essays in Legal History*, pp. 159–60.

Slayer's report: *víglýsing*. Information given by a manslayer that he has committed a homicide for which he assumes full responsibility. *Gul.*, cc. 156, 182, 240; *Frost.*, IV, c. 7.

Spindle gift: *rygjartó*. A tax levied on the housewives of the kingdom and paid in wool, hemp, or flax. It was abolished early in the twelfth century. *Frost.*, XVI, cc. 2–3.

Spiritual kinship: *guðsifjar*. "Kinship in God," which, the church believed, was formed when two or more persons shared in, or assisted at, certain religious rites of a sacramental character. In baptism and confirmation, therefore, all those who had ceremonial duties, the bishop, the priest, the children, and the sponsors, became related to each other in a spiritual sense. The importance of spiritual kinship in the older laws is that it was regarded as a bar to marriage between persons related in this way. *Gul.*, c. 26; *Frost.*, III, c. 8.

Staller: *stallari*. A prominent official at the royal court. Hertzberg seems to accept the suggested derivation of the title from *comes stabuli* or *stabularius*, master of the horse. *Gul.*, cc. 185, 200; *Frost.*, IV, c. 60.

Summer: *sumar*. The half-year beginning at "summer day" (*sumarmál*), April 14, and closing at "winter night" (*vetrnátt*), about October 14. *Gul.*, cc. 73, 81; *Frost.*, XIII, c. 1.

Summon: *stefna*. To give formal notice to some person, often an opponent in litigation, to be present for certain specified business at a certain place on a certain day. If the summons was to a man's own house, it was a "home summons" (*heimstefna*); if to a thing, it was a "thing summons" (þingstefna). *Gul.*, cc. 35, 46, 314.

Tenant (of land): *leiglendingr*. One who pays rent for land. The laws indicate that land was rarely leased for long terms; contracts for one year were apparently quite common. During the later centuries of the Middle Ages there was a continuous concentration of landed properties in the hands of the king, the church, and the local magnates, with the result that in the fourteenth century two-thirds, possibly three-fourths, of the Norwegian farmers were tenants. Johnsen, *Norges Bønder*, pp. 89–94; Keyser, *Norges stats- og retsforfatning*, pp. 346–54.

Tenure, land. *See* Lease, Mortgage, Odal, Purchase right, Tenant. Land might also be "sold" for a term of years; such land was called *stefnujǫrð*, literally "term land." The length of such a term seems ordinarily to have been fifteen years. During this period the farmer in possession was to all intents and purposes the owner of the land. *Gul.*, cc. 284, 286, 288.

Thegn: *þegn*. Any free subject of the king. *Frost.*, IV, c. 5.

Thing: *þing*. An assembly of free-born men convened to discuss the affairs of their community, or political unit, and to take action in the cases and on the subjects that were brought before it. Things were of many grades and ranged from the representative law things of the great jurisdictions to the petty assemblies of farmers summoned to hear the facts of a recent homicide. *See* Hertzberg, *Glossarium*, p. 739, where more than fifty different kinds of things are enumerated. Most of these were, no doubt, very much alike, the differences being chiefly in the type of business to be transacted by each body.

Thing token: *þingboð*, *þingsboð*. A token prepared and sent forth to summon the farmers to a thing. *Gul.*, cc. 131, 161; *Frost.*, I, c. 4; II, c. 23; V, c. 12. *See* Arrow.

Thirtieth morning: *þrítugsmorgunn*. An ale feast given by the heir of one deceased on the thirtieth morning after the decease. *See* Seventh-day ale. *Gul.*, cc. 23, 122.

Thrallborn: *þéborinn*, *þýborinn*. Born into slavery. In the case of a þéborinn child the father was most often a thrall, while one that was þýborinn was the child of a bondwoman by a free man and was acknowledged by the father as his child. *Gul.*, cc. 104, 115; *Frost.*, VI, cc. 5, 14, 21, 28.

Threefold oath: *lýrittareiðr*. An oath taken by the accused and two oath helpers to deny and refute an allegation. *Gul.*, c. 135, *et passim*.

Thumb ell: *þumalǫln.* The length of a line drawn from the elbow to the point of the thumb. *Frost.*, XIII, c. 21.

Trespass (and the fine for): *landnám. Gul.*, c. 81, *et passim.*

Twelvefold oath: *tylftareiðr.* An oath taken by the accused and eleven oath helpers to deny and refute an allegation. *Gul.*, cc. 132, 312; *Frost.*, IV, cc. 7, 14–15, 23–27.

Unauthorized labor: *áverki.* Labor that is not allowed; also the fruits of unpermitted labor, or the tools that are used by one who does such labor. *Gul.*, c. 75; *Frost.*, XIV, c. 1.

Uncle. In *Frost.*, VI (the wergeld system), this word is always used in the sense of paternal uncle except when otherwise indicated.

Upnám, Uppnám. Originally receiving or collecting a payment; later extended to include the men who received the payment. In one of the wergeld divisions of the Gulathing law the term is applied to the kinsmen just outside the circle of the baugamenn. These are formed into three groups, each of which is called an "upnám," since it receives certain payments when the wergeld is distributed. Its members are called *upnámamenn.* The term is also used for the money, or goods, that each group receives. *Gul.*, cc. 224, 228, 233–35.

Uterine: *sammœðra.* Of the same mother but not by the same father. *Gul.*, cc. 316–19; *Frost.*, VI, *passim.*

Wadmal, *vaðmál.* Coarse, heavy woolen cloth of domestic manufacture. It served many purposes, being even used as a standard of value: an ora was sometimes reckoned as the equivalent of six ells of wadmal. *Gul.*, cc. 57, 170, 235, 239.

BIBLIOGRAPHY

BIBLIOGRAPHY

Amira, Karl von, Das altnorwegische Vollstreckungsverfahren. München, 1874.

——— Grundriss des germanischen Rechts. Strassburg, 1897. Originally published in Paul's Grundriss der germanischen Philologie, V, Strassburg, 1890.

——— Nordgermanisches Obligationenrecht. 2 vols. Leipzig und München, 1882–96.

——— "Zur Textgeschichte der Frostuþingsbók." Germania, XXXII, 129–64. Wien, 1887.

Aubert, Ludvig M. B., "Bevissystemets udvikling i den norske criminalproces indtil Christian V's lov." Ugeblad for lovkyndighed, Christiania, 1864. A study of proof and evidence in the medieval and early modern legal systems in Norway.

——— Grundbögernes historie i Norge, Danmark, og tildels i Tyskland. Kristiania, 1892. A contribution to the legal history of real property.

——— Kontraktpantets historiske udvikling især i dansk og norsk ret [The Historical Development of Mortgages and Other Forms of Pledges Involving Contracts]. Kristiania, 1872.

——— De norske retskilder og deres anvendelse [The Sources of Norwegian Legal History and Their Application], I [no continuation]. Kristiania, 1877.

Bang, Anton Christian, Udsigt over den norske kirkes historie under Katholicismen [Survey of Norwegian Church History in Roman Catholic Times]. Kristiania, 1887.

Brandt, Frederik Peter, Forelæsninger over den norske retshistorie [Lectures on the History of Norwegian Law]. 2 vols. Kristiania, 1880, 1883.

——— "Nordmændenes gamle strafferet" [Criminal Procedure among the Northmen in Earlier Times]. Norsk historisk tidsskrift, Ser. I, Vol. IV (1877), 327–91; Ser. II, Vol. IV (1884), 20–113.

——— Om forelöbige retsmidler i den gamle norske rettergang [Preliminary Actions in Old Norwegian Legal Procedure]. Kristiania, 1862.

Brögger, Anton Wilhelm, Det norske folk i oldtiden [The Norwegian People in Prehistoric and Early Historic Times]. Oslo, 1925.

Bugge, Alexander, Studier over de norske byers selvstyre og handel [Studies in the Trade and Administration of the Norwegian Cities]. Kristiania, 1899.

Bull, Edvard, Leding [Coast Defense]. Christiania, 1920. A study in military administration.

Ericksen, Andreas Emil, "Om trældom i Norden" [Slavery in the North]. Nordisk Universitets-Tidsskrift, VII, nos. 3 and 4. Kjöbenhavn, 1861.

Flom, George Tobias (editor), Fragment A. M. 315 E of the Older Gulathing Law. Urbana, Ill., 1928.

Gjerset, Knut, History of the Norwegian People. 2 vols. New York, 1915.

Gjessing, Gustav Antonio, "En fremstilling af trældommens sandsynlige oprindelse hos Nordmændene" [A Presentation of the Probable Origin of Slavery among the Northmen]. Kristiania, 1862. Annaler for Nordisk Oldkyndighed.

Grágás, Islændernes Lovbog i Fristatens Tid. Oversat af Vilhjalmar Finsen. 4 vols. Kjöbenhavn, 1870.

Hansen, A. M., Oldtidens Nordmænd. Kristiania, 1907.

Heggtveit, Hallvard G., Trondhjem i fortid og nutid [Trondhjem, Past and Present]. Horten, 1897.

Hertzberg, Ebbe C. H., En fremstilling af det norske aristokratis historie indtil Kong Sverres tid [History of the Norwegian Aristocracy to the Reign of King Sverre]. Christiania, 1869.

——— "Den förste norske kongekroning, dens aarstal og ledsagende omstændigheder" [The First Coronation in Norway, Its Date and Attendant Circumstances]. Norsk historisk tidsskrift, Ser., IV, Vol. III (1905), 29–171.

——— "De gamle loves mynding" [*Mynding* in the Old Laws]. Kristiania, 1889. Kristiania Videnskabsselskabs afhandlinger, 1889, no. 3.

——— Grundtrækkene i den ældste norske proces [Outlines of the Oldest Form of Legal Procedure in Norway]. Kristiania, 1874.

——— "Lén og Veizla i Norges Sagatid" in Germanistische Abhandlungen zum LXX Geburtstag Konrad von Maurers. Göttingen, 1893. A study of quasi-feudal arrangements in medieval Norway.

——— Norges gamle love, V, glossarium. Christiania, 1895. A glossary to the old Norwegian laws prepared by Hertzberg with the assistance of Gustav Storm. A work of remarkable erudition.

Holmboe, Christopher Andreas, Das älteste Münzwesen Norwegens bis gegen Ende des 14. Jahrhunderts. Berlin, 1846.

Johnsen, Oscar Albert, Norges bönder [The Freemen of Rural Norway]. Kristiania, 1919.

——— De norske stænder [The Norwegian Estates]. Kristiania, 1906.

Keyser, Rudolf, Norges stats- og retsforfatning i middelalderen [The Legal and Constitutional System in Norway in the Middle Ages]. Christiania, 1867.

Larson, Laurence M., The King's Mirror (translation). New York, 1917.

——— "Witnesses and Oath Helpers in Old Norwegian Law," in Haskins Anniversary Essays, Boston, 1929.

Lehmann, Karl, Die Königsfriede der Nordgermanen. Berlin, 1886.

——— Verlobung und Hochzeit nach den nordgermanischen Rechten des früheren Mittelalters. München, 1882.

Mathiesen, Henrik, Det gamle Trondhjem: byens historie fra dens anlæg til erkestolens oprettelse [Old Trondhjem: the History of the City from Its Founding to the Establishment of the Metropolitan See]. Kristiania, 1897.

Maurer, Konrad von, Die Bekehrung des norwegischen Stammes zum Christenthum. 2 vols. München, 1855–56.

——— Die Eingangsformel der altnordischen Rechts- und Gesetzbücher. München, 1886.

——— "Die Eintheilung der älteren Frostuþingslǫg." Norsk historisk tidsskrift, Ser. II, Vol. VI (1888), 203–35

——— Die Entstehungszeit der älteren Frostuþingslǫg. München, 1875.

——— Die Entstehungszeit der älteren Gulaþingslǫg. München, 1872.

——— Island von seiner ersten Entdeckung bis zum Untergange des Freistaates. München, 1874.

——— Udsigt over de nordgermanske retskilders historie. Kristiania, 1878. Also published in Holtzendorffs Encyclopädie der Rechtswissenschaft, I, under the title: Ueberblick über die Geschichte der nordgermanischen Rechtsquellen (Leipzig, 1877).

——— Vorlesungen über altnordische Rechtsgeschichte. Leipzig, 1907–10.

Munch, Peter Andreas, Det norske folks historie [History of the Norwegian People]. 4 vols. Christiania, 1852–63.

Norges gamle love indtil 1387 [The Old Laws of Norway to 1387], edited by Rudolf Keyser, P. A. Munch, et al. 5 vols. Christiania, 1846–95. Vol. V is cited as Glossarium.

Olafsen, Olaf, Jordfælleskab og sameie [Joint Holdings and Common Cultivation]. Christiania, 1914.

Phillpotts, Bertha, Kindred and Clan in the Middle Ages and After. Cambridge, 1913.

Sars, Johan Ernst, Udsigt over den norske historie [General Survey of Norwegian History]. 4 vols. Christiania, 1874–77.

Schive, Claudius Jacob, Norges mynter in middelalderen [Norwegian Coinage in the Middle Ages]. Christiania, 1865.

Seebohm, Frederic, Tribal Custom in Anglo-Saxon Law. London, 1902.

Sievers, Eduard (editor), Die Tübinger Bruchstücke der älteren Frostuþingslǫg. Halle, 1886.

Steenstrup, Johannes, C. H. R., Danelag [Normannerne IV]. Kjöbenhavn, 1882.

Storm, Gustav, "Om lendermandsklassens talrighed i 12 og 13 aarhundred." Norsk historisk tidsskrift, Ser. II, Vol. IV (1884), 129–88. An attempt to estimate the number of barons in Norway in the twelfth and thirteenth centuries.

——— Sigurd Ranessöns proces. Kristiania, 1877.

Taranger, Absalon, Den angelsaksiske kirkes inflydelse paa den norske [The Influence of the Anglo-Saxon Ecclesiastical System on the Norwegian Church]. Kristiania, 1890.

——— "The Meaning of the Words *Oðal* and *Skeyting* in the Old Laws of Norway," in Essays in Legal History, edited by Paul Vinogradov. London, 1913.

——— "De norske folkelovböker (för 1263)" [The Norwegian National Codes (before 1263)], in Tidsskrift for retsvidenskap, XXXIX, 183–211, XLI, 1–68.

——— "Trondheimens forfatningshistorie" [The Constitutional History of Trondheim], in Kongelige Norske Videnskabers Selskabs skrifter, 1929, no. 5. Trondheim, 1930.

——— Udsigt over den norske retshistorie [General Survey of the History of Norwegian Law], I. Christiania, 1898.

Weinhold, Karl, Altnordisches Leben. Berlin, 1856.

Wergeland, Agnes Mathilde, Slavery in Germanic Society during the Middle Ages. Chicago, 1916.

Wilda, Eduard, Geschichte des deutschen Strafrechts. Halle, 1842.

Williams, Mary Wilhelmine, Social Scandinavia in the Viking Age. New York, 1920.

INDEX

INDEX

www.ingramcontent.com/pod-product-compliance
Ingram Content Group UK Ltd.
Pitfield, Milton Keynes, MK11 3LW, UK
UKHW051451290926
15471UKWH00008B/1139

9 781616 191047